Report Writing
for Business

Report Writing
for Business

NINTH EDITION

RAYMOND V. LESIKAR, PH.D.
Emeritus, Louisiana State
University

JOHN D. PETTIT, JR., PH.D.
Wichita State University

IRWIN

Chicago Bogotá Boston Buenos Aires Caracas
London Madrid Mexico City Sydney Toronto

Senior sponsoring editor: *Craig Beytien*
Associate editor: *Karen Mellon*
Senior marketing manager: *Kurt Messersmith*
Project editor: *Rita McMullen*
Production manager: *Bob Lange*
Interior designer: *Mercedes Santos/Annette Spadoni*
Cover designer: *Mercedes Santos/Maureen McCutcheon*
Cover illustrator: *Tim Lee*
Art studio: *Electra Graphics, Inc.*
Art coordinator: *Mark Malloy*
Compositor: *Weimer Graphics, Inc.*
Typeface: *10/12 Times Roman*
Printer: *R. R. Donnelley & Sons Company*

Library of Congress Cataloging-in-Publication Data

Lesikar, Raymond Vincent.
    Report writing for business / Raymond V. Lesikar, John D. Pettit.
—9th ed.
      p. cm.
    Includes index.
    ISBN 0-256-11565-6
    1. Business report writing.   I. Pettit, John D.   II. Title.
HF5719.L45   1995
808′.066651—dc20   94–12499

Printed in the United States of America
2 3 4 5 6 7 8 9 0 DO 1 0 9 8 7 6

To the memory of Lu Lesikar,
whose love, encouragement, and support
through this and all earlier editions
made her a part of this book.

Preface

This ninth edition of *Report Writing for Business* celebrates 34 years of report writing excellence, experience, and success for business professionals who will lead organizations into the 21st century. As such, the goal of this edition is the same one that has guided the success of the previous eight editions: to prepare students to write reports they must write in business. The text seeks to accomplish this goal by viewing report preparation as consisting of universal steps—defining the problem, collecting facts, organizing information, constructing the report, writing it, and such. These stages are appropriately seen as chapter titles in the text.

In preparing the text, we tried to retain the features that have made the book so successful over the years. To be sure, we did not want to tamper with a successful plan. But we made every effort to improve the content and structure of the book whenever practical, given its successful foundation features. Figuratively, we see the successive editions of *Report Writing for Business* as similar to the growth cycle of wildflowers. As one edition evolves into another, the text reseeds itself. And forthcoming editions expand, flourish, and prosper because of the presence of the past editions.

Although we view report writing as consisting of universal steps, we also recognize fully that reports differ widely by organization and company. To overcome this problem, we followed the assumption that although reports may differ, the principles of their construction are pervasive. Thus, the general teachings of the book may be easily adapted to the special report requirements of any organization. On the other hand, the text contains sufficient instruction to enable students to construct conventional reports.

As you read the book, you will note that *Report Writing for Business* addresses specifically the revolution in information technology occurring in business today. As we see it, reports are a logical response to the data explosion we see as a result of the computer. That is, reports relate data in meaningful ways to the information needs of business and more precisely to the solution of business problems.

Yet report writers in the last decade of the 20th century need clear thinking and diligent effort to produce effective reports just as much as report writers needed these same qualities earlier. The business environment with its technological dimensions provides exciting opportunities for creative problem solvers and their report writing skills that will extend well into the next century. *Report Writing for Business* intends to develop these report writing skills, tap the rich potential for creative problem solving, and firmly enhance the strong work ethic demanded by today's workplace.

Moreover, the text speaks directly to the complexities of business life in the transitions from the 20th to the 21st century. Indeed, living in general and professional life in particular are intriguing and challenging. Amid fluctuating security markets, unemployment issues, health care reform, corporate rightsizing, international conflict, media blitzes, and chuckholes in the information superhighway, we believe a book dedicated to providing for the information needs of business on a global basis is a worthwhile and significant venture. To meet the technological, organizational, international, and economic challenges at the turn of the 20th century, we made certain content changes and refinements in the text.

First, we added the most recent computer coverage to report writing topics wherever it applied. You will notice some of these additions as captions within chapters. Other applications are interwoven as paragraphs and parts of paragraphs within content coverages. We believe that this integrative approach is best because students can see at the exact point of coverage where and how computers apply to reports. Put differently, we do not believe that computer concepts and their application to reports are separable. It is our firm belief also that computers save people time and improve report quality. But they extend report writers' skills and abilities rather than replace them.

Second, we thoroughly revised Chapter 4, Library Research, to reflect technological developments in this data-collecting strategy. Because online data services and CD-ROMs exist in all major sources of business information, they are virtually impossible to list or classify. In fact, new sources of information quickly and regularly arise—daily, weekly, and monthly. For students who use library research for their reports, we suggest that they expect to find new and different sources that do not exist in print. In Chapter 4, we have focused only on those online and disk sources that presently exist for significant and established business data references.

Third, we prepared new problems (57 in all) that are realistic and stimulating to meet the ever-increasing demand for higher educational standards. Such problems should also confront students with the organizational realities of the report-writing situations they will encounter at the turn of the 20th century. Over the years, some students and professors have suggested we use actual company names in report cases to show realism of report situations. We have yet to be able to comply with this request because the problem situations would likely reflect negatively on the company involved in the report case. Certainly, that would not serve anyone's best interest. Accordingly, we have disguised actual companies in all report cases in the text. To be sure, however, the cases are realistic and reflect actual companies, their report needs, and their report problem situations.

Fourth, we made these additions to existing chapters: updated entries and sources of information in library research, added coverage of collaborative writing, revised documentation and bibliography material to emphasize the *Chicago Manual of Style* and to include MLA and APA formats, changed the long report example in Chapter 6, and renamed Chapter 12 to Cross-Cultural Communication and extended its coverage.

Moreover, we revised all chapters and examples to make sure they reflected current, modern report writing practice.

As we did in the eighth edition, we edited each chapter of the ninth edition to make certain that it read as an independent unit. Over the years, some professors have indicated a need to begin the writing coverages much earlier in their course designs. Although we believe there is a logical order of report preparation, we believe also that different chapter sequences are possible depending on the preferences of the professor. Those who want to begin writing earlier in their courses and to emphasize short reports can insert Chapters 9, 10, 11, and 12 immediately after Chapter 2. Those who prefer to stress the long, formal report can follow the normal chapter sequence. No doubt, there are combinations that can fit still other preferences.

The unique chemistry that brought us together in other writing projects continues to give synergized strength to this ninth edition of *Report Writing for Business*. With modest confidence, we sincerely feel that our combined efforts produced a text that could not have been prepared individually. The senior author brings a knowledge of teaching and writing to the partnership that spans six decades. The coauthor brings a vision and foresight acquired in research, writing, and teaching for 32 years. Cementing that professional relationship is a close personal friendship that respects the uniqueness of our individual contributions. Collectively, we believe that our combined talents have produced the most authoritative and complete text on the market.

Making a very special contribution to the content and writing of this book are scholars who reviewed the manuscript: Jolene Scriven, Northern Illinois University; Kenneth Pickard, California State University at Long Beach; Barbara Alpern, Walsh College; and David Covington, North Carolina State University. Their reviews were thorough and challenging. Also, Marie Flatley, our respected colleague at San Diego State University, allowed us to adapt her ideas on computer use to the specifics of report writing. And we are most grateful for her counsel, authoritative advice, and friendly encouragement of this writing project. To all of these dedicated professionals, we extend a personal thank you for their most valuable contributions.

Lastly, and most importantly, we acknowledge the personal contributions of our families. On the Lesikar side, Lu continued to give her love, patience, and understanding to this project in the last days of her life on this earth just as she did so graciously and unconditionally to many other writing efforts. For her lifetime of support, this book is dedicated to her. In addition, grateful appreciation is extended to Ray, Susan, Patti, and Stephanie. On the Pettit side, special gratitude goes to Suzanne, David, Melanie, and Jamie. The support and encouragement of these people so dear to us throughout the extensive work on this revision provided the positive climate for us to complete our task. Their endearing care and sensitivity helped us produce this ninth edition of *Report Writing for Business*.

Raymond V. Lesikar
John D. Pettit, Jr.

Contents in Brief

Contents

PART **4**   **Writing the Report**

P A R T 6   **Oral Reporting**

Preliminaries of Business Reports

CHAPTER 1
Orientation to Business Reports

CHAPTER 2
Development of Report-Writing Methods

P A R T *1*

Orientation to Business Reports

As you begin the study of a business subject, two questions are likely to come to mind: What is it I am about to study and how will it benefit me in my career? It is appropriate to answer these questions as a first step in your study of business report writing.

THE WHAT AND WHY OF REPORT WRITING

☐ WHAT ARE REPORTS?

Definitions of reports vary.

On first thought the answer to the question of what is report writing appears to be elementary. Certainly reports are commonplace in today's business world. Almost all organizations use them—businesses, government agencies, civic groups. Most use them extensively. In fact, it is unlikely that any modern organization of size could function without using reports. But in spite of the fact that reports are so commonplace, people do not agree on how to define them.

Our definition: an orderly and objective communication of factual information that serves some business purpose.

Definitions in current use range from one extreme to the other. By the broadest definition, a report is any representation of information ranging from the extremely formal to the highly informal. Narrower definitions limit reports to the more formalized presentations of information. For your use as a student of business reports, a definition approaching the narrower ones is best. Such a definition is the following: *A business report is an orderly and objective communication of factual information that serves some business purpose.*

The key words are orderly (care in preparation),

If you carefully inspect this definition, you can spot the identifying characteristics of a business report. As an **orderly** communication, a report is given some care in preparation. And care in preparation distinguishes a report from the casual, routine exchanges of information that continually occur in business. This is not to say that all reports are carefully prepared, but it does mean that they should be given at least something above minimum care in their preparation. Everyday oral exchanges of information, for example, do not classify as reports. Nor do the most casual handwritten notes.

objective (truth-seeking),

The **objective** quality of a report is its unbiased approach to the facts presented. The report seeks truth, regardless of its consequences. Because few people can be

3

thoroughly objective, it is true that report writers seldom achieve complete objectivity. Nevertheless, they must work for it. Certainly, some presentations disguised as reports are heavily persuasive, but they represent a specialized form of administrative communication. They are not business reports as we define them.

communication,

The word **communication** is broad by definition, concerning all ways of transmitting meaning (speaking, writing, drawing, gesturing, and such). For all practical purposes, however, business reports are either written or oral. And for reasons that will be given shortly, in today's complex business operations the more significant reports are written.

factual information (emphasis on events, records, data),

The basic ingredient of the report is **factual information**—events, records, and the various forms of data that are communicated in the conduct of business. In no way is the content fictional. Nor is there major stress on opinions, except in those rare cases when in the absence of facts authoritative opinions are the best information available. This statement does not mean that interpretations, conclusions, and recommendations (which may border on opinions) may not be included. They can and should be a part of most reports. But it does mean they should be either supported by fact or clearly labeled as opinion. As far as possible, the emphasis should be on fact.

and serves some business purpose.

Not all reports are business reports. Research scientists, medical doctors, ministers, students, and many others write reports. Thus, the need for the final phrase of the definition is obvious. To be classified as a business report, a report must **serve some business purpose.**

Examples of purposes are to solve a problem and to present information.

This purpose may be to solve a problem: Should X Company diversify its line? How can Y Company increase sales in the Northeast district? How can Z Company profitably use a computer? The purpose may be to present information needed in the conduct of business: a weekly report of a salesperson's activities, a summary of the day's production, an explanation of expenditures on a particular project, a description of the condition of a piece of equipment. In general, the purpose could concern the thousand and one areas of information a business needs in its operation.

This broad definition covers the many differences in reports.

Even though this definition of a business report is specific enough to be meaningful, it is broad enough to take into account the variations to be found in reports. For example, some reports do nothing more than present facts. Others go a step further by including interpretations. Still others proceed to conclusions and recommendations. There are reports formally dressed both in writing style and in physical appearance. And there are very informal reports. The definition given permits all these variations.

☐ WHY STUDY BUSINESS REPORT WRITING?

The second question "Why study business report writing?" may be answered from two standpoints. One is the standpoint of the companies for which the student will work some day. The other is the personal standpoint of the student. Convincing arguments support both positions.

Communication is vital to every part of today's business organization.

FROM A BUSINESS STANDPOINT   To understand how important report writing is to businesses, you need only note the amount of communication required in a business. As you know, today's complex business organizations feed on information. Throughout the organization, workers send and receive information. They process information by computers. They write messages. They fill out forms. They report orally—face to face and by telephone. More specifically, salespeople send in orders and weekly summaries of their activities. At the same time, they receive instructions and sales information from the home office. Production supervisors receive work orders, and they submit summaries of their production. Research specialists receive problems; later they communicate their findings to those who need the information. It is like this in every niche of the organization. Everywhere workers are receiving and sending information in the conduct of their work.

This communication takes various forms: oral, written, computer.

This information flow involves many forms of communication. Obviously, oral communication makes up a large part of it. In addition, there are all the various types of forms and records that are kept and exchanged. There are the storage and retrieval facilities that computers now provide. And, of course, there are the various forms of written communication. Among the written forms of business communication, reports play a very major role.

Reports play a major role among written communications.

That reports are vital in today's business operations is hardly a debatable point. Universally business executives recognize the importance of reports. Executives know they must have information in order to make decisions, and they know they get much of their information from reports. They know how important it is that the reports they receive be orderly and clear, for they need to get the information quickly and easily. The pressures for their time in business make quick and easy communication necessary. These general comments about the importance of reports, however, may not be convincing to traditionally wary students. They want, and have a right to expect, more concrete data. Fortunately, such data are not hard to find.

Convincing research results emphasize the importance of report writing.

The most convincing evidence of the importance of writing for business comes from surveys made over the past 40 years by researchers at a number of universities—Michigan State University, Ohio University, The University of Texas at Austin, University of Washington, University of California at Los Angeles, Louisiana State University, and Florida State University, to name a few.[1] Generally, these surveys sought to determine what business subjects are most important in training people for careers in business. Without exception, these studies found business writing, especially report writing, at or near the top. Typical of these investigations is a survey conducted at the University of Michigan.[2] This survey of 1,158 executives found business communication to be number one in importance for training future executives—clearly ahead of all the core business courses (such as finance, accounting, marketing, and management). Perhaps the most prominent and convincing of all is a three-year study commissioned by the American Assembly of Collegiate Schools of Business (AACSB). These words from the report capture the essence of the findings:

> Clearly, from university-based vantage points, the major weaknesses of baccalaureate graduates from business schools center around communication. Deans and faculty

---

[1] The authors have a file of over 50 such studies, including studies made by researchers from these schools.

[2] Herbert W. Hilderbrandt *et al.,* "An Executive Appraisal of Courses Which Best Prepare One for General Management," *The Journal of Business Communication,* 19, Winter, 1982, 5–15.

members were agreed that written and oral communication skills ranked as the number 1 and number 2 deficiencies of business undergraduates.[3]

FROM A PERSONAL POINT OF VIEW   While the foregoing facts are very convincing, we think the strongest argument for the study of business writing can be made from a personal advantage point. Proof of your personal gain is easily made from a logical interpretation of fact. The fact is that writing is important to business. Thus, your writing skills are apt to be rewarded personally. This conclusion is even more convincing when made through another line of reasoning.

This reasoning also begins with a simple statement of fact: The promotions you receive will be determined largely by the impressions you make on your superiors. You can impress your superiors in many ways, but mainly you can do so by your personal characteristics—appearance, job performance, and intellectual capacity for work. It is in this last-named area, intellectual capacity for work, that the writing skills come in.

Your satisfactory performance of work usually will be enough to communicate your intellectual capacity for promotions to rank-and-file positions. For promotions to high-level assignments, however, you will have to impress your superiors with your intellectual capacity for these assignments. You can make such impressions largely through your ability to communicate. And in business, this communicating often must be done in writing. Thus, the ability to write good reports and other business papers is a requisite for your advancement in business. If you do not have this ability, you are likely to be doomed to a mediocre role in business. This is true even if you happen to be capable intellectually in your field, because you will be judged mainly by the intellectual capacities you are able to communicate. What you cannot communicate is known only to you.

Proof of the value of writing to you in business could go on and on, for there is no shortage of supporting evidence. For your purposes, however, the foregoing presentation of fact and reason should be sufficient. Certainly, there can be no doubt that the businesses you will work for will need and expect you to have good writing skills. Nor should there be doubt that your writing skills can help you to advance in your career. Perhaps these observations will serve as incentives as you study the chapters that follow.

A REVIEW OF REPORT CLASSIFICATION

Since the first organized efforts to study the subject, scholars of report writing have advanced many classifications of reports. Each of these classification plans proposes to divide all reports written into distinct categories. A review of these classifications gives you an appropriate introduction to the study of report writing. We think such a review is appropriate for two main reasons.

Margin notes:

You stand to gain personally from your report-writing ability.

Good writing will impress your superiors with your intellectual capability.

This good impression will help you advance.

We may classify reports many ways.

---

[3] Lymon W. Porter and Lawrence E. McKibbon, *Management Education and Development: Drift or Thrust into the 21st Century?* New York: McGraw-Hill, 1988, 103.

First, a discussion of the ways of classifying reports will illustrate to you the variation in approaches to the subject. Reports are far from standardized. With tens of thousands of companies writing them and unknown scores of authorities determining their construction, they could not be otherwise. A knowledge of report classification gives you an insight into this complex picture.

A second benefit you will derive from reviewing report classification is that you will use the various classification terms in discussing report writing. As with most subjects, report writing has its own specialized terms—the technical language of the field, so to speak. Logically, you as a student of report writing should be acquainted with the vernacular of the subject. The terms used in classifying reports comprise much of this vernacular.

Knowing these classifications will help you appreciate the complexity of reports.

It also will enable you to talk about the subject.

☐ SUBJECT MATTER AS A BASIS FOR CLASSIFICATION

Possibly the simplest report classification you can use is one by subject matter. Obviously, all reports concern some subject. It is equally obvious that reports can be classified on the basis of some logical grouping of subjects.

The possibilities of grouping by subjects are almost limitless, being bound only by the infinite differences among report topics. Subject classifications, therefore, could be based on minute differences in content, or they could follow broader and more general lines. For example, in the field of accounting, distinctions in subject matter could provide classifications such as *cost, audit, tax,* and *finance.* But such divisions generally are not practical. A more practical and more widely used subject classification is one that follows broader lines—for example, one based on broad subject fields such as *accounting, management, economics, finance, engineering,* and *marketing.*

One classification is on the basis of subject matter: sales, tax, construction, and such.

☐ CLASSIFICATION BY TIME INTERVAL

Another way people often classify reports is by how frequently they occur. Some reports are written regularly—daily, weekly, monthly, or annually. These are often called **periodic** reports. Examples of this type are the routine weekly and monthly reports made by salespeople, the periodic summaries of progress in any large-scale operation, and the corporation's typical annual report of operations. Completing this classification are the **special** reports—reports prepared for a special assignment. By special assignment, we mean an assignment that is not likely to be repeated with any degree of regularity.

Classifications by time are periodic (regularly prepared) and special (not repeated).

☐ FUNCTIONAL CLASSIFICATION OF REPORTS

Possibly the most popular classification you can use is based on the function of reports. By this plan, reports are classified by what they do. On this functional basis, it is practical to classify reports into three groups—*informational, examination,* and *analytical.*[4]

Functional report types are

---

[4] Sometimes referred to as *problem-solving* reports.

(1) *informational*
(facts only),

(2) *examination* (facts
plus analysis and
interpretation), and

(3) *analytical* (facts,
analysis, interpretation,
and conclusions).

As the term implies, the **informational** report is a presentation of facts on the subject. It contains only the facts. It has no analyses and no conclusions.

The **examination** report carries the problem one step further than does the informational report. In the examination report, in addition to presenting the facts about the problem, the writer analyzes and interprets the data. But the writer's assistance stops here. There is no effort to follow the analysis to the point of concluding or of recommending. Any possible conclusion or recommendation to be derived from the information must be made by the reader, but doubtless the reader will be guided in these efforts by the writer's presentation of fact.

Like the examination report, the **analytical** report presents and analyzes data. But it goes a step further in that it also draws conclusions from the data. And when the problem warrants, it may even make recommendations. It is the most complete of all reports, covering all phases of a particular problem. It presents a problem in its entirety. It begins with an orientation and description of the problem; it presents the information gathered; and it analyzes and examines the information. From these analyses and examinations, it derives a conclusion or solution to the problem. Typically, an analytical report is written by one with good knowledge of the subject matter—one whose analyses are respected. These analyses are likely to form significant inputs in the decision-making process of the executives who read them.

☐ FORMALITY AS A DIVISION CRITERION

Still another area of variation that you can use for classification is the formality of the report. It is easy to see that the same degree of formality is not required in all report situations. A study addressed to an august body such as the U.S. Senate logically would be strictly formal in its makeup. On the other hand, a report written by one employee for the use of another employee of equal rank might be extremely informal. The differences between these two reports are sufficient to serve as a basis for classification. Two groups are commonly represented in this classification—*formal* and *informal.* By this classification, the term **formal** applies to all those reports that are dressed up physically and are appropriately worded to fit the requirements of a formal occasion. The term **informal** includes all reports with the makeup and wording requirements of an informal occasion. As you can see, there is a hazy and indefinite dividing line between the two types.

Classification by
formality gives us
(1) *informal* and
(2) *formal*

☐ DIVISION OF REPORTS BY PHYSICAL FACTORS

You can also use the physical makeup of reports to provide a simple and logical basis for grouping. We should note, however, that physical makeup is largely influenced by the formality of the situation and the length of the report. You should keep these two factors in mind while reviewing the following classification.

At the bottom of the formality and length scale is the **memorandum** report. Generally, it concerns a routine matter that must be transmitted within an organization. In the typical business situation, memorandum reports are written on specially prepared forms. Most common of these forms is one that begins with the headings "To, From, Subject" and has space provided below for informal presentation of the subject.

Physical differences
produce another
classification:

(1) *memorandum*
(routine, intracompany
message),

Other variations resemble questionnaires, providing space for routine presentation of specific information.

(2) *letter* (short topics in letter form),

Short topics with some need for formal or semiformal presentation are frequently submitted in the form of a **letter** report. From all outward appearances, they are letters, with all the physical properties of a typical business letter. They are classified as reports principally because of the nature of their content.

(3) *short* (medium topic, moderately formal),

Topics that are of medium or moderate length and have no great need for formal presentation usually are submitted in a form classified as a **short** report. Although there is no one set makeup of the short report, usually it is one that is minus much of the prefatory pages (title fly, contents pages, executive summary, and such) associated with more formal works.

(4) *long* (involved topic, formal).

At the top of this classification scale in formality and length is the **long** report. Long reports, as the term implies, concern presentations of relatively large problems. As a rule, such topics have some need for formal presentation. The typical long report is well supplemented with prefatory parts. Its contents are carefully organized and marked with headings. It may even require such supplementary parts as an appendix, bibliography, or index.

☐ WRITER-READER RELATIONSHIP AS A BASIS FOR GROUPING

Classified by writer-reader relationship, we have *administrative* (employee for a superior), *professional* (by outside specialist), and *independent* (for the public).

Classification arrangements have also been constructed on the basis of the relation between reader and writer. Although there is wide variation in the terms used in this division, possibly the most common are *administrative,*[5] *professional,* and *independent.*[6] **Administrative** reports are those reports officially written within a business organization to facilitate operations. **Professional** reports are submitted to an organization by outside specialists. For example, an outside management consultant may be called in to study a particular problem of a company. The consultant's findings, when presented in written form, would constitute a professional report. **Independent** reports are written for no particular group or person. Frequently, nonprofit research organizations publish such reports as a service to the public.

☐ CLASSIFICATIONS BY STATUS OF AUTHORSHIP

Classified by authorship status, we have *private* (for private business), *public* (by government groups), and *independent* (for no business or government group).

Another commonly used classification is one that distinguishes reports by the employment status of their authors. Reports written by those engaged in private business are logically referred to as **private** reports. Reports that originate through employees of public institutions (government groups, professional societies, colleges, and such) are known as **public** reports. Completing this classification is the **independent** report—one written by an individual without the authorization of any public or private group. For example, research scholars working on their own authority would present their findings in an independent report.

---

[5] Administrative reports are also known as *internal* reports.

[6] Professional and independent reports are sometimes referred to as *external* reports.

☐ MISCELLANEOUS REPORT TYPES

Various miscellaneous report types exist,

In addition to the terms used in the preceding classifications, scholars use numerous other terms to describe specific report types. Many in this group are known only within the narrow confines of a particular field, industry, or business. A few in this group, however, are so widely used as to warrant special review.

such as progress reports (status of a project),

The **progress** report is one of the best-known types used in industry. Actually, it is strictly an informational type of report. The information it presents is limited to the progress of some undertaking such as the construction of a bridge, an advertising campaign, or the operation of production machinery.

justification reports (support of a decision),

In recent years, the term **justification** report has become popular. It is a type of report that presents a decision to a particular problem—usually a short one. Its text contains a logical review of the points that affect the decision. This review, of course, justifies the author's decision.

recommendation and improvement reports.

Frequently in report-writing discussion, there is reference to the **recommendation** report. A recommendation report is nothing more than a variety of the analytical report referred to previously. Specifically, it is an analytical report that concludes with a recommendation. Another name for this type is the **improvement** report, although some authorities draw minor distinctions between the two terms.

☐ THE ROLE OF CLASSIFICATION IN STUDYING REPORTS

Classifications are useful, but we cannot study report writing by types.

As we noted previously, the conventional classifications are useful in describing reports. They also point out the wide variations that exist in approaches to the subject. It would not be logical, however, to study reports by types, as perhaps these classifications suggest.

Reports are integrally related. We use this concept in this book.

The basic principles used in any good report differ little. With small exceptions, the writing principles, the rules of logical organization, techniques of writing style and tone, and so on remain the same in all reports. Thus, any plan to study the subject by report types would be plagued with needless repetition. A more workable approach to the subject is one that treats all reports as being integrally related through their problem orientation, logical organization, use of proper writing techniques, and the like. Such an approach is followed in this book.

QUESTIONS

1. Review the definition of business reports given in the text. Bring out the key words in this definition, and discuss their significance in the study of report writing.

2. Does a person who conducts a one-person business need to know how to write a report for business purposes? A 10-person business? Fifty? One hundred?

3. Why is it important to you to be able to write good reports?

4. How do you interpret the survey findings presented in this chapter?

5. Assume that you have in your hands the following reports. Classify them on the basis of each of the classification schemes discussed in this chapter.

    a. An independent public accountant performs an annual audit of your business. A 20-page report is submitted on the results of the examination.

    b. Salespeople out on the road submit a weekly report of their activities to the sales manager. These reports are submitted on printed forms that provide for all the information required (number of calls, number of sales, travel mileage, and so on).

    c. The controller of a corporation prepares a yearly review of activities (production, marketing, finance, and such) for the stockholders, employees, and the public at large.

6. Inspect the reports in Figures 8–3 and 9–1 to 9–7 (excluding 9–6). Classify them by each of the classification schemes discussed in the chapter.

7. Why should the report student be concerned with report classification?

Development of Report-Writing Methods

The structure and techniques of report writing we present in this text are the products of years of development. From the earliest days of report writing, businesspeople have worked to develop the most practical and effective ways of communicating through reports. Their efforts have been influenced by two general needs. One is the information needs of business. The other is the needs of the communication process. Understanding these needs and how they have influenced report-writing methods is basic to your study of report writing.

INFORMATION NEEDS OF BUSINESS

Businesses function through communication.

Communication at the first work levels is light.

The higher work levels require more communication.

Businesses need information to function. Every worker, every supervisor, every staff employee must have information to do his or her job. In fact, there simply could be no organized productive effort without information.

At the first organizational levels, the need for information is relatively light. Assembly-line workers, for example, may require little more information than their work assignments. The same is true for janitors, gardeners, cooks, and others with routine assignments.

On the other hand, more involved work assignments at higher levels are likely to require more information. This is especially true for those assignments with administrative duties. Take, for example, the job of supervisor of a production department. The department's major goal, of course, is to produce—to make things. The supervisor's job is to guide the department toward this goal.

In guiding the department toward its goal, the supervisor must have a wide assortment of information. Of major importance is information on production needs—primarily production schedules, quotas, and the like. Also vital is information that tells of the progress of production—information such as data on output and quality of production. In addition, the supervisor needs information on the condition of the production equipment and of the workplace. He or she also needs information on the quality of the work done by each worker and of inventories of

13

raw materials and supplies. From other departments, the supervisor needs production and planning information in order to coordinate the department's efforts with the efforts of the total business. Also, the supervisor is likely to need all sorts of other information—information on the competition, new production techniques, new equipment, industry happenings, to name a few. We could continue the list indefinitely. The fact is plain and simple: this person needs a lot of information in order to do the job.

We could describe the information needs of other workers and supervisors; the effect would be the same. The obvious conclusion is that all members of all business organizations need information in order to do their jobs. There is no question about it. The need for information in business is great.

☐ A JUNGLE OF INFORMATION

Supplying information is a major business activity.

Because a business must have information if it is to function, supplying information is a major part of business activity. Of course, in this day of rapidly advancing technology, much of the information needed is communicated by computer. In progressive organizations, basic information needs are carefully planned—resulting in skillfully designed computer systems that receive and transmit information throughout the organization to those needing it. Even so, this planned information is only a part of the information needed—typically the routine part. Special needs and problems require much additional information.

Often too much information is supplied, creating a jungle of information.

Often an organization's information needs are more than adequately satisfied. This happens when reports contain more information than is necessary. The explanation for this tendency to oversupply information is apparent from simple observation. We human beings tend to over report when responding to information needs. We tend not to think in terms of what is needed, but in terms of what is available. The result is a jungle of information. The users of information have to search through this dense jungle for what they need. Obviously, searching wastes time; and in business, time is costly.

☐ EFFECTS ON REPORT WRITING

The information needs of business and the information jungle suggest that you (1) report selectively and

From the preceding discussion, you can understand that business needs information. But what is the relationship of these needs to report writing? More precisely, how have these needs affected the development of report writing? Two answers are apparent. First, writers have responded to the need to clear the jungle of information often found in business. As a result, modern report-writing instruction stresses reporting only the information needed and leaving out information not needed. It stresses organizing the information logically, as well as for quick and easy understanding. For example, it stresses placing major facts, analyses, and conclusions in positions of emphasis. It stresses using summaries at places that help readers to collect their thoughts. Current instruction also stresses using introductory and connecting parts to permit readers to begin reading a long report at any place and quickly get a bearing. In general, current report-writing methods stress the needs of reports to communicate the information needed for the work done in business.

(2) use the report structure developed over time to present information effectively.

Second, the development of report structure has been influenced by the information needs of business. The design of reports (see Chapters 8 and 9) actually helps readers find the information they need. For some examples, the text of a report may include headings (captions) placed at the beginnings of sections to help organize the information in the reader's mind and to guide the reader's thoughts through the information. Reports may have beginning summaries to give a quick review of highlights for readers too busy to look at all the details. They may include tables of contents that enable readers to find information quickly and easily. When the goal is to aid in decision making, the report structure may emphasize recommendations by placing them at the beginning where they stand out. Report writers may use forms of graphic presentation (charts, diagrams, pictures, maps, and such) to supplement the written word and to communicate quickly and effectively. They may use forward and backward references in the writing to tie together the parts of the report, thereby relating the report parts and ensuring the reader's quick understanding. The list could go on and on.

In summary, we can say that the report structure that has developed over the past makes information easy to find. It permits busy readers to go quickly to the facts needed and to ignore the information not needed. It enables them to find the minor, supporting details when these details appear to be useful. In general, it permits readers to get the information they need in the shortest time possible.

THE NEED TO COMMUNICATE

Understanding the communication process helps you understand report-writing techniques.

Much of the report-writing instruction we present in this text developed from the need to communicate. Reports, of course, are specialized forms of communication. And just as any other form of communication, they involve the communication process. It is not surprising, therefore, that writing techniques developed to make the communication process more effective in reports. In order to understand these developments, it will help if you first understand the communication process.

☐ THE COMMUNICATION PROCESS

Following is a two-person illustration that describes the process (you and Ms. Smith).

In describing the communication process, we shall use a situation involving two people. One is you. The other is a woman called Smith. Now, before we begin this description, we should note that the situation illustrated involves communication in general (not necessarily written reports). But as reports can be both written and oral, this general description is useful.

Smith sends a message to you.

It enters your sensory world, is picked up by your receptors (ears, eyes, touch), and goes to your brain.

SENSORY RECEPTORS AND THE SENSORY WORLD   We begin our description of the communication process with Smith communicating something to you. The message she sends may be in any of a number of forms—gestures, facial expressions, drawings, or, more likely, written or spoken words. Whatever its form, the message enters your sensory world.

By sensory world, we mean all that exists around you that your sensory receptors detect. The sensory receptors are those parts of your body (eyes, ears, nose) that record impressions (stimuli) from the world around you. In other words, your sensory world contains all that you feel, see, hear, or smell. From this sensory world, your receptors pick up stimuli and send them to your brain.

You should note, however, that your receptors cannot detect all that exists in the world around you. Just how much they can detect depends on a number of factors.

One determining factor is the ability of your individual sensory receptors to receive impressions. Not all receptors are equally sensitive. All ears do not hear equally well. Likewise, eyesights differ. So do abilities to smell. The other senses also vary from person to person.

Another determinant is your mental alertness. There are times, for example, when your mind is keenly alert to all that its senses can detect. There are other times when it is dull—in a stupor, a daydream, or the like.

Still another determinant is the will of your mind. In varying degrees, your mind has the ability to tune in or out events in the world of reality. In a noisy roomful of people, for example, you can select the conversation of a single person and keep out the surrounding noises.

When your sensory receptors record something from your sensory world, they relay it to your brain. Probably you would record the message Smith sent you in this way. But it could be joined by other messages your sensory receptors pick up from the world around you, such as outside noises, movements of objects, and facial expressions. In fact, your brain receives such messages in a continuous flow—a flow that may contract or expand, go fast or go slow, become strong or become weak.

THE PREVERBAL STAGE   This flow of stimulations into your mind begins the preverbal stage of communication. At this stage, the sensory perceptions pass through the filter of your mind, and your mind gives them meaning. Your filter is made up of all that has passed through your mind. Specifically, it is made up of all your experience, knowledge, bias, emotions—in fact, all you are and have been. Obviously, no two people have identical filters, for no two people have precisely the same experience, knowledge, bias, and such.

Because people's filters differ, meanings they assign to comparable perceptions also differ. One person, for example, may smile pleasantly when his or her filter receives the word *liberal;* another with sharply differing background may react with violent anger at the same word. In one person's filter, the word *butterball* rings a jolly note; in the filter of one who has long been troubled with weight problems, a negative connotation may occur. Even a salesperson's cheery "good morning" may produce sharply varying reactions. In a filter surrounded with happiness, the full positive meaning is received. A filter of a burdened, emotionally upset mind, on the other hand, may react with annoyance at these words that break into the mind's unhappy state.

THE SYMBOLIZING STAGE   Next in the communication process is the symbolizing stage. At this stage, your mind reacts to the filtered information it has received. If the filtered information produces a sufficiently strong reaction, your mind may elect to communicate some form of response by words, by gesture, by action, or by some other means.

When your mind does elect to communicate, it next determines the general meaning the response will take. This process involves the innermost and most complex

---

Side notes:

Your receptors do not detect all but vary in ability.

Mental alertness can hinder detection.

Also, the will of your mind is a factor.

When Smith's message enters your brain, it may be mixed with other sensory information.

The message passes through the filter of your mind, which gives it meaning. Your filter consists of the total content of your mind—experience, knowledge, bias, emotions.

Because people's filters differ, they give different meanings to a message.

Your mind reacts to the meaning it receives and may elect to respond.

Then, it determines the meaning of this response

workings of the mind and little is known about it. There is evidence, however, to indicate that one's ability here, and throughout the symbolizing stage, is related to one's mental capacities and to the extent to which one will permit the mind to react. Your ability to evaluate filtered information and formulate meaning is related to your ability with language. Ability with language equips you with a variety of symbol forms (ways of expressing meaning); and the greater the number of symbol forms in your mind, the more discriminating you can be in selecting them.

and converts this meaning into symbols (mainly words).

You end the symbolizing stage by encoding the meaning formed in your mind. That is, you convert your meanings into symbols, and you transmit the symbols. In most instances, your symbol form is words, either made as sounds or as marks on paper. You also may select gestures, movements, facial expressions, diagrams, and such.

The message you send enters Smith's sensory world, and the process is repeated.

THE CYCLE REPEATED   Transmittal of the encoded message ends the first cycle of the communication process. The transmitted signals next enter the sensory world that surrounds Smith; and then begins a second cycle, identical to the first. Now Smith picks up these symbols through her sensory receptors. They then travel through her nervous system to her brain. Here they are given meaning as they pass through her individual filter of knowledge, experience, bias, emotional makeup, and the like. The filtered meanings may also bring about a response, which Smith then formulates in her mind, puts in symbol form, and transmits. The process may continue indefinitely, cycle after cycle, as long as she and you want to communicate.

☐   **THE MODEL AND WRITTEN COMMUNICATION**

The process described generally applies to written communication, with these major exceptions:

Although the foregoing description of the communication process applies more specifically to face-to-face communication than to other forms, it generally describes written communications as well. But some significant differences exist.

(1) Written communication is more a creative effort,

EFFECTS ON CREATIVITY   Perhaps the most significant difference between face-to-face and written communication is that written communication is more likely to be a creative effort of the mind. That is, it is more likely to be thought out and less likely to be the spontaneous reaction to messages received. More specifically, the message in a written communication is more likely to be a result of stimuli produced by the mind than a result of outside stimuli picked up by the senses.

as in an involved report-writing situation.

In a report-writing situation, for example, before you begin work on the report, you have decided to communicate. Before you begin the task of communicating, you gather the information that will form the basis of your communication. Then, through logical thought processes, you encode the communication that will accomplish your communication objective. Thus, there is not likely to be an interchange of stimuli between you and your reader; nor is there likely to be any triggering of desires to communicate. The process is a creative and deliberate one.

A routine reporting situation is more like face-to-face communication.

On the other hand, a letter or memorandum situation can be an exception, at least to some extent. In a sense, this situation can be like a face-to-face situation in slow motion. Stimuli picked up by your receptors could produce a reaction that would bring about a communication response—in this case a written letter or memorandum. This message could, in turn, bring about a communication response in your reader's mind. Thus, a reply would be written. This reply could then bring about another reply from you. And the cycle could be repeated as long as each message brings about a communication response. Even so, letters and memorandums represent more deliberate and creative efforts than face-to-face communication.

(2) Time lapses are greater in written communication.

THE LAG OF TIME   The most obvious difference between face-to-face and written communication processes is the time factor. In face-to-face communication, the encoded messages move instantaneously into the sensory environments of the participants. In written communication, however, some delay takes place. Just how long the delay will be is indeterminate. Priority administrative announcements or telegrams may be read minutes after they are written. Routine letters require a day or two to communicate their content. Research reports may take weeks in communicating their information to the intended readers. All such written communications may be filed for possible reference in the indefinite future and may continue to communicate for months or years.

Feedback is slower.

The lag of time also makes a difference in the return information you get from communicating. Return information, commonly called feedback, helps you determine whether you are being understood. In face-to-face communication, feedback is easy to get. The participants are together. They can ask questions. They can observe facial expressions. They can repeat and simplify whenever it appears to be necessary. In written communication, feedback is slow at best. Often, it does not occur at all.

(3) Cycles in written exchanges tend to be fewer.

LIMITED NUMBER OF CYCLES   A third significant difference between face-to-face and written communication is the number of cycles that typically occur in a communication event. As previously noted, face-to-face communication normally involves multiple exchanges of symbols; thus, many cycles take place. Written communication, on the other hand, usually involves a limited number of cycles. In fact, most written communication is one-cycle communication. A message is sent and received, but none is returned. Of course, there are exceptions, such as letters and memorandums that lead to a succession of communication exchanges. But even the most involved of these would hardly match in cycle numbers a routine face-to-face conversation.

☐ SOME BASIC TRUTHS

The communication process reveals some basic truths.

Analysis of the communication process brings out three underlying truths, which are helpful to the understanding of communication in general and report writing in particular.

Because our mental filters differ, meanings sent may differ from meanings received.

MEANINGS SENT ARE NOT ALWAYS RECEIVED   First, meanings transmitted are not necessarily the meanings received. No two minds have identical filters. No two minds have identical storehouses of words, gestures, facial expressions, or any of the other symbol forms; nor do any two minds attach exactly the same meanings to all the symbols they have in common. Because of these differences, errors in communication are bound to occur.

MEANING IS IN THE MIND   A second underlying truth is that meaning is in the mind and not in the words or other symbols used. How accurately meaning is conveyed in symbols depends on how skilled one is in choosing symbols and how accurately the person receiving the symbols is able to interpret the meaning intended. Thus, you should look beyond the symbols used. You should consider the communication abilities of those with whom you want to communicate. When they receive your messages, they do not look at the symbols alone. They also look for the meanings they think you intended.

Meanings are in the mind—not in symbols.

COMMUNICATION IS IMPERFECT   Third is the basic truth that communication is highly imperfect. One reason for this imperfection is that symbols, especially words, are limited and at best are crude substitutes for the real thing. For example, the one word *man* can refer to any one of a few hundred million human males, no two precisely alike. The word *dog* stands for one of a countless number of animals varying sharply in size, shape, color, and in every other visible aspect. *House* can refer equally well to a shanty, a palatial mansion, and the many different structures between these extremes. The verb *run* tells only the most general part of the action it describes; it ignores the countless variations in speed, grace, and style. These illustrations are not exceptions; they are the rule. Words simply cannot account for the infinite variations and complexities of reality.

Because symbols are imperfect

Another reason for communication imperfection is that communicators vary in their ability to convey their thoughts. Some find great difficulty in selecting symbols that express their simplest thoughts; others are highly capable. Variations in ability to communicate obviously lead to variations in the precision with which thoughts are expressed.

and people differ in ability to communicate,

Although the foregoing comments bring to light the difficulties, complexities, and limitations of communications as a whole, we human beings do a fairly good job of communicating with one another. Even so, incidents of miscommunication occur frequently. Those people who attach precise meanings to every word, who feel that meanings intended are meanings received, and who are not able to select symbols well are apt to experience more than their share of miscommunication.

communication is far from perfect.

□   **RESULTING EMPHASIS ON ADAPTATION**

How the communication process influenced the development of report-writing techniques is easily derived from the preceding review. This review shows that communication is a unique event. It shows also that every mind (filter) is unique in its content—different from every other mind. No two people know the same words, nor do they know equally as much about all subjects. Obviously, these differences make communication difficult. Unless the symbols (mainly words) used have the same meanings in both minds, communication will suffer. Report writers of the past saw this problem. They developed the logical solution: adapt the message to the mind of the reader. Thus, adaptation has become a fundamental principle of good report writing.

The difficulties in communicating have led to an emphasis on adaptation.

By adapting to the readers, we mean using words and concepts that your readers understand. Adaptation involves first visualizing your readers—determining who they are, what they know about the subject, what are their educational levels, and how they think. Then, it involves tailoring the writing to fit these readers. The subject is discussed in greater detail in "Techniques of Readable Writing" (Chapter 10).

Adaptation means fitting the message to the reader's mind.

☐ DEVELOPMENT OF EMPHASIS ON READABILITY

Also, report writers have emphasized readability.

Emphasis on readability is a second major development resulting from report writers' efforts to improve the communication of reports. By readability, we mean that quality in writing that results in quick and easy communication. Readable writing communicates precisely—and with a single reading.

Research shows that different readability levels exist.

The concept of readability developed from scientific studies conducted over past years. These studies suggest that different levels of readability exist. More specifically, they show that for each general level of education there is a level of writing easily read and understood. Writing that is readable to one educational level can be difficult for those below that level. To illustrate, the general level of writing that is easy reading for the college graduate is difficult for those below his or her educational level. A level that is easy reading for the high school senior is difficult for those with less education. Readability levels exist for each general level of education. These levels may be measured by various formulas also developed through the readability research. Perhaps the best known of these, the Gunning Fog Index, is described in Appendix D. This formula is a useful tool in determining the level of one's writing.

Professionals write for specific levels. So should you.

The concept of readability is well known to professional writers, who long have been writing for varying levels of readership. The currently popular magazines, for example, aim at varying levels of readability. The *New Yorker* aims at about the level of a high school graduate. Magazines like *Reader's Digest* and *Time* are easy reading for those of eighth- and tenth-grade level. And at the bottom and aiming at third- to fifth-grade level of readership are an assortment of celebrity gossip magazines. As a report writer, you would do well to follow the professionals by adapting your messages to your readers.

Actually, writing readably is a form of adaptation.

Actually, writing readably for a given level of reader is a specialized form of adaptation. Thus, when you adapt, you are also working for readability. The concepts of adaptation and readability (see Chapter 10) form the foundations for the writing instructions in this book. It is comforting to know they are based on extensive research findings and they are tested techniques for improving communication.

ETHICS AND REPORT WRITING

Report writers also stress ethics.

In addition to stressing communication, report writers recognize the fact that their presentations can significantly affect others. Thus, they emphasize ethics in their work. Our review of report writing instruction will do the same.

Think about the meaning of ethics.

As you consider the subject of ethics, first think about what it means to be ethical. Then think about how ethics apply to report writing. Most probably, such words as *fairness, honesty, truth,* and *objectivity* come quickly to mind. All of these qualities are essential to ethics as they relate to report writing.

If you are ethical in the reports you prepare, you are fair and impartial in your presentation of facts. You keep an open mind and look at all sides of an issue. You present your report findings in a tone and style that fairly represent the facts. You

In reports, ethics mean you fairly present facts, keep an open mind, convey findings in appropriate tone and style, construct proper graphic aids, and overcome bias.

construct graphic aids that properly convey the report story, and you put aside any bias or prejudice you might have as you build your report on truth.

You achieve these ethical qualities in business reports through logical, rigorous, and diligent thinking. There is no substitute for it in reports. Remember, too, that ethical issues become quite visible for readers to observe in business reports—particularly those that are written. Others can see the results of faulty research methods, unjustified conclusions, one-sided arguments without factual support, overly large graphic aids, and the like.

You achieve ethics in reports through critical thinking.

Your ethical and professional responsibility is to face ethical dilemmas in report preparation with intensive thinking.

Ethical dilemmas will confront you often in the preparation of business reports. It is your ethical and professional responsibility to face these dilemmas with painstaking objectivity and critical, intensive thinking. In forthcoming chapters, we will remind you at selected places about the need for ethics in various stages of report preparation. But you should remember throughout your reading of this text that ethics exist through the intensity and objectivity of your thinking as you prepare professional business reports.

In Conclusion

The following chapters present the techniques developed to overcome the problems of communicating in reports.

In this quick review of the development of the structure and techniques of report writing, our goal has been to introduce subjects to you that will be covered in greater depth in following chapters. Another goal is to establish the point that the subject of report writing is not based on arm-chair theories or arbitrary rules and procedures. Rather, it is based on logical developments over long years of experimentation. You should keep this in mind as you read the remainder of this book.

Questions

1. Discuss and illustrate the differences in information needs of various work assignments in the business organization. Use illustrations other than those in the book.

2. Can a business ever have too much information? Discuss.

3. Discuss the ways the structure of a report can help satisfy information needs.

4. Give some examples of words that will have sharply differing meanings in different minds because of filter differences. Explain the differences.

5. Two college professors were discussing a theory developed by a leading scholar in their field. Said one to the other, "You are wrong in your interpretation of this point. Look here on page 37 of his book. These are his exact words, and the dictionary definitions prove that my interpretation is right." Said the other, "But I studied under the man three years. I have heard him discuss this point many times." Discuss this situation.

6. Thirty students in a classroom all hear the same lecture and read the same assignment. No two are likely to learn precisely the same material. Explain.

7. In an effort to emphasize a key point of communication, a professor asked a student to come before the class. The professor gave the student a sheet of paper on which appeared a line drawing of a geometric design. Then he asked the student to describe the design in words so that the other students could duplicate it. After long minutes of fruitless effort, the student gave up. Explain his difficulty.

8. Near the end of a working day, a supervisor walked through his shop. As he passed one of his machinists, he said, "I think you had better clean up around here." He said the same words to the next two machinists he passed. The first machinist immediately began tidying up his work area. The second man was embarrassed, but he agreed that he was overdue for a bath. The third man began to wonder how the boss found out that he had been telling dirty stories. Discuss from a communication point of view.

9. Trace the different meanings the following words could have under varying circumstances.

cat	pack	down	frame
stick	mark	drawl	hand
run	part	foot	head
club	chase	drive	key
bug	draft	form	

10. What is meant by "reader adaptation"?

11. What are "levels of readability"? What do they mean to the writer?

12. What does ethics mean for the report writer? Give some examples of unethical practices in business reports.

Problem Analysis
and Research

P A R T

2

Determining the Problem and Planning the Investigation

This chapter covers needs for a report, problem statement, and research plan.

Reports are written because someone needs information. Usually this need for information concerns a problem that must be solved. Thus, you will have to determine what the problem is before you can begin to work effectively on a report. Then, with the problem clearly in mind, you must work out a plan for getting the information you need to solve it. Next, you will carry out this research plan. A summary of the procedures for these basic steps appears in the following pages.

DETERMINATION OF NEED FOR A REPORT

Usually reports are assigned when an executive recognizes a need for information.

Your work on a business report usually begins when someone above you in the organization recognizes a need for a report. Logically, this someone is in a position to recognize need and has the authority to do something about it. Typically, this person is an executive who needs information in order to make a decision.

☐ A SUBJECTIVE PROCESS

Recognizing need is a subjective process done best by knowledgeable people.

Recognizing need is not a task for which there can be meaningful instruction. It is a highly subjective process, requiring an intimate knowledge of the subject. Authorities in every field know what topics need further investigation, whereas the novice does not. Competent chemists, for example, know what areas of chemistry need further research. So it is with competent physicists, geologists, and psychologists. And so it is with competent business administrators. They know the boundaries of business knowledge and where these boundaries should be pushed back. They know their own business and the business's needs for information. They know the information needs for their jobs, especially for the decisions they must make. On the basis of this knowledge, they determine the needs for reports.

☐ Two Types of Needs for Reports

Businesses need reports for two reasons: (1) to solve a problem, and

Generally a company needs business reports for two reasons. First, a company may have a special problem that needs solving. For example, a company may face problems such as determining which of two machines to buy, why sales in certain districts have dropped, whether a change in inventory method should be made, or what is the root of labor unrest at X Plant. To solve such problems, someone would need to gather all pertinent information, analyze it, and from the analysis arrive at an answer.

(2) to function properly.

Second, businesses need information in order to function properly. Proper functioning of today's complex business organizations requires vast quantities of information—production records, sales statistics, activity descriptions, personnel reviews, and the like. Modern business needs such information to facilitate decision making, to regulate production, to measure progress, and generally to coordinate and control its multiphased operations. Without adequate transmittal of information, modern business could not function. Reports serve as a major medium in transmitting this vital information.

☐ Three Ways of Assigning Reports

You may receive a report assignment in three ways: (1) by a direct request, (2) through standard operating procedures, and (3) through your initiative.

You are likely to receive a report-writing assignment in one of three ways. First, someone or some group may ask you, or a group of which you are a member, for information. As a member of a group, you may prepare the report collaboratively with other group members. The request may be in writing, usually in the form of a letter or a memorandum; or the request could be made orally. Second, you or your collaborative group may need to prepare a report as a result of your company's standard operating procedure. As we noted previously, many companies require that reports be used to transmit certain types of information within the organization. Third, you or your group could originate the report on your initiative. For example, you as an administrator may see a problem need, investigate the situation, collect information, analyze this information, and write a report. As an employee, you may see a need for collecting and passing on information. Or as an independent researcher, you may conduct an investigation on a topic and record the findings for any who might be interested.

Determining the Basic Problem

Your work on a report begins with a study of the problem.

After receiving the assignment, you must be sure you have the problem clearly in mind. In some situations, this is a simple and routine step that requires little effort. You may, for example, have worked on similar problems before; you may be intimately acquainted with the specific problem situation; or the problem may be a simple one. In other situations, the problem may be vaguely defined or complex. The more intricate and generally sophisticated such problems are, the more likely you are to misinterpret the objective. It is for problems such as these that the following suggestions for a problem determination procedure are given.

☐   GETTING THE PROBLEM CLEARLY IN MIND

You should get the problem clearly in mind by gathering and analyzing the information available.

You should begin the task of getting the problem in mind by carefully reviewing the information available. If the problem was assigned in writing, you should carefully study the written words for their most precise and likely meanings. In this effort, you may want to communicate further with those who asked you to research the problem. If the problem was orally assigned, you should probe and question the authorizers until you are certain of their intent. If you originated the research on the problem, then perhaps you have the task of clearing your thoughts.

☐   THE INFORMAL INVESTIGATION

You gather information through informal research,

Problem determination is not always the task of merely interpreting words. Frequently, you can clarify what the problem is only by having a thorough knowledge of the subject. If you do not already have such knowledge, you must acquire it. Typically, you acquire it through some form of preliminary information research. You can conduct this information investigation in any number of ways since there is no one best course. In fact, whatever method will provide the basic facts in a given case will suffice.

which involves talking to people, studying company records, and reading printed material.

Often your best course is to read about the subject from secondary sources—books, periodicals, brochures, and the like. Sometimes you can gain valuable background knowledge by searching through company records and documents. There are times when you can learn what you need to know by discussing the problem with people who know something about it. You may, for example, talk it over with your fellow workers, especially with those directly involved with the problem in their work situation. Or you may talk with authorities outside the company—private consultants, professors, government officials, and the like. If the problem is such that the opinions or practices of the general public are involved, you may just talk to people. In general, in your informal investigation you should use any source of information that will help you to understand the problem.

☐   CLEAR STATEMENT OF THE PROBLEM

Then you state the problem clearly, preferably in writing.

After you have the basic problem clearly in mind, you should put it in writing. Putting the problem in writing is good for many reasons. A written statement is permanently preserved; thus, you may refer to it time and again without danger of changes occurring in it. In addition, other people can review, approve, and evaluate a written statement, and their assistance may sometimes be valuable to you. Most important of all, putting the problem in writing forces you to do, and to do well, this basic initial task of getting the problem in mind. In this way, this requirement serves as a valuable form of self-discipline.

Your problem statement may be (1) an infinitive phrase, or

You can write the problem statement in one of three forms. One is the infinitive phrase. For example, if as a salesperson you must submit a summary of activities for the week, you might write the problem statement thus: *To present a summary of work activities for the week.* If you are a researcher assigned the task of reviewing and analyzing data on three low-priced cars to determine which is the best for a certain group, you might write this problem statement: *To determine whether Car A, Car B, or Car C is the best buy for middle-income families.*

(2) a question, or

The question is the second type of a problem statement. For the sales activity report previously described, you could write the problem statement in this question form: *How did I spend my work time last week?* And for the automobile study you could write it this way: *Is Car A, Car B, or Car C the best buy for the middle-class family?*

(3) a declarative statement.

A third and less popular form is the declarative statement. Although somewhat dull and not so goal-oriented as the other two, this form nevertheless gives a good indication of the problem. Using the two example situations previously described, you might write these problem statements: (1) *The company wants a summary of my work activities for last week,* and (2) *Cars A, B, and C will be compared in order to determine which one is the best buy for middle-income families.*

In all the preceding illustrations, the problem is unmistakably complete and clear. You cannot help but be aware of what the report must do. Were the statements not so clearly worded, they could very easily lead you to stray away from the goal. To illustrate the point, contrast the preceding statements on the automobile problem with this one: *To compare three cars as a guide to buying.* Obviously, this one describes the objective loosely. Although it implies that a conclusion will be reached, it ignores the goal of the comparison—to determine the best buy for middle-income families. Certainly this factor makes a significant difference in your route to your objective.

DETERMINING THE FACTORS

Next, you determine the factors of the problem. These may be subtopics of the main problem, hypotheses, or bases for comparison.

After stating the problem, you should turn to the mental task of determining the problem's needs. Within the framework of your logical imagination, you look for the factors of the problem. That is, you look for the subject areas that you must investigate in order to satisfy the overall objective. Specifically, these factors may be of three types. First, they may be merely subtopics of the broader topic about which the report is concerned. Second, they may be hypotheses that must be subjected to the test of investigation and objective review. Third, in problems that involve comparisons they may be the bases on which the comparisons are made.

The process is mental.

Obviously, this process is a mental one, involving the intricate workings of your mind. Thus, we may describe it only in the most general way. You begin the process by applying your best logic and comprehensive abilities to the problem. The same mental processes that helped you to comprehend the problem now should assist you in determining the structure of the solution.

☐   USE OF SUBTOPICS IN INFORMATIONAL AND SOME ANALYTICAL REPORTS

Subtopics of the overall subject are the factors in information reports.

If the problem concerns a need for information (with or without analysis), you should determine the subareas of information needed. That is, you should look for the topical breakdowns of the problem. By topical breakdowns, we mean the areas of information that must be covered—the subjects (topics) that the main problem involves. Perhaps this procedure is explained better by illustration.

The salesperson's report described in the foregoing example clearly is an informational type. It requires only a presentation of facts. Although there is no one best arrangement for these facts, they might well include such subareas as direct sales efforts, service expenses, promotion, prospect development, and competition activities. Thus, the analysis of the problem and its factors might take this form:

Problem statement:

To present a summary of work activities for the week

Factors:

1. Direct sales efforts

2. Service

3. Promotion

4. Prospect development

5. Expenses

6. Competitors' activities

Another example of factor breakdown for an information report is how to review a certain company's (say Company X) activities for the past year. This also could be a routine informational type of problem. That is, it could require no analyses, conclusions, or recommendations. But it could be analytical. It could require that each of the information areas covered be analyzed. It could even require that the analyses lead to an evaluation of the overall quality of the operation. In all of these cases, the mental process of determining factors involves determining the subdivisions of the overall subject. After thinking through the possibilities, you might arrive at this problem statement and factor analysis:

Problem statement:

To review the operations of Company X from January 1 through December 31

Factors:

1. Production

2. Sales and promotion

3. Financial status

4. Plant and equipment

5. Product development

6. Personnel

☐   **HYPOTHESES FOR PROBLEMS REQUIRING A SOLUTION**

Hypotheses (possible explanations) may be the factors in problems requiring solution.

By their nature, some problems require a solution. Typically, such problems seek an explanation of a phenomenon or the correction of a condition. In analyzing such problems, you must seek possible explanations or solutions. Such explanations or solutions are called *hypotheses*.

More precisely defined, hypotheses are tentative explanations of factual information. You advance them based on the information available and your knowledge of the subject area. The process is largely mental and is a product of your intelligence. After you have formulated your hypotheses, you conduct systematic research designed to prove or disprove the hypotheses.

The process is much the same as that followed by medical doctors in their efforts to cure patients of ailments. First, medical doctors collect information by inspecting the patients and asking questions about the symptoms—a procedure similar to the informal investigation. Then, with this information and their knowledge of medicine, the doctors mentally derive possible explanations for the ailment. A doctor may, for example, hypothesize that a patient's illness may be due to stomach ulcers. A second possible explanation—that gallstones are to blame—may be advanced. A third explanation may be advanced or perhaps four or more. With these hypotheses in mind, the doctor next conducts medical tests (X rays, blood analyses, and such) to prove or disprove the hypotheses.

If the doctor's research findings support one of the hypotheses, the likely answer to the problem has been found. If they do not, the doctor must make additional hypotheses and conduct additional tests. The doctor continues advancing hypotheses and testing them until there is proof that one is correct. Then, with the correct one identified, the doctor takes whatever action is necessary to cure the patient.

The procedure may be much the same in a business research situation. Illustrating this similarity is the case of a department store chain that wants to know why sales at one of its stores are dropping. In preparing this problem for investigation, you logically would begin by gathering information about the situation (the informal investigation). You would learn enough about the problem to enable you to work out a plan for solving it. You would begin the plan by clearly stating the problem, perhaps in these words:

Problem statement:
Why have sales declined at the Milltown Store?

Then, with this problem statement in mind, as well as the knowledge picked up through informal investigation of the problem, you would look for possible explanations. Perhaps you will pick up information that suggests competition in the area has become a major limiting factor. You might find information that supports the possibility that the Milltown economy might be changing, thus explaining the store's lost sales. Or you might discover that the store's management is at fault—there have been weak administration and merchandising. Thus, you might state the three hypotheses in this way:

1. Increased activity of competition in the store's trade area has caused a loss in sales.

2. Declining economic activity in the trade area explains the loss in sales.

3. The loss in sales is a result of weak administration and merchandising practices.

Next, you would design a research plan to test the three hypotheses. You may choose to test them one at a time or together. To get the information needed to test the hypothesis that competitors' increased activities have caused the sales decline, you might design a survey of consumers to determine changes in sources of supply, buying practices, attitudes, and such. To test the hypothesis that the sales decline is a result of a decrease in economic activity in the store's trade area, you might gather from government and industry sources all available data on the economic conditions. And to test the hypothesis that poor management is the cause of the decline, you might develop pertinent data through systematic observation of merchandising and administrative practices in the store.

After you have gathered these data, you would apply them to your hypotheses, using logic and appropriate statistical techniques. Your goal, of course, would be to test each hypothesis objectively, seeking with equal vigor to prove or disprove it.

Perhaps you would find one, two, or even three are valid. But it is also possible you would find that all are false. Then you would have to advance additional hypotheses and test them. And you would continue until you found a hypothesis that proves to be valid.

☐   BASES OF COMPARISON IN EVALUATION STUDIES

For evaluation problems, the bases for evaluating are the factors.

When the problem requires you to evaluate something, either singularly or by comparison with others, you must determine the bases for the evaluations. More specifically, you must determine the characteristics you will evaluate; and sometimes you must determine the criteria you will use in evaluating each characteristic.

The problem of a company seeking to determine in which of three cities it should locate its new factory illustrates this technique. In planning the work on this problem, you would begin by getting all the readily available information. You would learn from company officials what are the company's needs and requirements. If you do not already have such knowledge, you would learn from books, journals, specialists in the field, and so on the requirements for locating a plant. With this information in mind, you would write the problem statement; then you would determine its factors.

Writing the problem statement would be an easy task since the problem is a simple one. Something like this infinitive form would do the job:

Problem statement:

To determine whether Y Company's new factory should be located in City A, City B, or City C

Determining the factors would consist of identifying the bases for comparing the three cities. Obviously, these bases would be the characteristics of cities that make some more desirable for plant location than others. Perhaps in this case, availability of skilled labor is an important consideration. And it may be that the plant will use bulky raw materials, thus making availability of raw materials important. Similarly the bulky nature of the manufactured product might require more than the usual transportation; thus, quality of transportation facilities might be of major concern in the location decision. These and other location considerations similarly derived would make up the factors for this comparison study. Thus, your final breakdown of factors might look like this:

1. Availability of labor
2. Abundance of raw materials
3. Tax structure
4. Transportation facilities
5. Nearness to markets
6. Power supply
7. Community attitude

Also serving to illustrate this form of factor breakdown is the automobile selection problem described earlier. In selecting one of three automobiles as the best buy for middle-income families, you would need to determine in advance the bases for the decision. In this case, overall costs most certainly would be a major determinant, for middle-income consumers must be frugal. Performance would be another, and so would safety, durability, and perhaps even riding comfort. Thus, your problem statement and its factors might well take this form:

Problem statement:

To determine whether Car A, Car B, or Car C is the best buy for middle-income families

Factors:

1. Cost
2. Safety
3. Performance
4. Durability
5. Riding comfort

In either of the examples cited, you would gather data for each item (city, car) to be compared on each of the factors. Then, using these data, you could make comparisons. On the bases of these comparisons, you would develop your decisions.

☐   NEED FOR SUBBREAKDOWN

Sometimes the factors have factors of their own and may be broken down.

Each of the factors selected for investigation may have factors of its own. For example, in the preceding illustration concerning location of a new factory, you could cover the comparison of transportation facilities in the three cities with this breakdown of factors:

1. Water
2. Rail
3. Truck
4. Air

You could cover labor by these subfactors:

1. Skilled

2. Unskilled

And you could give these subfactors their own subfactors. For example, you could break down skilled labor by subfactors such as these:

1. Machinists

2. Plumbers

3. Pipe fitters

4. Welders

5. Electricians

These breakdowns of factors and subfactors could go on and on. You should continue to make them as long as they appear to be helpful to an understanding of the subject matter.

The value of this step of finding the factors of the problem is obvious: It serves as a guide to the investigation that follows. In addition, it gives the problem the first semblance of order.

CONSTRUCTING THE RESEARCH PLAN

Your next step is to plan the research that will get the information needed.

After deciding what information you need for the problem, you should turn your energies to the task of planning the research. In the more routine problems, your planning is likely to be quite simple. Research for a weekly sales report, for example, may require only collecting familiar data from personal records. When you write such reports, you hardly need to be conscious of a prescribed research procedure, for you are dealing with thoroughly familiar material.

Involved research plans should be in step-by-step detail.

In problems where the research needs are more complex, you are wise to construct a step-by-step research plan. For example, if you are seeking to learn consumer attitudes through a nationwide survey, you would need to chart a detailed course. The value of a detailed plan should be apparent. Certainly, a plan serves to bring order to your investigation, and you cannot make the larger, more complex investigations without order. By thinking out a course of action, you are likely to be aware of the possible errors and thus avoid them. A plan serves generally to clarify your thinking. In addition, it serves as a blueprint to be followed throughout the investigation.

Preferably you should write them in an order

In all but the simplest of investigations (such as those requiring only library research), you should write the plan. Not to write it would be to invite confusion, for most research plans are too involved for the mind to handle without help. Although the content and arrangement of the written plan need not follow any prescribed pattern, the plan usually follows the order in which the investigation progresses. The following checklist outline shows one acceptable arrangement:

such as the one illustrated here.

1. *The problem*

    Statement of the problem; its scope and limitations.

Factors (working hypotheses) or areas of information to be investigated.

Background material.

Limitations to the investigation (money, time, qualified people, and so on).

2. *Methodology*

Complete yet concise description of how the research is to be conducted.

If secondary research is to be employed: Would include description of basic sources to be consulted. May include a tentative bibliography.

If primary research is to be used: Would consist of a how-to-do-it description that goes through the procedure step by step. Contains sufficient detail to permit one to follow. For a survey, for example, planning may include topics such as sample design, selecting and training of workers, conduct of investigation, plan for pilot study, controls and checks, and time schedule of work.

3. *Handling the findings*

A description of how the findings will be prepared for application to the problem. Covers such activities as editing, classifying, tabulating, and verifying results.

4. *Reporting the results*

Any preliminary thinking concerning the procedure to be used in giving meaning to the findings and applying them to the problem. May include a tentative outline and a discussion of approach for final report.

The tentative working plan is important to the analysis of the report problem. But you must be familiar with basic research techniques before you can wisely construct a plan for solving report problems. Basic research techniques allow you to begin putting the work plan into practice by showing you how to collect facts that will form the basis of your report.

QUESTIONS

1. Discuss the needs for business reports. Give illustrations other than those in the text.

2. In what ways are problems assigned?

3. Write a clear statement of the problem and determine the factors involved in each of the following problem situations:
   a. A consumer research organization plans to test the three leading low-priced automobiles in an effort to determine which one is the best buy as a family car for the typical consumer.
   b. A national chain of dress shops wants to learn what qualities to seek in hiring sales personnel.
   c. A daily newspaper wants to know how well the various types of items in a typical issue are read.
   d. The sales division of a major national manufacturer compiles a semiannual report on its activities in all of its five sales districts.

      e.   A major soap manufacturer wishes to determine how its leading bath soap compares with its competition in the minds of consumers.

      f.   A distributor of a line of French perfumes is planning an advertising campaign. The company wants to know more about the people who are buying these perfumes. Such information will serve as a guide to slanting the distributor's advertising.

4.   Select and analyze one problem for hypothetical situations with factors that consist of *(a)* subtopics of information needed, *(b)* hypotheses, and *(c)* bases of comparison.

5.   Defend the logic of writing a detailed research plan.

Collecting Information: Library Research

Research gives you information and clarifies your perspective. It is a process of discovery that keeps you interested and makes you think.

You have analyzed the problem, defined the objectives, and determined what information you will need. Now you are ready to start the research that will provide facts for your report. This stage of your report writing can be especially challenging if you recognize from the outset its importance to your project. Research is a process of discovery that is interesting and rewarding for its own sake as well as for its contribution to your understanding of the subject you are investigating. It not only gives you the basic information you need, but it also helps you clarify your perspective and develop a context for your problem. Research prompts you to ask questions and to consider possible applications, alternatives, or relationships. It keeps you interested and makes you think.

Secondary research is research of materials someone else has developed.

There are two classifications of research: secondary and primary. Secondary research is research of materials someone else has developed and published in periodicals, brochures, reports, and such. In complex problems, you will frequently use secondary research in your informal investigation—even if you plan to develop most of your information through primary research.

Primary research is firsthand research and develops new information.

Primary research, as the term implies, is firsthand research. It brings about new findings or develops original information. You will use primary research when secondary information on your topic is incomplete, needs updating, or is simply not available.

To be effective as a report writer, you should be familiar with the methods most frequently used in both secondary and primary research. Because effective report writing should start with a review of what has been done on a subject, we will review the basics of secondary research first and then move on to primary research techniques in the following chapter.

CONDUCTING SECONDARY RESEARCH

Secondary research can be a rich source of information if you know what to look for and where to look.

Secondary research materials are potentially the least costly, the most accessible, and the most complete source of information. However, to take full advantage of what is available, you must know what you are looking for and where and how to find it.

That task can be a complex and challenging one. However, you can meet the challenge if you become familiar with the general arrangement of a library or other repositories of secondary materials and if you learn the aids to finding material in this arrangement. You will also need to devise a strategy for identifying and discovering the information you require. Research must be orderly if it is to be reliable and complete.

General reference sources can help you design a strategy.

Before you begin to design your complete and reliable strategy, you might want to consult some basic reference sources of business information. Four of them deserve mention. *Business Information Sources* by Lorna Daniells is probably the best single source. *The Basic Business Library: Core Resources* by Bernard S. Schlessinger; *Business Information: How to Find It, How to Use It* by Michael Lavin; and *Handbook of Business Information: A Guide for Librarians, Students, and Researchers* by Diane Wheeler Strauss are good sources as well. These reference guides will illustrate ways in which business information is organized and provide specific entries and annotation for a myriad of information sources. To locate them and to investigate particular entries, you will need to find and use a library.

FINDING PUBLICATION COLLECTIONS

A library is the natural place to begin secondary research.

The first step in an orderly search for secondary information is to determine where to begin. The natural place is, of course, a library. There are, however, different types of libraries offering different kinds of collections. Therefore, it is helpful to know the types of libraries available and to be familiar with their contents.

General libraries offer the public a wide variety of information sources.

General libraries are the best known and the most accessible. General libraries, which include college, university, and most public libraries, are called general to the extent they contain materials of all description. Many in this group, however, have substantial collections in certain specialized areas as well.

Special libraries have limited collections and limited circulation.

Libraries that limit their collections to one type or just a few types of material are considered **special libraries.** Many such libraries are private, though, and do not invite routine public use of their materials. Still, they frequently will cooperate on research projects they consider relevant and worthwhile.

Included in the special group are the libraries of private businesses. As a rule these collections are designed to serve the sponsoring company, and they provide excellent information in the specialized areas of the company's operations. Company libraries are not as accessible as other specialized types, but a letter of inquiry explaining the nature and purpose of a project or a letter of introduction from someone known to the company can help you gain access to material you need.

Special libraries are also maintained by various types of associations—trade organizations, professional and technical groups, chambers of commerce, and labor unions, for example. Like company libraries, association libraries may provide excellent coverage of highly specialized areas. Although they develop collections principally for members or research staff, association libraries frequently make resources available to others engaged in reputable research.

A number of public and private research organizations also maintain specialized libraries. Research divisions of big-city chambers of commerce and the bureaus of research of major universities, for example, keep extensive collections of material covering statistics and general information for a local area. State agencies collect similar data. Again, though these materials are developed for a limited audience, they are often made available upon request.

Consult a directory to determine what special libraries offer.

Now, how do you determine what these research centers and special libraries offer and whom to contact for permission to use their collections? Several guides are available in the reference department of most general libraries. Particularly helpful in identifying information available in research centers is *The Research Centers Directory*. Published by Gale Research Company, it lists research activities, publications, and services of over 12,000 university-related and other nonprofit organizations. It is supplemented between editions by a related publication, *New Research Centers*.

Gale Research also publishes two comprehensive guides to special library collections. *The Directory of Special Libraries and Information Centers* describes the contents and services of selected information centers, archives, special, and research libraries. Each entry includes the address and telephone number of the facility and the name and title of the individual in charge. A companion guide, *Subject Directory of Special Libraries and Information Centers,* organizes the same information by subject.

TAKING THE DIRECT APPROACH

Begin your research using the direct approach. Look up the information you need.

When you have found the appropriate library for your research, you are ready for the next challenge. With the volume of material available, how will you find what you need? If you know nothing about how material is arranged in a library, you will waste valuable time on a probably fruitless search. However, if you are familiar with certain basic reference materials, you may be able to proceed directly to the information you seek. And if the direct approach does not work, there are several effective indirect methods of finding the material you need.

Consider both print and electronic sources in your research.

In the past, you could begin these direct and indirect strategies by accessing only printed secondary sources. With today's computer technology, you can begin by accessing electronic sources as well. For every listing of a secondary information source in the following pages, there is likely to be an online or CD-ROM source. New electronic sources originate regularly, instantly, and continuously. Thus, you should consider secondary sources mentioned in this chapter as starting points in your search for business information. At best, the categories of secondary sources used are broad terms that include both print and electronic sources. You should use them as beginnings of your research work but never final destinations.

Taking the direct approach is advisable when it is quantitative or factual information you seek. The reference section of your library is where you should start. There, either on your own or with the able assistance of a research librarian, you can discover any number of timely and comprehensive sources of facts and figures. Though you cannot know all of these sources, as a business researcher you should be familiar with certain basic ones.

□ ENCYCLOPEDIAS

Encyclopedias offer both general and detailed information.

Encyclopedias are the best known sources of direct information and are particularly valuable when you are just beginning a search. They offer background material and other general information to give you a helpful introduction to the area under study. Individual sections are written by experts in the field and frequently include a short bibliography.

Of the popular general encyclopedias, two are worthy of special mention. The *Encyclopedia Americana* is exceptionally good for American use, particularly with its coverage of statistical and technological material. The *Encyclopaedia Britannica* is good overall, having as an additional benefit the *Micropaedia,* a companion set that summarizes and cross-references material in the main volumes. Both encyclopedias are supplemented with yearbooks that keep the series up to date.

A number of specialized encyclopedias are also helpful, including *The Encyclopedia of Economics, The Encyclopedic Dictionary of Accounting and Finance, The Encyclopedia of Banking and Finance,* and *The Encyclopedia of Management.* Articles include definitions, background information, analyses of trends and statistical data, as well as selected bibliographies.

□ BIOGRAPHICAL DIRECTORIES

Biographical directories offer information about influential people.

A direct source of biographical data about a leading figure of today or the past is a biographical directory. Best known are *Who's Who in America* and *Who's Who in the World,* annual publications that summarize the lives of living people who have achieved some degree of prominence. Sketches include vital statistics, educational background, career activities, memberships, and writings. Similar publications provide coverage by geographical area: *Who's Who in the East, Who's Who in the Midwest,* for example.

Specialized publications will help you find information on individuals in particular professions. *Who's Who in Finance and Industry* provides brief sketches of prominent people in business and finance, as do *Standard & Poor's Register of Corporations, Directors, and Executives* and the *Reference Book of Corporate Managements.* Other business-oriented biographical sources include *Who's Who of American Women, Who's Who in the Securities Industry, The Rand McNally International Bankers Directory, Who's Who in Insurance,* and *Who's Who in Venture Capital.* Nearly all business and professional areas are covered by some sort of biographical directory.

☐ **ALMANACS**

Almanacs provide factual and statistical information.

Almanacs are handy guides to factual and statistical information. Simple, concise, and selective in their presentation of data, they should not be underestimated as references. *The World Almanac and Book of Facts* is an excellent general source of facts and statistics. If it is business and investment data you need, the *Irwin Business and Investment Almanac* provides comprehensive coverage of timely information. And if you are investigating a particular state or region, an almanac published by the local newspaper is a reliable source of facts and figures. Almanacs are published annually, so their contents are always up to date.

☐ **TRADE DIRECTORIES**

Trade directories publish information about individual businesses and products.

For information about individual businesses or the products they make, buy, or sell, directories are the references to consult. Directories are compilations of details in a specific area of interest and are variously referred to as catalogs, listings, registers, or source books. Some of the more comprehensive directories are indispensable in general business research. For example, the *Million Dollar Directory: Leading Public and Private Companies* series, published by Dun & Bradstreet, identifies approximately 160,000 U.S. companies with a net worth of $500,000 or more. The 23-volume *Thomas Register of American Manufacturers* is a reference of 145,000 manufacturers and services, their company profiles, and detailed product information from 2,000 catalog files.

There are literally thousands of directories in publication, and they vary widely in scope, detail, and organization. To determine what directories are available in a particular field, you will find two guides especially helpful. The first, the aptly named *Directories in Print* published by Gale, lists and describes approximately 14,000 general commercial and manufacturing directories; directories of individual industries, trades, and professions; and databases that have directory features. It now contains 4,000 foreign directories as well. The second, *Guide to American Directories,* records over 8,000 major U.S. industrial, professional, and mercantile directories.

☐ **GOVERNMENT PUBLICATIONS**

The federal government publishes an extensive selection of research materials.

The federal government publishes literally hundreds of thousands of titles each year. Surveys, catalogs, pamphlets, periodicals—there seems to be no limit to the information various bureaus, departments, and agencies collect and make available to the public. The challenge of working with government publications, therefore, is finding your way through this wealth of material to the specifics you need. That task can sometimes be very complex and require indirect research methods. However, if you are familiar with a few key sources, the direct approach will often be productive.

Monthly catalogs list the research each agency publishes.

It is sometimes helpful to consult the *Monthly Catalog of U.S. Government Publications.* Issued by the Superintendent of Documents, it includes a comprehensive listing of annual and monthly publications and an alphabetical index of the issuing agencies. The catalog also indicates which of the publications have been distributed to public, college, state, or government-agency libraries. (Libraries designated to receive copies of federal publications are called Federal Depository Libraries. You may want to make sure the library you select for your research is so designated.)

Department of Commerce censuses and surveys include information important to business research.

Routinely available, however, are a number of Department of Commerce publications that are invaluable to business research. The *Census of Population* and *Census of Housing,* issued every 10 years, summarize the results of population and housing unit counts taken at the beginning of each decade. Population data are broken down demographically by age, sex, race, ethnicity, employment status, occupation, and income, among other criteria, and geographically by categories that include region, state, and congressional districts. Housing figures are recorded in terms of units, costs, fuel use, and so forth.

Every five years, the Bureau of the Census publishes the *Census of Governments* and the following economic census reports: *Census of Retail Trade, Census of Manufacturers, Census of Agriculture, Census of Construction Industries, Census of Transportation, Census of Service Industries, Census of Wholesale Trade,* and *Census of Mineral Industries.* Important intercensal reports include the monthly *Housing Starts* series and the *Annual Survey of Manufacturers.* Both are available in depository libraries.

The *Statistical Abstract of the United States* is yet another useful reference offered by the Bureau of the Census. Published annually, it is the standard summary of statistics on the social, political, and economic organization of the United States. The Department of Commerce also issues the monthly *Survey of Current Business,* which provides data on industrial production, commodity prices, domestic and foreign trade, wages, and similar topics of interest to the business researcher.

The Department of Labor and the Federal Reserve System feature data and analyses business researchers find useful.

Publications of the Department of Labor's Bureau of Labor Statistics are also very useful and readily available references. *The Monthly Labor Review* is a highly regarded government periodical that publishes articles on employment, wages, productivity, and such. Also, *The Federal Reserve Bulletin,* published monthly by the Federal Reserve System, contains statistics on developments in the U.S. economy and articles on the impact of economic changes.

☐ **BUSINESS SERVICES**

Private business services collect and publish data. Many such reports are available in public and university libraries.

Business services are private organizations that supply a variety of information to business practitioners, especially investors. Libraries also subscribe to their publications, giving the business researcher ready access to yet another source of valuable, timely data.

Moody's Investors Service, one of the best known of such organizations, publishes annually a *Manual* in each of eight business areas: transportation, industrials, OTC (over the counter) industrials, OTC unlisteds, international, public utilities, banks and finance, and municipals and governments. These reports summarize financial data and operating facts of all major American companies, providing the information an investor needs to evaluate the investment potential of individual securities or of fields as a whole. Semiweekly and weekly *News Reports* supplement these manuals. *Standard Corporation Descriptions,* a bimonthly publication, covers over 12,000 companies with listed and unlisted securities. It is published in loose-leaf form. Also in loose-leaf form, *Value Line Investment Survey* reports on 1,700 companies in about 95 industries. This advisory service also has weekly additions.

Two additional business service organizations that are especially helpful are Predicasts, Inc., and Gale Research Company. Predicasts, Inc., provides separate business services, although it is best known for its publications featuring forecasts and market data by country, product, and company *(World-Regional-Casts* and *World-Product-Casts).* The *Predicast F&S Index United States* indexes and abstracts articles from business-oriented publications and thus is an excellent general reference tool. *Predicast Basebook* is helpful in market research, offering time series data that reflect the cyclical sensitivity of various products and industries. Its source directory, compiled annually and supplemented quarterly, contains bibliographical information on worldwide information sources.

Similarly, Gale Research Company provides a long list of services to business researchers. In addition to the directories previously mentioned, Gale publishes the *Encyclopedia of Business Information Sources,* which includes 21,000 entries on subjects and references to handbooks, encyclopedias, almanacs, dictionaries, and other sources of information. Additional Gale publications are *Encyclopedia of Associations* and *Encyclopedia of Information Systems and Services.*

□ INTERNATIONAL SOURCES

Statistical information for the international business environment is available in a wide range of documents.

In today's global business environment, we often need information outside our borders. Many of the sources we have discussed have counterparts with international information. *Principal International Businesses* lists basic information on major companies located over the world. *Major Companies of Europe* and *Japan Company Handbook* are two sources providing facts on companies in their respective areas. The *International Encyclopedia of the Social Sciences* covers all important areas of social science, including biographies of acclaimed persons in these areas. General and specialized dictionaries are available, too. *The Multilingual Commercial Dictionary* and the *International Business Dictionary in Nine Languages* include commonly used business terms in several languages. You will even be able to find trade names in the *International Trade Names Dictionary* published by Gale Research. For bibliographies and abstracts, available sources include *International Business Reference Sources, Business International Index,* the *Foreign Commerce Handbook,* and several more. Even statistical information is available in sources such as the *Index to International Statistics, Statistical Yearbook,* and *Worldcasts.* In addition, libraries usually contain many references for information on international marketing, exporting, tax, and trade.

□ LOOSE-LEAF SERVICES AND AUDIO TAPES

Loose-leaf services offer updates on law, tax, and personnel/labor.

Two other sources of business information for the secondary researcher are loose-leaf services and audio tapes. For keeping up-to-date on business law and tax issues, Commerce Clearing House and Prentice Hall, Inc., offer excellent loose-leaf publications with weekly and biweekly supplements that bring together legal rules, orders, and decisions on a particular topic. The Bureau of National Affairs provides the same type of service for personnel and labor information.

Audio tapes provide information in nonbook form.

Audiocassette tapes supply nonbook information on articles, seminars, interviews, books, and speeches. You can listen to these tapes in an office, at home, in a car, or while jogging. Usually, almost all business topics are covered through them. A good bibliography to consult for audio tapes is *On Cassette: A Comprehensive Bibliography of Spoken Word Audiocassettes*, published by R. R. Bowker. This annual volume identifies over 44,000 audio cassettes from more than 400 producers.

USING INDIRECT METHODS

When you cannot find secondary materials directly, try the indirect approach. Start by preparing a bibliography of sources that may include the material you need.

If you cannot move directly to the source of information you need, you must then find the data through indirect methods. The first step in this approach is preparing a bibliography, or list of prospective sources. Gathering the publications in your bibliography and systematically checking them for the information you are seeking are the second and third steps, respectively.

Gather all available publications. Check each systematically for the information you require.

These last two steps are elementary but nonetheless important. Your acquisition of secondary materials must be thorough. You should not depend solely on the material you find on the shelves of your library. Use interlibrary loan services or database searches; send away for company or government documents. Your check of the sources you gather must be thorough, too. For each source, review the pages cited in your bibliographic reference. Then, take some time to learn about the publication. Review the table of contents, index, and endnotes or footnotes related to the pages you are researching. You should be familiar with both the source and the context of all information you plan to report; they are often as significant as the information itself.

However, the first step, preparing the bibliography, is still the most demanding and challenging step in indirect research. It is therefore helpful to review what this task involves.

☐ SEARCHING FOR PREPARED BIBLIOGRAPHIES

Try to find a prepared bibliography. It will save you time and trouble.

You should begin your own bibliography by looking for one that has already been prepared. Lists of published materials are available through a number of sources, and finding such a list may save you the time and trouble of developing a bibliography from scratch.

Start your search in the reference section of your library. Prepared bibliographies are sometimes published as reference books, and individual entries often include a description of the reference. In the reference section, you may also find bibliographies compiled by associations or government agencies. Encyclopedias are also a helpful source of published materials; most articles conclude with a brief bibliography.

Another way to discover prepared bibliographies is to consult texts, articles, and master's and doctor's theses that deal with your subject. If books include bibliographies, it is so noted on their cards in the card catalog. Academic studies routinely

| FIGURE 4-1 | A typical library main menu screen using an electronic catalog |

```
          Welcome to the SDSU Library
          Public Access Catalog (the PAC)

You may search for library materials by any of the following:

          A > AUTHOR
          T > TITLE
          W > KEYWORDS in TITLES
          S > SUBJECT
          J > JUVENILE BOOKS
          C > CALL #

          R > RESERVE Lists
          I > Library INFORMATION
          D > Disconnect

     Choose one (A,T,W,S,J,C,R,I,D) :
```

include complete bibliographies. Articles present the most challenging task, for not all list their sources. However, since those that do are likely to include listings that are very timely and selective, it is worth the trouble to check articles individually.

☐   **USING THE LIBRARY CATALOG**

The library catalog is another resource for developing a bibliography.

If you are not able to locate a prepared bibliography, or if the bibliographies you have identified are inadequate, you must set about developing your own list of prospective sources. Here the library catalog is very helpful.

Library catalogs list the holdings of each library.

If the catalog you are using is composed of cards, it offers three distinct ways of identifying and locating desired references: by author, by title, and by subject. However, today many libraries are using electronic catalogs, giving you numerous ways to locate sources. As you can see from the main menu screen of one system in Figure 4–1, in some ways electronic catalogs are similar to card catalogs. You can still locate sources by author, title, and subject. But the electronic catalogs give you more main options and more options within each choice. The options you have will depend on the system installed and the way your librarians decided to set it up.

Understanding how the catalog systems work will help you gather information efficiently.

Two options you need to understand clearly are *keywords in titles* and *subject.* When the *keywords in titles* option is selected, the system will ask you for the keywords and then search only the titles for those keywords. This means that the items it finds will likely be on the subject you need. However, it misses all those whose titles do not contain the words you keyed in. For example, if you wanted to know more about cross-cultural communication, using keywords in title would find only items with those exact words in the title. It would miss titles with the words *intercultural communication, international communication,* and *global communication.* If you did multiple searches

FIGURE 4-2   **An electronic catalog screen showing a system's search for intercultural communication**

```
You searched for the SUBJECT: intercultural communication
99 entries found, entries 1-8 are:                          CALL #
Intercultural Communication
      1  Advertising international : the privati HF5821 .K3213 1991
      2  The alchemy of English : the spread, fu PE2751 .K3 1986
      3  American communication in a global soci E840.2 .F57
      4  American communication in a global soci E840.2 .F57 1987
      5  America's mass media merchants          P92.U5 R4
      6  Anthropological other or Burmese brothe GN345 .S66 1992
      7  The Asian mind game : unlocking the hid HD58.6 .C474 1991
      8  BaFa BaFa : a cross culture simulation. SG-99




      Please type the NUMBER of the item you want to see, or
      F > Go FORWARD            A > ANOTHER Search by SUBJECT   J > JUMP
      R > RETURN to Browsing    D > DISPLAY Title and Author
      N > NEW Search            L > LIMIT this Search
      Choose one (1-8,F,R,N,A,D,L,J)
```

using all the similar terms you could think of, it would still miss those titles without the keywords, such as Robert Axtell's *Dos and Taboos Around the World.*

The subject search, on the other hand, is broader. Using the subject *intercultural communication,* you will find items on the subject, whether or not the exact words are indicated in the title. For example, you might find a management book with a chapter on *intercultural* communication; however, the book's emphasis might be on something else, such as crisis management or conflict resolution.

The electronic catalog never gets tired. If you key in the words accurately, it will always produce a complete and accurate list of sources. Let us look at a few results from a subject search on *intercultural* communication. Notice in Figure 4–2 that the system found 99 sources. That is more than you really want, so you decide to select the option shown at the bottom of the screen to limit your search. This system then gives you some options for limiting your search (see Figure 4–3). You decide to limit the search by year, telling the electronic catalog system you want it to find all sources after 1990 (see Figure 4–4). As you can see in Figure 4–5, nine entries were found. When you ask the system to display the title and author, it brings up the screen shown in Figure 4–6. Not only will you find the title and author, but you will also find complete bibliographic information, the call number, and the status along with subjects which this book fits. Furthermore, the system gives you the option of browsing through other books nearby on the shelf.

The library catalog is a useful source of information for your library's holdings. Learning to use it will save you time and make your searches efficient and effective.

| FIGURE 4–3 | **Electronic catalog screen illustrating options for limiting a search** |

```
You searched for the SUBJECT: intercultural communication
99 entries found, entries 1-8 are:                        CALL #



          You may limit your search by any of the following:

                    L > LANGUAGE
                    M > MATERIAL type
                    A > Words in the AUTHOR
                    T > Words in the TITLE
                    S > Words in the SUBJECT
                    P > PUBLISHER
                    Y > YEAR of publication
                    R > RETURN to Browsing

          Choose one (L,M,A,T,S,P,Y,R)
```

| FIGURE 4–4 | **Electronic catalog screen that shows time as a search limit and other menu options** |

```
You searched for the SUBJECT: intercultural communication
99 entries found, entries 1-8 are:                        CALL #
   YEAR of publication AFTER 1990



              F > FIND items with above limits

              A > AND   (Limit further)
              O > OR    (Expand retrieval)
              R > RETURN to Previous Screen

              Choose one (F,A,O,R)
```

☐   **USING PERIODICAL INDEXES**

To identify articles for your list of prospective sources, consult a periodical index.

The card catalog helps you identify books for your bibliography. To identify articles published in newspapers, magazines, or journals, you will need to consult an index, either a general one or one that specializes in the field you are researching. Indexes are available in the reference section of most libraries and are regularly updated.

If you are like most business researchers, you will start your search for periodical literature with the *Business Periodicals Index*. Issued monthly and cumulated yearly, this guide covers 345 major business periodicals and indexes by subject headings and company references. It also lists articles on a wide variety of business areas, indus-

FIGURE 4-5   **Electronic catalog screen with alphabetic entries determined by limiting search by years**

```
You searched for the SUBJECT: intercultural communication LIMITED TO AFTER 1990
9 entries found, entries 1-8 are:                          CALL #
Intercultural Communication
    1   Advertising international : the privati HF5821 .K3213 1991
    2   Anthropological other or Burmese brothe GN345 .S66 1992
    3   The Asian mind game : unlocking the hid HD58.6 .C474 1991
    4   Bridging differences : effective interg HM258 .G838 1991
    5   The Bushman myth : the making of a Nami DT1558.S38 G67 1992
    6   Cultures and organizations : software o HM258 .H574 1991
    7   Intercultural communication : a reader  HM258 .I52 1991
    8   Profiting in America's multicultural ma HF5718 .T457 1991




Please type the NUMBER of the item you want to see, or
F > Go FORWARD                    A > ANOTHER Search by SUBJECT
R > RETURN to Browsing            D > DISPLAY Title and Author
N > NEW Search                    J > JUMP
Choose one (1-8,F,R,N,A,D,J)
```

tries, and trades. A partial list of the business areas includes accounting, advertising, banking, communications, computer technology and applications, economics, finance, industrial relations, insurance, international business, management, marketing, and public relations. *The Business Periodicals Index* online counterpart is WILSONLINE. Its two CD-ROM products are WILSONDISC: BPI and *Wilson Business Abstracts.*

Another guide you will find useful is the *Predicasts F&S Index United States,* which covers business-oriented periodicals, newspapers, and special reports. It includes company, product, and industry information as well as information on corporate activities, new products and technologies, and on social and political developments with business implications. Each entry contains a brief abstract of the article as well as bibliographical notations.

A third index that may be helpful to you is the *PAIS International in Print,* which lists by subject information relating to economics and public affairs. Its sources are extensive. They include, in addition to books and periodicals, pamphlets and reports published by associations and businesses as well as materials issued by the government.

There are a number of useful specialized indexes as well. For the best known business-oriented newspaper, there is the *Wall Street Journal Index,* and for the acknowledged newspaper of record, the *New York Times Index.* For research in marketing, there are two useful listings: *Findex* and *Marketing Information: A Professional*

FIGURE 4–6   **Electronic catalog screen showing complete bibliographic information and availability**

```
You searched for the SUBJECT: intercultural communication LIMITED TO AFTER 1990

AUTHOR        Thiederman, Sondra B.
TITLE         Profiting in America's multicultural marketplace : how to do
                business across cultural lines / by Sondra Thiederman.
PUBLISHER     New York : Lexington Books ; Toronto : Maxwell Macmillan Canada ;
                New York : Maxwell Macmillan International, c1991.
DESCRIPTION   xxiv, 262 p. / 24 cm.
NOTE(S)       Includes bibliographical references (p. [253}) and index.
SUBJECT(S)    Business communication.
              Intercultural communication.
CALL #        HF5718 .T457 1991.



        LOCATION              CALL #                        STATUS
1 >  Book Stacks          HF5718 .T457 1991                 AVAILABLE

R > RETURN to Browsing            A > ANOTHER Search by SUBJECT
F > FORWARD browse                Z > Show Items Nearby on Shelf
B > BACKWARD browse               S > SHOW items with the same SUBJECT
N > NEW Search
Choose one (R,F,B,N,A,Z,S)
```

Reference. If you are doing accounting research, you are well advised to consult the *Accountants' Index.* And if you are interested in economics, you will find relevant listings in the *Social Sciences Index.* Rounding out this selection of readily accessible indexes is the familiar *Reader's Guide to Periodical Literature,* which is useful in very general research.

Microfilm and microfiche store information on film.

Most libraries offer newspapers and periodicals on microforms. Microforms save space for libraries and exist in two types—microfilm and microfiche. Microfilms are films of published words that can be read on special microfilm equipment. The film is available on reels. Microfiche sheets contain photographically reduced pages of published works with greater reduction than microfilm. They, too, require special equipment to read and print. Both of these forms of microcopying are important sources of information for business researchers.

☐ **SEARCHING DATABASES**

Computers offer the most advanced method of conducting secondary research. As you know, the capacity of computers to collect and retrieve information has expanded phenomenally over the past decade. Business research has been a primary beneficiary of these advances. Much information routinely recorded in printed form and accessed through directories, encyclopedias, bibliographies, indexes, and the

Computers organize and store vast amounts of data in file collections. Called databases, there are two types: (1) online and (2) CD-ROM.

like is now collected and stored in computer files as well. When these files, known collectively as databases, are in turn accessed by computer, the result is research that can be more extensive and complete than any conducted through traditional means. You may access databases in two ways: (1) through *online* information retrieval systems that use a terminal connected to a large mainframe computer usually through telephone lines, and (2) through CD-ROMs (compact disk—read only memory) that use microcomputers.

Online databases access information stored in mainframe computers. They provide many materials essential to business.

Online databases (those accessed through online searches) are usually produced by private information services and offer a variety of materials essential to business. For example, Dialog Information Services (DIALOG) includes in its selection more than 500 bases. Four other vendors, Bibliographic Retrieval System (BRS), Data-Star, Dow Jones, and Mead/Nexis offer many of the same information files. In addition, prominent business resources, including the *Harvard Business Review, The New York Times,* and Standard & Poor's, now offer computer access to their data and files. You can find 5,000 online databases listed and briefly described in the *Directory of Online Databases.*

Many libraries offer facilities for online computer searches of databases.

Most public, college, and university libraries offer online database searching service for a fee that reflects the computer time employed and the number of items identified. Before you begin the search, you will need to work closely with trained staff to design a strategy that will use computer time effectively and retrieve only relevant information. However, considering the potential advantages of computer-assisted research, the cost of the service is a small price to pay. For an excellent discussion of the online search process, you can read Part III of *Introduction to Reference Sources* by William A. Katz.

Check to determine which services offer complete copies of articles.

Many online sources offer researchers complete copies of the articles they list. Some, however, do not. An excellent source to consult for those that do offer full text services is *Fulltext Sources Online*, edited by Ruth M. Ornstein. This resource notes periodicals, newspapers, and newsletters that are available in full text online. More specifically, the directory tells which vendors and their specific databases are in full text, for what time period the full text offering is available, and how often the database is updated.

CD-ROM databases use microcomputers with special features and compact disks.

CD-ROM databases use microcomputers with special features such as compact disk drives, coin box connections, and laser printers to access stored information on compact disks. For example, *ABI/Inform* offers abstracts on compact disks of 800 business and management periodicals that have been published since 1985. Most CD-ROM services are available only after 1985 because the technology was developed about that time. Since then, however, they have become a permanent part of library resources. You may consult *Directory of Portable Databases*, a semiannual publication by Gale Research, for descriptions of CD-ROM products, diskettes, and such.

The two forms complement one another.

These two database forms complement rather than compete with one another. Online systems provide more capacity and faster processing of information. CD-ROM, however, is less expensive. Thus, CD-ROM disk systems are available to users on a monthly, quarterly, or semiannual basis. If researchers need more current information, they can use an online database that is edited daily or weekly.

Computer-assisted research is becoming routine in report preparation.

As you can see, computer technology in information storage and retrieval continues to expand. Because of this growth, computer-assisted research is unquestionably becoming a routine step in the research process of preparing business reports.

☐ RECORDING INFORMATION

Keep track of the sources you gather in an orderly way.

In the past, researchers used a card system to help them keep track of the sources they identified. This card system can be combined with and adapted to a computer system quite easily. The manual system of organization required that the researcher complete two sets of cards. One set was simply a bibliography card set, containing complete information about sources. A researcher numbered these cards consecutively as the sources were identified. A second set of cards contained the notes from each source. Each of these cards was linked to its source through the number of the source in the bibliography card set.

Since the computer systems in today's libraries often allow users to print the citations they find from the indexes and databases, it makes the most sense to number the source on the printout rather than recopy it to a card. Not only is it usually more legible than one's handwriting; it is also complete. Some writers will cut their printouts apart and tape them to a master sheet. Others will enter these items in databases they build. With the widespread use of notebook and laptop computers, many researchers are taking notes on computers rather than cards. These notes can be linked to the original source by number as in the manual system.

No matter whether you use a manual, combined, or computer system, using one is essential.

☐ USING PHOTOCOPY SERVICES

Photocopy research findings if it is helpful.

The widespread availability of photocopy equipment may make it more convenient for you to make copies of your research findings than to summarize them on note cards. Photocopying can be especially useful when you need to record information verbatim or when all or nearly all the information in the reference source pertains to your topic. When you photocopy material, you will need to develop a system that allows you to record bibliographical information and keep related information together as we discussed in notetaking procedure earlier.

QUESTIONS

1. Suggest a hypothetical research problem that would make good use of a specialized library.

2. What specialized libraries are there in your community? What general libraries?

3. Under what general condition is it likely that investigators may be able to proceed directly to the printed source of the information sought?

4. Distinguish between the contents of encyclopedias and biographical directories.

5. Describe the contents and name the issuing branch of the following publications of the federal government.
    a. *1990 Census of the United States*
    b. *Survey of Current Business*
    c. *The Monthly Labor Review*
    d. *Statistical Abstract of the United States*

6. Describe the contents of the following indexes to published material.
    a. *Reader's Guide to Periodical Literature*
    b. *Predicast F & S Index United States*
    c. *Business Periodicals Index*
    d. *PAIS International in Print*
    e. *Monthly Catalog of U.S. Government Publications*
    f. *New York Times Index*

7. Explain how database searches can help you collect facts for business reports.

8. In which of the indexes is one most likely to find information on the following subjects?
    a. Labor-management relations
    b. Innovation in sales promotion
    c. Accident proneness among workers
    d. Recent advances in computer technology
    e. Trends in responsibility accounting
    f. Labor unrest in the 1800s
    g. Events leading to enactment of a certain tax measure in 1936
    h. Textbook treatment of business writing in the 1930s
    i. Viewpoints on the effect of deficit financing by governments
    j. New techniques in office management

9. Discuss how photocopying equipment can assist you in collecting data from library sources.

Collecting Information: Primary Research

The first step in primary research is to review secondary materials. Determine what information already exists.

Because of the wealth of secondary sources, you should look first for what is available in published form on a problem you wish to research. Otherwise you may spend valuable time and effort developing information that already exists. However, you may not always find what you are looking for, or what is available may be inappropriate or incomplete. Or there may not be any secondary information on your problem. Under these circumstances it is appropriate to get your information firsthand through what is called *primary research*. There are four basic methods of primary research:

1. Search through company records.
2. Experimentation.
3. Observation.
4. Survey.

The nature of the information you need for your research problem will determine which procedure—or combination of procedures—you will use.

SEARCH THROUGH COMPANY RECORDS

Company records are an excellent source of firsthand information.

Since many of today's business problems involve various phases of company operations, a company's internal records are frequently a source of important information. Production data, sales records, merchandising information, accounting records, and the like are useful to investigate.

There are no set rules on how to go about finding and gathering information through company records. Record-keeping systems vary widely from company to company. However, you are well advised to keep the following standards in mind as you conduct your investigation. First, as in all types of research, you must have a clear idea of the type of information you need. Undefined, open-ended investigations are not

Make sure you (1) have a clear idea of the information you need, (2) understand the terms of access and confidentiality, and (3) cooperate with company personnel.

appreciated—nor are they particularly productive. Second, make sure you understand clearly the ground rules under which you are allowed to review materials. Matters of confidentiality and access should be resolved before you start. And third, if you are not intimately familiar with a company's records yourself, cooperate in your investigation with someone who is. The complexity and sensitivity of such materials require they be reviewed in their proper context.

RESEARCH THROUGH THE EXPERIMENT

Experimentation develops information by testing variable factors.

The experiment is a very useful technique in business research. Originally a technique perfected in the sciences, the experiment is an orderly form of testing. In general, it is a form of research in which you systematically manipulate one variable factor of a problem while holding constant all the others. You measure quantitatively or qualitatively any changes resulting from these manipulations. You then apply your findings to the problem.

For example, suppose you are asked to conduct research for a company that wants to determine whether a new package design will lead to more sales. You might start by selecting two test cities, taking care they are as nearly alike as possible on all characteristics that might affect the problem. After making the selection, you would secure information on sales in the two cities for a specified period before the experiment. Next you would introduce the new package design in one city, and in the other, continue to sell the product in the old package. For a second specified period, you would keep careful sales records and monitor all other factors that might affect the experiment. Specifically, you would check to make sure advertising, economic conditions, competition, and such remained unchanged. Thus, when the experimentation period was over, you could attribute any differences you found between the sales of the two cities to the change in package design.

Keep nonexperimental variables constant. If they change in any way, note the changes when you report experiment results.

The need for keeping constant all variables other than those that are the subject of the experiment cannot be emphasized enough. All too frequently researchers violate this basic rule and reach false conclusions. However, there are times when even the most conscientious researchers find it impossible to keep constant all variables concerned. In such cases they try to compensate for the unwanted variations and qualify their conclusions with an explanation of how these other changes may have affected the results.

Design each experiment to fit the problem.

Each experiment should be designed individually to fit the requirements of the problem. Nonetheless, a few basic designs underlie most experimental procedures. Becoming familiar with two of the most common procedures—the before-after and the controlled before-after—will give you a framework for understanding and applying this primary research technique.

☐ THE BEFORE-AFTER DESIGN

The simplest form of experiment is the before-after design. In this plan, you select a test group of subjects and measure the variable in which you are interested. Next you introduce the experimental factor. After a specified period of time, during which the

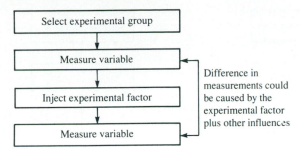

FIGURE 5–1   **The before-after experiment**

Select experimental group

↓

Measure variable

↓

Inject experimental factor

↓

Measure variable

Difference in measurements could be caused by the experimental factor plus other influences

---

The before-after experiment is the simplest design. You use just one test group.

experimental factor has presumably had its effect, you again measure the variable in which you are interested. If there are any differences between the first and second measurements, you may assume the experimental factor plus other influences are the cause. Figure 5–1 illustrates this basic design.

Consider the following application. Assume you are conducting research for a retail store to determine the effect of point-of-sale advertising. As a first step, you select a product for the experiment, Brand Y razor blades. Second, you record sales of Brand Y blades for one week, using no point-of-sale advertising. Then you introduce the experimental variable—the Brand Y display. For the next week, you again record sales of Brand Y blades, and at the end of the second week, compare results. Any increase in sales would presumably be explained by the introduction of the display. That is, if 500 packages of Brand Y blades were sold in the first week, and 600 the second, you conclude the 100 new sales can be attributed to point-of-sale advertising.

The changes recorded in a before-after experiment may not always be attributed to the experimental factor alone.

You can probably anticipate the major shortcoming of this design. It is simply not logical to assume the experimental factor explains all the difference in sales between the first week and the second. Sales could change for a number of other reasons—changes in weather, holiday, or other seasonal influences on business activity, other advertising, and so on. At best you can determine for sure only that point-of-sale advertising *could* influence sales. It may be just one of several influences, however.

□ **CONTROLLED BEFORE-AFTER DESIGN**

In the controlled before-after experiment you use two identical test groups. You introduce the experimental factor into one group, then compare the two groups. Any difference you can attribute to the experimental factor.

To account for influences other than experimental factors, you may use designs more complex than the before-after plan. These designs attempt to measure the other influences by including some means of control. The simplest of this type of experiment is the controlled before-after plan.

In the controlled before-after plan, you select not one group, but two. One group is selected to be the experimental group; the other serves as the control. Before introducing the experimental factor, you measure in each group the variable to be tested. Then you introduce the experimental factor into the experimental group only.

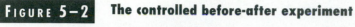

FIGURE 5-2   **The controlled before-after experiment**

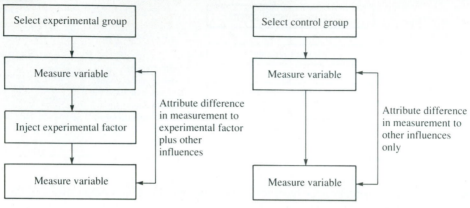

When the period allotted for the experiment is over, you measure again in each group the variable being tested. Any difference between the first and second measurements in the experimental group can be explained by two possible causes—the experimental factor and other influences. But the difference between the first and second measurements in the control group can be explained only by other influences, for this group was not subjected to the experimental factor. Thus, comparing the "afters" of the two groups will give you a measure of the influence of the experimental factor. This design appears in diagram form in Figure 5–2.

It is possible to modify the point-of-sale application. For example, you can select two groups: Brand Y blades and Brand X blades and record the sales of both blades for one week. Next, you introduce point-of-sale displays for Brand Y only and record sales for both Brand Y and Brand X for a second week. At the end of the second week, you compare results. Whatever difference you find in Brand Y sales and Brand X sales will be a fair measure of the experimental factor, independent of what changes may have been brought about by outside influences.

For example, if 400 packages of Brand X blades are sold the first week and 450 packages the second, the increase of 50 packages (12.5 percent) can be attributed to influences other than the experimental factor, the display. If 500 packages of Brand Y blades are sold the first week and 600 the second, the increase of 100 packages can be attributed to both the display and outside factors. To distinguish between the two, you note that outside factors accounted for the 12.5 percent increase in the sales of Brand X blades. Because of the experiment control, you attribute 12.5 percent of the increase in Brand Y sales to outside influences as well. An increase of 12.5 percent on a base of 500 sales is 63 sales, indicating that 63 of the 100 additional Brand Y sales are the result of outside influences. However, the sale of 37 additional packages of Brand Y blades can be directly attributed to point-of-sale advertising.

OBSERVATION AS A RESEARCH TECHNIQUE

Research by observation involves watching phenomena and recording results.

Like experimentation, observation is a technique perfected in the sciences, and it, too, can be useful in business research. Simply stated, observation is seeing with a purpose. It consists of watching certain phenomena involved in a problem and recording systematically what is seen. In observation, you do not manipulate the details of what you observe; you take note of situations exactly as you find them.

This form of observation does not involve experimentation.

Note that observation as an independent research technique is different from the observation you use in recording the effects of variables introduced into a test situation. In the latter case, observation is a step in the experiment, not an end in itself. The two methods, therefore, should not be confused.

To see how observation works as a business technique, consider this situation. You are a grocery supplier who wants to determine how shoppers are responding to a new line of foods. A review of sales records would certainly give some information, as would a survey of store patrons. However, observing customers as they shop may reveal important information you might overlook using alternative techniques.

Similarly, observation can prove useful if you are a researcher for a public interest organization interested in determining the extent to which automobile safety belts are used. Simply observing drivers as they enter their vehicles and prepare to drive off will reveal a great deal of information about how many and what kind of drivers "buckle up."

Observation can be helpful in conducting preliminary research. For example, if you are an office manager interested in designing a more efficient working area, you might begin the project by observing how personnel use the current office layout.

☐ PLAN OF THE OBSERVATION

Observation requires a systematic procedure for observing and recording.

Like all primary research techniques, observation must be designed to fit the requirements of the problem being considered. However, the planning stage generally requires two steps. First, you construct a recording form; second, you design a systematic procedure for observing and recording the information.

The form should enable you to record details quickly and accurately.

The recording form may be any tabular arrangement that permits quick and easy recording of the information observed. Though observation forms are hardly standardized, one commonly used arrangement (see Figure 5–3) provides a separate line for each observation. Captions at the top of the page mark the columns in which the observer will place the appropriate mark. The form identifies characteristics to be observed and requires the recording of such potentially important details as the date, time, and place of the observation as well as the name of the observer.

An effective observation system ensures the collection of complete and representative information.

The observation procedure may be any system that ensures the collection of complete and representative information. Again, there is no standardized method. But the basics of any effective procedure include a clear focus, well-defined steps, and provisions for ensuring the quality of the information collected. For example, in a problem of determining what style of clothing men wear in a certain city, the procedure would include a detailed schedule of observation for all appropriate sections of the city. It would specify times for the observations, with provisions made for weather

FIGURE 5-3   Excerpt of a common type of observation recording form

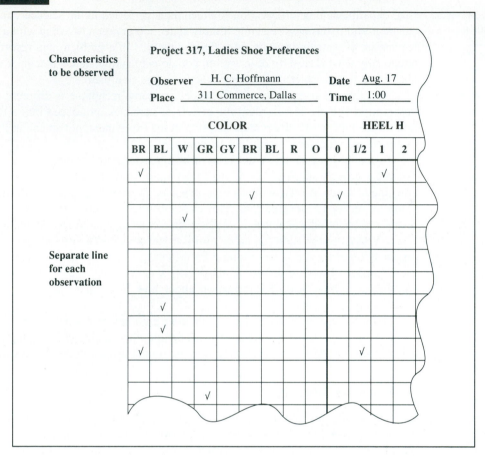

and other contingencies. Additionally, it would include detailed observing instructions, telling each observer precisely what to do; and it would cover all possible complications the observer might encounter. In short, the procedure would be so thorough that it would leave no major question relevant to the problem unanswered.

☐ LIMITATIONS OF OBSERVATION

Observation merely records behavior. It does not reveal motive.

Offsetting the advantages of observation are two limitations. The first is inherent in the technique itself. Observation by definition limits you to what you can see and thus offers no reliable way for you to determine why subjects do what they do. Some researchers maintain that opinions, attitudes, and the like can be interpreted from overt acts. However, such interpretations are highly speculative and undercut the objectivity and accuracy that are the strengths of the technique. Therefore, for problems that require psychological information about a given group of subjects, observation is inappropriate, unless, of course, it is used in conjunction with an interview or a survey.

Observation can be costly, however.

The second limitation is a pragmatic one: observation can be costly. The cost depends upon the elaborateness of the situation and the frequency of the activities being observed. Something simple, like stationing an observer on a busy downtown street to observe characteristics of the shoes worn by passersby, could be done at relatively little expense. Assigning an observer to an automobile dealership to record the actions of individual shoppers will be considerably more costly in terms of the time required to complete each observation. (Recent advances in video equipment, however, offer opportunities for more cost-efficient observation, especially when the equipment is used in conjunction with computer-readable recording forms.)

RESEARCH THROUGH THE SURVEY

Certain information you can determine best by asking questions.

The premise of the survey as a method of primary research is simple: You can best determine certain types of information by asking questions. Such information includes personal data, opinions, evaluations, and other material that is important in and of itself. The survey may also include information necessary to plan, interpret, or supplement an experiment or observation study.

Decide which survey format and delivery will be most effective in developing the information you need.

There are a number of decisions to make about the survey once you have decided to use it for your research. First is the matter of format. Questions can range from spontaneous inquiries to carefully structured interrogatories. Next is the matter of delivery. Questions can be posed in a personal interview, asked over the telephone, or presented in printed form.

Also decide whom to interview. If the subject group is large, select a sample.

But most important is the matter of whom to survey. Except for situations where the number of people involved in a problem under study is relatively limited, not everyone who has information to contribute can do so. You thus have to select a sample of respondents to represent the group as a whole and to do so as accurately as possible. There are several ways to select that sample, as you shall see.

☐   SAMPLING THEORY AS A BASIS FOR SURVEYING

Your sample must be both reliable and representative.

Sampling theory forms the basis for most survey research, though it has any number of additional applications as well. Buyers of grain, for example, judge the quality of a multiton shipment by examining a few pounds. Quality control supervisors spot-check a small percentage of products ready for distribution to determine whether production standards are being met. County fair judges take a little taste of each entry of home-made jam to decide which will win a blue ribbon.

The premise for these and all sampling cases is the general law that a sufficiently large number of items taken at random from a larger number of items will have the characteristics of the group. Implicit in this law are first, the principle of sample reliability, and second, the principle of sample representativeness. Both are fundamental to the accurate use of sampling in primary research.

PRINCIPLE OF SAMPLE RELIABILITY   Sample reliability is a matter of numbers. More specifically, it is a matter of selecting a number of items sufficient to stabilize sample response. If you select too few, your sample is likely to include chance errors that will exaggerate the diversity in the response. However, as you increase the number of items, these errors tend to offset each other, and the diversity levels off. When that leveling point is reached, both your sample and its response can be considered reliable.

A reliable sample is large enough to eliminate chance errors.

The reliability of a sample should be determined one response at a time. That means if you are conducting a 10-question survey, you technically should use 10 separate reliability tests, one for each question. However, it is seldom necessary to be so exacting. Testing a few key questions, particularly those requiring the highest degree of accuracy, is usually sufficient to determine the reliability of the survey as a whole.

Test for sample reliability one question at a time.

If you are familiar with statistics, you can test sample reliability by determining the average of individual responses and measuring the standard deviation from that average. The smaller the standard deviation, the lower the probability of error in the sample and its response. (A review of this method is included in Appendix C.) However, there are also a number of nontechnical methods you may use, including the cumulative frequency test.

The standard deviation measures the reliability of sample size.

The cumulative frequency test is reasonably simple. Assume you want to determine the reliability of a sample of respondents who have completed a questionnaire. Begin by collecting the completed forms, arranging them in random order, and dividing them into equal groups of 50, 100, or whatever number appears to be appropriate. Then select one question for your test. Tally for the first group its responses to each alternative answer and convert each tally to a percentage of the total responses given.

The cumulative frequency measures sample reliability, too.

Now move to the second group. Count its responses to each alternative answer. But this time combine these tallies with the corresponding tallies of the first group and compute the percentage for the cumulative total. Add the tallies for the third group to those of the first and second and compute the percentage for the new cumulative total. Do the same for each succeeding group until all groups are included. And, as you proceed, plot the cumulative percentages on a graph.

The percentages are likely to plot an erratic pattern at first. However, as the group totals are accumulated, the pattern will tend to stabilize. When the plot line straightens out and begins to run parallel to the base line, you may assume the answer is reliable and the sample is, too, at least as it relates to the question you have selected. To determine the reliability of the sample for the questionnaire as a whole, you will have to test several key questions and compare their graphs.

To illustrate this technique, let's say you have completed a survey of 1,200 homemakers and decided that one of the most significant questions in your questionnaire is one asking whether the respondent prefers Product A to Product B. The alternative answers are yes, no, and no opinion. Assume further that you have decided to divide your surveys into 12 groups of 100 and to test the yes answers.

TABLE 5–1	Application of cumulative frequency test (12 groups of 100, yes answers to product preference question)

Group Number	Yes Answers in Group	Cumulative Yes Answers	Cumulative Percentage of Yes Answers
1	74	74	74
2	56	130	65
3	59	189	63
4	44	233	58
5	66	299	60
6	57	356	60
7	68	424	61
8	52	476	60
9	49	525	58
10	57	582	58
11	63	645	58
12	56	701	58

In the first group of questionnaires, you find that 74 respondents or 74 percent have marked yes as their answer. Plot 74 on your graph. In the second group, you count 56 yes answers. Add these 56 to the 74 in the first group. The cumulative total is 130 or 65 percent of the 200 responses tallied. Plot 65 percent on your graph.

In the third group are 59 yeses. Adding them to the 130 recorded in the first two groups gives you a cumulative total of 169 affirmative answers or 63 percent of the 300 responses you have counted. Plot 63 percent on your graph. And so you continue to record and cumulate the responses of all 12 groups as indicated in Table 5–1 and to plot them as indicated in Figure 5–4. You will note that a leveling off at 58 percent occurs after the 10th group, indicating that both your sample and its response are reliable. You can in fact conclude that of all homemakers familiar with Product A and Product B, 58 percent prefer Product A.

A representative sample reflects the composition of the group from which it is selected.

PRINCIPLE OF REPRESENTATIVENESS Sample representativeness is a matter of composition rather than numbers. It requires that the sample selected to represent a group reflect the composition of that group in every way possible. To determine the opinion of the general public on a political issue, therefore, you obviously could not derive your sample from individuals who sign petitions or who write letters to government officials. Their level of interest, education, and motivation will make them singularly unrepresentative of the public at large. But you would have a similar, if more subtle, credibility problem using a telephone directory as a source. Any sample drawn from its listings will have a disproportionately small number of low-income families.

However, you can design a sample representative of the general public or of any group you are studying by selecting one of five basic sampling techniques.

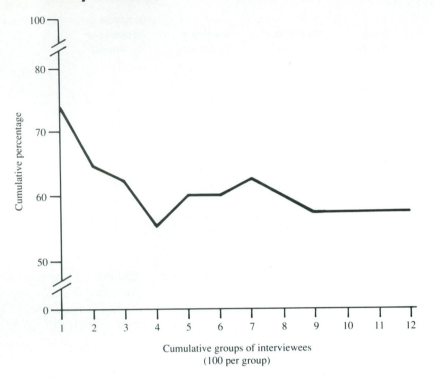

FIGURE 5–4 **Cumulative frequencies plotted (illustrating tendency to flatten out as stability is reached)**

☐ THE TECHNIQUES OF SAMPLING

The techniques most commonly used to construct representative samples are random sampling, stratified random sampling, systematic sampling, quota sampling, and area sampling. Each of these techniques has advantages in certain situations and limitations in others. Your first task in designing a representative sample, therefore, is to decide which technique is best suited to your research problem.

In random sampling, every item in the subject group has an equal chance of being selected.

RANDOM SAMPLING   Random sampling is the technique assumed in the general law of sampling. By definition, it is the sampling technique that gives every member of the group under study an equal chance of being included. To assure equal chance, you must first identify every member of the group and then, using a list or some other convenient format, record all the identifications. Next, through some chance method, you select the members of your sample.

For example, if you are studying the job attitudes of 200 assembly line workers and determine that 25 interviews will give you the information you need, you might make out a name card for each worker, place the 200 cards in a container, mix them up, and draw out 25. Since each of the 200 employees has an equal chance of being selected, your sample will be random and can be presumed to be representative.

STRATIFIED RANDOM SAMPLING   Stratified random sampling consists of subdividing the group under study and making random selections within each subgroup. The size of each division is usually proportionate to that division's percentage of the whole. In situations where a subgroup is too small to yield meaningful findings, however, you may have to select a disproportionately large sample. (Of course, when the study calls for statistics on the group as a whole, each enlarged sample must be reduced, and the subgroup's actual proportion restored.)

In stratified random sampling, the group is subdivided and the sample selected randomly from each subgroup.

Assume, for example, you are attempting to determine the curriculum needs of 5,000 undergraduates at a certain college and you have decided to survey 20 percent of the enrollment or 1,000 students. To construct a sample for this problem, first divide the enrollment list by academic concentration: business, liberal arts, nursing, engineering, and so forth. Then draw a random sample from each of these groups, making sure the number you select from each concentration is proportionate to the percentage of the total undergraduate enrollment that concentration represents. That is, if 30 percent of the student body are majoring in business, you will randomly select 300 business students for your sample. If 40 percent of the enrollment are liberal arts majors, you will randomly select 400 for your sample. And so on.

If another part of your research calls for an in-depth study of individual majors as well, you can, for this aspect of your project, expand the sample of a small concentration. Architecture, for example, might comprise 2 percent of the college's total enrollment, but you consider 20 students too few to give meaningful findings about that department. For this part of your study, and this part only, you can therefore increase the number of students surveyed to 40 or 50 or whatever number you decide will be meaningful.

SYSTEMATIC SAMPLING   Systematic sampling, though not random in the strictest sense, is random for all practical purposes. It is the simple technique of taking selections at constant intervals (every *n*th unit) from a list of the items under study. The interval used is, as you might expect, a matter of the size of the list available and the sample size desired. For example, if you want a 10 percent sample of a list of 10,000, you might select every 10th item on the list.

In systematic sampling, the items are selected from the subject group at constant intervals.

However, your sample would not really be random. By virtue of its designated place on the original list, every item does not have an equal chance of being selected. To correct that problem, you might use an equal-chance method to determine what *n* to use. Thus, if you selected the number 7 randomly, you would draw the numbers 7, 17, 27, and so on to 9,997 to make up your sample. Or, if you wanted to draw every 10th item, you might first scramble the list and then select from the revised list numbers 10, 20, 30, and so on to 10,000 and make up your sample that way.

Select the interval randomly or scramble the order of the subject group if you want your systematic sample to be random.

QUOTA SAMPLING   Quota sampling is a nonrandom technique. Also known as controlled sampling, it is used whenever the proportionate makeup of the universe under study is available. The technique requires that you refer to the composition of the universe in

TABLE 5–2	**Alternative quota sample**			

	Number in Universe	Percent of Total	Number to Be Interviewed
Total student enrollment	4,000	100	400
Sex:			
Men students	2,400	60	240
Women students	1,600	40	160
Fraternity, sorority membership:			
Members	1,000	25	100
Nonmembers	3,000	75	300
Marital status:			
Married students	400	10	40
Single students	3,600	90	360
Class rank:			
Freshmen	1,600	40	160
Sophomores	1,000	25	100
Juniors	800	20	80
Seniors	400	10	40
Graduates	200	5	20

Setting quotas assures the sample reflects the whole. Choose items randomly within each quota.

designing your sample, selecting items so your sample has the same characteristics in the same proportion as the original group. Specifically, it requires that you set quotas for each characteristic you want to consider in your research problem and make certain the quotas are met. Because you sample until you meet your quotas, not every item in the universe has an equal chance of being chosen. Of course, the characteristics selected for determining makeup should have some bearing on the research problem.

Let's say you want to survey a college student body of 4,000, using a 10 percent sample. As Table 5–2 illustrates, you have a number of alternatives for determining the makeup of your sample, depending on the focus of your research. Keep in mind, though, no matter what characteristic you select, the quotas the individual segments represent must total 100 percent; and the number of items in the sample must total 400.

For an area sample, draw items from the subject group in stages. Select randomly at each stage.

AREA SAMPLING   Area sampling consists of drawing items for a sample in stages. It is appropriate when the area to be studied is large and when that area can be broken down into progressively smaller components. For example, if you want to draw an area sample for a certain city, you may use census data to divide the city into homogeneous districts. Using an equal-chance method, you then select a given number of districts to include in the next stage of your sample. Each of the districts you select you in turn divide into subdistricts—city blocks, for example. Continuing the process, you randomly choose a given number of the blocks selected and subdivide each of them into households. Finally, using random sampling once more, you select the households that will comprise the sample you will actually use in your research.

Area sampling is not limited to geographical divisions, however. It is adaptable to any number of applications. For example, it is an appropriate technique to use in a survey of workers in a given industry. An approach you may take in this situation is to list all companies involved in the industry and randomly select a given number of companies from that list. Then, using organization units and selecting randomly at each level, you break each of the companies down into divisions, departments, sections, and so on until you finally identify the workers you will survey.

□   CONSTRUCTING THE QUESTIONNAIRE

The object of your questionnaire is to develop accurate and relevant information.

Constructing a questionnaire is just as important as designing a sample. It is not enough that a sample is reliable and representative; to make a meaningful contribution, a group selected to participate in this form of primary research must be asked questions that will reveal accurate, relevant information about the problem under investigation.

First, review the problem; then plan how to address it.

The quality of a sample's response is affected by virtually every aspect of a questionnaire: how individual questions are phrased, in what order they are presented, through what format, and so on. Therefore, the first step in designing a questionnaire is to review the research problem; the next step is to plan in detail how that problem might most effectively be addressed.

Here are some guidelines for making sure your questionnaire develops meaningful information.

What you are hoping to develop in your questionnaire is accurate information that relates meaningfully to your research. That is always, as the accountants say, your bottom line. You should keep that objective in mind as you decide the overall strategy of your survey. You should keep it in mind as well as you move on to the specifics of designing and organizing individual items in your questionnaire. The following approach will help you meet that goal.

SELECT THE TYPES OF QUESTIONS   Questions appropriate for a written questionnaire or for a questionnaire administered orally can be classified into two broad types: open and closed. Closed questions offer a choice of replies. Respondents indicate their answers by underlining, checking off, or, in the case of oral questionnaires, telling the recorder which alternatives they choose. Open questions invite free answers. Respondents reply in their own words, writing their responses in longhand or dictating them.

Open questions invite respondents to answer in their own words.

Closed questions invite respondents to choose among alternative answers. Formats include dichotomous and multiple-choice questions.

Closed questions include dichotomous questions, which offer two alternatives, and multiple-choice questions, which offer three alternatives or more. Typical responses to a dichotomous question are true or false, yes or no, favor or oppose, A or B. Such answers are, or should be, mutually exclusive. Alternative answers to multiple-choice questions are frequently a list of names, numbers, or statements from which respondents are instructed to select one or sometimes more than one, depending on the question. Multiple-choice questions also may offer respondents a scale on which to indicate their responses or ask them to rate or rank a series of alternatives.

Closed questions are easier to administer. The answers are easier to compile.

There are decided advantages to using closed questions in a questionnaire. From the respondent's view, closed questions are relatively easy and quick to answer. They require no writing or elaboration and thus circumvent such writing and speaking deterrents as natural reticence, embarrassment, inarticulateness, or just plain laziness.

From the questioner's point of view, closed questions offer responses that are easy to compile and quantify. They take less time to administer and interpret and enable the questioner to reach a relatively large number of respondents at comparatively little expense.

However, closed questions limit responses and are impersonal.

However, using closed questions has disadvantages, too. Closed questions are impersonal and arbitrary; they reveal nothing of reactions, rationales, and other individual aspects of responses; they limit respondents to choices someone else has defined and force them to speak in a voice other than their own.

Open questions reveal respondents' understanding and convictions, but require sensitivity and objectivity in interpreting responses.

In contrast, open questions encourage individualized answers, which may, depending on the research problem, be worth the additional effort of all parties involved. Open questions best fit issues where the logic and process of responses are at least as important as the responses themselves. They provide contexts, offer perspectives, and reveal levels of understanding and conviction that otherwise could not be known. But they also challenge the sensitivity and the objectivity of whoever interprets the responses. All the advantages of open questions can therefore be lost if the interpreter is not up to the task.

Ask respondents only about what they have experienced, what they can recall, and what they are willing to reveal.

Ask Questions That Can Be Answered   In addition, determine what type of information you can reasonably expect to elicit from your respondents. Such information includes that which is within their experience, that which they can recall, and that which they are willing to provide.

To illustrate, assume you are designing a questionnaire to determine how well traditional detergents are competing with a new variety of soap products with bleach and fabric softener. Key criteria are cleanliness, softness, and, since the detergents with additives cost more, price. However, you cannot ask questions like which type leaves clothes cleaner, which leaves clothes softer, or which is the better value—not without first establishing that your respondents have bought and used both varieties and are at least in a position to make meaningful comparisons. The information you need must be within their experience.

By the same token, even if you do establish that your respondents have bought and used both types, you cannot ask them to name for you the brand of the first box of each variety they bought, the store where they bought it, or the price they paid for it. Though such details may be very important to you in determining, say, the beginning of brand loyalty or the reasons for change, they are not distinctive enough for the respondents to recall. You will thus have to take another approach to elicit the information you want.

You will also have to forgo asking questions of a personal nature. These can range from matters of age, income, and marital status to personal health habits, such as the number of times clothing items are worn before they are washed. Few respondents are willing to provide such information. Therefore, if your research requires a profile of the typical buyer of either the traditional or the innovative detergents, you will have to develop such information through indirect means and settle for reasonable estimates. Presenting age and income ranges will help with demographics. Asking the number of adults in the household will assist with marital status. As for the frequency of wearings before washings, you might ask a series of impersonal questions about what respondents perceive to be common practice before requesting them to describe their own.

Use familiar and neutral vocabulary.

CHOOSE THE MOST EFFECTIVE PHRASING   Give careful attention to the phrasing of your questions, too. There are several potential pitfalls in question wording that can result in misleading or inaccurate information. Using unfamiliar or suggestive vocabulary and structuring questions so they imply a preferred response are likely problem areas. For example, it is meaningless to ask respondents if the detergent they use is bio-degradable unless you can be sure they know a biodegradable product is one that breaks down naturally after use. Indeed, you should not use the word *detergent* if you suspect your respondents know laundry products only as soap. Select words that are appropriate for the education and experience of your sample.

Using suggestive language poses a different kind of problem. Many words have connotations that can influence respondents' answers. For example, words like *safe, pure, environment,* and *value* encourage respondents to respond positively; whereas words like *dangerous, chemical, pollution,* and *expense* encourage them to respond negatively. To avoid the possibility of either influence, use words that are as neutral as possible.

Avoid leading questions—questions that influence responses.

Questions that invite approval or disapproval or in any way affect responses are called leading questions. Using suggestive language is only one cause. Using names is another. For example, asking who uses Wave detergent will likely result in an exagger-ated estimate of Wave users. Asking what brand of detergent respondents use will provide more accurate results.

Leading questions are also caused by references to prestige, authority, or popular attitudes. For example, phrases like *doctors recommend, professional women say,* or *most people agree* included in a question about laundry products will invariably result in distorted responses. Some respondents may identify with the statements; others may be intimidated by them. Either way, the answers will lack the accuracy and candor a reliable study requires. The easiest way to avoid this type of influence is to eliminate all such biased expressions from your questions.

Requiring affirmative or negative answers can also result in a leading question. For example, asking respondents if they prefer laundry detergents with additives to laundry products without additives is likely to evoke a less accurate response than asking them which they prefer, laundry detergents with additives or laundry products without additives. Similarly, asking respondents to agree or disagree with an affirma-tive statement (Clothes come out cleaner when you use a detergent with bleach) or a negative statement (Clothes do not come out cleaner when you use a detergent with bleach) will not reveal information as accurately as asking them whether clothes come out cleaner (a) when they use a detergent with bleach or (b) when they use a detergent without bleach.

Focus open questions clearly. Where necessary, elicit information in stages.

SELECT THE MOST EFFECTIVE STRUCTURE   Structure your questions carefully, open questions as well as closed. Open questions need a clear focus; closed questions need a selection of answers that are complete, consistent, and do not overlap. For example, avoid asking vague open questions like, "What is your opinion of laundry products with bleach and softening additives?" The responses will be superficial at best. Decide what you really want to know and then phrase your open question so it will reveal that information. And be willing to elicit information in stages. To illustrate, if you want to determine what features of the new type of detergents the public seems initially to be responding to, ask, "What did you expect of a detergent with additives when you first bought the product?" Then, if you want to learn about the competition your traditional detergent may be facing, follow up with, "In what ways did the product meet or exceed your expectations?" and, "In what ways did it fall short of what you expected?"

Structure closed questions to reveal one item of information at a time.

Decide what information you are seeking when you structure closed questions, too. And again, be willing to elicit information in stages. A common problem in structuring questions is writing double-barreled questions that ask for two items of information at once. An example of a double-barreled question is, "Does detergent with bleach get clothes clean without fading the fabric?" If your respondents answer no, will they mean that the product does not get clothes clean, that it fades the fabric, or both? Take the items one at a time. "Does detergent with bleach get clothes clean?" is one question. "Does detergent with bleach fade the fabric?" is another.

Be sure there are just two possible alternatives in a dichotomous question, and be sure they do not overlap.

When you are writing dichotomous questions, be sure the two answers you present are the only alternatives possible. Otherwise you will be forcing your respondents to make a false choice. Be sure, too, that the choices you present are mutually exclusive. A question that illustrates both problems is, "Do you wash your clothes at home or do you use a laundry service?" First, the inquiry does not take into account respondents who wash their clothes at the local laundromat. And second, it does not allow for respondents who use both alternatives, and, for that matter, unstated others as well. If you want to know in general what facilities your respondents use for getting their clothes clean, present a multiple-choice question listing all possible methods and invite respondents to indicate which they use. If you want, however, to know which they use most frequently, ask them to indicate one answer or to rank the alternatives in order of frequency of use.

Similarly, include all possible choices in multiple-choice questions and make sure no alternatives overlap.

Look out for incomplete or overlapping alternatives when you design multiple-choice questions, too. And consider for both dichotomous and multiple-choice questions the effect of introducing "don't know," "no opinion," or "other" alternatives. If you omit them when they are necessary, your respondents may select an inappropriate answer or not answer at all. However, if you include them when they are unnecessary, your respondents may evade the question. Defining your purpose clearly and knowing your sample will help you make the proper decision.

Use a scaling technique to measure attitudes or opinions. Ranking measures relatively; rating measures individually.

For measuring attitudes or opinions, use a scaling technique instead of a multiple-choice question. Scales offer respondents more flexibility and thus elicit more precise answers. Two simple techniques are ranking, which measures relatively, and rating, which measures individually.

Both techniques require a question or statement followed by a list of alternatives. In ranking, you ask your sample to number or letter the alternatives in an order appropriate to the question: importance, difficulty, or preference, for example. The numbering (1, 2, 3 . . .) or lettering (A, B, C . . .) logically proceeds from "most" to "least" or "highest" to "lowest." To determine the relative importance of product features in the purchase of laundry detergent, therefore, ask your respondents to rank

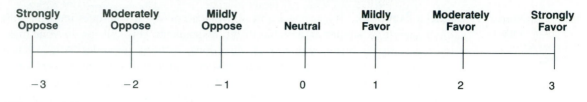

FIGURE 5-5   **Example of a rating scale**

What is your opinion of current right-to-work legislation?

Strongly Oppose	Moderately Oppose	Mildly Oppose	Neutral	Mildly Favor	Moderately Favor	Strongly Favor
-3	-2	-1	0	1	2	3

alternative features (price, scent, effect on fabrics, and so forth) in the order they consider them when deciding which laundry product to buy.

To measure the importance of these features individually, develop a scale (1. Very important; 2. Fairly important; 3. Not important) and ask your sample to rate each alternative accordingly. Three gradients are sufficient for this question, but other questions may need more. Be sure to provide enough gradients to make distinctions meaningful. (See Figure 5–5.)

Vary scales to avoid patterning responses.

Scales can be set up graphically as well as numerically. They can measure virtually any range of contrasting attitudes or qualities. Because scales are so versatile and potentially so revealing, you may want to use them frequently. If you use several scales in a questionnaire, however, randomly vary the poles so that negative answers will not, for example, be always on the left or the beginning of the scale and positive on the right or the end. By the same token, if you use one scale for several questions, randomly pose some questions negatively and others affirmatively. Otherwise you may encourage a pattern in your sample's responses (all answers on the left or all *A*s) that will undermine the accuracy of your results.

The layout should facilitate recording, tabulating, and analyzing responses.

PLAN THE PHYSICAL LAYOUT   Pay careful attention to the design of your questionnaire. Plan the overall physical layout to facilitate recording, analyzing, and tabulating answers. Give clear and consistent directions for closed questions, and keep to a minimum the space you provide for answers to open questions.

Order questions logically. Be aware of how order may influence responses.

Consider the order of questions, too. There should be a logic not just to what you ask, but also to when you ask it. Begin, for example, with questions that are interesting or easy to answer and introduce more challenging questions later. (Easy questions typically require brief, impersonal, or factual answers.) Develop a sequence that will encourage respondents to give complete and candid answers. But at the same time, be sensitive to the effect each question will have on those that follow. Otherwise you may unwittingly lead or pattern responses.

A brief introduction may be helpful. Include the purpose of the survey, directions for completing it, and other appropriate information.

DEVELOP AN APPROPRIATE INTRODUCTION   Consider carefully the introduction to your questionnaire. A few lines at the top of the page may be sufficient, or you may need to attach a cover letter. It depends upon what you want to explain to your respondents and in how much detail. For example, you may identify yourself, define the purpose of the survey, and indicate how respondents will benefit from the study. You may also include a general set of directions and let respondents know whether they should sign their names or answer anonymously. Keep in mind, however, how these items may influence responses and omit or adjust as necessary.

CONDUCT A PILOT STUDY   If it is reasonably convenient, pilot test your questionnaire with a small sample as similar as possible to the respondents you will use in your main study. Look for problems with format, directions, wording, or order. After such a review, you may decide to turn an open question into a multiple-choice query or to substitute simple vocabulary for specialized terms. Remember, though, to test your revisions as well. Continue to make adjustments until you are reasonably sure your survey is reliable.

Test your questionnaire with a small sample. Make necessary corrections.

☐   **PLANNING THE PERSONAL INTERVIEW**

When you research by personal interview, as the terminology indicates, you gather information through oral questioning. There are two interview formats from which to choose: structured and unstructured. The structured interview is formal and standardized; it follows a pattern of questions. The unstructured interview is informal and highly individualized; interviewers develop questions as they go along and probe respondents' answers with follow-up inquiries.

In a structured interview, you ask prepared questions. In an unstructured interview, you make up your questions as you proceed.

Research by interview has a number of principles in common with research by written questionnaire. All research interviews, for example, require a reliable, representative sample. And the structured interview uses the same techniques as the written questionnaire does for developing and ordering questions. (The techniques for developing questions in an unstructured interview need more complex explanation than can be provided in this text.) Therefore, what shall concern you here are the delivery of questions and the methods of recording verbal responses.

Interviews and questionnaires have similar research requirements.

NEED FOR CARE IN INTERVIEWING   Your objective in using interviewing is no different from your objective in using any research technique: to develop meaningful information. Therefore, you have to take care that your results are accurate and check your procedures at virtually every step. Though each research problem has individual requirements, there are a number of common precautionary measures you should consider.

Your objective in an interview is to develop meaningful information.

First, select interviewers carefully. Start with the most basic of requirements: Potential interviewers should be intelligent, honest, and willing to work. In addition, they should be able to relate to your respondents and your respondents to them. City dwellers, for example, are not likely to get as much information from farmers as individuals who speak the farmer's language. Thus, before you select interviewers for your research problem, decide to what age, sex, physical appearance, social background, and education level your sample is likely to respond well. The characteristics, of course, will vary with each problem.

Select competent interviewers who relate well to respondents.

Second, develop standard questioning procedures and test thoroughly to make sure procedures are followed. Any variation in how questions are introduced, ordered, or phrased can affect the accuracy of answers. In instances that require interviewers to observe and interpret in addition to asking questions, procedures must be particularly

Test questioning procedures thoroughly, and prepare detailed instructions for interviewers.

clear. What you must do, therefore, is anticipate all probable situations your interviewers may encounter and prepare instructions to cover them. For best results, write an explicit, detailed instruction sheet and distribute it to all prospective investigators with directions that they read it thoroughly before they start to interview.

Supervise interviewers in the field.

Third, devise a plan for supervising your interviewers in the field. For, even if you select your investigators carefully and outline their duties clearly, there is still the possibility of error that only close supervision can avoid. Check regularly for basic as well as more complicated mistakes. At the very least, make sure all interviewers are conducting their research as scheduled and recording their data as instructed. You may want to supervise smaller projects yourself; in larger projects you will probably have to set up teams of researchers and delegate the responsibility. However, to make the most of any additional investment in personnel, have your supervisors serve also as leaders, giving directions as well as making sure they are carried out. In many respects, supervising is the most important step because an interviewer who is lazy or incompetent can compromise an entire investigation.

Flexibility is the primary advantage of the interview.

STRONG AND WEAK POINTS OF THE PERSONAL INTERVIEW   The greatest strength of the personal interview is its flexibility. Interviewers can do much more than just read questions. They can pass out pictures or product samples for respondents to examine, or distribute cards from which respondents select their answers. In this way they can involve respondents actively in the answering process and keep their interest. Interviewing also enables questioners to clarify directions and encourage respondents to develop answers. Furthermore, interviewers can clarify responses themselves by noting the tone respondents use, as well as recording expressions, gestures, and other potentially revealing aspects of responses.

The potential for influencing responses is the primary disadvantage.

However, the greatest strength of the personal interview is potentially its most serious weakness. Interviewers may unwittingly—or intentionally—influence responses. There are any number of opportunities, both subtle and overt, for such bias. Tone of voice, inflection, body language, personal image, and the like may encourage some responses and discourage others. Indeed, in certain circumstances, respondents may respond more to the questioner than to the questions, especially when they perceive the interviewer as someone they want to impress, positively or negatively. Careful selection, training, and supervision of interviewers will minimize the potential for such compromising effects.

Interviews are the most effective way to develop information about attitudes and preferences.

Certain types of information can be gathered more effectively through the personal interview than through other primary research methods. Interviews are, for example, a revealing source of objective information about data respondents are likely to recall—information about policies, techniques, procedures, and the like. Interviews are also useful in more subjective areas, such as attitudes, preferences, and tastes; they are frequently the basis of research for opinion surveys and interpretive studies.

Interviews can be costly, however.

There are certain practical limitations you must consider in selecting the interview as a research method, however. First, interviews can be expensive. Personnel and administrative costs are high; even volunteer interviewers have to be trained, supervised, and reimbursed for expenses. And then there is the potential problem of time. Interviews are usually one-on-one. If interviewees can be selected randomly from a single, accessible site, the research can be completed quickly. However, if quota or stratified sampling is required, if sites are scattered, or if each respondent can be interviewed by appointment only, the research will take considerably longer. Therefore, weigh both the schedule and the budgetary requirements of your research carefully in your decision to include interviews in your primary research.

☐ THE TELEPHONE AS A RESEARCH TOOL

Interviewing by telephone is comparatively quick and inexpensive.

Interviewing by telephone is a variation of the personal interview. However, as you might expect, asking questions over the telephone redefines the relationship between the interviewer and interviewee and raises a new set of potential advantages and disadvantages.

A significant advantage of telephone interviews is speed. You can reach large numbers of interviewees quickly and thus save time. For example, if you are conducting research about business executives or other professionals, you do not have to travel to a variety of sites or languish in waiting rooms to interview subjects. You can call them directly. And you will obviously save a good deal of money in the process, especially if your study group is concentrated in a toll-free calling area.

Another significant advantage of telephone interviewing is the possibility of using a truly random sample. That assumes, of course, all members of the group you are sampling are telephone subscribers and all telephones are identified. When every item in a universe is known and accessible, it is a simple process to devise a representative sample of the whole.

Keep in mind, however, that telephone subscribers are not necessarily representative of American society. Not everyone has a telephone. Low-income families or families living in very rural areas, for example, would be underrepresented in any study of American society as a whole. (How recent competition among telephone service providers may affect the percentage of the population owning telephones and subscribing to a telephone system is hard to say.)

However, telephone interviews provide no chance for observation, and they compete for one's attention with other surveys and with sales campaigns.

There are other limitations to telephone interviewing, too, You cannot observe respondents as they answer your questions, and you are not likely to be able to hold their attention as long. As a result, you miss much of the context of responses and must settle for fewer questions that are also less complex than those you might have asked in a face-to-face interview.

Finally, telephone interviewing has been used increasingly in recent years for sales and promotion as well as for research. Soliciting by telephone, a technique that uses personal or automated telephone calls to attract new buyers of products or services, has become common in some areas, frequently to the annoyance of those who are called. Many potential respondents, therefore, have come to view uninvited calls as inconvenient, even intrusive. To minimize resistance to your request for a telephone interview, schedule calls at a reasonable time, let your respondents know right away who you are and why you are calling, and politely ask for their cooperation. Even so, be prepared for a hostile few who will give incomplete answers or simply hang up.

☐ **SURVEY BY MAIL**

Mail questionnaires are yet another popular method of surveying. The procedure here is outwardly simple. You mail questionnaires to respondents; they complete them and mail them back to you. But, as you might expect, the process involves a little more than a simple exchange of a form. The questionnaire, for example, is usually accompanied by a cover letter that explains the survey, encourages complete and candid answers, and sets a deadline for returning responses. A stamped, addressed envelope is customarily included to facilitate returns. Reminder and acknowledgment letters are frequently part of the mail survey process as well.

MAIL SURVEY ADVANTAGES   The mail questionnaire has two initial advantages: it makes (1) wide geographic coverage possible at (2) comparatively little cost. For those reasons, the method is particularly effective in reaching small, widely scattered groups. If you wanted to survey the members of a college class five years after graduation, for example, personal interviews would involve a great deal of time and expense, with travel costs, time in transit, and the like. Telephone interviews would be considerably less time-consuming and less costly. But using the mail would be the most efficient and economical method of all.

> Mail surveys offer wide geographic coverage at relatively low cost.

Another advantage is the lack of interviewer bias. Respondents deal with a mail questionnaire directly, and they record their own responses. Still, this advantage remains such only if the researcher makes sure directions are clear, questions are sound, and respondents are able to work independently. Any confusion, evasion, or misrepresentation that might invalidate responses will not be detected until the questionnaires are returned, if it is detected at all.

> Mail surveys eliminate interviewer bias.

A mail questionnaire allows respondents to answer questions when they have the time, the resources, and the motivation. For surveys that require specialized information or detailed, deliberative answers, therefore, a mail questionnaire is more appropriate than a face-to-face or a telephone interview. But that advantage is lost if the level of detail required is not made clear or if the respondents lack time or inclination to make the effort expected.

> Respondents can complete the mail survey at their convenience.

A final advantage of the mail questionnaire is that it lends itself to sound sampling techniques, provided the mailing lists available are representative of the group to be studied. However, that benefit has its limitations, too, for the selection of a sound sample for mailing does not assure a sound sample of returns, as you will see.

> Mail surveys lend themselves to random distribution.

MAIL SURVEY DISADVANTAGES   Offsetting these advantages are significant drawbacks that can make a mail questionnaire inappropriate for some studies. Part of planning a survey, therefore, requires anticipating the potential effect of these shortcomings.

First, there is the possibility of a biased or nonrepresentative sample. Although you may mail your questionnaire to a representative sample, not all who receive questionnaires will return them. Those who do are likely to be respondents who feel strongly in one way or another about the topic and thus are not truly representative of the group you are attempting to study. It helps somewhat to design your questionnaire to encourage maximum results or to send reminders to late respondents. Even so, you

> However, those returning the survey may not comprise a reliable or representative sample.

should be prepared for a less than 100 percent response and make provisions for suitable corrections in your analysis.

Mail surveys are less expensive than other survey techniques, but they are far from inexpensive.

A second possible problem is expense. To be sure, mail questionnaires are less costly to administer than personal or telephone interviews. But they are far from free. The actual cost per response is directly related to the percentage of respondents replying. For example, assuming the cost of each questionnaire mailed (including two-way postage, processing, handling, and cost of stationery) is a conservative $1.25, a return of 10 percent (about average) would mean a cost of $12.50 per return. A return of 5 percent would raise the cost to $25.00. Such returns and even lower are not uncommon in some fields. However, keep in mind the cost per return does diminish if the percentage of returns increases. That fact should be even more of an incentive for you to encourage as complete a response from your sample as possible.

They offer no opportunity for observation.

The lack of opportunity for observation is a third possible drawback of the mail questionnaire. Observing respondents is sometimes necessary to obtain the context of replies. You can detect from tone of voice or from nonverbal communication the full meaning of answers. And being with respondents makes it possible to explain or interpret difficult questions. However, using a mail questionnaire limits you to recording just what respondents write and makes you totally dependent upon the instructions as stated. By carefully selecting and wording questions, you can minimize such limitations; but you are not likely to eliminate them.

There may be a delay in receiving responses.

Finally, there is the potential problem of delay in receiving results. Mail service is sometimes slow; and not all respondents will complete or return questionnaires right away. Therefore, if you want information quickly, a mail questionnaire may be less effective than other forms of primary research that allow direct access to respondents and require immediate replies.

☐ THE PANEL SURVEY

The panel survey studies the responses of a designated group over time.

The panel survey is a series of group interviews conducted over a period of time. Most typically, the panel is a continuing study with the same group answering questions on the same subject indefinitely. The questioning can be conducted in any of the three formats previously discussed: the personal interview, the telephone interview, or the questionnaire.

Panel members may be chosen randomly or selected personally.

Members of a panel are selected in much the same fashion as respondents in a conventional personal interview. For routine studies concerning the actions or reactions of a given universe, they are selected randomly, using recognized sampling techniques. However, for studies that require expert opinion, members of the panel may be selected individually and subjectively. For example, to determine consumer preferences for a study of laundry detergents, a quota, random, or area sampling could be used to determine a panel that represents the consuming public. However, to predict how the public will respond to a new form of packaging for an established detergent product, a carefully selected panel of psychologists might be more appropriate.

The experiment is one type of panel interview.

There are two general forms of the panel interview. One is an experiment of sorts. Researchers first interview the panel on the subject of concern; then they make the phenomenon under study occur. Finally, they conduct another interview with the same group to see if any changes have been brought about as a result of introducing the phenomenon.

For example, a company that wants to measure the effect of its efforts to change its image might start by interviewing a panel on its feelings about the current public image of the company. Next, the company will begin its intensive public relations campaign. After a given period of time, during which it is presumed no other image-influencing factor will be introduced, company researchers will interview the panel again. Any changes, positive or negative, between the first and the second interview the company can attribute to the effect of its public relations campaign. If there is no change, the company can assume the campaign has had essentially no effect.

But more common is the continuing study.

A second and more popular form of the panel is the continuing study. Here panelists serve as a sounding board or as a means of providing information on an ongoing basis. The Marketing Research Corporation of America, for example, gets information monthly from a standing panel of families on such topics as expenditures by product, by brand, and by geographic area.

The panel interview is a relatively inexpensive method to identify changes over time.

The most significant advantage of the panel as a primary research tool is that it allows you to measure change over time. In addition, it is a relatively inexpensive survey form, since it usually involves small groups of respondents who are both available and willing to be interviewed.

However, panel membership runs the danger of becoming nonrepresentative.

But the panel survey has its disadvantages, too. First, the panel runs the risk of becoming nonrepresentative over time. Sometimes the problem is attrition or turnover. Original panelists may move, resign, or otherwise leave the study. If you are conducting a panel survey of apartment dwellers, for example, it may be impossible to keep the composition of the group stable. But sometimes the problem is the lack of attrition or turnover. In this case, if you are conducting a panel survey of college students, you would not want to retain individual panelists after graduation since they would no longer be true representatives of the group you set out to study.

A second disadvantage of the panel survey is the bias that can come as a result of being a panelist. Members may begin to take a special interest in the issues involved or become self-conscious about their role, essentially anticipating and preparing for their questions. Or just the opposite may happen. They may become complacent about or disinterested in the issues and give inaccurate or incomplete answers. If either change occurs, the membership can no longer be considered representative or its responses reliable.

QUESTIONS

1. What advice would you give an investigator who has been assigned a task involving analysis of internal records of several company departments?
2. Define experimentation. What does the technique of experimentation involve?
3. Explain the significance of keeping constant all factors other than the experimental variable of an experiment.

4. Give one example each of problems that can best be solved through (*a*) before-after designs and (*b*) controlled before-after designs. Explain your choices.

5. Discuss the limitations in using experiments in business.

6. Define observation as a research technique.

7. Select an example of a business problem that can be solved best by observation. Explain your choice.

8. Using your imagination to supply any missing facts you may need, develop a plan for the experiment you would use in the following situations.

   a. The Golden Glow Baking Company has for many years manufactured and sold cookies packaged in attractive boxes. It is considering packaging the cookies in plastic bags and wants to conduct an experiment to determine consumer response to this change.

   b. The Miller Brush Company, manufacturers of a line of household goods, has for years sold its products on a house-to-house basis. It now wants to conduct an experiment to test the possibilities of selling through conventional retail outlets.

   c. A national chain for food stores wants to know whether it would profit by doubling the face value of coupons. It is willing to pay the cost of an experiment in its research for an answer.

   d. The True Time Watch Company is considering the use of automated sales displays ($9.50 each) instead of stationary displays ($4.50 each) in the 2,500 retail outlets that sell True Time watches. The company will conduct an experiment to determine the relative effects on sales of the two displays.

   e. The Marvel Soap Company has developed a new cleaning agent that is unlike current soaps and detergents. The product is well protected by patent. The company wants to determine the optimum price for the new product through experimentation.

   f. National Cereals, Inc. wants to determine the effectiveness of advertising to children. Until now, it has been aiming its appeal at the homemaker. The company will support an experiment to learn the answer.

9. Using your imagination to supply any missing facts you may need, develop a plan for research by observation for these problems.

   a. A chain of department stores wants to know what causes differences in sales by departments within stores and by stores. Some of this information it hopes to get through research by observation.

   b. Your university wants to know the nature and extent of its automobile parking problem.

   c. The management of an insurance company wants to determine the efficiency and productivity of its data entry department.

   d. Owners of a shopping center want a study to determine shopping patterns of their customers. Specifically, they want to know such things as what parts of town the customers come from, how they travel, how many stores they visit, and so on.

    e. The director of your library wants a detailed study of library use (what facilities are used, when, by whom, and so on).

    f. The management of a restaurant wants a study of its workers' efficiency in the kitchen.

10. Using your imagination to supply any missing facts you may need, develop a plan for research by survey for these problems.

    a. The American Restaurant Association wants information that will give its members a picture of its customers. The information will serve as a guide for a promotion campaign designed to promote restaurant eating. Specifically, it will seek such information as who eats out, how often, where they go, how much they spend. Likewise, it will seek to determine who does not eat out and why.

    b. The editor of your local daily paper wants a readership study of his publication. That is, he wants to know just who reads what.

    c. An organization of tobacco companies wants to learn the current trend in tobacco use. They want to know such information as how many people are smoking, how many have stopped, how many new smokers there are, and so on.

    d. The American Association of Publishers wants a survey of reading habits of the American people. They want to know who reads what, how much, when, where, and so on.

11. Give examples of sampling problems that can make best use of random sampling. Do the same for quota and area sampling.

12. Construct three leading questions. Explain why they are leading.

13. Rewrite the questions in 12 above so that they do not lead the reader.

14. Assume you need information on the following subjects, and you have reason to believe the people in your sample will be reluctant to give it to you. How would you attempt to get this information?

    a. Family income

    b. Age

    c. Reading habits

    d. Morals

    e. Personal cleanliness

15. Give an illustration of how a question asking for opinion could be substituted by one asking for fact.

16. What would be the effect of memory on questions concerning these matters?

    a. Articles read in a periodical

    b. Expenditures for recreation

    c. Clothing worn at one's wedding

    d. Reasons for purchasing an automobile

    e. An automobile accident

17. Discuss the pros and cons of using telephone, personal interview, and mail survey techniques for each of the problems listed in question 10.

18. Point out violations of the rules of good questionnaire construction in the following questions. The questions do not come from the same questionnaire.

   a.   How many days on the average do you wear a pair of socks before changing?

   b.   (The first question in a survey conducted by Fortune cigarettes.) Have you ever smoked a Fortune cigarette?

   c.   Do you consider the ideal pay plan to be one based on straight commission or straight salary?

   d.   What kind of gasoline did you purchase last time?

   e.   How much did you pay for clothing in the past 12 months?

   f.   Check the word below that best describes how often you eat dessert with your noon meal.

   Always
   Usually
   Sometimes
   Never

P A R T 3

Structure of Reports

Organizing Information and Constructing the Outline

Clear reports are those that are well organized.

Akey criterion of a clear business report is its organization. A report that communicates effectively is one with facts and parts in an orderly arrangement. Thus, you must give significant thought to the facts and report parts as you construct your report.

Classify, edit, and tabulate primary research results before you attempt to apply them.

It is likely, however, that your information will be in various states of order depending on the methods you used to collect it. Material collected through an orderly form of bibliographical research should be arranged by subjects and ready for application to the problem. But you need to classify, edit, and tabulate information collected through primary research before you can apply it to the problem.

CLASSIFYING DATA

Use logic to determine which results should be grouped.

Classifying data means grouping research results by some logical basis—for example, time, quantity, and place. In primary research problems, you usually classify information before you edit and tabulate it.

Classification is a simple enough process. Let's say you have completed a questionnaire survey of 500 college students, asking them the open question, "What do you expect your annual income to be one year after graduation?" Predictably, there will be 500 individual responses. To make your findings more meaningful, therefore, you might arrange the answers by broad quantitative groups: under $15,000, $15,000 to $20,000, $20,000 to $25,000, and $25,000 and over.

The same survey might include a question to determine the undergraduates' motives in pursuing a college education. Of the many varied responses to "Why am I seeking a college degree?" most could be classified into such categories as professional goals, personal goals, or philosophical goals.

In either instance, the information is brought together or reduced to make it more workable and understandable. Thus, you can see the two chief reasons for

81

classifying data: (1) you can bring significant relationships of data to light and (2) you can simplify data and make them that much easier to interpret.

In some primary research, you can classify data as you collect them.

It is possible in some primary research to do the classifying and the related tasks of editing and tabulating while you are collecting your information. In these situations, you must either predetermine the grouping plan or base the groups on early or anticipated information. When the subject is fairly simple and you know it well, this early determination of the classification plan can be easy. With more complex or less familiar areas of investigation, however, it can be difficult and may result in costly, time-consuming corrections.

EDITING AND TABULATING

Check data for errors. Determine which results you can use and which you cannot.

Editing is the step that logically follows classifying. Here you examine all the data collected, looking for possible inconsistencies or omissions, making corrections whenever possible, and generally preparing the forms for tabulation. You may have to discount answers to a rating question, for example, because respondents ranked rather than rated the alternatives. Or you may want to qualify the results of a question that only a small percentage of your respondents answered.

Count results and reduce them to an orderly form.

The process of interpreting the forms and looking for errors is largely a subjective one and requires that you know the subject matter thoroughly. Obviously, the quality of the adjustments or revisions that result is no better or worse than the quality of your editing.

Tabulating, which is the next step, is the procedure of counting survey answers or observed responses and compiling them systematically. It is the process of reducing the findings to an orderly and understandable form.

Do complex tabulations by computer, if you can.

For large scale surveys, tabulation should really be done by computer. The results are entered into a database, whereupon retrieving and sorting information become simply a matter of giving appropriate instructions to the computer. The instructions that carry out these functions can be especially designed for the project or can be available as a standardized software package. The details of how to use a computer are beyond the scope of this text. But do not overlook the increasing opportunities to employ this method of tallying your results. If you cannot use a computer yourself, the chances are good you can find economical computer assistance in this aspect of your work. The time you save and the accuracy you gain are usually well worth the cost.

Simple tabulations you can do by hand.

However, for smaller surveys or for studies where computer assistance is not available, you will have to tabulate by hand. You can use something as basic as the cross-five technique, which is counting by marks and making every fifth mark across the preceding four (卌); or you can devise a simple system of your own. If you are going to tally by hand, though, it is a good idea to prepare your questionnaires or response sheets in advance, using color coding or symbols you can recognize easily as you conduct your count.

CONSTRUCTING THE REPORT OUTLINE

You are now ready to construct the outline.

After you have given the information collected a preliminary workable order, your next logical step is to arrange the findings into a more formal order appropriate for communicating. Specifically, you must construct the report outline.

The report outline, of course, is the plan for the writing task. It is to the writer what the blueprint is to the construction engineer or what the pattern is to the dressmaker. In addition to serving as a guide, the outline forces you to think before writing. And when you think, your writing is likely to be clear.

Outlines should be written. They serve as tables of contents and captions.

Although this plan may be either written or mental, you should write it in all but the shortest of problems. In longer reports, where tables of contents are needed, the outline forms the basis of this table. Also, in most long reports, and even in some short ones, the outline topics may serve as guides to the reader when placed within the report text as captions (or heads).

☐   PATTERNS OF REPORT ORGANIZATION

You should decide on a sequence: (1) indirect, (2) direct, or (3) chronological.

After you have your information ready for outlining and before you begin the task of outlining, you should decide on which writing sequence or pattern to use in the report. The possible sequences you can choose from are many, but they fall into two basic patterns—*indirect* (also called logical or inductive) and *direct* (also called psychological and deductive). Some authorities suggest a third order, the *chronological* arrangement. Actually this order really is a special form adaptable to either the logical or psychological order. Although the emphasis at this stage of report preparation is on the selection of a sequence for the whole of the report, these patterns are useful guides to constructing any writing unit, be it a sentence, paragraph, major section, or the whole.

Indirect order moves from known to unknown—typically introduction, body, conclusion (or summary).

INDIRECT ORDER   In the **indirect** arrangement, the findings are in inductive order— moving from the known to the unknown. Preceding the report findings are whatever introductory material is necessary to orient the reader to the problem. Then come the facts, possibly with their analyses. And from these facts and analyses, summary or concluding statements are derived. In some problems, a recommendation section may also be included. Thus, in report form this arrangement is typified by an introductory section, the report body (usually made up of a number of sections), and a summary, conclusion, or recommendation section.

An illustration of this plan is the following report of a short and rather simple problem concerning a personnel action on a subordinate. For reasons of space economy, the illustration presents only the key parts of the report.

> Numerous incidents during the past two months appear to justify an investigation of the work record of Clifford A. Knudson, draftsman, tool design department. . . .
>
> The investigation of his work record for the past two months reveals these points:
>
> 1.   He has been late to work seven times.
> 2.   He has been absent without acceptable excuse for seven days.
> 3.   On two occasions, he reported to work in a drunken and disorderly condition.
> 4.   And so on.

> The foregoing evidence leads to one conclusion: Clifford A. Knudson should be fired.

Direct order begins with the most important information (conclusions, recommendations, main facts).

DIRECT ORDER   Contrasting with the logical sequence is the **direct** arrangement. This sequence presents the subject matter in deductive fashion. Summaries, conclusions, or recommendations come first and are followed by the facts and analyses they are drawn from. A typical report following such an order would begin with a presentation of summary, conclusion, and recommendation material. The report findings and the analyses from which the beginning section derives comprise the following sections.

> Clifford A. Knudson, draftsman, tool design department, should be fired. This conclusion is reached after a thorough investigation brought about by numerous incidents during the past two months. . . .
>
> The recommended action is supported by this information from his work record for the past two months:
>
> 1.   He has been late to work seven times.
> 2.   He has been absent without acceptable excuse for seven days.
> 3.   On two occasions, he reported to work in a drunken and disorderly condition.
> 4.   And so on.

Chronological order is an order based on time (past to present, present to past).

CHRONOLOGICAL ORDER   In the **chronological** arrangement, the findings are in an order based on time. Obviously, such an arrangement is limited to problems that are of an historical nature or in some other way are related to time. The time pattern followed may be from past to present, from present to past, from present to future, or from future to present. A report following an order of time may begin with an introductory section or with a summary, conclusion, or recommendation. In other words, the chronological order is generally combined with either of the two preceding orders. Therefore, it is the arrangement of the findings (the report body) to which the chronological sequence is usually applied.

> Clifford A. Knudson was hired in 1992 as a junior draftsman in the tool design department. For the first 18 months, his work was exemplary, and he was given two pay increases and a promotion to senior draftsman. In January of 1994, he missed four days of work, reporting illness, which was later found to be untrue. Again, in February. . . .
>
> All of these facts lead to the obvious conclusion: Clifford A. Knudson should be fired.

☐ **SYSTEMS OF OUTLINE SYMBOLS**

This conventional symbol system is commonly used in marking the levels of an outline.

Various authorities have prescribed guides and procedures for outlining. The gist of most of this procedure is that the material to be presented should be divided into separate units of thought and that some system of arabic, roman, or alphabetical symbols should join the units. The most common system of outline symbols is the conventional form.

I. First degree of division
   A. Second degree of division
      1. Third degree of division

> *a.* Fourth degree of division
> > (1) Fifth degree of division
> > > (*a*) Sixth degree of division

This numerical (or decimal) system also is used.

A second system of symbols is the numerical (sometimes called *decimal*) form. This system uses arabic numerals separated by decimals. The numerals show the order of division. The succession of decimals shows the steps in the division process. Illustration best explains the procedure.

1. First degree of division
    1.1 Second degree of division
        1.1.1 Third degree of division
            1.1.1.1 Fourth degree of division
2. First degree of division
    2.1 Second degree of division
        2.1.1 Third degree of division (first item)
        2.1.2 Third degree of division (second item)
            2.1.2.1 Fourth degree of division (first item)
            2.1.2.2 Fourth degree of division (second item)

☐ THE NATURE AND EXTENT OF OUTLINING

You should construct the outline to meet the objective of the report.

In general, you build the outline around the objective of the investigation and your findings. With the objective and findings in mind, you build a mental structure of your report. In this process, you hold large areas of facts and ideas in mind, shifting them around until the most workable arrangement comes about. This workable arrangement is the order that will present the findings in their clearest and most meaningful form.

When you reach this stage, you probably have done some work on the outline.

The extent of the outlining task will differ from problem to problem. In fact, in many instances you will do much of the work long before you consciously begin the task of constructing an outline. The early steps of defining the problem and determining its subproblems may lay the groundwork for final organization. If you used a questionnaire or other form in gathering information, possibly its structure has given the problem some order. The preliminary analysis of the problem, along with the tasks of classifying and tabulating the findings, and possibly preliminary interpretations of the findings, may have given you the general idea of the report story to be written. Thus, when you begin to construct the outline, the work to be done may be in varying degrees of progress. The task of outlining will never be the same for any two problems. Even so, a general and systematic procedure for outlining may prove helpful.

☐ ORGANIZATION BY DIVISION

Look at outlining as a division process.

This procedure is based on the concept that outlining is a process of dividing. The subject of division is the whole of the information gathered. Thus, you begin to organize by seeking an appropriate and logical way to divide all your collected information.

You divide the whole into parts, the parts into subparts, the subparts into subparts, etc.

After you have divided the whole of the information into comparable parts, you may further divide each of the parts. Then, you may further divide each of these subparts, and you may continue to divide as far as it is practical to do so (Figure 6–1). Thus, in the end you may have an outline of two, three, or more levels (or stages) of division. You designate these levels of division in the finished outline by some system of letters or numbers, such as the two systems previously discussed.

☐   **DIVISION BY CONVENTIONAL RELATIONSHIPS**

Time, place, quantity, and factor are the bases for division.

In dividing the information into subparts, you are trying to find a means of division that will produce equal and comparable parts. Time, place, quantity, and factors are the general bases for these divisions.

When the information has a time basis, division by time is possible.

DIVISION BY TIME PERIODS   Whenever the information assembled has some chronological aspect, you can organize your material by time. In such an organization, the divisions of the whole are periods of time. Usually, the periods follow a time sequence. Although a past-to-present and present-to-past sequence is the rule, variations are possible. The time periods you select need not be equal in length, but they should be comparable in importance. Of course, determining comparability is a subjective process and is best based on the facts of the one situation.

A report on the progress of a research committee serves to illustrate this possibility. You could break down the time period covered by such a report into the following comparable subperiods.

The period of orientation, May–July

Planning the project, August

Implementation of the research plan, September–November

In addition to illustrating a time breakdown of a problem, this example shows a logical division of subject matter. Each of the three time periods contains logically related information (orientation, planning, implementation). Similarly, the following breakdown of a report on the history of a company is made up of logical time periods. As in the preceding example, you may further subdivide each of these parts into smaller time units.

Struggle in the early years (1887–1901)

Growth to maturity (1902–29)

Depression and struggle (1930–39)

Wartime shifts in production (1940–45)

Postwar prosperity (1946–76)

Industry dominance (1977–present)

The years ahead

You could arrange the happenings within each period in the order of their occurrence. Close inspection may reveal additional division possibilities.

FIGURE 6–1   Procedure for constructing an outline by process of division

I Introduction	I A	I A
II	B	B
	C	C
	II A	II A 1 etc.
		2
	B	B 1
		2
III		3
	III A	III A 1 etc.
		2
	B	B 1
		2
	C	C 1
IV		2
	IV A	IV A 1 etc.
		2
	B	B 1
		2
		3
V Summary, conclusion, recommendation	V A	V A
	B	B

Step 1	Step 2	Step 3	etc.
Divide the whole into comparable parts. This gives the roman numbered parts of the outline. Usually an introduction begins the outline. Some combination of summary, conclusion, recommendation ends it.	Divide each roman section. This gives the A, B, C headings.	Then divide each A, B, C heading. This gives the 1, 2, 3 headings.	Continue dividing as long as it is practical to do so.

When the information is related to geographic location, a place division is possible.

PLACE AS A BASIS FOR DIVISION   If the information collected has some relation to geographic location, a place division is possible. Ideally, the division would be such that like characteristics concerning the problem exist within each geographic area. Unfortunately, place divisions are hampered because political boundary lines and geographic differences in characteristics do not always coincide.

A report on the sales program of a national manufacturer illustrates a division by place. You could organize the information in this problem logically into these major geographic areas:

New England   Southwest   Rocky Mountain

Atlantic Seaboard   Midwest   Pacific Coast

South

Another illustration of organization by place is a report on the productivity of a company with a number of manufacturing plants. In organizing this problem, you could make the company's plants the major divisions of the report. Then, you could break down each plant by space subdivisions—this time by sections, departments, divisions, or such.

The following outline excerpt illustrates one such possibility:

Millville Plant:

    Production

        Planning and production control

        Production department A

        Production department B

        Production department C

        And so on

    Sales

        Sales office A

        Sales office B

        Sales office C

        And so on

    Finance

        Credit and collection

        Comptroller

        And so on

    Personnel

        Salary administration

        Employment

        And so on

Bell City Plant:

Production

And so on

DIVISION BASED ON QUANTITY   You can also divide your report by quantity whenever the information involved has quantitative values. To illustrate, an analysis of the buying habits of a segment of the labor force could very well break down by income groups. Such a division might produce the following sections:

Under $10,000

$10,000 to under $15,000

$15,000 to under $20,000

$20,000 to under $25,000

$25,000 to under $30,000

$30,000 and over

Another example of division on a quantitative basis is a report of a survey of men's preferences for shoes. Because of variations in preferences by ages, an organization by age groups appears logical. Perhaps a division such as the following would result:

Youths, under 18

Young adult, 18–30

Adult, 31–50

Senior adult, 51–70

Elderly adult, over 70

FACTORS AS A BASIS FOR ORGANIZATION   Factor breakdowns are not so easily seen as the preceding three possibilities. Frequently, problems have little or no time, place, or quantity aspects. Instead, they require investigation of certain information areas in order to meet the objective. Such information areas may consist of a number of questions that must be answered in solving a problem. Or they may consist of subjects that must be investigated and applied to the problem.

An example of a division by factors is a report that seeks to determine the best of three cities for the location of a new manufacturing plant. In arriving at this decision, your procedure would be to compare the three cities on the basis of the factors that affect the plant location. Thus, you might arrive at this logical organization plan:

Worker availability

Transportation facilities

Public support and cooperation

Availability of raw materials

Taxation

Sources of power

Another illustration of organization by factors is a report advising a manufacturer whether to begin production of a new product. As you can see, this problem has little time, place, or quantity considerations. Thus, you would reach your decision on the basic question by carefully considering the factors involved. Among the more likely factors are these:

Production feasibility

Financial considerations

Strength of competition

Consumer demand

Marketing considerations

☐ COMBINATION AND MULTIPLE DIVISION POSSIBILITIES

Sometimes combinations of time, place, quantity, and factor are logical.

Not all division possibilities are clearly time, place, quantity, or factor. In some instances, you will need to use some combinations of these bases of division. In the case of a report on the progress of a sales organization, for example, you could arrange the information collected by a combination of quantity and place:

Areas of high sales activity

Areas of moderate sales activity

Areas of low sales activity

Although not so logical, the following combination of time and quantity is also a possibility:

Periods of low sales

Periods of moderate sales

Periods of high sales

Multiple organization possibilities can occur.

Some problems can be organized in more than one way. For example, take the problem of determining the best of three towns for locating a new manufacturing plant. It could be organized by towns or by the bases of comparison. Organized by towns, the bases of comparison likely would be the second-level headings:

This plant location problem is organized by place.

II. Town A
   A. Worker availability
   B. Transportation facilities
   C. Public support and cooperation
   D. Availability of raw materials
   E. Taxation
   F. Sources of power
III. Town B
   A. Worker availability
   B. Transportation facilities
   C. Public support and cooperation

  D. Availability of raw materials
  E. Taxation
  F. Sources of power
IV. Town C
  A. Worker availability
  B. And so on

Organized by bases of comparison, towns likely would be the second-level headings:

Here it is organized by factors (the basis of comparison).

II. Worker availability
  A. Town A
  B. Town B
  C. Town C
III. Transportation facilities
  A. Town A
  B. Town B
  C. Town C
IV. Town support and cooperation
  A. Town A
  B. Town B
  C. Town C

The second plan is better because it makes comparison easy.

At first glance, both plans appear to be logical. Close inspection, however, shows that organization by towns is not good, for it separates the information that must be compared. For example, to find out which town has the best worker availability, one would have to look at three different parts of the report. In the second outline, the information to be compared is close together.

Even though one of them is not good, these two plans show that some problems can be organized in more than one way. When more than one way is possible, you must compare the possibilities carefully to find the one that best presents the report information.

□ INTRODUCTORY AND CONCLUDING SECTIONS

The preceding discussion deals with the body of the report.

To this point, the organized procedure discussed has concerned primarily the arrangement of the information gathered and analyzed. It is this portion of the report that comprises what is commonly referred to as the report body. To this report body, you will usually append two additional major sections.

An introduction may precede it, and a summary or conclusion may follow it.

At the beginning of a major report, you may have an introduction to the presentation (the reason the examples above begin with II rather than I), although some forms of today's reports eliminate this conventional section. You may also add to each report a final major section in which you bring the objective to a head. Such a section may be little more than a summary in a report in which the objective is simply to present information. In other instances, it may be the section in which you draw together the major findings or analyses to form a final conclusion. Or possibly, in this section you may develop a recommended line of action based on the foregoing analysis of information.

☐ WORDING OF THE OUTLINE

When the outline will appear in the report, take care in wording it.

As the outline in its finished form is the report's table of contents and may also serve as caption guides to the paragraphs throughout the written text, you should take care in constructing its final wording. In this regard, you should review a number of conventional principles of construction. Following these principles will enable you to produce a logical and meaningful outline of your report.

You may use topic or talking captions. Topic captions give only the subject of discussion.

TOPIC OR TALKING CAPTION?   In selecting the wording for the captions, you have a choice of two general forms—the topic and the talking caption. Topic captions are short constructions, frequently one or two words in length, which do nothing more than identify the topic of discussion. The following segment of a topic caption outline is typical of its type.

II. Present armor unit
    A. Description and output
    B. Cost
    C. Deficiencies
III. Replacement effects
    A. Space
    B. Boiler setting
    C. Additional accessories
    D. Fuel

Talking captions identify the subject and tell what is said about it.

Like the topic caption, the talking caption (or popular caption, as it is sometimes called) identifies the subject matter covered. But it goes a step further. It also indicates what is said about the subject. In other words, the talking captions summarize, or tell the story of, the material they cover, as in the following illustration of a segment of a talking outline.

II. Operation analyses of armor unit
    A. Recent lag in overall output
    B. Increase in cost of operation
    C. Inability to deliver necessary steam
III. Consideration of replacement effects
    A. Greater space requirements
    B. Need for higher boiler setting
    C. Efficiency possibilities of accessories
    D. Practicability of firing two fuels

Further illustrating the difference between topic and talking captions are the following two outlines.

A Report Outline of Captions That Talk

I. Orientation to the problem
    A. Authorization by board action
    B. Problem of locating a woolen mill
    C. Use of miscellaneous government data

    D. Logical plan of solution
- II. Community attitudes toward the woolen industry
  - A. Favorable reaction of all cities to new mill
  - B. Mixed attitudes of all toward labor policy
- III. Labor supply and prevailing wage rates
  - A. Lead of San Marcos in unskilled labor
  - B. Concentration of skilled workers in San Marcos
  - C. Generally confused pattern of wage rates
- IV. Nearness to the raw wool supply
  - A. Location of Ballinger, Coleman, and San Marcos in the wool area
  - B. Relatively low production near Big Spring and Littlefield
- V. Availability of utilities
  - A. Inadequate water supply for all but San Marcos
  - B. Unlimited supply of natural gas for all towns
  - C. Electric rate advantage of San Marcos and Coleman
  - D. General adequacy of all for waste disposal
- VI. Adequacy of existing transportation systems
  - A. Surface transportation advantages of San Marcos and Ballinger
  - B. General equality of airway connections
- VII. A final weighting of the factors
  - A. Selection of San Marcos as first choice
  - B. Recommendation of Ballinger as second choice
  - C. Lack of advantages in Big Spring, Coleman, and Littlefield

A Report Outline of Topic Captions

- I. Introduction
  - A. Authorization
  - B. Purpose
  - C. Sources
  - D. Preview
- II. Community attitudes
  - A. Plant location
  - B. Labor policy
- III. Factors of labor
  - A. Unskilled workers
  - B. Skilled workers
  - C. Wage rates
- IV. Raw wool supply
  - A. Adequate areas
  - B. Inadequate areas
- V. Utilities
  - A. Water
  - B. Natural gas
  - C. Electricity
  - D. Waste disposal

VI. Transportation
   A. Surface
   B. Air
VII. Conclusions
   A. First choice
   B. Alternative choice
   C. Other possibilities

Talking captions help to communicate the report's message.

You can usually choose between topic and talking captions, although some companies have specific requirements for their reports. Topic captions are the conventional form. Because they have the support of convention, they are most often used in industry, especially in the more formal papers. Talking captions, on the other hand, while relatively new, are gaining rapidly in popularity. Because they emphasize the main points in the report, they help the readers get the message quickly, thus saving time. They are recommended as the superior form, but either is correct.

Captions at a level of division should be grammatically parallel.

PARALLELISM OF CONSTRUCTION   Because of the many choices available, you will likely construct outlines that have a mixture of grammatical forms. Some report writers believe such a mixture of forms is acceptable and each caption should be judged primarily by how well it describes the material it covers. The more precise and scholarly writers disagree, saying mixing caption types is a violation of a fundamental concept of balance.

For example, if caption II is a noun phrase, so should be captions III, IV, etc.

This concept of balance can be expressed in a simple rule—the rule of parallel construction. It states that all coordinate captions should be of the same grammatical construction. That is, if the caption for one of the major report parts (say part II) is a noun phrase, all equal-level captions (parts III, IV, V, and so on) must be noun phrases. And if the first subdivision under a major section (say part A of II) is a sentence, the captions coordinate with it (B, C, D, and so on) must be sentences.

The following segment of an outline illustrates violations of the principle of parallel construction.

A. Machine output is lagging (sentence)

B. Increase in cost of operations (noun phrase)

C. Unable to deliver necessary steam (decapitated sentence)

You could correct this parallelism error in any one of three ways: by making the captions all sentences, all noun phrases, or all decapitated sentences. If you want all noun phrases, you could write captions such as these:

A. Lag in machine output

B. Increase in cost of operations

C. Inability to deliver necessary steam

Or as all sentences, you could write them like this:

A. Machine output is lagging

B. Cost of operations increases

C.   Boiler cannot deliver necessary steam

Another violation of parallelism is apparent in the following example:

A.   Income distribution becoming uniform (decapitated sentence)

B.   Rapid advance in taxes (noun phrase)

C.   Annual earnings rise steadily (sentence)

Again, you could correct the error by selecting any one of the captions and revising the others to conform with it. As sentences, they would appear like this:

A.   Income distribution increases uniformly

B.   Taxes advance rapidly

C.   Annual earnings rise steadily

When revised as noun phrases, they would take this form:

A.   Uniform increase in income distribution

B.   Rapid advance in taxes

C.   Steady rise in annual earnings

As decapitated sentences, they would read this way:

A.   Income distribution becoming uniform

B.   Taxes advancing rapidly

C.   Annual earnings rising steadily

Make the talking captions concise.

CONCISENESS IN WORDING   As a general rule, your talking captions should be the shortest possible word arrangements that can also meet the talking requirement. Although the following captions talk well, their excessive lengths obviously affect their roles in communicating the report information:

> Appearance is the most desirable feature that steady users of cigarette lighters look for.

> The two drawbacks of lighters mentioned most often by smokers who use matches are that lighters get out of order easily and frequently are out of fluid.

> More dependability and the ability to hold more lighter fluid are the improvements most suggested by both users and nonusers of cigarette lighters.

Obviously, the captions contain too much information. Just what should be left out, however, is not easily determined. Much depends on the analysis the writers have given the material and what they have determined to be most significant. One analysis, for example, would support these revised captions.

> Appearance most desirable feature

> Dependability primary criticism

> Fuel capacity most often suggested improvement

Repeating words in captions can be monotonous.

VARIETY IN EXPRESSION   In the report outline, as in all forms of writing, you should use a variety of expressions. You should not overuse words, since too-frequent repetition is monotonous, and monotonous writing is not pleasing to the reader. The following outline excerpt illustrates this point:

A. Chemical production in Texas

B. Chemical production in California

C. Chemical production in Louisiana

Talking captions are not likely to be monotonous.

As a rule, if you make the captions talk well, there is little chance of monotonous repetition occurring. It is unlikely that your successive sections would be presenting similar or identical information. That is, captions that are really descriptive of the material they cover are not likely to use the same words. As an illustration of this point, the outline topics in the foregoing example can be improved simply through making the captions talk:

A. Texas leads in chemical production

B. California holds runner-up position

C. Rapidly gaining Louisiana ranks third

QUESTIONS

1. Assume you have interviewed a representative group of the student body of your school on the subject of total out-of-pocket expenditures of students during the academic year. Making any logical assumptions, discuss the categories into which your findings might possibly be classified.

2. What should you consider in deciding between machine and hand tabulation of research data?

3. Explain the relationship of the report outline to the finished report.

4. What are the basic patterns of report organization? Can you see advantages and shortcomings in these patterns? Discuss.

5. Describe the two conventional systems of symbols used in outlining the report. Illustrate each to the sixth level of subdivision.

6. Discuss the concept of outlining as a process of division.

7. By what four relationships may the information on a subject be divided? Illustrate each.

8. Select a problem (different from the text illustrations) that has at least two division possibilities. Evaluate each of the possibilities.

9. Assume you are working on a report on the history of manufacturing in the northeastern section of the United States. What division possibilities would you consider in organizing this problem? Discuss the merits of each.

10. What are talking captions? Topic captions? Illustrate each by example (different from those in the text).

11. Point out any violations of grammatical parallelism in the following subheads of a major division of a report.
    a. Sporting goods shows market increase
    b. Modest increase in hardware volume
    c. Automotive parts remains unchanged
    d. Plumbing supplies records slight decline

12. The following subheads of a major division of a report are not all parallel in grammatical construction. Correct them.
    a. Predominance of cotton farming in southern counties
    b. Livestock paces farm income in the western region
    c. Wheat crop dominant in the north region
    d. Truck farming leads in central and eastern section

13. Correct another set of headings:
    a. High rate of sales in District III
    b. District II ranks second
    c. District IV reports losses
    d. District I at the bottom

14. Correct yet another set of headings:
    a. Need for improved communication
    b. Alternative plans considered
    c. Complicating factor of qualified personnel
    d. Selection of education plan

15. Elaborate on the need for variety of expression on the outline headings. Back up your presentation with illustrations.

16. Mark the point of error in the following portion of a report outline. Explain the error.
    a. Initial costs differ little
    b. Brand B has best trade-in value
       1. Brand A is a close second
    c. Composite costs favor brand B

17. Work up a tentative outline for a report problem in Appendix A that your instructor chooses.

Interpreting Information

Interpretation is deriving logical meaning from information to solve a report problem. It exists throughout report preparation.

You interpret throughout the process of preparing a business report. Interpretation begins when you state the problem, and it continues as you collect facts and organize them. But facts alone do not solve the report problem. If the problem is to be solved, you must examine facts as they relate to your report situation. You must derive logical meaning from the facts—meaning that helps to solve the report problem. This highly subjective process of deriving logical meaning from facts to solve a problem is called **interpretation.**

AN APPROACH TO INTERPRETATION

When you have the information in logical order, you are ready to begin the task of analyzing and interpreting the information in terms of applications to the problem. Your objective throughout the information-gathering process, after all, was to develop meaningful information. Now it is time to see what you have discovered.

Your effectiveness as an interpreter depends upon your experience, analytical skills, and ability to be objective.

Interpretation is perhaps the most challenging of the research steps. It would be ideal to have a set of rules for reading your data and determining what they mean; however, there is no such formula. The capacity to interpret is highly individualized. It depends upon your knowledge of the subject and your native ability to analyze, see connections, draw conclusions, and the like. It depends also upon the complexity of the research problem. You therefore determine your approach to interpretation on a case-by-case basis. But your objective in all cases is an analysis that is perceptive, comprehensive, fair, and ethical.

To reach that objective, you will find a review of the fundamentals of interpretation helpful. It is the type of information you will likely learn through experience and is offered here in anticipation of what you need to know as you set about your early efforts to analyze data.

The fundamentals may logically be grouped into five areas:

1. Expectations that lead to interpretation error.

2. Fallacious procedures in interpretation.

3. Attitudes and practices conducive to sound interpretation.

4. Techniques in interpreting for the reader.

5. An orderly procedure for interpretation.

EXPECTATIONS AND INTERPRETATION ERROR

Do not let your expectations affect your objectivity.

After you have completed your research, you naturally are eager to learn the results. You may be apprehensive, hopeful, or just curious about what your data will reveal. You may want the results to justify your effort, especially if that effort has been extensive. It may be that you have a vested interest in the outcome or that you are working against a deadline. Whatever the circumstances, as you undertake this important step of interpretation, be aware of how your expectations may affect the quality of your analysis.

There are three errors in interpretation that commonly result from expectations about the results of research. Knowing about them in advance may help you avoid them.

☐ DESIRE FOR THE SPECTACULAR

Resist exaggerating the meaning of results.

Anticipation is a very strong element at the beginning of any interpretation process. Just about every researcher would be delighted to make a startling first-time discovery, to find incontrovertible evidence of a point long suspected, or to develop revolutionary new insight into an old problem. To achieve modest results, therefore, may be something of an anticlimax. But modest results are more likely, and you must resist the tendency to exaggerate.

You may not necessarily learn this reserve by example. Survey results published in the general media, for instance, are frequently overstated. A slight shift in voter preferences, a small percentage change in buying patterns, a fraction of a point adjustment in standardized test scores all make headlines. And it is not uncommon for these results to be refuted with great fanfare a short time later by minuscule swings in the opposite direction.

But assume you are reviewing your own research, perhaps a before-and-after study to determine the impact of a dramatic new advertising campaign. Assume further you discover a small increase in sales. Regardless of what the popular or professional climate might be, you must take care not to exaggerate the consequence of the change. Obviously, you will welcome any sign of a positive effect. But no matter how eager you or anyone else is to learn the advertising is working, you will have to wait for more substantial survey results to confirm its effectiveness.

☐ BELIEF THAT CONCLUSIONS ARE ESSENTIAL

Be prepared to admit your data may be inconclusive.

Another cause of error in interpretation is the belief there must be an answer to every question—and a final, definitive answer at that. This is not necessarily true. There are too many variables in the research process to guarantee absolute certainty. Even so, you may be tempted to make definite interpretations simply because you think you will be evading a basic issue if you do not.

For example, let's say you are conducting a consumer survey for a soft-drink company and 3 percent of your respondents volunteer the information that they detect an unpleasant aftertaste after drinking one of the company's diet beverages. You will be making a mistake if you take it upon yourself to interpret that response. If you conclude there is no problem with aftertaste because so low a percentage indicated there was, you are ignoring the fact that not all those interviewed had an opportunity to express their opinions on this point. By the same token, if you interpret the 3 percent response as significant because it was volunteered, you risk exaggerating the problem. What you should do, therefore, is conduct a second survey that includes a question about the residual flavor of the drink in question.

You may sometimes have to qualify an interpretation, letting your reader know that more than one interpretation of certain data is possible. And sometimes you may simply be unable to interpret the data, either because you lack the technical expertise or because you have insufficient background in the subject under study. But whether you have more than one conclusion or none, accept your incapability rather than make arbitrary or capricious statements about what your data mean. Your credibility, if that is what you are worried about, will be threatened far less by an admission of doubt or a recommendation for further study than it will by an erroneous conclusion.

□ **ACCEPTANCE OF LACK OF EVIDENCE AS PROOF TO CONTRARY**

Do not interpret lack of contrary evidence as proof a proposition is true. Similarly, do not interpret lack of positive evidence as proof a proposition is false.

If you believe that when you cannot prove a proposition its opposite must be true, you are likely to make a third common error in interpretation. In a court of law, for example, the prosecution has the burden of proof to establish a defendant's guilt. If the prosecution does not offer sufficient proof, the trial judge or the jury concludes not that the defendant is innocent, but that there is insufficient evidence to find the accused guilty beyond a reasonable doubt. Not guilty is not the same as innocent, as is occasionally made clear when a defendant who has been found not guilty later admits the crime.

Similarly, in business, if you have no data to prove that a proposed advertising campaign will be successful, you cannot conclude it will fail. Or because you have no evidence to prove that a person is a good credit risk, you cannot assume the person is a poor risk. Your best option in both instances is to seek additional data. If that is impossible, you may have to suspend the campaign only because there is insufficient evidence to support it and it would be illogical to do otherwise. The same holds true for denying credit.

Keep in mind this basic proposition: Evidence must support every conclusion. A conclusion that cannot be supported cannot be made, at least not logically. And the evidence used to support a conclusion must be substantial and affirmative.

FALLACIOUS INTERPRETATION PROCEDURES

A fallacious interpretation violates the rules of logic.

A fallacy is an error in reasoning. It occurs where a discussion claims to conform to the rules of sound argument but in fact does not. A fallacy may be a deliberate violation of the rules of logic, or it may be accidental. If it is deliberate, it is unethical.

The fallacy may also be obvious or subtle. In any case, it has no place in the interpretation of research results.

Certain fallacies are more likely to occur in interpretation than others. Knowing what they are will help you avoid errors that will undermine your most careful efforts to present accurate and meaningful information.

☐ BIAS IN INTERPRETATION

Avoid conscious bias and be sensitive to unconscious bias.

Bias in interpretation results from preconceptions about the information being analyzed. These preconceptions, which may be favorable or unfavorable, conscious or unconscious, seriously compromise the integrity of research by influencing how data will be selected and emphasized. Conscious bias is flatly unethical. Unconscious bias reflects the limitations of the analyst. Of the two, unconscious bias is the more dangerous, for it is difficult for the researcher to detect and correct.

Unconscious bias may be personal: a researcher who has experienced an on-the-job injury may be less than impartial in interpreting a survey determining attitudes toward job safety. It may be cultural: a researcher brought up in the traditional work ethic may unintentionally slant an analysis of a survey of the chronically unemployed. It may be professional: an accountant trained in the last-in-first-out method of determining inventory valuation may not be entirely receptive to evidence supporting a different method.

There is no single remedy for bias, except to be constantly aware of the possibility it exists. And keep in mind there is no excuse for interpretation bias that has roots in racial, sexual, ageist, ethnic, or religious prejudice.

☐ COMPARISON OF NONCOMPARABLE DATA

Compare only data that are logically related.

One of the most common procedures you will perform in interpretation is comparing data. Indeed, comparisons are the foundation of the majority of your trends and conclusions. It is critical, therefore, that you take care to compare data that are logically related. Otherwise, the entire point of your research may be lost.

For example, it makes little sense to compare salaries for a group of workers unless you first establish a common definition of jobs and responsibilities. Similarly, if you are interested in comparing the quality of education in various countries, you will reach no meaningful conclusions if you ignore differences in the process by which students are selected for the various levels of their respective system. Or, if you want to determine how housing costs of today compare with those of two decades ago, you have to take into account the effect of inflation if you want a true measure of change.

☐ CAUSE-EFFECT CONFUSION

Do not confuse coincidence or sequence with cause.

Interpretation error sometimes results from a mistaken assumption that a cause-effect relationship exists between sets of data. You are likely to make that error if you do not distinguish between association and causation.

One type of association you are likely to confuse with causation is correlation. A classic illustration of this error is measuring the traffic flow over the Brooklyn Bridge and recording the times of tidal changes. Even if you were to find a high correlation between the two sets of data (for example, every time the tide changes there occurs an increase in traffic), to suggest there is a causal relationship between traffic and tide is foolish.

A second type of association you may confuse with causation is sequence. It is the mistake of supposing because one event precedes another, the first causes the second. This error in logic is called the *post hoc fallacy*. Obviously, it is mere superstition. (If a black cat crosses your path, you will have bad luck.) But it is also the illogic that enables many a chief executive officer who happens to arrive at a company just as the climate is right for expansion to claim full credit for increases in production and sales.

☐ UNRELIABLE DATA

Use only data you can validate as fact.

An interpretation can be no more reliable than the information on which it is based. Reliable data are those that are statistically sound. They are collected through sound research methodology and by competent researchers. Usually, reliable data are facts; that is, they are verifiable truths as contrasted with opinions, which are attitudes of the mind.

Although it is not always possible to determine the reliability of information gathered, you should handle questionable information with extreme care. Only information that is unquestionably reliable is worthy of interpretation. In no case are interpretations better than the data from which they are derived.

Consider the importance of reliability in medical research. Before a new drug is offered to the general public, it must be carefully tested to determine if it is both effective and safe. Imagine the consequences if the sample or the test period are insufficient. If investigators determine the product has no discernible effect, the public may be denied the latest wonder drug. If, instead, the investigators determine the product achieves, as far as they can tell, its desired effect, the public may be lulled into a false confidence, or worse, exposed to a whole new set of health hazards.

☐ UNREPRESENTATIVE DATA

Make sure both your data source and your data selection are representative.

Often interpretations are based on data not representative of the subject under study. The problem could be either the data source or the data selection.

One common problem with data source is, again, the size and composition of the sample. Interpreters who equate quantity of respondents to quality of results, for example, are likely to reach false conclusions. So too are those who ignore how the respondents were selected. In reality, a small bit of representative data is far superior to great amounts of unrepresentative data.

Compare, for example, the representatives of two types of polls popular during recent election campaigns. One is a television survey that invites viewers to indicate their choice of candidate by calling one of two or more telephone numbers displayed on the television screen. Each call thus registers a "vote." The other is also a telephone survey, but here the respondents are randomly selected from current voting lists and are called by neutral pollsters.

The number of calls in the first type of survey can easily outnumber the number of calls in the second. But which results would you rely on? The decision is easy when you consider the potential for nonrepresentation in the first format. Those who call obviously have a strong preference; furthermore, there is no provision for multiple "votes" from the same caller, no way of verifying the callers' eligibility to vote, and so on.

The problem with data selection can occur even if the sample itself is representative. The interpreter must consider a representative sample of the available data, as it were, making sure to include all results necessary to give an accurate reading of the information gathered. For example, an interpreter who fails to take into account "no opinion" responses can seriously misconstrue the results of an attitude survey.

☐   NEGLECT OF IMPORTANT FACTORS

Consider all factors that may affect the research problem.

You can also make errors in interpretation by reviewing only one factor in a complex problem of many factors. And complex problems are the rule rather than the exception in most research. You must take care, therefore, to look for all possible factors that affect the problem and give all these factors their due weight in the analysis.

For example, what would you make of a study of collegians that revealed a positive correlation between spending money and earning grades? That is, those who spend money freely earn higher grades than those who do not. You can speculate, if you choose. Perhaps the free spenders are subsidized in some way, so they do not have to devote potential study hours to part- or full-time jobs. Or maybe they come, for the most part, from higher income families and are reaping the benefits of strong academic and cultural backgrounds. But speculation is not valid interpretation. You need accurate data on employment, family background, and other factors like age, course of study, and so on before you can determine whether the correlation is anything more than coincidence.

ATTITUDES AND PRACTICES CONDUCIVE TO SOUND INTERPRETING

Interpretation is the application of clear thinking to the information gathered, and clear thinking follows the rules of logic. You can avoid a major misreading of your data, therefore, by anticipating potential errors in logic as you begin to interpret and by checking for fallacies as you proceed.

But sound interpretation is not simply a matter of routinely reviewing logic. It is also a matter of attitude and practice, both of which are highly individualized and determined largely by experience. How critically and judiciously you approach a problem, how willingly you consult with others, and how thoroughly you test your results have a great deal to do with how truthful, ethical, and perceptive your interpretation will be. And if your testing of quantitative information includes statistical aids, so much the better.

☐ CULTIVATION OF A CRITICAL POINT OF VIEW

Play the role of critic throughout your research.

Cultivating a critical point of view is essential in research and reporting. It is very tempting to be an advocate of your own work, especially since you have invested so much of your time and effort. But you have to be a critic of it as well. For every interpretation you posit, consider the possible arguments against it. Play the role of skeptic. Identification of all possible objections can only strengthen what you finally report.

☐ MAINTENANCE OF THE JUDICIAL ATTITUDE

Or play the role of judge. In either case, do not act as the advocate of your own work.

It is not enough simply to identify objections, however; you need to resolve them as well. And here you have another role to play, that of judge. Review your points and counterpoints objectively and decide which are the true readings of the data. You cannot let such elements as popularity or convenience determine which arguments you accept and which you reject. You certainly cannot allow whatever personal interests you may have intrude. Your primary responsibility is to deal fairly and ethically with your reader. Again, like a judge, you must leave no stone unturned in your search for truth.

☐ CONSULTATION WITH OTHERS

Consult with experts and critics.

Even though you may be well qualified in the field you are investigating, the chances that you know all there is to know in that field are slim. You have a great deal to gain, therefore, by talking over problems, appraisals, and interpretations with others in the field. You may profit, too, by submitting your ideas to an ardent critic. Then, armed with the critic's views, you are in a much better position to interpret opinions.

It is a rare situation in which the work of one mind cannot be improved through the assistance of others. If it does nothing else, talking over a research problem with someone will give you greater confidence in what you finally report.

☐ TESTING OF INTERPRETATIONS

To look critically at all sides of an issue is sometimes not enough. What you should do is actually test your interpretations. Unfortunately, few interpretations can be tested conclusively, for the means of testing are largely subjective. Even so, the fact that interpretations are tested at all should enhance their credibility. There are two subjective tests that are appropriate for any interpretation.

Ask yourself if your interpretations make sense.

The first is the test of experience and reason. You simply ask, "Does this interpretation appear reasonable in light of what is known or has been experienced?" Obviously, your answer will depend on how much you know and how well you reason. But most of the time you can tell whether what you conclude basically "makes sense."

For example, if you are studying the effect of education upon future earnings and find an inverse relationship between the two, check your study carefully. Though there are individual cases where someone with a below average education has an income well above average or vice versa, experience suggests a positive correlation between level of schooling completed and income.

The second test of an interpretation is the negative test. In a sense, it is a corollary to the critical point of view. You propose an interpretation exactly opposite from the interpretation you are considering and examine it in light of all available evidence. Your next steps, obviously, are to review the examination results, compare them to the examination results of the original, and decide which of the two interpretations is the more reasonable.

To illustrate, assume you are an English professor who has just completed a survey of student reading habits at your university. Most of the students, you find, list among the books and articles they have read material that is considered good by accepted literary standards. It certainly would be encouraging to conclude that the quality of the material collegians at your institution read is high. But, posing a competing interpretation might alert you to data you overlooked in your initial review. It could very well be that the students in your study actually read a great deal of low-quality literature as well. In that case, you may have to amend your complimentary conclusion considerably.

☐ USE OF STATISTICAL AIDS TO INTERPRETATION

Frequently, the information you gather in research is quantitative—that is, expressed in numbers. In their raw form, such data can be voluminous, consisting of tens, hundreds, even thousands of figures. If you want to use such figures effectively, you must first find ways of reducing them so you can grasp their general meaning. The science of statistics provides many methods of analyzing data; and as a writer of business reports, you should be familiar with at least the most common.

Explaining statistics is obviously beyond the scope of this text, but here is a brief sample of the topics you should know. Of greatest use to you as an investigator are the various measures of central tendency—the mean, median, and mode. These measures seek to find one value of a series that appropriately describes the whole. Then there are the measures of dispersion—range, variance, and standard deviation. These measures help to describe the spread of a series of data. Ratios (expression of one quantity as a multiple of another) and probabilities (the number of times something will probably occur over the range of possible occurrences) are also useful in simplifying and interpreting data. If you need to review these and other useful concepts, you will find them described in any standard statistics textbook.

☐ USE OF COMPUTERS IN INTERPRETATION

You will find several computer tools useful in analyzing data. Often, combining raw numbers gives you a different way to view facts and provides a clearer picture of their meaning. Today, the user-friendly quality of some very sophisticated statistical software permits you to have easy access to these resources without advanced computer knowledge. Some programs will query you about the nature of your data and recommend which statistical tests to use. Also, most spreadsheet software will compute basic statistics that allow you to obtain meaningful interpretations of data.

Graphics software may also assist.

As we will see in more detail in Chapter 15, graphics software can help you in interpreting information. First, graphics reveal trends and relationships in data that are often difficult to picture from raw facts. Accordingly, graphics enable you to interpret your data more accurately and meaningfully. Second, graphics software can help you explain what the data mean. For example, through a graphic you can direct a reader to look at dotted and dashed lines for the last five years, noting the trend of profits. In addition, using the options available in most graphics packages, you can create clear, attractive graphics without being an artist.

Sound thinking should govern their use.

These computer aids to interpretation, along with the other interpretation practices and attitudes discussed, should help you to give your readers the meanings you derive from the facts. Even so, you must use them with good logic and sound thinking. As you know, computers are no better than the people who use them.

INTERPRETING FOR THE READERS

Put yourself in your readers' place and explain results in appropriate context and detail.

When you have thoroughly interpreted your research so you understand it, you must take your assignment as business reporter one important step further—namely, to convey your interpretation so your readers understand it as well. Keep in mind that your readers are likely to be less informed about the problem under investigation than you are. You may have to explain points basic to you in language and detail they can understand. You may have to review the context of the problem. Your readers will probably want to know what led up to the research and why the research was necessary. In short, you will have to put yourself in your readers' place and make all adaptations necessary to communicate what you have learned from your research. Communicating your findings is, after all, the final objective of your effort.

Stress logic and evidence as you explain findings.

The task of communicating is easier if you guide the readers carefully and deliberately through your reading of the data. Let them benefit from what you have learned, sparing them the trial-and-error process you covered. Stress the logic of your findings and point out the evidence behind them. Communication is most effective when it is based on confidence.

ORDERLY PROCEDURE IN INTERPRETING

Each relationship among researcher, problem, and reader is unique. Therefore, there can be no standard plan for the actual process of interpretation. But there are certain steps common to all effective interpretation procedures, regardless of the dynamics of the individual project. You should consider them as you prepare your approach.

☐ RELATE INFORMATION TO THE PROBLEM

Show clearly how findings relate to the research problem.

Your first step in orderly interpretation is relating the information collected to the phase of the problem it affects. There is no set way to do this. Sometimes one small bit of information plays a paramount role in the problem, while in other instances large quantities of information need to be combined in order to shed light on a single minor point. In still others, a maze of comparisons and cross-comparisons is necessary to reveal just one aspect of the study. Therefore, you must be alert for a variety of possible relationships between your data and the problem. Your search must be exhaustive.

☐ MAKE ALL PRACTICAL INTERPRETATIONS

Consider all plausible interpretations.

Next, you should make all plausible interpretations of the relationships you have discovered. Ignore no interpretation with merit. In some instances, you may advance a number of interpretations for one piece of information. In others, you may find only one interpretation. Your efforts here should be orderly and, again, thorough. An error of omission at this point could very well affect the problem as a whole.

☐ REEVALUATE INTERPRETATIONS

Review and challenge the interpretations you are considering.

The third step is to review carefully all the interpretations you have developed. It is a good idea to use the two subjective tests here. Evaluate each interpretation in the light of existing evidence. And challenge each with a counter-interpretation as well.

☐ SELECT INTERPRETATIONS WITH MOST MERIT

Then select the interpretations that have the firmest grounding in fact and logic.

In the fourth step, select the interpretations that appear, on the basis of your evaluation, to have the most merit. Those that do not fare so well should be dropped or at least qualified by an explanation.

☐ DERIVE CONCLUSIONS FROM THE INTERPRETATIONS

Develop logical conclusions from your interpretations.

Finally, from the interpretations you have retained, develop conclusions. What you are doing here is taking the interpretation process one step further, interpreting the interpretations, as it were. The conclusions must follow logically from, and be limited to, the meanings and explanations you have derived from the data.

If it is appropriate, make clear and specific recommendations for action.

And if your problem calls for recommendations as well, go the next step down the interpretation ladder. Recommendations are, in a sense, interpretations drawn from the conclusions. They are the lines of action to which conclusions logically point and, as such, are the ultimate test of the effectiveness of your research. Recommendations, of course, are not guarantees. But if they are the result of informed, objective analysis at each step of the process, they should identify among all possible options those activities with the most reasonable chance of success.

QUESTIONS

1. Discuss the need for interpretation in most report problems.

2. Discuss the common expectations that can produce interpretation error. Illustrate each with realistic examples different from those in the text.

3. Distinguish between unconscious and conscious bias. Comment on the effects of each on the interpretation of report information.

4. Explain the error of comparing noncomparable data. Illustrate with original examples.

5. In reply to criticisms of the living conditions of his troops in a foreign encampment, an army general replied with some interesting statistical comparisons. One of these comparisons showed that the annual death rate of his men was less than 17 per 1,000—about the same as that for the capital city of the homeland. Evaluate this comparison.

6. What is cause-effect error? Illustrate with original examples.

7. Explain how the reliability of data is related to their representativeness. Illustrate with original examples.

8. A survey of smoking habits among college students revealed that grades made by nonsmokers were generally higher than those made by heavy smokers. A conclusion that smoking caused low grades was reached. Do you agree? Explain your viewpoint.

9. In a report on living standards of production workers at an aircraft plant, the following statement was made: "Of those employees in the $650-to-$800-per-week group who employ maids, 50 percent are past 40 years of age." What is the interpretation fallacy that most likely occurred here?

10. A report on students in public elementary schools produced data showing that the health of the students was correlated with the grades they made. Grades of students with defective eyes, ears, and teeth were found generally to be lower than grades of children without these defects. Would it be logical to generalize that physical defects cause the retardation of students? Are there other factors that might contribute to low grades?

11. Using company records covering a five-year period, a business executive concluded that most productive salespeople were in the 35-to-40-age bracket. Explain what the executive could do to test this interpretation.

12. Discuss the interpretation fallacies present in the following cases.
    a. A study produced data that showed U.S. college students to be far behind their comparable groups in European countries. The conclusion was made that the educational systems in these European countries are superior to that in the United States.
    b. A politician concluded that in his incumbent opponent's 20 years as mayor of a city, the city's expenditures had increased an exorbitant 280 percent.

c. The editor of a leading magazine for business executives reported that unsolicited letters received from readers justified a conclusion that the public favored stronger government controls over unions.

d. When questioned about their feelings concerning a certain personnel policy of the company, 14 percent of the employees interviewed strongly supported the policy, 62 percent showed little or no concern about it, and 24 percent disapproved of it. A management report concluded that the policy should be continued, since 76 percent did not oppose it. The union objected to this conclusion.

e. Records compiled at a certain university showed that students who had majored in engineering received an average of $150 per month more in beginning salary than business graduates. An analyst concluded that careers in engineering are more rewarding monetarily than are careers in business.

f. A campus survey at a midwestern university showed that 92 percent of the students of Christian faith favored a certain issue, whereas only 33 percent of the Hindu students favored the matter. The conclusion reached was that Christians and Hindus were far apart on this matter.

g. A top executive in a department store chain assembled statistics on sales by stores. The executive then concluded that those store managers who had achieved the best percentage gains were the best managers and should be so rewarded.

h. A report writer found data showing that sales of soft drinks were correlated with vacation travel. It was concluded that soft-drink sales were heavily affected by vacations.

Constructing the Formal Report

There are many
variations in makeup.

Once your outline is in finished form, you plan the makeup of your report. This task is complicated by the fact that reports are far from standardized in physical arrangement. The variations are countless. In fact, report types in use are so numerous as to almost defy meaningful classification. Even so, to determine the makeup of a specific report, you should know the possibilities available. Thus, you should be acquainted with a workable approach to the makeup of all reports.

OVERALL VIEW OF CONTENT

The following
classification plan
illustrates the general
structure of reports.

It pictures report
structure as a stairway.
Long, formal reports are
at the top.

As reports become
shorter and less formal,
changes occur.

The title fly drops out.

The executive summary
and letter of transmittal
are combined.

Such an approach is presented in the following paragraphs. It should be pointed out, though, that the concept of this approach is quite general. It does not account for all possible reports, nor the countless minor variations in report makeup. But it should help you grasp the relationship among all reports.

To understand this relationship, you might view the whole of reports as resembling a stairway, as illustrated in Figure 8–1. At the top of this stairway is the formal, full-dress report (Step 1). This is the form used when the problem is long and the problem situation is formal. This report contains a number of *prefatory parts* (parts that appear before the report text). Typically, prefatory parts include the title fly, title page, letters of transmittal and authorization, table of contents, and executive summary.

As the need for formality decreases and the problem becomes smaller, the report's makeup also changes. Although these changes are far from standardized, they follow a general order.

First, the title fly drops out (Step 2). This page contains only the title, and the title information appears on the next page. Obviously, the title fly is used strictly for reasons of formality.

Next, the executive summary and transmittal letter are combined (Step 3). At this stage, the report problem usually is short enough to permit its summary in a relatively short space.

111

FIGURE 8–1   **Progression of change in report makeup as formality requirements and length of the problem decrease**

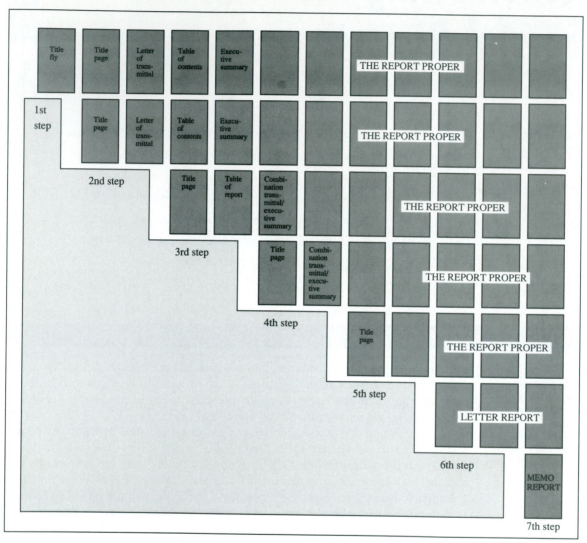

Next, the table of contents is omitted.

In the next step, the table of contents drops out (Step 4). The table of contents, being a guide to the report text, serves little value in a short report. Certainly, a guide to a 100-page report is necessary, but a guide to a 1-page report is illogical. Somewhere between these extremes exists a dividing point. You should follow the general guide of including a table of contents whenever it appears to have some value for the reader.

The combination letter of transmittal and executive summary drops out, forming the popular *short report*.

The next step is the letter report, then the memorandum.

This progression of structure is general.

As formality and length requirements continue to decrease, the combined letter of transmittal and executive summary drops out (Step 5). Thus, the report now has only a title page and report text. The title page remains because it serves as a useful cover page. In addition, it contains the most important identifying information.

Below this short-report form is a report that reinstates the letter of transmittal and executive summary and presents the entire report in the form of a letter—hence, the letter report (Step 6). Finally, for short, even more informal problems, the memorandum (informal letter) form may be used (Step 7). Illustrated at the end of this chapter and Chapter 9 are these steps in the progression: Step 1, Figure 8–3; Step 5, Figure 9–1; Step 6, Figure 9–2; Step 7, Figures 9–3, 9–4, and 9–5.

As previously mentioned, this analysis of report change is at best general and perhaps oversimplified. Many actual business reports fall between the steps. Most, however, generally fit within this framework. Knowledge of this relationship of length and formality should help you as you plan your reports.

ORGANIZATION AND CONTENT OF FORMAL REPORTS

Length and formality characterize long reports.

Be a report architect—design parts of a long report to fit one situation.

The first parts to be designed are the prefatory ones. Long reports usually contain all of them.

In determining which prefatory parts to include, you should know their roles and content.

Long, formal reports are highly important. They usually concern major investigations, which explains their length. Also, they typically are written for high-level administration, which explains their formality.

In constructing a long, formal report, you should view your task much as an architect views a design problem. You have a number of components with which to work. Your task is to select and arrange components to meet the requirements of the given situation.

In this case, the first components are the report's prefatory parts. As we noted in our review of the structure of reports (Figure 8–1), the longest, most formal report contains all of these parts. As length and formality requirements decrease, some of the parts drop out. Thus, as the architect of the report, you must decide which parts are needed to meet the length and formality requirements of your situation.

To make this decision—and carry it out—you must first know the parts. Thus, in the following paragraphs we shall review them. In addition, we shall review the remaining structure of the longest, most formal report. For convenience, our review arranges the parts by groups. First are the prefatory parts—those most related to the report's formality and length. Then comes the report proper, which, of course, is the meat of the report—the report story. The final group consists of appended parts. These parts contain supplementary materials—information that is not essential to the report but may be helpful to some readers. In summary, our review follows this pattern:

Prefatory parts

Title fly

Title page

Letter of authorization

Letter of transmittal, preface, or foreword

Table of contents and table of illustrations

Executive summary

Report proper

Introduction

Report findings (usually presented in two or more major divisions)

Summaries, conclusions, or recommendations

Appended parts

Appendix

Bibliography

As we proceed through our review of these parts, it will be helpful to study Figure 8–3 at the end of this chapter. Also, it will help to look in Chapter 13 for examples of page form.

☐   THE PREFATORY PARTS

TITLE FLY   First among the possible prefatory report pages is the **title fly** (see page 123). It contains only the report title. Simple to construct, the title fly is included solely for reasons of formality. Because the title appears again on the following page, the title fly really is somewhat repetitive. But most books have one—and so do most formal reports.

Although constructing the title fly is simple, composing the title is not. In fact, on a per-word basis, the title typically requires more time than any part of the report. This is as it should be, for titles must be carefully worded. Their goal is to tell at a glance what the report covers—and what it does not. A good title fits the report like a glove. It covers all of the report information snugly—no more, no less.

For completeness of coverage, you should build your title around the five *W*s: **who, what, where, when,** and **why.** Sometimes, you may add **how** to this list. In some problems, however, not all of the *W*s are essential to complete identification. Nevertheless, they serve as a good checklist for completeness. For example, a title of a report analyzing the Lane Company's 199*x* advertising campaigns might be constructed as follows:

Who: Lane Company

What: Analysis of advertising campaigns

Where: Not essential

When: 199*x*

Why: Implied

Thus, the title emerges: "Analysis of the Lane Company's 199*x* Advertising Campaigns."

The title fly (the first prefatory part) contains only the title.

Carefully word report titles to show report contents.

Consider who, what, when, where, why, and how when phrasing a title. Not all will apply.

One- or two-word titles are too broad. Subtitles can aid conciseness.

Obviously, you cannot write a completely descriptive title in a few words—certainly not in one or two. Extremely short titles are, as a rule, vague. They cover everything but touch nothing. Yet it is your objective to achieve conciseness in addition to completeness; thus, you must also seek the most economical word pattern consistent with completeness. Occasionally, in your effort to be concise and complete, you may want to use subtitles. Here is an example: "A 19xx Measure of Employee Morale at Pfeifer's Mossback Plant: A Study Based on a Survey Using the Semantic Differential."

The *title page* includes the title, the receiver, and the writer of the report.

TITLE PAGE   Like the title fly, the **title page** (see page 124) presents the report title. But it displays other information essential to the report's identification. In constructing your title page, you should include complete identification of yourself and the authorizer or recipient of the report. You may also include the date of writing, particularly if the time identification is not made clear in the title. The title page is mechanically constructed and is precisely illustrated in Chapter 13.

Include the *letter of authorization* if authorization was written.

LETTER OF AUTHORIZATION   A report may be authorized orally or in writing. If yours is authorized in writing, you should insert a copy of this document (usually a letter or memorandum) after the title page. If your report is authorized orally, you may review the authorization information in the letter of transmittal, introductory section, or both.

Write the letter in direct order.

The primary objective of the **letter of authorization** is to authorize the researcher to begin the investigation. In addition, the letter contains a brief statement of the problem, with some indication of the limiting factors, together with the scope of the investigation and the limitations, if any. Perhaps the use of the report might also be mentioned, as well as when the report is needed and how much the cost of preparation will be. The letter may follow any of a number of acceptable organization patterns. The following outline describes one acceptable in arrangement and content:

Consider this arrangement: authorization, explanation of purpose, scope of the problem, and limitations/special points.

1.   Direct, clear authorization of the investigation.

2.   Explanation of the objective in unmistakable words.

3.   Description of problem areas requiring investigation. This description may be an explanation of the problem subdivisions.

4.   Limitations (such as time and cost) and special instructions.

Transmittal letters also are written in direct order.

LETTER OF TRANSMITTAL, FOREWORD, PREFACE   Most formal reports contain some form of personal communication from writer to reader (see page 125). In most business cases, the **letter of transmittal** makes this contact. In some formal cases, particularly where the report is written for a group of readers, a foreword or preface performs this function.

Begin by transmitting the report. Identify subject, authorization facts, and such.

The letter of transmittal, as its name implies, is a letter that transmits the report to the reader. Since this major message is essentially positive, you should write the letter in direct style; that is, in the beginning you should transmit the report directly, without explanation or other delaying information. Thus, your opening words should say, in effect, "Here is the report." Tied to or following this statement of transmittal usually is a brief identification of the report's subject matter and possibly an incidental summary reference to the authorization information (who assigned the report, when, etc.).

Sometimes the executive summary and letter of transmittal are combined (summary following transmittal).

If you choose to combine the letter with the executive summary, as you may in some forms of reports, the opening transmittal and identification may be followed by a quick review of the report highlights, much in the manner described in the following discussion of the executive summary. But whether the letter of transmittal does or does not contain an executive summary of the report text, generally you should use it to make helpful and informative comments about the report. For example, you may suggest how the report information may be used. You may suggest follow-up studies, point out special limitations, or mention side issues of the problem. In fact, you may include anything that will help your reader understand the report.

Individual letters permit you to personalize. Do so.

Except in very formal instances, the transmittal letter allows you to more or less chat with your readers. Such a letter may well reflect the warmth and vigor of your personality. Generally, you should use enough personal pronouns (*you, I, we*) to create a friendly aura. A warm note of appreciation for the assignment or a desire to further pursue the project may mark your close.

Forewords and *prefaces* are similar to transmittals. They follow no set organization plan.

Minor distinctions sometimes are drawn between **forewords** and **prefaces,** but for all practical purposes they are the same. Both are preliminary messages from writer to reader. Although usually they do not formally transmit the report, forewords and prefaces do many of the other things that letters of transmittal do. Like transmittal letters, they seek to help the reader appreciate and understand the report. For example, they may include helpful comments about the report—its use, interpretation, follow-up, and the like. In addition, prefaces and forewords frequently contain expressions of indebtedness to those who helped in the research. Like letters of transmittal, they usually are written in the first person, but seldom are they as informal as some letters. Arrangement of the contents of prefaces and forewords follows no established pattern.

The *table of contents* gives headings and page numbers. A list of illustrations may also be needed.

TABLE OF CONTENTS AND LIST OF ILLUSTRATIONS   If your report is long enough to warrant a guide to its contents, you should give it a **table of contents** (see page 126). This is the report outline in its finished form with page numbers. If the report has a number of tables, charts, illustrations, and the like, you may set up a separate **list of illustrations** (see page 127). The mechanics of constructing both of these units are fully described in Chapter 13.

The *executive summary* condenses the report.

EXECUTIVE SUMMARY   The **executive summary,** also called the *synopsis, epitome,* and *précis* (see page 128), is the report in miniature. It concisely summarizes all of the report's essential ingredients. It includes all the major facts as well as the primary analyses and conclusions derived from them. It is designed chiefly for the busy executive who may not have time to read the whole report; but it may also serve as a preview or review for those who will thoroughly read the report text.

Its length is about one eighth of the report. Use concise, lively writing.

In constructing the executive summary, you simply reduce the parts of the report in both order and proportion. Because your objective is to cut the report to a fraction of its length (usually less than one eighth), much of your success will be determined by your skill in directness and word economy. With space at a premium, loose writing obviously will be costly. But in your efforts to be concise, you are likely to adopt a dull writing style. Thus, you must work hard to give the executive summary a touch of color and style.

FIGURE 8–2   **Diagram of the executive summary in normal order and in direct order**

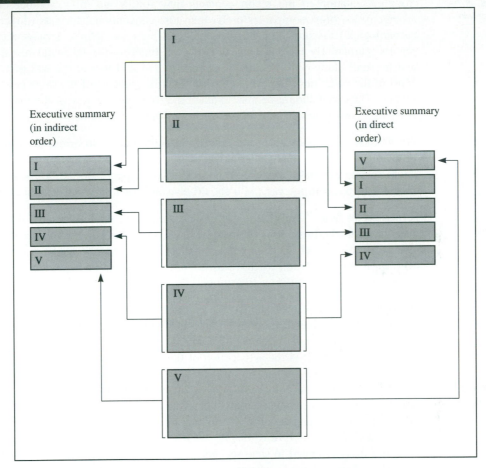

Executive summary (in indirect order)

Executive summary (in direct order)

Either direct or indirect order is appropriate.

Although most executive summaries present the report in normal order (typically from introduction to conclusion), many report writers now favor a more direct opening (see Figure 8–2). Such a plan shifts the major findings, conclusions, or recommendations to the major position of emphasis—the beginning. From this direct beginning, the summary moves to the introductory parts and then through the report in normal order.

The executive summary should be sufficiently detailed to cover everything significant.

Although the terms *executive summary, synopsis, epitome,* and *précis* are essentially synonyms, some authorities make distinctions. Particularly, they view the executive summary as a longer and more detailed summary than the others. Our view is that the beginning summary of a report should be sufficiently detailed to cover everything significant. Such a summary justifies the term *executive summary.*

☐   THE REPORT PROPER

Arrangements of the report proper vary.

Your presentation of the report contents may follow any of a number of general arrangements. Most companies prefer the more conventional formats (direct, logical, chronological) discussed in Chapter 6. Some prefer a definite arrangement for all reports, particularly technical ones. Two such reports—the technical research paper and the staff study—are illustrated in Figures 9–4 and 9–6 at the end of Chapter 9. Most of the variations, however, are simply rearrangements of the same general information. Thus, you should be able to adapt the following review of the makeup of the body of a conventional logical-order report to other arrangements.

The *introduction* prepares the reader to receive the report. Consider the following content possibilities:

INTRODUCTION   The purpose of the report's **introduction** is to orient the reader to the problem at hand. In this undertaking, you may include scores of topics—in fact, anything that will help your reader understand and appreciate the problem. Although the content possibilities vary, you should consider the following general topics.

(1) *Authorization facts* (report origin).

1. Origin of the Report   The first part of your introduction might include a review of the facts of **authorization.** Some writers, however, omit this part. If you decide to use it, you will present such facts as when, how, and by whom the report was authorized, who wrote the report, and when it was submitted. This section is particularly useful for reports that have no letter of transmittal.

(2) *Purpose* (goal, objective).

2. Purpose   A vital part of almost every report you will write is a description of the **purpose** of your investigation. The purpose of the report (also called *objective, problem, object, aim, goal, mission, assignment, proposal,* or *project*) is whatever the report seeks to do. It is the satisfaction of the need that began the investigation. The need may be of long- or short-term value or a combination of both.

It is commonly stated in infinitive or question form.

You may state the purpose of your report in an infinitive phrase (" . . . to propose standards of corporate annual reports") or in the form of a well-phrased question ("What retail advertising practices do Centerville consumers disapprove of?"). Whatever you believe does the best job of explaining what your report seeks to do is what you want.

You may also need to state secondary, or collateral, purposes in this section. If a major problem is solved, collateral values are achieved. By stating these values, you help convince the reader of your report's worthiness. In other words, you should use a positive approach by telling what the solved problem can do for your reader. For example, an investigation of employee morale would involve looking into various explanations of morale: adequacy of communication, compensation, work environment, and administration.

(3) *Scope* (boundaries of the problem).

3. Scope   If the scope of the problem is not clearly covered in any of the introductory sections, you may need to include it in a separate section. By **scope,** we mean the boundaries of the problem. In this section, you should describe the exact coverage of the problem in good, clear language. Thus, you tell your reader exactly what is and is not a part of the problem.

(4) *Limitations* (hindrances to the report goal).

4. Limitations   With some problems, you will find limitations that are sufficiently important to warrant presenting them as a separate section of the introduction. By **limitations,** we mean anything that in some way has impeded the investigation or had a deterring effect on the report. The illustrative list of limitations to a report investigation problem might include an inadequate supply of money for conducting the investigation, insufficient time for doing the work, unavoidable conditions that hampered objective investigation, or limitations inherent to the problem under investigation.

(5) *History* (how the problem developed).

5. Historical Background   Sometimes a knowledge of the **history** of the problem is essential to understanding the report. Therefore, you may need to include in your introduction a section on this topic. Your general aim in this part is to acquaint your reader with some of the issues involved, principles raised, and values that might be realized if more research were done. Also, in this section you may orient the reader and clarify the report situation. This better understanding will help the reader and you to solve some of the problems that may arise in the future.

(6) *Sources and methods of collecting data* (how you got the facts).

6. Sources and Methods of Collecting Data   It is usually advisable to tell the reader how you collected the report information, whether through library research, interviewing, or such. If you used library research, for example, you may mention the major publications consulted. If you used interviewing, your description may cover such areas of the survey as sample determination, questionnaire construction, procedures followed, facilities for checking returns, and so forth. Whatever the technique used, you should describe it in sufficient detail to allow the reader to evaluate the quality of your research.

(7) *Definitions* (of unfamiliar terms and usages).

7. Definitions   If in the report you use words likely to be unfamiliar to the reader, you should define these words. One practice is to define each word on its first use in the report text. A more common practice, however, is to set aside a special section in the introduction for **definitions.**

(8) *Preview* (plan of the report).

8. Report Preview   In long reports, you should use the final section of the introduction to **preview** the report layout. In this section, you should tell the reader how the report will be presented—what topics will be taken up first, second, third, and so forth. Even more important, you should give the reasons why you followed this plan. In this way, you give your readers a clear picture of the road ahead so they may logically relate the report topics as they read them.

Choose and combine from this list to custom fit your introduction.

As previously noted, the sections discussed are listed only for the purpose of suggesting possible introduction content. In few reports will you need all of the topics mentioned. In some instances, you will be able to combine some of the topics; in others, you may split them into additional sections. In summary, you should tailor your introduction to fit the one report.

The report *body* presents and analyzes the information gathered.

THE REPORT BODY   The part of the report that presents the information collected and relates it to the problem is the report **body** (see pages 130–136 of Figure 8–3). Normally, it comprises the bulk of the report's content. In fact, in a sense this part *is* the report. With the exception of the conclusion or recommendation section that follows, the other parts of the report are attached parts. It is the report body to which most of the comments in this text pertain.

THE REPORT ENDING   You may end your report in any of a number of ways: with a summary, a conclusion, a recommendation, or a combination of the three.

Informational reports usually end with a *summary* of major findings.

1. Ending Summary   For some reports, particularly those that do little more than present information, you may include an **ending summary** of the major findings. Frequently, these reports have minor summaries at the end of each major division. When you follow this practice, your final summary should simply recap these summaries.

The ending summary is less complete than an executive summary.

You should not confuse the ending summary with the executive summary. The executive summary is a prefatory part of the report; the ending summary is part of the report text. Also, the executive summary reviews the entire report, usually from beginning to end. The ending summary reviews only highlights of facts.

Reports that seek an answer end with a *conclusion.*

2. Conclusions   Some reports must do more than present information; they must analyze the information in light of the problem and from there reach a conclusion. A report **conclusion** answers what you said you wanted to accomplish in your problem statement. The conclusion typically comes at the end of the report, although it may be placed first in the direct (psychological) arrangement.

The structure for presenting conclusions varies by problem.

For easy reference, you may tabulate your conclusions. But their arrangement is open to question. Sometimes you will feel the most important ones should be placed first; other times you will want to list them according to the arrangements discussed in the findings. Also, you may combine them with recommendations. In some cases—such as where the conclusion is obvious—you may omit it and present only a recommendation.

Include *recommendations* when readers want or expect them.

3. Recommendations   The **recommendations** are the writer's section. Here you state your interpretations based on the conclusions. A recommendation specifies a course of action to take. Of course, you need not state your recommendations if you are not asked to; but if you are asked, you should state them completely, including who should do what, when, where, why, and, sometimes, how.

Also, state alternative actions for the reader.

You may include alternative courses of action. But you should state your preferences. Since you are familiar with the findings, you should not leave your readers on the horns of a dilemma. You should state the desired action and then leave the readers to choose their own course. Since you are likely to be in a subordinate position, you should give your advice for your superiors to accept.

☐ **APPENDED PARTS**

Add an appended part when needed.

Sometimes it is desirable to append special sections to the report. The presence of these parts is normally determined by the specific needs of the problem concerned.

The *appendix* contains information that indirectly supports the report.

APPENDIX   The **appendix,** as its name implies, is a section tacked on. You use it for supplementary information that supports the body of the report but has no logical place within it. Possible contents might be questionnaires, working papers, summary tables, additional references, other reports, and so on.

As a rule, you should not include in the appendix the charts, graphs, sketches, and tables that directly support the report. Instead, you should place them in the

Information that directly supports the report belongs in the main text.

body of the report where they support the findings. Reports are best designed for the reader's convenience. Obviously, it would not be convenient for readers to thumb through many pages to find appendix illustrations to the facts they read in the report body.

Include a *bibliography* if you used printed sources.

BIBLIOGRAPHY   When your investigation heavily uses library research, you should include a **bibliography** (a list of the publications consulted). The construction of this formal list is described in Chapter 14.

SUMMARY REVIEW OF REPORT CONSTRUCTION

In summary, it is with these ingredients that you can build the report described at Step 1 in Figure 8–1. By systematically dropping and changing some of these ingredients, you can adapt your reports to meet the formality needs of each situation. This description, of course, is simplified. Many companies prescribe differing report arrangements. Some, for example, may remove acknowledgments from the letter of transmittal or preface and place them in a separate section. They may break up the executive summary and present recommendations, conclusions, and findings in separate prefatory sections. And some may include special prefatory sheets for intercompany routing purposes. Nevertheless, the progression described captures the nature of the relationship of all reports. It should serve as a good general guide in planning them.

QUESTIONS

1. Discuss the effects of formality and problem length on the model of report makeup described in Figure 8–1.
2. Select three of the report problems in Appendix A (preferably the long ones) and write a report title for each. Use the title checklist to explain and defend your title.
3. It has been said that the shorter a report is, the longer its title needs to be. Do you agree? Defend your decision.
4. Discuss the content of the title page. Why is this page the last of the prefatory parts to leave the report?
5. Discuss the contents of the letter of transmittal.
6. Explain the differences between a letter of transmittal and a foreword or preface. Why would you use each?
7. Discuss and justify the differences in writing style in the letter of transmittal and the text of the report.
8. What determines whether a report should have a table of contents?
9. Tell how to construct an executive summary.
10. Discuss the objectives of the introduction to a report.

11. How would the introduction of a report written for only one reader who knows the problem well differ from that written for a dozen readers, some of whom know little about the problem?

12. What effect does the life of a report (the time it is kept on file) have on the introduction content?

13. Discuss each of the introduction topics mentioned in the text, bringing out the considerations that would determine the use of each.

14. Why is it important that the sources of information used and the methods of investigation followed be fully described?

15. What is meant by the "limitations" of a report problem?

16. Explain the content and role of a preview in the introduction of a report.

17. Name and distinguish between the conventional types of report endings. Explain in what types of reports each should be used.

18. What is the role of the appendix in a report?

19. When should a report have a bibliography?

| FIGURE 8–3 | **Illustration of a long, formal report** |

This long, formal report presents the findings of an observational study of successful and unsuccessful salespeople to determine the differences in how each group works. The results will be used to revise the content of the company's sales training program. Because the report is extensive and the situation formal, the report has all the major prefatory parts. The significant statistical findings are effectively emphasized by graphics.

Title fly

The title includes the essentials of the 5 W's.

SALES TRAINING RECOMMENDATIONS FOR ARMOR MOTORS

BASED ON A 1994 STUDY OF COMPANY SALES ACTIVITIES

FIGURE 8-3   *(continued)*

Title page

<u>SALES TRAINING RECOMMENDATIONS FOR ARMOR MOTORS</u>

<u>BASED ON A 1994 STUDY OF COMPANY SALES ACTIVITIES</u>

Prepared for

*Here the essential
facts of
authorization are
provided.*

Mr. Peter R. Simpson, Vice President for Sales
Armor Motors, Inc.
72117 North Musselman Road
Dearborn, MI 48126

Prepared by

Ashlee P. Callahan
Callahan and Hebert Research Associates
Suite D, Brownfield Towers
212 North Bedford Avenue
Detroit, MI 48219

November 17, 1994

FIGURE 8–3   *(continued)*

Letter of
transmittal

November 17, 1994

Mr. Peter R. Simpson
Vice President for Sales
Armor Motors, Inc.
72117 North Musselman Road
Dearborn, MI 48126

Dear Mr. Simpson:

The letter begins
directly, with the
authorization.

Here is the report on the observational study of your salespeople
you asked us to conduct last August 17.

Pertinent comments
help the reader
understand and
appreciate the
research.

As you will see, our observations pointed to some specific needs
for sales training. Following the procedure we agreed to, we will
prepare an outline of these needs in a revised curriculum plan that
we will submit to your training director December 4. We are
confident that this curriculum plan will aid in correcting the
shortcomings in your sales force.

A goodwill comment
ends the letter.

We at Callahan and Hebert appreciate having this assignment. If
you should need any assistance in interpreting this report or in
implementing our recommendations, please call on us.

Sincerely yours,

Ashlee P. Callahan

Ashlee P. Callahan
Senior Research Associate

FIGURE 8–3   *(continued)*

A review of the problem facts prepares the reader to receive the report.

The three areas of sales work investigated logically form the main headings.

Subfactors of the work areas make logical second-level headings.

Note the parallel wording of the headings.

Note also the talking quality of the second-level headings.

FIGURE 8–3   *(continued)*

*List of charts
(a continuation
of the table of
contents)*

LIST OF CHARTS

*A list of the
graphics in the
report appears
here, with
complete titles
that describe
content.*

FIGURE 8–3   *(continued)*

<table>
<tr><td>

Executive summary

Following the direct-order plan, this executive summary places the recommendations first. Highlights of the supporting findings follow.

The remaining paragraphs summarize the major findings in the order presented in the report.

Note that the important facts and figures are present.

The significant comparisons and conclusions are emphasized throughout.

</td><td>

<u>Executive Summary</u>

Conclusions drawn from this study suggest that these topics be added to Armor's sales training program:

1. Negative effects of idle time
2. Techniques of cultivating prospects
3. Development of bird dog networks
4. Cultivating repeat sales
5. Projection of integrity image
6. Use of moderate persuasion
7. Value of product knowledge

Supporting these recommendations are the following findings and conclusions drawn from an observational study comparing sales activities of productive and marginal salespeople.

The data show that the productive salespeople used their time more effectively than did the marginal salespeople. As compared with marginal salespeople, the productive salespeople spent less time in idleness (28% vs. 53%). They also spent more time in contact with prospects (31.3% vs. 19.8%) and more time developing prospects (10.4% vs. 4.4%).

Investigation of how the salespeople got their prospects showed that because floor assignments were about equal, both groups profited about the same from walk-ins. The productive group got 282; the marginal group got 274. The productive group used bird dogs more extensively, having 64 contacts derived from this source during the observation period. The marginal group had 8. The productive salespeople also were more successful in turning these contacts into sales.

Observations of sales presentations revealed that the productive salespeople displayed higher integrity, used pressure more reasonably, and knew the product better than the marginal salespeople. Of the 20 productive salespeople, 16 displayed images of moderately high integrity (Group II). The marginal group members ranged widely with 7 in Group III (questionable), and 5 each in Group II (moderately high integrity) and Group IV (deceitful). Most (15) of the productive salespeople used moderate pressure, whereas the marginal salespeople tended toward extremes (10 high pressure, 7 low pressure). On the product knowledge test, 17 of the productive salespeople scored excellent and 3 fair. Of the marginal members, 5 scored excellent, 6 fair, and 9 inadequate.

vi

</td></tr>
</table>

FIGURE 8—3   *(continued)*

*Report text
(introduction)*

SALES TRAINING RECOMMENDATIONS FOR ARMOR MOTORS

BASED ON A 1994 STUDY OF COMPANY SALES ACTIVITIES

THE PROBLEM AND THE PLAN

Incidentals of Authorization and Submittal

*These
authorization
facts identify the
participants in
the report.*

This study of Armor salespeople's sales activities is submitted to Mr. Peter R. Simpson, Vice President for Sales, on November 17, 1994. As specified by written agreement dated August 28, the investigation was conducted under the direction of Ashlee P. Callahan of Callahan and Hebert Research Associates.

Objective of Sales Training Improvement

*Here the writer
explains the
problem clearly
and precisely.*

The objective of the study was to find means of improving the effectiveness of Armor salespeople. The plan for achieving this objective involved first determining the techniques and characteristics of effective selling. This information then will be used in improving Armor's sales training program.

Use of Observational Techniques

The methodology used in this investigation was an observational study of Armor salespeople. Specifically, the study employed the time-duty technique, which is a unique means of observing work performance under real conditions. A detailed description of this technique is a part of the proposal approved at the August meeting and is not repeated here. Specific items relative to the application of this method in this case are summarized below.

*A brief review
of methodology
permits the
reader to judge
the research.*

Two groups of 20 Armor salespeople were selected for the observation—a productive and a marginal group. The productive group was made up of the company's top producers for the past year; the marginal group comprised the lowest producers. Only salespeople with three years or more of experience were eligible.

A team of two highly trained observers observed each of the salespeople selected for a continuous period of five working days. Using specially designed forms, the observers recorded the work activities of the salespeople. At the end of the observation period, the observer conducted an exit interview, recording certain demographic data and administering a test of the salesperson's knowledge of Armor's automobiles.

1

FIGURE 8–3   *(continued)*

2

<u>A Preview of the Presentation</u>

A description of the presentation prepares the reader for what follows.

In the following pages, the findings and analysis appear in the arrangement discussed at the August meeting. First comes a comparison of how the productive and the marginal salespeople spend their work time. Second is an analysis of how the productive and the marginal salespeople find their prospects. Third is a comparative analysis of the observable differences in sales presentations of the two groups. Conclusions drawn from these comparisons form the bases for recommendations of content emphasis in Armor's sales training program.

ANALYSIS OF WORK TIME USE

From this point on, the presentation of findings, with comparisons and analysis, pursues the report objective.

The time-duty observation records were examined to determine whether differences exist between the productive and marginal salespeople in their use of work time. Activities were grouped into four general categories: (1) idleness, (2) contacting prospects, (3) finding prospects, and (4) miscellaneous activities. This examination revealed the following results.

<u>Negative Effect of Idle Time</u>

As shown in Chart 1, the productive salespeople spent less work time in idleness (28%) than did the marginal salespeople (53%). Further

Here and elsewhere, note the use of graphics at places near their discussion in the text.

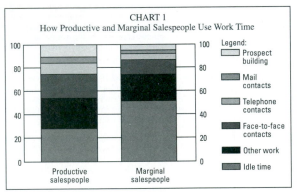

CHART 1
How Productive and Marginal Salespeople Use Work Time

Legend:
- Prospect building
- Mail contacts
- Telephone contacts
- Face-to-face contacts
- Other work
- Idle time

FIGURE 8-3 *(continued)*

*Report text
(continued)*

3

examination of the observations reveals that the top five of the 20 productive salespeople spent even less time in idleness (13%); and the bottom five of the marginal salespeople spent more time in idleness (67%). Clearly, these observations suggest the predictable conclusion that the successful salespeople work more than their less productive counterparts.

Correlation of Prospect Contacting and Success

The productive salespeople spent more time contacting prospects face to face, by telephone, and by mail (31.3%) than did the marginal salespeople (19.8%). The specific means of making these contacts show similar differences. The productive and marginal salespeople spent their work time, respectively, 23.2% and 13.5% in face-to-face contacts, 4.8% and 2.0% in mail contacts, and 8.3% and 4.6% in telephone contacts. These data lend additional support to the conclusion that work explains sales success.

*The text
presents the
data thoroughly
yet concisely —
and with
appropriate
comparisons.*

Vital Role of Prospect Building

During the observation period, productive salespeople spent more than twice as much time (10.5%) as marginal salespeople (4.4%) in building prospects. Activities observed in this category include contacting bird dogs and other lead sources and mailing literature to old and prospective customers.

Necessity of Miscellaneous Activities

Both the productive and marginal salespeople spent about a fourth of their work time in miscellaneous activities (tending to personal affairs, studying sales literature, attending sales meetings, and such). The productive group averaged 25.2%; the marginal group averaged 22.5%. As some of this time is related to automobile sales, the productive salespeople would be expected to spend more time in this category.

*A section
summary helps
the reader
identify and
remember the
major findings.*

Summary-Conclusions

The preceding data reveal that the way salespeople spend their time affects their productivity. Productive salespeople work at selling. In sharp contrast with the marginal salespeople, they spend little time in idleness. They work hard to contact prospects and to build prospect lists. Like all automobile salespeople, they spend some time in performing miscellaneous duties.

DIFFERENCES IN FINDING PROSPECTS

*This and the
other major
sections begin
with helpful
introductory
comment.*

A comparison of how productive and marginal salespeople find prospects and measurement of the productivity of these methods was a second area of investigation. For this investigation, the observations were classified by the four primary sources of prospects: (1) walk-ins, (2) bird dogs and other referrals, (3) repeat customers, and (4) other. Only prospects that were

FIGURE 8-3   *(continued)*

contacted in person or by telephone during the observation period were
included. Prospects were counted only once, even though some were
contacted more than once.

<u>Near Equal Distribution of Walk-ins</u>

As expected, most of the contacts of both the productive and marginal
salespeople were walk-ins. Because both groups had about equal floor
assignments, they got about the same number of prospects from this source.
As illustrated in Chart 2, the productive members got 282 (an average of 14.1
each), and the marginal members got 274 (an average of 13.7 each)

*Note how the use
of color adds
interest as well as
helps the reader
visualize the
comparisons in
the graphics.*

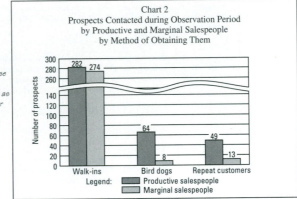

Chart 2
Prospects Contacted during Observation Period
by Productive and Marginal Salespeople
by Method of Obtaining Them

Although both groups got about the same number of prospects from walk-ins,
the productive salespeople got better results. A review of sales records shows
that the productive salespeople averaged 2.6 sales per week from walk-ins; the
marginal salespeople averaged 2.2. The difference, although appearing slight,
represents roughly 16 automobiles per year.

<u>Value of Cultivating Old Customers</u>

Returning old customers and friends referred by them constitute the second
most productive source of prospects. During the observation period, the

FIGURE 8-3   *(continued)*

Report text
(continued)

5

productive salespeople had contacts with 49 such prospects; the marginal salespeople had 13. The productive salespeople also had better sales success with these prospects, turning 40 of them into sales — an average of two per week. The marginal group members made sales to seven of these prospects — an average of .35 per person. These differences appear to be a direct result of effort (or lack of it) in maintaining contacts with customers after the sale.

Limited Effectiveness of Using Bird Dogs

Contacts from bird dogs comprise the third largest group, producing 64 total contacts for the productive and 8 for the marginal salespeople. Sales from this source totaled 9 for the productive salespeople and 2 for the marginal salespeople — an average of .45 and .1 sales per person, respectively. Although not large in terms of volume, these data explain much of the difference between the two groups. The use of bird dogs involves work, and the willingness to work varies sharply between the two groups.

Note how talking headings help emphasize the major findings.

Scant Use of Other Techniques

Other prospect gaining techniques were little used among the salespeople observed. Techniques long discussed in industry sales literature such as cold-spearing, placing written messages on automobile windshields, and random telephoning produced no prospects for either group during the observation period. All of the salespeople observed noted that they had used these techniques in the past, but with little success. The lack of evidence in this study leaves unanswered the question of the effectiveness of these techniques.

Summary–Conclusions

The obvious conclusion drawn from the preceding review of how prospects are found is that the productive salespeople work harder to get them. Although both groups get about the same number of walk-ins, the successful ones work harder at maintaining contacts with past customers and at getting contacts from a network of bird dogs and friends.

OBSERVABLE DIFFERENCES IN PRESENTATIONS

Differences in the sales presentations used constituted the third area of study. Criteria used in this investigation were (1) integrity, (2) pressure, and (3) product knowledge. Obviously, the first two of these criteria had to be evaluated subjectively. Even so, the evaluations were made by highly trained observers who used comprehensive guidelines. These guidelines are described in detail in the approved observation plan.

FIGURE 8–3   *(continued)*

Report text
(continued)

6

Positive Effect of Integrity

The evaluations of the salespeople's integrity primarily measured the apparent degree of truthfulness of the sales presentations. The observers classified the images of integrity they perceived during the sales presentations into four groups: Group I -- Impeccable (displayed the highest degree of truthfulness), Group II -- Moderately High (generally truthful, some exaggeration), Group III -- Questionable (mildly deceitful and tricky), Group IV -- Deceitful (untruthful and tricky).

Here and elsewhere, text references tell the reader when to observe the charts.

Of the 20 productive salespeople observed, 16 were classified in Group II (see Chart 3). Of the remaining four, 2 were in Group I and 2 in Group III.

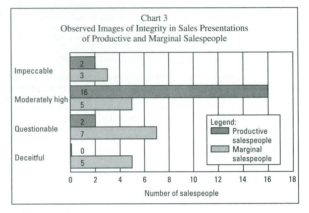

Chart 3
Observed Images of Integrity in Sales Presentations
of Productive and Marginal Salespeople

Distribution of the marginal salespeople was markedly different: 3 in Group I, 5 in Group II, 7 in Group III, and 5 in Group IV. Clearly, integrity was more apparent among the productive salespeople.

Apparent Value of Moderate Pressure

Measurements (by observation) of pressure used in the sales presentations were made in order to determine the relationship of pressure to sales success. Using the guidelines approved at the August meeting, the observers classified

FIGURE 8–3   *(continued)*

*Report text
(continued)*

7

each salesperson's presentations into three categories: (1) high pressure, (2) moderate pressure, and (3) low pressure. The observers reported difficulties in making some borderline decisions, but they felt that most of the presentations were easily classified.

Of the 20 productive salespeople, 15 used moderate pressure, 3 used low pressure, and 2 used high pressure (see Chart 4). The 20 marginal salespeople

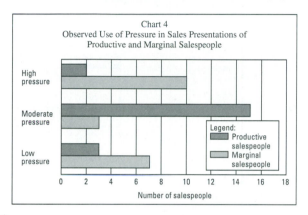

Chart 4
Observed Use of Pressure in Sales Presentations of
Productive and Marginal Salespeople

*The facts are not
just presented.
They are
compared and
conclusions are
drawn from
them.*

presented a different picture. Only 3 of them used moderate pressure. Of the remainder, 10 used high pressure and 7 used low pressure. The evidence suggests that moderate pressure is most effective.

Necessity of Product Knowledge

Product knowledge, a generally accepted requirement for successful selling, was determined during the exit interview. Using the 30 basic questions developed by Armor management from sales literature, the observers measured the salespeople's product knowledge. Correct responses to 27 or more of the questions was determined to be excellent, 24 through 26 was fair, and below 24 was classified as inadequate.

The productive salespeople displayed superior knowledge of the product with 17 of the 20 scoring excellent. The remaining 3 scored fair (see Chart 5).

FIGURE 8-3   (continued)

Scores for product knowledge were sharply different in the marginal salesperson group. Although 5 of them scored excellent, 6 scored fair, and 9 scored inadequate.

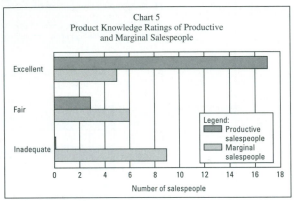

*Note how text
and charts work
closely together
to present the
information.*

These data point to an apparent weakness in training or a lack of individual preparation.

<u>Summary-Conclusions</u>

*Another
summary-
conclusion
brings the
section to a
close.*

The preceding presentation reveals some basic differences in the sales presentations of the productive and marginal salespeople. The productive salespeople displayed higher integrity (though not the highest). They used moderate pressure, whereas the marginal people tended toward high or low extremes. Also, the productive people knew their products better.

RECOMMENDATIONS FOR TRAINING

The conclusions reached in preceding sections suggest certain actions that Armor Motors should take in training its sales force. Specifically, the instruction should be altered to include the following topics:

*From the
summary-
conclusions of
the preceding
three sections the
recommendations
are derived.*

1. Importance of minimizing idle time.

2. Sales rewards from productive work (mailing literature, telephoning, cultivating prospects, etc.).

FIGURE 8–3   *(concluded)*

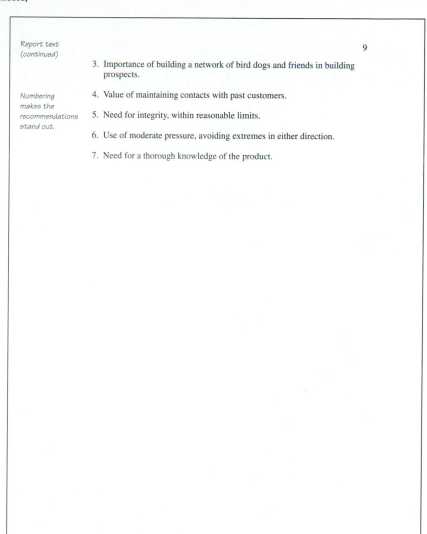

*Report text
(continued)*   9

3. Importance of building a network of bird dogs and friends in building
   prospects.

*Numbering
makes the
recommendations
stand out.*

4. Value of maintaining contacts with past customers.

5. Need for integrity, within reasonable limits.

6. Use of moderate pressure, avoiding extremes in either direction.

7. Need for a thorough knowledge of the product.

Constructing Short and Special Reports

Most of the business reports you are likely to write will be short and informal.

Most of the reports you are likely to write in business and industry are short and informal. To be sure, you may write long formal reports—you may even write them often—but more common by far will be reports that are less extensive and less complex. Such reports tend to be brief and more personal. They are developed within a short time and deal with problems relatively limited in scope. Some are specialized reports, with prescribed functions and formats. Becoming familiar with the basic types of these short and specialized reports is, therefore, an important part of your preparation as a business report writer.

Short reports are similar to long reports, but there are differences.

Short reports have a great deal in common with long reports. The writing style and the techniques of organization are similar. So, too, are the requirements for reliable research and logical reasoning. But certain differences do exist, as we will see.

MAJOR DIFFERENCES BETWEEN SHORT AND LONG REPORTS

Four major differences exist between short and long reports.

Specifically, four differences between short and long reports stand out as most significant. Short and special reports have less need for introductory material, tend to use the direct order, employ a more personal writing style, and include fewer coherence aids.

☐ LESS NEED FOR INTRODUCTORY MATERIAL

(1) Shorter reports need little introductory material.

One major content difference in the shorter report forms is their minor need for introductory material. Most reports at this level concern day-to-day problems. Thus, they have a short life. They are unlikely to be kept on file for posterity. They are intended for only a few readers, those who know the problem and its background. The readers' interests are in the report findings and any action they will lead to.

But include as much introduction as is needed to prepare the reader for the report.

This is not to say that all shorter forms have no need for introductory material. In fact, some have very specific needs. In general, however, the introductory need in shorter, more informal reports is less than that for more formal, longer types. But no rule applies across the board; each situation should be analyzed individually. In each case, you must cover whatever introductory material is needed to prepare your reader to receive the report. In some shorter reports, an incidental reference to the problem, authorization of the investigation, or such will do the job. In some extreme cases, you may need a detailed introduction comparable to that of a more formal report. There are also reports that need no introduction whatever. In such cases, the nature of the report serves as sufficient introductory information. For example, a personnel action by its very nature explains its purpose. So do weekly sales reports, inventory reports, and some progress reports.

□ PREDOMINANCE OF DIRECT ORDER

(2) Usually shorter reports begin directly—with conclusions or recommendations.

Because they usually are more goal oriented, shorter, more informal reports are likely to use the direct order of presentation. In other words, such reports typically are written to handle a problem—to make a specific conclusion or recommendation for action. This conclusion or recommendation is of such relative significance that it overshadows the analysis and information that support it. Thus, it deserves a lead-off position.

Sometimes, but not often, longer reports are written in the direct order.

The longer forms of reports also may use a direct order. In fact, many do. The point is, however, that most do not. Most follow the logical (introduction-body-conclusion) order. As one moves down the structural ladder toward the more informal, shorter reports (see Figure 8–1), however, the need for direct order increases. At the bottom of the ladder, direct order is more the rule than the exception.

Use the direct order when the conclusion or recommendation will serve as a basis for action.

Your decision on whether or not to use the direct order is best based on a consideration of your readers' likely use of the report. If the readers need the report conclusion or recommendation as a basis for taking an action, directness will speed their efforts. A direct presentation will permit them to quickly receive the most important information. If they have confidence in your work, they may choose not to read beyond this point and can promptly take the action the report recommends. Should they desire to question any part of the report, however, it is there for their inspection. The obvious result will be saving the valuable time of busy executives.

Use indirectness when you must take the reader through the analysis.

On the other hand, if there is reason to believe that your readers will want to arrive at the conclusion or recommendation only after a logical review of the analysis, you should organize your report in the indirect (logical) order. This arrangement is especially preferable when your readers do not place their full confidence in your work. You then take your readers through the facts and their analysis before giving them your conclusions or recommendations. Your readers thus can see the soundness of your reasoning. If you are a novice working on a new assignment, for example, you will be wise to lead your readers to your recommendations or conclusions by using the logical order.

☐ MORE PERSONAL WRITING STYLE

(3) Personal writing is common in shorter reports because they (a) involve personal relationships, (b) concern a personal investigation, and (c) are routine.

Although the writing styles of all reports have much in common, the writing in shorter reports tends to be more personal; that is, shorter reports are likely to use the personal pronouns *I, we, you,* and such rather than a third-person approach.

The explanation of this tendency toward personal writing in short reports should be obvious. First, short-report situations usually involve personal relationships. Short reports tend to be from and to people who know one another and typically communicate informally when they meet and talk. Second, short reports by nature are apt to involve a personal investigation. The finished work represents their writers' personal observations, evaluations, and analyses. The writers are expected to report them as their own. Third, the problems that short reports address tend to be the day-to-day, routine ones. It is logical to report them informally, and personal writing tends to produce this effect.

Write impersonally (a) when your reader prefers it and (b) when the situation is formal.

Your selection of personal versus impersonal style should be based on the circumstances of the situation. You should consider the expectations of those who will receive the report (see Chapter 11). If they expect formality, you should write impersonally. If they expect informality, you should write personally. Second, if you do not know the readers' preferences, you should consider the formality of the situation. Convention favors impersonal writing for most formal situations.

From this analysis, it should be apparent that either style can be appropriate for reports ranging from the shortest to the longest. The point is, however, that short-report situations are more likely to justify personal writing.

☐ LESS NEED FOR A FORMAL COHERENCE PLAN

(4) Long reports need sentences and paragraphs in key places for coherence.

Longer reports need a formal coherence plan to make the parts stick together (see Chapter 11). In other words, because of the complexities arising from their length, you must make an effort to relate the parts. Otherwise, the paper will read like a series of disjointed, minor reports. What you do is use summaries and introductory, forward-looking sentences and paragraphs in key places. In this way, the reader will be able to see how each part of the report fits into the whole scheme of things.

Shorter reports show coherence through a logical organization plan.

The shorter the report becomes, the less it needs a formal coherence plan. In fact, in the extremely short forms (such as memorandums and letter reports), little in the way of wording is needed to relate the parts. In such cases, the information is so brief and simple that a logical, orderly arrangement clearly shows the plan of presentation.

Need for a coherence plan, not report length, should determine its use.

Although formal coherence plans are less frequently used in the short forms of reports, the question of whether to include them should not be determined by length alone. Instead, the matter of need should guide you in your choice. Whenever your presentation contains organizational complexities that can be made clear by summarizing, introducing, and relating parts, you should include these elements. Thus, need rather than length is the major determinant. But it is clearly evident that need for formal coherence plans lessens as report length decreases.

SHORT FORMS OF REPORTS

Following is a review of the more popular short reports.

As we noted earlier, the short forms of reports are by far the most numerous and important in business. In fact, the three types represented by the bottom three steps of the stairway in Figure 8–1 make up the bulk of the reports written in business. Thus, a review of each type is in order.

☐   THE SHORT REPORT

The *short report* consists of title page and report text.

One of the more popular short-report types is the conventional **short report.** Representing the fifth step in Figure 8–1, this report consists of only a title page and the report text. Its popularity may be explained by the impression of moderate formality it gives. Inclusion of the one most essential prefatory part gives the report at least a minimal appearance of formality and does so without the tedious work of preparing the other prefatory pages. It is ideally suited for the short but moderately formal problem.

Usually, it is in direct order, beginning with a summary.

Like most of the less imposing forms of reports, the short report may be organized in either the direct or indirect order, although direct order is by far the more common plan. As Figure 9–1 at the end of the chapter illustrates, this plan begins with a quick summary of the report, including and emphasizing conclusions and recommendations. Such a beginning serves much the same function as the executive summary of a long, formal report.

The introduction comes next, followed by the findings and analyses, and finally conclusions.

Following the summary come whatever introductory remarks are needed. As noted previously, sometimes this part is not needed at all. Usually, however, there follows a single paragraph covering the facts of authorization and a brief statement of the problem and its scope. After the introductory words come the findings of the investigation. Just as in the longer report forms, the findings are presented, analyzed, and applied to the problem. Finally comes the conclusion and, if needed, a recommendation. The conclusion and recommendation may come at the end, even though they also may appear in the beginning summary. Sometimes omitting a summary or conclusion would end the report too abruptly, halting the flow of reasoning before it reached its logical goal.

The mechanics of constructing the short report are much the same as those for the longer, more formal types. As illustrated in Figure 9–1, this report uses the same form of title page and has the same layout requirement. Like long reports, it uses headings. But because of the report's brevity, the headings rarely go beyond the two-division level—in fact, one level is most common. Like any other report, its use of graphic aids, appendix, and bibliography depends on its need for them.

☐   LETTER REPORTS

Letter reports are reports in letter form.

The second more common short form of report is the letter report (see Figure 9–2). As the term implies, a **letter report** is a report written in letter form. It is used primarily to present information to someone outside the company, especially when it is to be sent by mail. For example, a company's written evaluation of a credit customer may well be presented in letter form and mailed to the one who requests it. An outside consultant may write a report of analyses and recommendations in letter form. An organization officer may elect to report certain information to the membership in letter form.

Usually they cover short problems.

Normally, letter reports present the shorter problems—typically, those that can be presented in three or four pages or less. But no hard and fast rule exists on this point. Long letter reports (10 or more pages) have been used successfully many times.

Typically, they are written in personal style.

As a general rule, letter reports are written personally (using *I, you,* and *we* references). Of course, exceptions exist, such as when one is preparing such a report for an august group—say, a committee of the U.S. Senate or a company's board of directors. Other than this point, the writing style recommended for letter reports is much the same as that for any other report. Certainly, clear and meaningful expression is a requirement for all reports.

They may be organized in the indirect order (beginning with a brief introduction).

Letter reports may be arranged in either the direct or indirect order. If the report is to be mailed, there is some justification for using an indirect approach. Because such reports arrive unannounced, an initial reminder of what they are, how they originated, and such is in order. A letter report written to the membership of an organization, for example, may appropriately begin with these words:

> As authorized by your board of directors last January 6, this report reviews member company expenditures for direct-mail selling.

They may also be written in the direct order, in which case a subject line gives introductory facts.

If you elect to begin a letter report in the direct order, a subject line will be appropriate. The subject line consists of some identifying words, which appear at the top of the letter, usually immediately after or before the salutation. Although subject lines are formed in many ways, one acceptable version begins with the word *Subject* and follows it with descriptive words that identify the problem. As the following example illustrates, this identifying device helps to overcome any confusion the direct beginning may otherwise cause the reader:

> *Subject:* Report on direct-mail expenditures of Association members, authorized by board of directors, January, 1994
>
> Association members are spending 8 percent more on direct-mail advertising this year than they did the year before. Current plans call for a 10 percent increase for next year.

Organization of letter reports is much like that of longer reports.

Regardless of which beginning is used, the organizational plan for letter reports corresponds to those of the longer, more formal types. Thus, the indirect-order letter report follows its introductory buildup with a logical presentation and analysis of the information gathered. From this presentation, it works to a conclusion, recommendation, or both. The direct-order letter report follows the initial summary-conclusion-recommendation section with appropriate introductory words. For example, the direct beginning illustrated above could be followed with these introductory words:

> These are the primary findings of a study authorized by your board of directors last January. As they concern information vital to all of us in the association, they are presented here for your confidential use.

Following such an introductory comment, the report presents the supporting facts and their analyses. The writer systematically builds up the case that supports the opening comment.

The letter report ends on a goodwill note.

With either order, a letter report may close with whatever friendly goodwill comment is appropriate for the one occasion.

☐ MEMORANDUM REPORTS

Memorandum reports are widely used as internal written messages.

Because of their adaptability, **memorandum reports** (illustrated in Figures 9–3, 9–4, 9–5, and 9–7) are the most widely used reports in business. They are internal messages; that is, they are written by one person in an organization to another person in the organization.

Most are written informally.

Most memorandum reports are communications between people who know each other. For this reason, they are usually written informally. Even so, some are formal, especially when the intended reader is high in the organization's administration. In fact, some memorandum reports have captions and graphic aids.

Memorandum reports need little introductory information.

Because memorandum reports usually concern routine, day-to-day problems, they have little need for introductory information. In fact, they frequently begin reporting with no introductory comment. Besides, the standard format takes care of announcing the subject.

They are written on special stationery.

Memorandum reports are usually presented on standardized interoffice memorandum stationery. The words *Date, To, From,* and *Subject* appear at the top, usually just below the company heading. All the essential material is thus identified immediately. Printed memorandum reports may carry a written signature or the writer's initials as a form of courtesy or verification. But, because of the *From* heading, a printed signature is superfluous.

SPECIAL REPORT FORMS

Some special report forms deserve review.

Of the conventional special reports, the proposal, the staff report, the corporate annual report, the audit report, and the technical report are among the most widely used. As a business report writer, you should be familiar with the general purpose and requirements of each.

☐ THE PROPOSAL

Proposals vary in length.

Whether proposals belong in a discussion of short reports is debatable because they are not always short. In fact, they can range from just a few pages to several volumes. We discuss proposals here primarily as a matter of convenience.

A *proposal* is a presentation for consideration.

PROPOSALS DEFINED By definition, a **proposal** is a presentation for consideration of something. Some proposals fit this definition well—for example, a company's proposal to merge with another, an advertising agency's proposal to promote a product, a city's proposal to induce a business to locate in its area. But other proposals are more precisely described as appeals or bids for grants, donations, and sales of goods or services—a college professor submits a request for research funds to a government agency, a community organization submits a request to a philanthropic foundation for help in building a drug rehabilitation facility, or a company submits a bid for its products or services.

Proposals are made by individuals or organizations to individuals or organizations.

Usually a proposal is written, but it can be oral. It may be made by an individual or an organization (including the business organization); and it may be made to any of a variety of individuals or organizations (government agencies, foundations, businesses). It could even be made internally—by one part of a business to another part or to the management of the business. For example, a department might make a proposal to management outlining its needs for new equipment.

They may be invited or prospecting.

INVITED OR PROSPECTING   Proposals may be invited or prospecting. Invited means an organization announces it will make an award and is seeking applications for it. A government agency might have funds to award for research projects; a foundation might wish to make grants for educational innovations; a business might want competing suppliers to bid on a product or service it needs. These organizations would then announce to interested parties that they seek proposals for these awards. Typically, their announcements describe their needs and specify the requirements the proposals should cover.

In business, invited proposals usually follow meetings.

In business situations, invited proposals usually follow preliminary meetings between the parties involved. For example, a business might have a certain need for production equipment. Its representative would then initiate contact with likely suppliers of this equipment. At these meetings, the representatives would discuss the needs thoroughly. The meetings would end with an invitation for each supplier to submit a proposal for fulfilling the needs with its equipment. In a sense, this proposal is a bid supported by the documentation and explanation needed for conviction.

Prospecting proposals are like sales letters.

Prospecting proposals are much like rational sales letters. They amount to descriptions of what the writer or writer's organization could do if given an award by the reader's organization. For example, a university department might wish to seek funding to develop a new curriculum in international management. It then might write proposals to philanthropic foundations describing the curriculum, outlining its financial needs for implementing it, and proposing that the foundation award the funds needed. Or a business engaged in supplying a unique service might submit unsolicited a description of its services with specific applications to a business that might use these services. Such proposals differ from rational sales letters primarily in physical form (they are in report form, not letter form). When products or services are being proposed, they may differ also by being specifically adapted to the reader's business.

Formats vary from memorandum to long report form.

FORMAT AND ORGANIZATION   The physical arrangement and organization of proposals vary widely. The simplest proposals resemble formal memorandums (see Figure 9–5). Internal proposals (those written for and by people in the same organization) usually fall in this category, although exceptions exist. The more complex proposals may take the form of a full-dress long report, including prefatory parts (title pages, letter of transmittal, table of contents, executive summary), text, and an assortment of appended parts. Most are somewhere between these extremes.

Select the form appropriate for your case.

Because of wide variations in makeup, you would be wise to investigate carefully before designing a particular proposal. In your investigation, try to determine which form is conventional among those who will read it. Look to see what those before you have done in similar situations. In the case of invited proposals, review the announcement thoroughly looking for any clues concerning what the inviting organization prefers. If you are unable to follow any of these courses, design a form based on your knowledge of report structure. Your design should be one that you believe is best for the one case.

Formality needs vary. Do what is appropriate.

FORMALITY REQUIREMENTS   The formality requirements of proposals vary. In some cases (a university's proposal for a research grant, for example), strict formality is expected. In others (such as a manufacturing department's proposal to the plant manager to change a production procedure), informality is in order. As in other reports, the decision should be based primarily on the relationship between the parties involved. If the parties are acquainted personally, informality is appropriate. If they are not, a formal report usually is expected. An exception would be made in any case in which formality is expected regardless of the relationship of the participants.

Determine content by reviewing needs. If invited, review invitation.

CONTENT   You should consider the needs of the individual case in determining content of a proposal. In the case of an invited (solicited) proposal, review the facts of the proposal announcement, if in writing. If the proposal follows an oral meeting, review your recollections of the meeting or the notes taken at the meeting. Usually, such a review will tell you what is wanted. In fact, some written invitations even give a suggested plan for the proposal. It is highly important that you follow such guidelines; in competitive situations, the selection procedure frequently involves checking off and rating each point given in the invitation.

In uninvited, use judgment in determining needs.

If you are making a proposal uninvited, you will have to determine what the readers need to know. As each case will have different needs, you will have to use your best judgment.

Consider these eight content possibilities:

Although content possibilities vary widely, you should consider including the eight topics listed below. They are broad and general, and you should combine or subdivide them as needed to fit the facts of your case.

1. Report purpose and problem (a good beginning topic).

1. Report purpose and the problem   An appropriate beginning consists of a statement of the purpose (to present a proposal) and the problem (for training Dunn Company sales personnel in demonstration techniques). If the report is in response to an invitation, it should tie in with the invitation (as described in the July 10 announcement). The problem should be stated clearly, in the way described in Chapter 3. This proposal beginning illustrates these recommendations:

> As requested at the July 10 meeting with Alice Burton, Thomas Cheny, and Victor Petrui in your Calgary office, the following pages present Murchison and Associates' proposal for reducing turnover of field representatives. Following guidelines established at the meeting, the plan involves determining job satisfaction of the current sales force, analyzing exit interview records, and comparing company compensation and personnel practices with industry norms.

Uninvited proposals must gain interest quickly.

If the proposal is submitted without invitation, its beginning has an additional requirement: It must gain interest. As noted previously, uninvited proposals are much like sales letters. Their intended readers are not likely to be eager to read them. Thus, their beginnings must overcome readers' reluctance. An effective way of doing this is to start with a brief summary of the proposal and its highlights, emphasizing benefits. This beginning of an unsolicited proposal sent by a restaurant consultant to prospective clients illustrates this technique:

> The following pages present a proven plan for operations review that will (1) reduce food costs, (2) evaluate menu offerings for maximum profitability, (3) increase kitchen efficiency, (4) improve service, and (5) increase profits. Mattox and Associates propose to achieve these results through their highly successful procedures that involve analysis of guest checks and invoices and observational studies of kitchen and service work.

2. Background.

2. Background Sometimes a review of background information is helpful to an understanding of the problem. A college's proposal for an educational grant, for example, might benefit from a review of the college's involvement in the area in which the grant would be applied. A company proposing a merger with another company might review industry developments that make the merger desirable. Or a chief executive officer proposing reorganization of a company's administration to the board of directors might present the background information that explains the need for reorganization.

3. Need.

3. Need Closely related to background information is the need for what is being proposed. Background facts may be used to establish need. But because need can be presented without background support, we list it separately.

4. Plan description.

4. Description of plan The heart of the proposal is the description of what the writer proposes to do. This is the primary message. It should be presented concisely, in clear and orderly fashion.

5. Particulars (time schedules, costs, performance standards, equipment and supplies needed, and such).

5. Particulars A part of the plan description, but discussed separately for emphasis, are the particulars of the proposal. By particulars, we mean the specifics—time schedules, costs, performance standards, means of appraising performance, equipment and supplies needed, guarantees, personnel requirements, and such. What is needed in a given situation depends on the unique requirements of the case. But in any event, the description should anticipate and answer the readers' questions.

6. Ability to deliver.

6. Evidence of ability to deliver Sometimes the proposing organization must establish its ability to perform. Thus, it must show its credentials. This means presenting information such as qualifications of personnel, evidence of success in similar cases, adequacy of equipment and facilities, description of operating procedures, and evidence of financial status. Whatever will be helpful in support of the organization's ability to carry out what it proposes should be used.

7. Benefits of the proposal (especially if selling needed).

7. Benefits of the proposal The good things that would result from the proposal are also content possibilities, especially if the readers must be convinced. Reader benefits are important in sales writing. And as we have noted, proposals can be much like sales presentations. The greater the need to persuade, the more you should stress benefits. However, the writing in proposals is more objective and less flamboyant than that in sales literature.

A college's request for funding to establish a program for minorities could point to the disadvantaged students that would be given bright futures. A proposal to offer a consulting service to restaurant operations could stress improved work efficiency, reduced employee theft, savings in food costs, increased profits, and such.

8. Concluding comments (words directed toward next step).

8. Concluding comments The proposal should not end abruptly but with words directed to the next step—acting on the proposal. One possibility is to present a summary review of highlights. An offer to present other information that might be needed is another possibility. So is an urge (or suggestion) to act on the proposal.

☐ THE STAFF REPORT

The *staff report* follows a fixed organizational plan that leads to a conclusion.

One of the most widely used reports in business is the **staff report.** Patterned after a form traditional to the technical fields, the staff report is well adapted to business problem solving. Its arrangement follows the logical thought processes used in solving conventional business problems. Although the makeup of this report varies by company, the following arrangement recommended by a major metals manufacturer is typical:

One typical staff report has these parts: (1) identifying information, (2) summary, (3) objective, (4) facts, (5) discussion, (6) conclusions, and (7) recommendations.

Identifying information: As the company's staff reports are written on intra-company communication stationery, the conventional identification information *(Date, To, From, Subject)* appears at the beginning.

Summary: For the busy executive who wants the facts fast, a summary begins the report. Some executives will read no further. Others will want to trace the report content in detail.

The problem (or objective): As do all good problem-solving procedures, the report text logically begins with a clear description of the problem—what it is, what it is not, what its limitations are, and the like.

Facts: Next comes the information gathered in the attempt to solve the problem.

Discussion: Analysis of the facts and applications of the facts and analyses to the problem follow. (Frequently, the statement of facts and their discussion can be combined.)

Conclusions: From the preceding discussion of facts come the final meanings as they apply to the problem.

Recommendation: If the problem's objective allows for it, a course of action may be recommended on the basis of the conclusion.

Perhaps the major users of staff reports are the branches of the armed forces. This report is standardized throughout all branches. As shown in Figure 9–6, the military version differs somewhat from the business arrangement just described.

☐ THE CORPORATE ANNUAL REPORT

The *corporate annual report* details a company's financial activities and plans.

The **corporate annual report** is a comprehensive account of a company's finances and operations. It explains the company's financial standing, summarizes the activities of the year just completed, and describes plans for the year to come. Each report has as its objective to explain the business enterprise to a diverse readership: the investor, the employees, and the public. It is thus a challenging document to write and an instructive one to read. Though you are not likely to develop corporate annual reports yourself, you can expect to refer to them frequently in your business career. It makes sense, therefore, to know how to read and to use them.

Annual reports provide excellent examples of effective report-writing techniques.

All corporate annual reports include basic accounting data required by the Securities and Exchange Commission and by listings agreements with the major stock exchanges. But companies are increasingly aware of the effectiveness of annual reports, both as public service information documents and as public relations tools. You can thus learn a great deal about style, graphics, and other elements of business communication by studying these very professional examples of business writing.

☐ THE AUDIT REPORT

Short- and long-form *audit reports* are well known in business.

Short-form and long-form **audit reports** are well known to accountants. The short-form report is perhaps the most standardized of all reports—if, indeed, it can be classified as a report. Actually, it is a statement verifying an accountant's inspection of a firm's financial records. Its wording seldom varies. Illustrations of this standard form can be found in almost any corporate annual report.

Long-form audit reports vary in form.

Composition of the long-form audit report is as varied as the short form is rigid. In fact, a national accounting association, which made an exhaustive study on the subject, found practices to be so varied that it concluded that no typical form exists. Although it covers a somewhat simple and limited audit, the audit report illustrated in Figure 9–7 shows one acceptable form.

☐ THE TECHNICAL REPORT

Technical reports differ primarily in subject matter.

Although it generally follows the plan of the conventional formal report, the **technical report** has some unique characteristics. The technical report differs from other reports primarily in its subject matter. Its exact makeup varies from company to company, but the following description typifies this form.

Their prefatory parts are similar to those in conventional formal reports.

The beginning pages of the technical report are much like those of the traditional formal report. First come the title pages, although frequently a routing or distribution form for intracompany use may be worked into or perhaps added to them. A letter of transmittal is likely to come next, followed by a table of contents and illustrations. From this point on, however, the technical report is likely to differ from the traditional report in two respects: (1) beginning summary and (2) text organization.

However, their summaries may be in different parts.

Instead of the executive summary, the technical report may present the summary information in a number of prefatory sections. There may be, for example, separate sections covering findings, conclusions, and recommendations. Parts of the conventional introductory material also may be presented in prefatory sections. The "objective" is the most likely part in this area, although "method" is also a widely used section.

Also, they may be organized in a predetermined order.

The text of the technical report usually begins with introductory information. The remaining information may be organized much like that in any conventional report, or it may follow a predetermined and somewhat mechanical arrangement. One such arrangement is the following:

Introduction

Methodology (or methods and materials)

Facts

Discussion

Conclusion

Recommendations

☐ THE PROGRESS REPORT

Progress reports review the progress of an activity.

As its name implies, a progress report presents a review of progress made on an activity. For example, a fund-raising organization might prepare weekly summaries of its efforts to achieve its goal. Or a building contractor might prepare for a customer a report on progress toward completing a building. Typically, the contents of these reports concern progress made, but they may also include such related topics as problems encountered or anticipated and projections of future progress.

Their formats vary.

Progress reports follow no set form. They can be quite formal, as when a contractor building a large manufacturing plant reports to the company for which the plant is being built. Or they can be very informal, as in the case of a worker reporting by memorandum to his or her supervisor on the progress of a task being performed. Some progress reports are quite routine and structured, sometimes involving filling in blanks on forms devised for the purpose. Most, however, are informal, narrative reports, as illustrated by the example in Figure 9–3.

QUESTIONS

1. What are the major differences in the construction of the short and long reports?
2. Why do the shorter forms of reports usually require less introductory material than do the longer reports?
3. Defend the use of direct order in the shorter forms of reports.
4. What should determine whether one should use the direct order in a report?
5. Explain the logic of using personal style in some reports.
6. What should determine whether one should use personal style in a report?
7. What should determine whether one should use coherence aids in a report?

8. Describe the structure of a typical short report.

9. Distinguish between letter and memorandum reports.

10. Discuss and illustrate (with examples other than those in the text) two contrasting types of beginnings for the letter report.

11. Define proposals. What should be included in them?

12. "To be successful, a proposal must be persuasive. This quality makes the proposal different from most short reports (which stress objectivity)." Discuss.

13. Describe the makeup of the traditional staff report. Can you think of any advantages of this plan?

14. Discuss the purposes of the typical corporate annual report.

15. How do technical reports differ from other business reports? How are they similar?

FIGURE 9–1   Illustration of a short report

RECOMMENDATIONS FOR DEPRECIATING DELIVERY TRUCKS

BASED ON AN ANALYSIS OF THREE PLANS

PROPOSED FOR THE BAGGET LAUNDRY COMPANY

Submitted to

Mr. Ralph P. Bagget, President
Bagget Laundry Company
312 Dauphine Street
New Orleans, Louisiana   70102

Prepared by

Charles W. Brewington, C.P.A.
Brewington and Karnes, Certified Public Accountants
743 Beaux Avenue
New Orleans, Louisiana 70118

April 16, 19—

FIGURE 9-1   (continued)

RECOMMENDATION FOR DEPRECIATING DELIVERY TRUCKS

BASED ON AN ANALYSIS OF THREE PLANS

PROPOSED FOR THE BAGGET LAUNDRY COMPANY

I. Recommendations and Summary of Analysis

The Reducing Charge method appears to be the best method to depreciate Bagget Laundry Company delivery trucks. The relative equality of cost allocation for depreciation and maintenance over the useful life of the trucks is the prime advantage under this method. Computation of depreciation charges is relatively simple by the Reducing Charge plan but not quite so simple as computation under the second best method considered.

The second best method considered is the Straight-Line depreciation plan. It is the simplest to compute of the plans considered, and it results in yearly charges equal to those under the Reducing Charge method. The unequal cost allocation resulting from increasing maintenance costs in successive years, however, is a disadvantage that far outweighs the method's ease of computation.

Third among the plans considered is the Service Hours method. This plan is not satisfactory for depreciating delivery trucks primarily because it combines a number of undesirable features. Prime among these is the complexity and cost of computing yearly charges under the plan. Also significant is the likelihood of poor cost allocation under this plan. An additional drawback is the possibility of variations in the estimates of the service life of company trucks.

II. Background of the Problem

Authorization of the Study. This report on depreciation methods for delivery trucks of the Bagget Laundry Company is submitted on April 16, 19—, to Mr. Ralph P. Bagget, President of the Company. Mr. Bagget orally authorized Brewington and Karnes, Certified Public Accountants, to conduct the study on March 15, 19—.

Statement of the Problem. Having decided to establish branch agencies, the Bagget Laundry Company has purchased delivery trucks to transport laundry back and forth from the central cleaning plant in downtown New Orleans. The Company's problem is to select from three alternatives the most advantageous method to depreciate the trucks. The three methods concerned are Reducing Charge, Straight-Line, and Service-Hours. The trucks have an original cost of $7,500, a five-year life, and trade-in value of $1,500.

Method of Solving the Problem. In seeking an optimum solution to the Company's problem, we studied Company records and reviewed authoritative literature on the subject. We also applied our best judgment and our experience in analyzing the alternative methods. We based all conclusions on the generally accepted business principles in the field. Clearly, studies such as this involve subjective judgment, and this one is no exception.

1

FIGURE 9-1   *(continued)*

2

<u>Steps in Analyzing the Problem.</u> In the following analysis, our evaluations of the three depreciation methods appear in the order in which we rank the methods. Since each method involves different factors, direct comparison by factors is meaningless. Thus our plan is that we evaluate each method in the light of our best judgment.

III. <u>Marked Advantages of the Reducing Charge Method</u>

Sometimes called Sum-of-the-Digits, the Reducing Charge method consists of applying a series of decreasing fractions over the life of the property. To determine the fraction, first compute the sum of years of use for the property. This number becomes the denominator. Then determine the position number (first, second, etc.) of the year. This number is the numerator. Then apply the resulting fractions to the depreciable values for the life of the property. In the case of the trucks, the depreciable value is $6,000 ($7,500–$1,500).

As shown in Table I, this method results in large depreciation costs for the early years and decreasing costs in later years. But since maintenance and repair costs for trucks are higher in the later years, this method provides a relatively stable charge over the life of the property. In actual practice, however, the sums will not be as stable as illustrated, for maintenance and repair costs will vary from those used in the computation.

Table I

DEPRECIATION AND MAINTENANCE COSTS FOR
DELIVERY TRUCKS OF BAGGET LAUNDRY FOR 19X0–19X4
USING REDUCING CHARGE DEPRECIATION

End of Year	Depreciation	Maintenance	Sum
1	5/15 ($6,000) = $2,000	$ 100	$ 2,100
2	4/15 ($6,000) = 1,600	500	2,100
3	3/15 ($6,000) = 1,200	900	2,100
4	2/15 ($6,000) = 800	1,300	2,100
5	1/15 ($6,000) = 400	1,700	2,100
	$6,000	$4,500	$10,500

In summary, the Reducing Charge method uses the most desirable combination of factors to depreciate trucks. It equalizes periodic charges, and it is easy to compute. It is our first choice for Bagget Laundry Company.

FIGURE 9-1   (continued)

3

IV. Runner-up Position of Straight-Line Method

The Straight-Line depreciation method is easiest of all to compute. It involves merely taking the depreciable value of the trucks ($6,000) and dividing it by the life of the trucks (5 years). The depreciation in this case is $1,200 for each year.

As shown in Table II, however, the increase in maintenance costs in later years results in much greater periodic charges in later years. The method is not usually recommended in cases such as this.

Table II

DEPRECIATION AND MAINTENANCE COSTS FOR
DELIVERY TRUCKS OF BAGGET LAUNDRY FOR 19X0–19X4
USING STRAIGHT-LINE DEPRECIATION

End of Year	Depreciation	Maintenance	Sum
1	1/5 ($6,000) = $1,200	$ 100	$1,300
2	1/5 ($6,000) = 1,200	500	1,700
3	1/5 ($6,000) = 1,200	800	2,100
4	1/5 ($6,000) = 1,200	1,300	2,500
5	1/5 ($6,000) = 1,200	1,700	2,900
	Totals $6,000	$4,500	$10,500

In addition, the Straight-Line method generally is best when the properties involved are accumulated over a period of years. When this is done, the total of depreciation and maintenance costs will be about even. But Bagget Company has not purchased its trucks over a period of years. Nor is it likely to do so in the years ahead. Thus, Straight-Line depreciation will not result in equal periodic charges for maintenance and depreciation over the long run.

FIGURE 9–1   *(concluded)*

4

V. Poor Rank of Service-Hours Depreciation

The Service-Hours method of depreciation combines the major disadvantages of the other ways discussed. It is based on the principle that a truck is bought for the direct hours of service that it will give. The estimated number of hours that a delivery truck can be used efficiently according to automotive engineers is computed from a service total of one-hundred thousand miles. The depreciable cost ($6,000) for each truck is allocated pro rata according to the number of service hours used.

The difficulty and expense of maintaining additional records of service hours is a major disadvantage of this method. The depreciation cost for the delivery trucks under this method will fluctuate widely between first and last years. It is reasonable to assume that as the trucks get older more time will be spent on maintenance. Consequently, the larger depreciation costs will occur in the initial years. As can be seen by Table III, the periodic charges for depreciation and maintenance hover between the two previously discussed methods.

Table III

DEPRECIATION AND MAINTENANCE COSTS FOR
DELIVERY TRUCKS OF BAGGET LAUNDRY FOR 19X0–19X4
USING SERVICE-HOURS DEPRECIATION

End of Year	Estimated Service-Miles	Depreciation	Maintenance	Sum
1	30,000	$1,800	$ 100	$1,900
2	25,000	1,500	500	2,000
3	20,000	1,200	900	2,100
4	15,000	900	1,300	2,200
5	10,000	600	1,700	2,300
	100,000	$6,000	$4,500	$10,500

The periodic charge for depreciation and maintenance increases in the later years of ownership. Another difficulty encountered is the possibility of a variance between estimated service hours and the actual service hours. The wide fluctuation possible makes it impractical to use this method for depreciating the delivery trucks.

The difficulty of maintaining adequate records and increasing costs in the later years are the major disadvantages of this method. Since it combines the major disadvantages of both the Reducing Charge and Straight-Line methods, it is not satisfactory for depreciating the delivery trucks.

FIGURE **9–2**   **Illustration of a letter report**

INTERNATIONAL COMMUNICATION ASSOCIATION

3141 Girard Street · Washington, D.C.

January 28, 19—

Board of Directors
International Communication Association

Dear Members:

Subject: Recommendation of Convention Hotel for the 19— Meeting

RECOMMENDATION OF THE LAMONT

The Lamont Hotel is my recommendation for the International Communication Association meeting next January. My decision is based on the following summary of the evidence I collected. First, the Lamont has a definite downtown location advantage, and this is important to convention goers and their spouses. Second, accommodations, including meeting rooms, are adequate in both places, although the Blackwell's rooms are more modern. Third, Lamont room costs are approximately 15% lower than those at the Blackwell. The Lamont, however, would charge $400 for a room for the assembly meeting. Although both hotels are adequate, because of location and cost advantages the Lamont appears to be the better choice from the members' viewpoint.

ORIGIN AND PLAN OF THE INVESTIGATION

In investigating these two hotels, as was my charge from you at our January 7th meeting, I collected information on what I believed to be the three major factors of consideration in the problem. First is location. Second is adequacy of accommodations. And third is cost. The following findings and evaluations form the basis of my recommendation.

THE LAMONT'S FAVORABLE DOWNTOWN LOCATION

The older of the two hotels, the Lamont is located in the heart of the downtown business district. Thus it is convenient to the area's two major department stores as well as the other downtown shops. The Blackwell, on the other hand, is approximately nine blocks from the major shopping area. Located in the periphery of the business and residential area, it provides little location advantage for those wanting to shop. It does, however, have shops within its walls that provide virtually all of the guest's normal needs. Because many members will bring spouses, however, the downtown location does give the Lamont an advantage.

FIGURE 9–2   *(concluded)*

Board of Directors   -2-   January 28, 19—

ADEQUATE ACCOMMODATIONS AT BOTH HOTELS

Both hotels can guarantee the 600 rooms we will require. As the Blackwell is new (since 1988), its rooms are more modern and therefore more appealing. The 69-year-old Lamont, however, is well preserved and comfortable. Its rooms are all in good repair, and the equipment is modern.

The Blackwell has 11 small meeting rooms and the Lamont has 13. All are adequate for our purposes. Both hotels can provide the 10 we need. For our general assembly meeting, the Lamont would make available its Capri Ballroom, which can easily seat our membership. It would also serve as the site of our inaugural dinner. The assembly facilities at the Blackwell appear to be somewhat crowded, although the management assures me that it can hold 600. Pillars in the room, however, would make some seats undersirable. In spite of the limitations mentioned, both hotels appear to have adequate facilities for our meeting.

LOWER COSTS AT THE LAMONT

Both the Lamont and the Blackwell would provide nine rooms for meetings on a complimentary basis. Both would provide complimentary suites for our president and our secretary. The Lamont, however, would charge $400 for use of the room for the assembly meeting. The Blackwell would provide this room without charge.

Convention rates at the Lamont are $55–$65 for singles, $65–$75 for double-bedded rooms, and $68–$80 for twin-bedded rooms. Comparable rates at the Blackwell are $65–$75, $75–$85, and $80–$95. Thus the savings at the Lamont would be approximately 15% per member.

Cost of the dinner selected would be $16.00 per person, including gratuities, at the Lamont. The Blackwell would meet this price if we would guarantee 600 plates. Otherwise, they would charge $18. Considering all of these figures, the total cost picture at the Lamont is the more favorable one.

Respectfully,

Willard K. Mitchell

Willard K. Mitchell
Executive Secretary

FIGURE 9–3   **Illustration of a progress report in memorandum form**

MEMORANDUM

THE **M**URCHISON **C**O. **I**NC.

July 21, 19—

TO: William T. Chysler
           Director of Sales

FROM: James C. Calvin, Manager   _gcc_
           Millville Sales District

SUBJECT: Quarterly Report for Millville Sales District

SUMMARY HIGHLIGHTS

After three months of operation I have secured office facilities, hired and developed
three salespeople, and cultivated about half the customers available in the Millville
Sales District. Although the district is not yet showing a profit, at the current rate of
development it will do so this month. Prospects for the district are unusually bright.

OFFICE OPERATION

In April I opened the Millville Sales District as authorized by action of the Board of
Directors last February 7th. Initially I set up office in the Three Coins Inn, a motel on
the outskirts of town, and remained there three weeks while looking for permanent
quarters. These I found in the Wingate Building, a downtown office structure. The
office suite selected rents for $940 per month. It has four executive offices, each
opening into a single secretarial office, which is large enough for two secretaries.
Although this arrangement is adequate for the staff now anticipated, additional
space is available in the building if needed.

PERSONNEL

In the first week of operation, I hired an office secretary, Ms. Catherine Kruch. Ms.
Kruch has good experience and has excellent credentials. She has proved to be very
effective. In early April I hired two salespeople—Mr. Charles E. Clark and Ms. Alice
E. Knapper. Both were experienced in sales, although neither had worked in apparel
sales. Three weeks later I hired Mr. Otto Strelski, a proven salesperson whom I
managed to attract from the Hammond Company. I am still searching for someone
for the fourth subdistrict. Currently I am investigating two good prospects and hope
to hire one of them within the next week.

FIGURE 9–3   *(concluded)*

William T. Chysler   2   July 21, 19—

PERFORMANCE

After brief training sessions, which I conducted personally, the salespeople were assigned the territories previously marked. And they were instructed to call on the accounts listed on the sheets supplied by Mr. Henderson's office. During the first month Knapper's sales totaled $17,431 and Clark's reached $13,490, for a total of $30,921. With three salespeople working the next month, total sales reached $121,605. Of the total, Knapper accounted for $37,345, Clark $31,690, and Strelski $52,570. Although these monthly totals are below the $145,000 break-even point for the three subdistricts, current progress indicates that we will exceed this volume this month. As we have made contact with only about one half of the prospects in the area, the potential for the district appears to be unusually good.

FIGURE 9–4   Illustration of a technical memorandum report

MEMORANDUM   the **Crowell Company, inc.**

TO: Charles E. Groom   *ESP*   June 3, 19—

FROM: Edmund S. Posner

SUBJECT: Graff Lining Company's use of Kynar pipe lining

Following is the report you requested January 9 on the Graff Lining Company's process of using Kynar for lining pipe. My comments are based on my inspection of the facilities at the Graff plant and my conversations with their engineers.

Dimension limitations

Graff's ability to line the smaller pipe sizes appears to be limited. To date, the smallest diameter pipe they have lined in 10-foot spool lengths is 2 inches. They believe they can handle $1\frac{1}{2}$-inch pipe in 10-foot spools, but they have not attempted this size. They question their ability to handle smaller pipe in 10-foot lengths.

This limitation, however, does not apply to fittings. They can line $1\frac{1}{2}$-inch and 1-inch fittings easily. Although they can handle smaller sizes than these, they prefer to limit minimum nipple size to 1 inch by 4 inches long.

Maximum spool dimensions for the coating process are best explained by illustration:

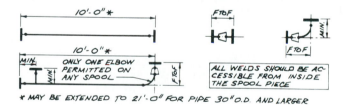

* MAY BE EXTENDED TO 21'-0" FOR PIPE 30" O.D. AND LARGER

FIGURE 9-4   (continued)

Graff corrects defects found. If the defect is small, they correct by retouching with sprayer or brush. If the defect is major, they remove all the coating by turning and reline the pipe.

<u>Recommendations for piping</u>

Should we be interested in using their services, Graff engineers made the following recommendations. First, they recommend that we use forged steel fittings rather than cast fittings. Cast fittings, they point out, have excessive porosity. They noted, though, that cast fittings can be used and are less expensive. For large jobs, this factor could be significant.

Second, they suggest that we make all small connections, such as those required for instruments, in a prescribed manner. This manner is best described by diagram:

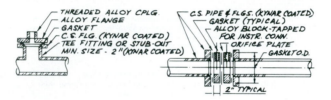

Graff engineers emphasized this point further by illustrating a common form of small connections that will not work. Such connections are most difficult to coat. Pinhole breaks are likely to occur on them, and a pinhole break can cause the entire coating to disbond. A typical unacceptable connection is the following:

FIGURE 9–4   *(continued)*

Charles E. Groom   3   June 3, 19—

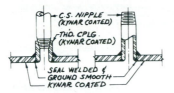

Preparation of pipe for lining

Graff requires that all pipe to be lined be ready for the coating process. Specifically, they require that all welds be ground smooth (to avoid pitting and assure penetration). Because welds are inaccessible in small pipe, they require forged tees in all piping smaller than 4 inches. In addition, they require that all attachments to the pipe (clips, base ells, etc.) be welded to the pipe prior to coating.

The lining procedure

The procedure Graff uses in lining the pipe begins with cleaning the pipe and inspecting it for cracked fittings, bad welds, etc. When necessary, they do minor retouching and grinding of welds. Then they apply the Kynar in three forms: primer, building, sealer. They apply the building coat in as many layers as is necessary to obtain a finished thickness of 25 mils. They oven bake each coat at a temperature and for a time determined by the phase of the coating and the piping material.

Inspection technique

Following the coating, Graff inspectors use a spark testing method to detect possible pinholes or other defects. This method is best explained by illustration:

FIGURE 9–4 *(concluded)*

Charles E. Groom   4   June 3, 19—

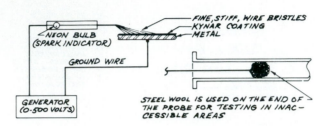

A third recommendation is that we establish handling procedures to protect the coated pipe. As the Kynar coating will chip, we would need to make certain that we protect all flange spaces. Also, we would need to be careful in shipping, handling, storing, and erecting the pipe.

FIGURE 9–5   Illustration of a short proposal

MEMORANDUM

TO: Helen S. Hobson   DATE: May 19, 19—

FROM: Ross H. Jefferson *RHJ*

SUBJECT: Sponsored membership in the Association for Business
Communication

As you requested May 17, following is my proposal for Stoner to sponsor
my membership in the Association for Business Communication (ABC).

Description of ABC

The primary professional organization in business communication, ABC is
dedicated to keeping its members informed of the latest developments in
business communication practice and theory. It informs its members through
two quarterly publications: The Journal of Business Communication
(research and theory) and The ABC Bulletin (practice). In addition, the
Association holds an annual meeting as well as regional meetings
throughout the United States and Canada. Papers presented at these
meetings cover both the current theoretical and practical topics in business
communication.

Founded in 1936, ABC now has 2,258 members, including 939 institutions. Of the individual memberships, most (1,043) are academics from the
United States and Canada. But 103 are business professionals. Companies
represented include IBM, AT&T, Exxon, Imperial Oil, State Farm Insurance,
McDonnell Douglas, and Aetna Insurance. In addition, 124 members are
from countries outside North America. ABC's diverse membership provides
an effective exchange of experience and knowledge.

Benefits of Membership

Membership in ABC would benefit Stoner as well as me personally. The
meetings and the publications would enable me to bring the latest
communication knowledge to my editorial work. ABC would be especially
helpful in my assignments involving teaching communication to our
employees, for much of its emphasis is on teaching techniques. Also,
membership in ABC would enhance Stoner's image. ABC is a prestigious
organization, and its membership includes the corporate elite. In addition,
meeting with the members of other companies and exchanging ideas would
help me do a better job of directing Stoner's communication activities.

FIGURE 9-5 *(concluded)*

Helen S. Hobson   2   May 19, 19—

Costs of Membership

ABC annual dues are $40, which includes subscriptions to the Journal and the Bulletin. The costs of attending the meetings would vary with the meeting sites. For this year, the approximate costs for the international meeting in San Diego would be $700 (registration, $80; transportation, $330; hotel, $180; meals, $90; miscellaneous, $20). For the regional meeting in Houston it would be $570 (registration, $70; transportation, $150; hotel, $200; meals, $120; miscellaneous, $30). The total cost for this year would be $1,310.

Recommended Action

Based on the preceding information, I believe that membership in ABC offers us benefits well worth the cost. Thus, I recommend that Stoner sponsor my membership on a one-year trial basis. At the end of this year, I would review actual benefits received and recommend whether or not to continue membership.

FIGURE 9–6   Military form of staff study report

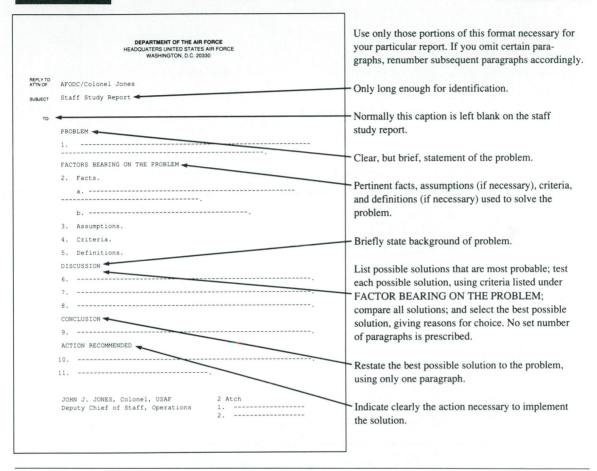

DEPARTMENT OF THE AIR FORCE
HEADQUATERS UNITED STATES AIR FORCE
WASHINGTON, D.C. 20330

REPLY TO
ATTN OF: AFODC/Colonel Jones

SUBJECT: Staff Study Report ◄

TO: ◄

PROBLEM ◄

1.   --
---.

FACTORS BEARING ON THE PROBLEM ◄

2.   Facts.
      a. ---
-----------------------------------.
      b. ---------------------------------------.

3.   Assumptions.

4.   Criteria.

5.   Definitions.

DISCUSSION ◄

6.   --.

7.   --.

8.   --.

CONCLUSION ◄

9.   --.

ACTION RECOMMENDED ◄

10.   --.

11.   -------------------------------.

JOHN J. JONES, Colonel, USAF   2 Atch
Deputy Chief of Staff, Operations   1. ------------------
                                     2. ------------------

Use only those portions of this format necessary for your particular report. If you omit certain paragraphs, renumber subsequent paragraphs accordingly.

Only long enough for identification.

Normally this caption is left blank on the staff study report.

Clear, but brief, statement of the problem.

Pertinent facts, assumptions (if necessary), criteria, and definitions (if necessary) used to solve the problem.

Briefly state background of problem.

List possible solutions that are most probable; test each possible solution, using criteria listed under FACTOR BEARING ON THE PROBLEM; compare all solutions; and select the best possible solution, giving reasons for choice. No set number of paragraphs is prescribed.

Restate the best possible solution to the problem, using only one paragraph.

Indicate clearly the action necessary to implement the solution.

FIGURE 9–7   Illustration of a long-form audit report

TO: William A. Karnes   DATE: May 3, 19—

FROM: Auditing Department

SUBJECT: Annual Audit, Spring Street Branch

Introduction

Following is the report on the annual audit of the Spring Street branch. Reflecting conditions existing at the close of business May 1, 19—, this review covers all accounts other than Loans and Discounts. Specifically, these accounts were proofed:

Accounts Receivable	Savings
Cash Collateral	Suspense
Cash in Office	Series "E" Bonds
Collections	Tax Withheld
Christmas Club	Travelers Checks
Deferred Charges	

Condition of Accounts

All listing totals agreed with General Ledger and/or Branch Controls except for these:

Cash in Office . . . . $1.17 short
Tax Withheld . . . .   .21 short
Travelers Checks . . . .   .97 short

Exceptions Noted

During the course of the examination the following exceptions were found:

Analysis. The branch had 163 unprofitable accounts at the time of the audit. Losses on these accounts, as revealed by inspection of the Depositors Analysis Cards, ranged from $7.31 to $176.36 for the year. The average loss per account was $17.21.

Proper deductions of service charges were not made in 73 instances in which the accounts dropped below the minimum.

Bookkeeping. From a review of the regular checking accounts names were recorded of customers who habitually write checks without sufficient covering funds. A list of 39 of the worst offenders was submitted to Mr. Clement Ferguson.

FIGURE 9–7   *(continued)*

A check of deposit tickets to the third and fourth regular checking ledgers revealed six accounts on which transit delays recorded on the deposit tickets were not correctly transferred to the ledger sheets.

During the preceding month on 17 different accounts the bookkeepers paid items against uncollected funds without getting proper approval.

Statements. Five statements were held by the branch in excess of three months:

Account	Statement Dates
Curtis A Hogan	Sept. through April
Carlton I. Breeding	Dec. through April
Alice Crezan	Nov. through April
Jarvis H. Hudson	Jan. through April
W.T. Petersen	Dec. through April

Paying and Receiving. During the week of April 21–27, tellers failed to itemize currency denominations on large (over $100) cash deposits 23 times. Deposits were figured in error 32 times.

Savings. Contrary to instructions given after the last audit, the control clerk has not maintained a record of errors made in savings passbooks.

The savings tellers have easy access to the inactive ledger cards and may record transactions on the cards while alone. When this condition was noted in the last report, the recommendation was made to set up a system of dual controls. This recommendation has not been followed.

Safe Deposit Rentals. Rentals on 165 safe deposit boxes were in arrears. Although it was pointed out in the last report, this condition has grown worse during the past year. Numbers of boxes by years in arrears are as follows:

2 to 3 years	87
3 to 4 years	32
4 to 5 years	29
over 5 years	17
Total	165

Stop payments. Signed stop payment orders were not received on three checks on which payment was stopped:

Account	Amount	Date of Stop Payment
Whelon Electric Company	$317.45	Feb. 7, 19--
George A. Bullock	37.50	April 1, 19--
Amos H. Kritzel	737.60	Dec. 3, 19--

FIGURE 9–7   *(concluded)*

<u>Over and Short Account</u>. A $23.72 difference between Tellers and Rock Department
was recorded for April 22. On May 1 this difference remained uncorrected.

William P. Bunting

William P. Bunting
Head, Auditing Department

Copies to:

W.F. Robertson
Cecil Ruston
W.W. Merrett

Writing the Report

PART 4

Techniques of Readable Writing

Your research and applications must be communicated effectively.

Of all the tasks you must perform as a report writer, communicating the report story to those who should receive it is the most critical. Regardless of how well you work on other parts of the report, unless you communicate the results of your efforts, you will fail in your objective. And communicating is not easy.

THE FUNDAMENTAL NEED FOR ADAPTATION

For writing to be clear, it must be adapted to the reader.

Study of the communication process (see Chapter 2) reveals that communication is not a precise activity. Some degree of miscommunication is the rule rather than the exception. Also, communication involves fitting the message to the audience—that is, using words and concepts the audience knows and understands. This approach to communication is called *adaptation*. It is a fundamental concept that should govern your use of all the writing suggestions offered in the following pages.

Begin by visualizing your reader.

The first step in adapting your own writing is to visualize your readers. Determine such things as who your readers are, how much they know about the subject, what educational levels they have achieved, and how they think. With these images of your readers in mind, tailor every aspect of your writing—especially vocabulary, sentence structure, tone, and style—to fit the audience.

For a readership with mixed knowledge and abilities, write so the lower levels can understand and the higher levels can maintain interest.

Your task is relatively simple when you are writing to a single reader or a homogeneous group of readers. But what if you are writing to a group with varying characteristics? What if, say, your audience is comprised of people ranging from college graduates to grade school graduates? The obvious answer is to aim at the lowest level of the group; they must not be excluded. But at the same time, it makes sense to present your work in a manner that will maintain the interest of the higher levels, too. Simple, even elementary writing can—and should—have broad reader appeal.

If you are better educated or better informed on the subject area than your readers are, adaptation does mean simplification. A company executive writing to rank-and-file employees, for example, must write in the everyday words the employees understand. Likewise, a technician writing to a nontechnical audience has to simplify the vernacular other technicians would understand and expect. An unadapted technical report would be virtually incomprehensible to a lay audience. As the following examples show, few technical writers were better aware of this fundamental rule than the late Dr. Albert Einstein. In writing on a technical subject to a nontechnical audience, he skillfully adapted his language and approach:

> What takes place can be illustrated with the help of our rich man. The atom M is a rich miser who, during his life, gives away no money (energy). But in his will, he bequeaths his fortune to his sons M′ and M″, on condition that they give to the community a small amount, less than one thousandth of the whole estate (energy or mass). The sons together have somewhat less than the father had (the mass sum M′ and M″ is somewhat smaller than the mass M of the radioactive atom). But the part given to the community, though relatively small, is still so enormously large (considered as kinetic energy) that it brings with it a great threat of evil. Averting that threat has become the most urgent problem of our time.[1]

But when writing to fellow scientists, he wrote in words they understood and expected:

> The general theory of relativity owes its existence in the first place to the empirical fact of the numerical equality of the inertial and gravitational mass of bodies, for which fundamental fact classical mechanics provided no interpretation. Such an interpretation is arrived at by an extension of the principle of relativity to co-ordinate systems accelerated relatively to one another. The introduction of co-ordinate systems relative to inertial systems involves the appearance of gravitational fields relative to the latter. As a result of this, the general theory of relativity, which is based on the equality of inertia and weight, provides a theory of the gravitational field.[2]

Also illustrating this fundamental principle of adaptation are the financial sections of the annual reports of some of our major corporations. In attempting to communicate the financial information, some companies see their stockholders as being uninformed on matters of finance. Perhaps they see their rank-and-file readers as people who have had no business experience. Their communication might read like this:

> Last year, your company's total sales were $117,400,000, which was slightly higher than the $109,800,000 total for the year before. After deducting for all expenses, we had $4,593,000 left over for profits, compared with $2,830,000 for 1993. Because of these increased profits, we were able to increase your annual dividend payments per share from the 50 cents paid over the last 10 years.

Some companies visualize their stockholders in an entirely different light. They see them as being well informed in the language of finance. Perhaps they misjudge their readers, or maybe they fail to consider their readers' knowledge. In any event, these companies present their financial information in a somewhat technical and sophisticated manner, as illustrated by this example:

> The corporation's investments and advances in three unconsolidated subsidiaries (all in the development stage) and in 50 percent owned companies was $42,200,000 on

---

[1] Albert Einstein, *Out of My Later Years*, New York: Philosophical Library, Inc., 1950, 53.

[2] Albert Einstein, *Essays in Science*, New York: Philosophical Library, Inc., 1934, 50.

December 31, 1993; and the excess of the investments in certain companies over net asset value at dates of acquisition was $1,760,000. The corporation's equity in the net assets as of December 31, 1993, was $41,800,000 and in the results of operations for the year ended December 31, 1993 and 1992, was $1,350,000 and $887,500. Dividend income was $750,000 and $388,000 for the years 1993 and 1992, respectively.

Adaptation underlies all that will be said about communicating.

The preceding discussion shows that adaptation is basic to communication—so basic, in fact, that you will need to refer to it as you study the writing instructions in the pages ahead. For example, much of what we say about writing technique will stress simplicity—using simple words, short sentences, and brief paragraphs. You will need to think of simplicity in terms of adaptation. Specifically, you will need to keep in mind that what is simple for one person may not be simple for another. Only if you keep in mind the logical use of adaptation will you fully understand the intended meaning of this instruction.

SUPPORT OF THE READABILITY STUDIES

Readability is determined primarily by word choice and sentence length. But paragraph length can be a factor, too.

Readability studies conducted over past years (see Chapter 2) strongly support the need for adaptation. They show conclusively that writing that communicates is writing that fits the reading ability of the reader. More precisely, these studies show that readability of writing is determined mainly by two major factors. One is word choice. The other is sentence length. We will review these two factors in the following section and include yet a third factor, paragraphing. Although not so directly addressed by the readability studies, paragraphing also affects how readable a report will be.

Do not apply writing techniques mechanically. Use good judgment.

As you consider these three techniques, remember that you should not apply them mechanically. Writing, as we have stressed so often in this text, is not routine work to be done by the numbers, rules, or formulas. It is better approached as an art. In all forms of art, mastery of techniques is a prerequisite to good performance. The art of writing requires you not only to master the techniques, but to apply them with good judgment as well.

WORD SELECTION

Selecting the right words is a part of adaptation.

In general, your task as a writer is to produce in your reader's mind the meanings you have formulated in your mind. You do this mostly through words. Thus, your task as a writer is largely one of selecting words that relate your intended meanings as precisely as possible.

The very nature of words, however, makes this task difficult. Just look at an unabridged dictionary to see what a challenge finding exact wording can be. The difficulty is intensified by the complexity of word meanings. Words are at best inexact symbols of meanings. A single word may have a dozen dictionary definitions. In fact, it is said that the 500 most commonly used English words have a total of 14,000 dictionary definitions. Then there are the countless shades of differences in meanings words acquire in use. And if that were not confusing enough, words are frequently used inexactly; and those meanings have to be sorted out from the confusing array of denotations and connotations as well.

These difficulties are identified not to discourage you, but to impress upon you how important it is to make your best efforts to overcome them. Some specific suggestions follow.

☐   SELECT WORDS THE READER UNDERSTANDS

Use words that mean the same to your reader as they do to you.

To write to communicate, you must use words that mean the same to your reader as they do to you. In business, this requirement frequently translates to simplifying your writing. That does not mean using a primer style; and it certainly does not mean being condescending to your readers. What the requirement does demand is that you write in words your readers expect and understand. Find common ground of meaning among the varied options and define carefully any difficult or confusing terms. This advice is as sound for a technician writing for a technical audience as it is for an astronaut writing for grade school students.

Some degree of simplification is the key to quick and correct communications. Readability studies support simplified writing (see Chapter 2). They show conclusively that writing communicates best when it is slightly below the comprehension level of the reader. Specifically, they show that simplification is achieved through a general preference for the familiar over the unfamiliar, for the short over the long, and for the nontechnical over the technical word. Although these distinctions between words overlap considerably, they are worth discussing separately for reasons of emphasis.

Strong, vigorous words will improve your reader's understanding of and confidence in your writing.

USE STRONG, VIGOROUS WORDS   Like people, words have personality. Some words are strong and vigorous; some are dull and weak; and others fall between these extremes. If you aspire to be an effective writer, you should be constantly aware of these differences. Become a student of words and select your vocabulary to produce just the right effect. *Tycoon*, for example, is a more forceful description of someone who has made it in business than *eminently successful business executive. Bear market* makes a point about what is happening on the stock exchange more emphatically than *generally declining market.* And *boom* gives a stronger impression of an improvement in the economy than *period of business prosperity.* Skilled writers make strong words predominate. Vigorous words will move readers through difficult writing quickly and smoothly, leave them with a clear understanding of what the point is, and inspire a confidence in your judgment and authority.

The verb is the strongest form of speech, followed by the noun.

Of all the forms of speech, the verb is the strongest, followed by the noun. The verb is the action word, and action by its very nature commands interest. Nouns, of course, are the doers of action—the characters in the story, so to speak. As doers of action, they also attract the reader's attention.

Contrary to what many novice writers think, adjectives and adverbs should be used sparingly. These words add length to the sentence, distracting the reader's attention from the key nouns and verbs. As Voltaire phrased it, "The adjective is the enemy of the noun." Furthermore, modifiers, as these words are called, introduce subjectivity into evaluations and qualify definitive statements. Therefore, in writing that requires objectivity and authority, as report writing does, they should be kept to a minimum.

PREFER THE FAMILIAR TO THE UNFAMILIAR WORD   As a general rule, the familiar everyday words are the best to use in report writing. Of course, what is everyday usage to you may be high-level talk to others. Thus, the suggestion to use familiar language is really an application of the principle of adapting your writing to your reader.

> Familiar words communicate more effectively than unfamiliar words do.
>
> Avoid words that make your writing appear stuffy and pompous.

Unfortunately, many business writers resist this simple advice. They seem to believe that everyday language is not "important" enough. Rather than writing naturally, they write stiffly and pompously. For example, they use the word *endeavor* rather than *try*. They do not *find out;* they *ascertain*. They *terminate* rather than *end;* they *utilize* instead of *use*. And so on. Using large, unfamiliar words is not the way to impress your readers.

> Use the same vocabulary you would use if you were conversing with your reader.

There is nothing wrong with using hard words when they are appropriate to the subject and the audience. Perhaps your best advice is to use the vocabulary you would use in face-to-face discussion of the report content with your intended reader. Another good rule of thumb is to use the simplest words that carry the thought without insulting your reader's ability to understand the topic.

The communication advantage of familiar words over the formal, complex ones is obvious in the following contrasting examples.

Formal and Complex	**Familiar Words**
The conclusion ascertained from a perusal of the pertinent data is that a lucrative market exists for the product.	The data studied show that the product is in good demand.
The antiquated mechanisms were utilized for the experimentation.	The old machines were used for the test.
Company operations for the preceding accounting period terminated with a substantial deficit.	The company lost much money last year.

> Generally, short words communicate more effectively than long. There are exceptions, however.

PREFER THE SHORT TO THE LONG WORD   Short words tend to communicate better than long words. Certainly, there are exceptions. Some long words like *hypnotize, hippopotamus,* and *automobile* generally are well known; some short words like *verd, vie, id,* and *gybe* are understood only by a few. On the whole, however, there is a clear correlation between word length and word difficulty. Also, the heavier the proportion of long words to short words, the harder the writing is to understand. This is true even when the reader understands the long words. As readability studies clearly show, a heavy proportion of long words slows the reading and makes understanding difficult. Thus, when you are writing your report, use long words with caution. Make certain the long words you do use are well known to your readers. And even if they are, keep them in proportion; they should not dominate the text.

The following contrasting sentences clearly show the effect of long words on writing clarity. Educated readers are likely to understand long words, but the high proportion of long words makes for heavy reading. Without question, the simple versions communicate better.

Heavy or Long Words	Short and Simple Words
A decision was *predicated* on the *assumption* that an *abundance of monetary funds was forthcoming.*	The decision was *based* on the *belief* that there would be *more money.*
They *acceded* to *the proposition* to *terminate* business.	They *agreed* to *quit* business.
During the preceding year the company *operated at a financial deficit.*	*Last year* the company *lost money.*
Prior to accelerating productive operation, the foreman inspected the machinery.	*Before speeding up production,* the foreman inspected the machinery.
Definitive action was *effected subsequent to* the reporting date.	*Final* action was *made after* the reporting date.

USE SPECIALIZED WORDS WITH CAUTION   Every field has its own specialized language. If you are in the field, much of that language is a part of your everyday working vocabulary. Certainly, it is logical to use jargon when you are writing to others in your field. Even so, overusing specialized words can make reading difficult. Frequently, jargon is made up of long and high-sounding words, which, when used heavily, dull the writing and make the message hard to understand. The difficulty seems to increase as the proportion of technical words increases. The following sentence written by a physician illustrates this point:

> It is a methodology error to attempt to interpret psychologically an organic symptom, which is the end-result of an intermediary change of organic processes, instead of trying to understand these vegetative nervous impulses in their relation to psychological factors, which introduce a change of organic events resulting in an organic disturbance.

No doubt the length of this sentence contributes to its difficulty, but the heavy proportion of technical terms does not help. The conclusion that may be drawn here is obvious. Writers in a specialized field may use specialized terms in writing to others in the field, but they should use such words in moderation.

In writing to those outside of the field, specialists must use the language of the lay readers. Physicians might well refer to a *cerebral vascular accident* in writing to fellow physicians, but *stroke* is what nonmedical readers will understand. Accountants who write to nonaccountants might want to consider the appropriateness of terminology like *accounts receivable, liability,* and *surplus.* Though such expressions are elementary in accountancy, the general public may have little idea what they mean. But substitute *how much is owed the company, how much the company owes,* and *how much was left over,* and the general public will understand completely.

One last point about jargon. Some writers use specialized terms, like unfamiliar language, to make their writing sound "important." Jargon, they believe, identifies them with the sophistication of a specialized area of knowledge or influence and thus makes what they say sound sophisticated and important as well. Using specialized

All fields have specialized terms that are useful for communicating with others in the field.

If you are writing to a lay audience about a specialized area, make appropriate adjustments in your vocabulary.

Never try to impress your reader with jargon.

language in this way does impress the reader, but certainly not the way the writer intends.

□   BRING THE WRITING TO LIFE WITH WORDS

Lively writing keeps the reader's attention.

To communicate effectively, you must keep your reader's undivided attention. What you are writing about will, of course, have a great deal to do with how well you succeed. But a lively topic is certainly no guarantee of success. Dull writing can cause a reader to lose interest no matter what the subject is.

How to bring your writing to life and make it interesting is one of the greatest challenges in writing. Whole texts have been written on the topic, and the most effective writers are those who never abandon their personal efforts to meet that challenge. However, even if you are a novice report writer, you can enliven your writing considerably by using concrete words, emphasizing action, and employing simple grammatical constructions. We will review these techniques one at a time.

Concrete words are specific words.

USE CONCRETE WORDS   Concrete words are simple words that describe sensual experience, cite specifics, and otherwise create vivid, detailed images in the minds of the readers. They are the opposite of abstract words, which describe intangible experience, cite theories, phenomena, and other nonspecifics, and evoke only vague impressions. Concrete words have a direct appeal to the readers; abstract words have an indirect appeal. Concrete words hold the readers' interest because they relate directly to the readers' experience and the readers can understand them readily. Abstract words discourage readers' interest because they require considerable intellectual effort with no guarantee of complete or correct understanding.

We could go on with the contrast, but the point should already be clear: for reasons of speed, clarity, certainty, and ease, readers prefer the concrete. So, if you want your report to attract and keep readers' attention, favor concrete words in your writing. It is as simple as that.

Concreteness means simplicity.

To a large extent, concrete words are the short, familiar words previously discussed. The readers know what these words mean because the words are familiar and their meanings are both simple and precise. For example, this sentence is filled with long, unfamiliar words:

The magnitude of the increment of profits was the predominant motivating factor in the decision to expand merchandise options.

Written in shorter and more familiar words, the idea becomes more concrete:

We decided to try out new lines because we made so much money last year.

It means exactness, too.

But concreteness involves more than simplicity. Some very simple expressions can be abstract. For example, a chemist writing up the results of an experiment might refer to a *nauseous odor*. The word choice here is not difficult to comprehend, but what, really, does it tell the reader? Certainly not as much as does reporting the substance *smelled like decaying fish*. Most readers can vividly imagine the odor, and some may actually express their revulsion by making faces as they read.

One of the best-known examples of concreteness is in the advertising claim that Ivory soap is "99.44 percent pure." Had the advertisement used abstract words such as "Ivory is very pure," few customers would have been impressed. But the company used specific words, and millions took notice. Similar differences in abstract and concrete expressions are evident in the following.

Abstract	Concrete
A sizable profit	A 22 percent profit
Good accuracy	Pinpoint accuracy
The leading student	Top student in a class of 90
The majority	53 percent
In the near future	By Thursday noon
A work-saving machine	Does the work of seven people
Easy to steer	Quick steering
Light in weight	Featherlight

PREFER ACTIVE TO PASSIVE VERBS   Of all the parts of speech, verbs are the strongest. And verbs are at their strongest when they are in the active voice. Thus, if you want the best in vigorous and lively writing, make extensive use of active-voice verbs.

In active voice, the subject does the action. In passive voice, it receives the action.

Active-voice verbs show their subject doing the action. They contrast with the verbs in the passive form, which show subjects being acted upon. The following sentences illustrate the distinction.

Active.   The auditors inspected the books.

Passive.   The books were inspected by the auditors.

The first example clearly is the stronger, because it is the simpler and the more direct. The doers of the action act, and their verb is short and clear; they also occupy the most emphatic place in the sentence. In the second example, however, the helping verb *were* dulls the verb, and the doers are relegated to a prepositional phrase at the end of the sentence. The following sentences give additional proof of the superior effectiveness of the active voice.

Passive	Active
The new process *is believed* to be superior by the investigators.	Investigators *believe* the new process is superior.
The policy *was enforced* by the committee.	The committee *enforced* the policy.
The office *will be inspected* by Mr. Hall.	Mr. Hall *will inspect* the office.
A gain of 30.1 percent *was recorded* for soft-line sales.	Soft-line sales *gained* 30.1 percent.
It *is desired* by this office that this problem *be brought* before the board.	This office *desires* that the secretary *bring* this problem before the board.
A complete reorganization of the administration *was effected* by the president.	The president completely *reorganized* the administration.

Passive voice does have its place, however. It gives you a way to vary sentence structure and to shift emphasis.

In no way should you interpret this emphasis on active voice to mean that passive voice should be eliminated or that it is incorrect. It certainly is grammatically correct. It provides an opportunity to vary sentence structure; and it offers another option for expressing ideas in the third-person style. Most important, it permits you to shift emphasis from the doer to the object of the action, and, if you eliminate the prepositional phrase, to omit any reference to the doer at all. Therefore, there are times when passive voice is actually preferable to active.

Consider the following examples, where the identification of the performer is unimportant, and the emphasis is properly on the object of the action.

Advertising is often criticized for its effect on prices.

Petroleum is refined in Texas.

In the following examples, the performer is unknown; passive voice is again appropriate.

The equipment has been sabotaged seven times during the past year.

Anonymous complaints have been received.

In the next sentences, the writer prefers not to name the doer.

The surveillance was conducted over a period of two weeks.

The funds were restored before the end of the month.

In these last two illustrations, the writer identifies the doer but downplays the doer's role in the event.

Responsibility for the miscalculations has been assumed by the financial officer.

The position was refused by the candidate who was our first choice.

Know when and how to use passive voice effectively.

The passive voice is only a problem when writers use it indiscriminately. Writers who use the indirect way of expressing an action when the direct way would be much clearer and more interesting are, for the most part, ill-advised as to the true function of passive voice. They lose their readers by forcing them to find their way through unnecessarily convoluted expressions. Such writing also suggests that the writer is reluctant to make the kind of emphatic statements that result from active voice. If a writer is not committed to what he or she says, why should a reader be interested?

Avoid camouflaged verbs. You camouflage a verb by changing it to a noun form and then adding action words.

AVOID OVERUSE OF CAMOUFLAGED VERBS Closely related to the problem of overusing abstract words and passive voice is the problem of using camouflaged verbs. A verb is camouflaged—or hidden—when it appears in the sentence as an abstract noun rather than an active-voice verb. For example, in the sentence, "Elimination of the excess material was effected by the crew," the noun *elimination* is developed from the verb *eliminate*. Although there is nothing intrinsically wrong with nouns made from verbs, in this case, the noun inappropriately has the most emphatic place in the sentence. A more effective phrasing uses the pure verb form: "The crew eliminated the excess material." Likewise, it is stronger to *cancel* than to *indicate a cancellation,* to *consider* than to *give consideration to,* and to *appraise* than to *make an appraisal.* Here are additional illustrations of the point.

Camouflaged Verbs	Clear Verb Form
Amortization of the account was effected by the staff.	The staff amortized the account.
Control of the water was not possible.	They could not control the water.
The new policy involved the standardization of the procedures.	The new policy involved standardizing the procedures.
Application of the mixture was accomplished.	They applied the mixture.

From these illustrations and those of the discussion of passive voice come two helpful writing rules: (1) where appropriate, write of people doing things, not of things being done and (2) express that action directly. Write so that your readers will be able to visualize the activity and either identify with it or react to it. Consider the following versions of the same event:

> The committee unanimously approved the merger.
>
> The committee gave its unanimous approval to the merger.
>
> The merger was approved unanimously by the committee.

In the first version, the readers can almost see the voting process. The action is clear and emphatic. That emphasis is lost, and the mental image blurred, with each ensuing rendition.

☐   SELECT WORDS FOR PRECISE COMMUNICATION

Effective writing requires a thorough knowledge of language.

If you are going to write clearly, you will obviously have to have some mastery of language—enough at least to enable you to convey your meaning precisely. Unfortunately, it is all too easy to take knowledge of language for granted. Selecting words mechanically, using them without thinking of what they are really communicating, or even using words without knowing what they mean—these problems all result from presuming the content of your report will more or less speak for itself. Be assured it will not. If you do not give careful attention to language, even your most insightful comments will seem fuzzy.

Become a student of words. Study language and learn shades of difference in meanings of similar words.

Thus, to be a good writer, you must become a student of words. Learn precise meanings of words. Learn, too, the shading of meanings of words or of groups of words. For example, be aware that *fewer* refers to numbers of items and individuals and that *less* refers to amount, value, or degree. (It is *fewer absentees,* but *less absenteeism; fewer customers,* but *less demand.*) Be aware also of words that identify absolutes—like *unique, full,* or *perfect*—and cannot use traditional comparatives. Something cannot be more unique, less full, or most perfect. But something can be described as more nearly unique, less nearly full, or most nearly perfect. This sort of precision in the use of language suggests to your reader you have taken equal care in the preparation of all other areas of the report.

By the same token, be aware of the connotation of words. Though they share similar dictionary definitions, the words *secondhand, used, recycled,* and *antique* suggest very different meanings to your reader. *Slender* implies an attribute quite different from *skinny,* and *to claim* implies more to the reader than either *to report* or *to say* does.

Use correct idiom. Idiom is the way in which ideas are expressed in a language. There is little reason to some idioms, but violations will offend the reader.

In your effort to be a precise writer, you need to use the correct idiom. By *idiom* we mean the way we say things in our language. Much of our idiom has little rhyme or reason. But if we want to be understood correctly, we should follow it. For example, what is the logic in the word *up* in this sentence: "Look up her name in the directory"? There really is none. This is just the wording we have developed to cover this meaning. It is correct idiomatic usage to say "independent of " and incorrect to say "independent from." But there is no real justification. Similarly, you "agree to" a proposal, but you "agree with" a person. You are "careful about" an affair, but you are "careful with" your money. So it is with these additional illustrations:

Faulty Idiom	Correct Idiom
authority about	authority on
comply to	comply with
enamored with	enamored of
equally as bad	equally bad
in accordance to	in accordance with
in search for	in search of
listen at	listen to
possessed with ability	possessed of ability
seldom or ever	seldom if ever
superior than	superior to

SUGGESTIONS FOR NONDISCRIMINATORY WRITING

Avoid words that discriminate against minorities and women.

Although discriminatory words are not directly related to writing clarity, our review of word selection would not be complete without some mention of them. By discriminatory words, we mean words that do not treat all people equally and with respect. More specifically, they are words that refer negatively to groups of people, especially minorities (racial, religious) and women. Such words run contrary to acceptable views of fair play and human decency. They have no place in business reports.

We often use discriminatory words without bad intent.

Many discriminatory words are a part of the vocabularies we have acquired from our environments. We often use them innocently, not realizing how they affect others. We can eliminate discriminatory words from our vocabularies by examining them carefully and placing ourselves in the shoes of those to whom they refer. The following review of the major forms of discriminatory words should help you achieve this goal.

☐   AVOID WORDS THAT STEREOTYPE BY RACE OR NATIONALITY

Words depicting minorities in a stereotyped way are unfair and untrue.

Words that stereotype all members of a group by race or nationality are especially unfair. Members of any minority vary widely in all characteristics. Thus, it is unfair to suggest that Jews are miserly, that Italians are Mafia members, that Hispanics are lazy, that blacks can do only menial jobs, and so on. Unfair references to minorities are sometimes subtle and not intended, as in this example: "We conducted the first marketing tests in the ghetto areas of the city. Using a sample of 200 black families, we. . . . " These words unfairly suggest that only blacks are ghetto dwellers.

Words that present members of minorities as exceptions to stereotypes are also unfair.

Also unfair are words suggesting that a minority member has struggled to achieve something that is taken for granted in the majority group. Usually well intended, words of this kind can carry subtle discriminatory messages. For example, a reference to a "neatly dressed Hispanic man" may suggest that he is an exception to the rule—that most Hispanics are not neatly dressed, but here is one who is. So can references to "a generous Jew," "an energetic Puerto Rican," "a hardworking black," and "a Chinese manager."

Eliminate such references to minorities by treating all people equally and by being sensitive to the effects of your words.

Eliminating unfair references to minority groups from your communication requires two basic steps. First, you must consciously treat all people equally, without regard to their minority status. You should refer to minority membership only in those rare cases in which it is a vital part of the message to be communicated. Second, you must be sensitive to the effects of your words. Specifically, you should ask yourself how those words would affect you if you were a member of the minorities to which they are addressed. You should evaluate your word choices from the viewpoints of others.

☐ AVOID SEXIST WORDS

Many words in our language suggest male dominance. Avoid using them.

Even more prevalent in today's business reports than words that discriminate against minorities are sexist words—words that discriminate against women. As you may know, many of the words used in English suggest male superiority. This condition is easily explained: Our language developed in a male-dominated society. For reasons of fair play, you would do well to avoid sexist words. Suggestions for avoiding some of the more troublesome sexist words follow.

Avoid using the masculine pronouns (he, him, his) for both sexes.

MASCULINE PRONOUNS FOR BOTH SEXES   Perhaps the most troublesome sexist words are the masculine pronouns (*he, his, him*) when they are used to refer to both sexes, as in this example: "The typical State University student eats *his* lunch at the cafeteria." Assuming that State is coeducational, the use of *his* suggests male supremacy. Historically, of course, the word *his* has been classified as generic—that is, it can refer to both sexes. But many businesspeople do not agree and are offended by the use of the masculine pronoun in such cases.

You can do this (1) by rewording the sentence;

You can avoid the use of masculine pronouns in such cases in three ways. First, you can reword the sentence to eliminate the offending word. Thus, the illustration above could be reworded as follows: "The typical State University student eats lunch at the cafeteria." Here are other examples:

Sexist	Nonsexist
If a customer pays promptly, *he* is placed on our preferred list.	A customer who pays promptly is placed on our preferred list.
When an unauthorized employee enters the security area, *he* is subject to dismissal.	An employee who enters the security area is subject to dismissal.
A supervisor is not responsible for such losses if *he* is not negligent.	A supervisor who is not negligent is not responsible for such losses.

Sexist	Nonsexist
When a customer needs service, it is *his* right to ask for it.	A customer who needs service has the right to ask for it.

(2) by making the reference plural;

A second way to avoid sexist use of the masculine pronoun is to make the reference plural. Fortunately, the English language has plural pronouns (*their, them, they*) that refer to both sexes. Making the references plural in the examples given above, we have these nonsexist revisions:

If customers pay promptly, *they* are placed on our preferred list.

When unauthorized employees enter the security area, *they* are subject to dismissal.

Supervisors are not responsible for such losses if *they* are not negligent.

When customers need service, *they* have the right to ask for it.

or (3) by substituting neutral expressions.

A third way to avoid sexist use of *he, his,* or *him* is to substitute any of a number of neutral pronouns. The most common are *he or she, he/she, s/he, you, one,* and *person.* Using neutral expressions in the problem sentences, we have these revisions:

If a customer pays promptly, *he or she* is placed on our preferred list.

When an unauthorized employee enters the security area, *he/she* is subject to dismissal.

A supervisor is not responsible for such losses if *s/he* is not negligent.

When service is needed, *one* has the right to ask for it.

Neutral expressions can be awkward; so use them with caution.

You should use such expressions with caution, however. They tend to be somewhat awkward, particularly if they are used often. For this reason, many skilled writers do not use some of them. If you use them, you should pay attention to their effect on the flow of your words. Certainly, you should avoid sentences like this one: "To make an employee feel he/she is doing well by complimenting her/him insincerely confuses her/him later when he/she sees his/her coworkers promoted ahead of him/her."

Avoid words suggesting male dominance.

WORDS DERIVED FROM MASCULINE WORDS   As we have noted, our male-dominated culture affected language development. Many of our words are masculine even though they do not refer exclusively to men. Take *chairman,* for example. This word can refer to both sexes, yet it does not sound that way. More appropriate and less offensive substitutes are *chair, presiding officer, moderator,* and *chairperson.* Similarly, *salesman* suggests a man, but now many women work in sales. *Salesperson, salesclerk,* or *sales representative* would be better. Other sexist words and nonsexist substitutes are as follows:

Sexist	Nonsexist
man-made	manufactured, of human origin
manpower	personnel, workers
congressman	representative, member of Congress
businessman	business executive, businessperson
mailman	letter carrier, mail carrier
policeman	police officer
fireman	fire fighter

Sexist	Nonsexist
fisherman	fisher
cameraman	camera operator

Not all man-sounding words are sexist.

Many words with *man, his,* and the like in them have nonsexist origins. Among such words are *manufacture, management, history,* and *manipulate.* Also, some clearly sexist words are hard to avoid. *Freshperson,* for example, would not serve as a substitute for *freshman.* And *personhole* is an illogical substitute for *manhole.*

Do not use words that lower the role of women.

Words That Lower Women's Status   Thoughtless writers and speakers use expressions belittling the status of women. You should avoid such expressions. To illustrate, male executives sometimes refer to their female secretaries as *my girl,* as in this sentence: "I'll have my girl take care of this matter." Of course, *secretary* would be a better choice. Then there are many female forms for words that refer to work roles. In this group are *lady lawyer, authoress, sculptress,* and *poetess.* You should refer to women in these work roles by the same words that you would use for men: *lawyer, author, sculptor, poet.*

Examples of sexist words could go on and on. But not all of them would be as clear as those given above, for the issue is somewhat complex and confusing. In deciding which words to avoid and which to use, you will have to rely on your best judgment. Remember that your goal should be to use words that are fair and that do not offend.

Sentence Construction

Effective sentence construction indicates clear and orderly thinking.

Arranging words into sentences that communicate clearly and easily is another important goal for you as a report writer. Each sentence should express a complete thought in the form of either a statement or a question. At a minimum, it should tell or ask what a subject is or does. But, as you know from your studies of grammar, through phrases and clauses it can tell or ask a great deal more. Whether simple or complicated, an effective sentence is the product of clear and orderly thinking. Sentence construction is thus another important index of the thoroughness and logic of the report itself.

The techniques of good thinking do not reduce to routine steps, procedures, formulas, or the like, for the process is too little understood. But the sentences that result from good thinking do have clearly discernible characteristics. Knowing what those characteristics are, therefore, can give you some general guidelines for constructing your own statements and questions.

☐   Keep Sentences Short

More than any other characteristic of a sentence, length is most clearly related to sentence difficulty. The longer a sentence is, the harder it is to understand. The explanation of this relationship is simple. The human mind can hold at one time only a

The longer the sentence, the harder it is to understand. So keep sentences short.

limited amount of subject matter. When more than that amount is presented in a single package, the mind cannot grasp it all—at least not in a single reading. Therefore, if you want to make sure your readers comprehend what you are presenting, you must give the material to them a small amount at a time.

Sentences of 16 to 18 words are appropriate for middle-level readers.

The amount of data and number of relationships you can set before your readers at once depends upon their reading level. Most current authorities agree that sentences aimed at the middle level of adult American readers should average 16 to 18 words in length. For more advanced readers, the average can be higher. And it must be lower for those of lower reading ability. Of course, these length figures do not mean that sentences of six or so words are taboo, nor do they prohibit sentences of 30 words or so. Length contributes to sentence variety. Furthermore, short sentences provide a means of emphasizing facts you consider important, and long sentences allow you to deemphasize materials you do not want to make particularly conspicuous. But, for routine sentences, aim for the sentence length that is appropriate for your audience's reading level.

The effects of sentence length are apparent in the following sentences. Note in each instance how much more effectively the shorter version makes its point.

Long and Hard to Understand

This memorandum is being distributed with the first-semester class cards, which are to serve as a final check on the correctness of the registration of students and are to be used later as the midsemester grade cards, which are to be submitted prior to November 16.

Some authorities in personnel administration object to expanding normal salary ranges to include a trainee rate because they fear that probationers may be kept at the minimum rate longer than is warranted through oversight or prejudice and because they fear that it would encourage the spread from the minimum to maximum rate range.

Regardless of their seniority or union affiliation, all employees who hope to be promoted are expected to continue their education either by enrolling in special courses to be offered by the company, which are scheduled to be given after working hours beginning next Wednesday, or by taking approved correspondence courses selected from a list, which may be seen in the training office.

Short and Clear

The accompanying cards will serve now as a final check on student registration. Later you will use them for midsemester grades, which are due before November 16.

Some authorities in personnel administration object to expanding the normal salary range to include a trainee rate for two reasons. First, they fear that probationers may be kept at the minimum rate longer than is warranted through oversight or prejudice. Second, they fear that it would in effect increase the spread from the minimum to the maximum rate range.

Regardless of their seniority or union affiliation, all employees who hope to be promoted should continue their education in either of two ways. (1) They should enroll in special courses to be given by the company. (2) They should take approved correspondence courses selected from the list that may be seen in the training office.

☐ USE WORDS ECONOMICALLY

Another way to shorten sentences is to use words economically.

Of the many ways in which every thought may be expressed, the shorter ways are usually the best. In general, shorter wordings save the reader time; they are clear; and they make more interesting reading. Thus, to write effectively means to write economically. As a report writer, you should strive to express your material in as few words as possible, making sure, of course, that your final versions are complete as well as concise.

Learning to use words economically is a continuing effort. The most effective report writers constantly edit their work for wordiness, always on the lookout for more efficient ways to express each thought. Although they realize economy of writing style depends largely upon the subject, they nonetheless know from practice certain types of expression are uneconomical no matter what the material. The more common types of wordy expression you can learn to recognize as well. The following sections explain what they are and how you might correct them.

Avoid wordy phrases. Substitute shorter expressions.

CLUTTERING PHRASES   There are many phrases in our language, particularly in the language we use in business, that can be replaced by shorter expressions. Although each replacement saves only a word or two, these little savings build up over an entire document. The overall effect of editing a business report for wordiness can thus be significant.

As the following sentences illustrate, the shorter substitutes are more effective:

The Long Way	Short and Improved
In the event that payment is not made by January, operations will cease.	*If* payment is not made by January, operations will cease.
In spite of the fact that they received help, they failed to exceed the quota.	*Even though* they received help, they failed to exceed the quota.
The invoice was *in the amount of* $50,000.	The invoice was *for* $50,000.

Here are other contrasting pairs of expressions:

Long	Short
Along the line of	Like
For the purpose of	For
For the reason that	Because, since
In the near future	Soon
In accordance with	By
In very few cases	Seldom
In view of the fact that	Since, because
On the occasion of	On
With regard to, with reference to	About

Eliminate words that add no meaning.

SURPLUS WORDS   Words that add nothing to the sentence meaning should be eliminated. In some instances, however, taking out such words requires recasting the sentence. In the following sentences, note how such editing is done.

Contains Surplus Words

It will be noted that the records for the past years show a steady increase in special appropriations.

There are four rules *that* should be observed.

In addition to these defects, numerous other defects mar the operating procedure.

His performance was good enough *to enable him* to qualify for the promotion.

The machines *that were* damaged by the fire were repaired.

By *the* keeping *of* production records, they found the error.

Surplus Words Eliminated

The records for past years show a steady increase in special appropriations.

Four rules should be observed.

Numerous other defects mar the operating procedure.

His performance was good enough to qualify him for promotion.

The machines damaged by the fire were repaired.

By keeping production records, they found the error.

Avoid roundabout ways of saying things. Talking around a point suggests you are tentative or evasive.

ROUNDABOUT CONSTRUCTION   Of the many ways of writing a point, some are direct; others are roundabout. The direct ways are more effective in report writing because they suggest confidence, conviction, and candor. The writer appears to be holding nothing back. Roundabout construction, on the other hand, implies tentativeness or evasiveness. The writer, for some reason, seems reluctant to tell all.

Although there are many varieties of roundabout expression, the following illustrations clearly show the general nature of this type of writing problem. (Note that roundabout construction is in many respects a category of excess wording.)

Roundabout

The departmental budget *can be observed to be decreasing* each new year.

The union is *involved in the task of reviewing* the seniority provision of the contract.

The president is *of the opinion that* the tax was paid.

It is essential that the income be used to retire the debt.

The supervisor should *take appropriate action to determine* whether the time cards are being inspected.

The price increase will *afford the* company *an opportunity* to retire the debt.

During the time she was employed by this company, Miss Carr was absent once.

He criticized everyone he *came in contact with.*

Direct and to the Point

The departmental budget *decreases* each year.

The union is *reviewing* the seniority provision of the contract.

The president *believes* that the tax was paid.

The income *must* be used to retire the debt.

The supervisor *should determine* whether the time cards are being inspected.

A price increase will *enable* the company to retire the debt.

While employed by this company, Miss Carr was absent once.

He criticized everyone he met.

Unnecessary repetition has a negative effect. It suggests you lack concern or respect for your reader.

UNNECESSARY REPETITION   Redundancy violates effective writing principles. Repetition is particularly annoying to readers because it suggests a lack of respect for readers and lack of concern for their time. Some cases imply that the readers have a limited vocabulary or intellectual capacity. Words must be defined on the spot and ideas must be restated—or so the repetition would make it seem. Other instances of redundancy occur simply because the writer does not take the time to edit his or her work carefully.

Effective repetition, however, emphasizes and connects key ideas.

When used correctly, repetition does have its place in report writing. It is a powerful device for both transition and emphasis. Used incorrectly, however, it is cumbersome and distracting. The following contrasting examples show typical instances of redundancy and illustrate how it can be corrected.

Needless Repetition	**Repetition Eliminated**
The provision of section five *provides* for a union shop.	Section five provides for a union shop.
The assignment of training the ineffective worker is *an assignment* he or she must carry out.	Training the ineffective worker is an assignment he or she must carry out.
Modern, up-to-date equipment will be used.	Modern equipment will be used.
In the office they found supplies *there* that had never been issued.	In the office they found supplies that had never been issued.
He reported for work Friday *morning at 8 A.M.*	He reported for work Friday at 8 A.M.
In my opinion I think the plan is sound.	I think the plan is sound.
One must not neglect the *important essentials.*	One must not neglect the essentials.

☐ GIVE FACTS PROPER EMPHASIS

Determine the emphasis of each point in your report and communicate it in your writing.

The numerous facts, assumptions, analyses, conclusions, and such that you should include in a report vary in their importance to the report objective. Some, such as conclusions, play major roles. Other areas supply supporting details. Still others are only incidental. Your task as a writer is to determine the importance of each bit of information in your report and to communicate this emphasis in the writing. Giving the facts proper emphasis is largely a matter of sentence design.

Let us review some rules of emphasis. As you already know, verbs are more emphatic than nouns; and both are more emphatic than modifiers. You may also know that clauses carry more weight than phrases and that independent clauses carry more weight than dependent clauses. To continue, words placed at the beginning of a sentence have more impact than words placed at the end or in the middle, respectively. Simple, shorter sentences carry more emphasis than longer, involved ones. Finally, a sentence placed at the beginning of a paragraph receives more attention than a sentence placed at the end; and an end sentence receives more attention than a sentence placed in the middle.

Know which parts of speech, grammatical construction, and sentence and paragraph position give emphasis to a point.

Knowing the effect of grammatical weight and position enables you to control your presentation of facts and analyses very skillfully. There are any number of options you may choose, depending upon what you wish to emphasize and to subordinate. Keep in mind, however, that your decisions should be consistent with the logic of your material and the demands of your problem.

The illustration below indicates what happens when you do not show the relative importance of various facts in a report. As you can see, the writer tries to give each item special emphasis when logic indicates they are not equally important. In addition, placing every fact in its own simple sentence results in writing that is elementary to the point of being ridiculous.

> The Mann building was inspected on October 1. Mr. George Wills inspected the building. Mr. Wills is a vice president of the company. He found that the building has 6,500 square feet of floor space. He also found that it has 2,400 feet of storage space. The new store must have a minimum of 6,000 square feet of floor space. It must have 2,000 square feet of storage space. Thus, the Mann building exceeds the space requirement for the new store. Therefore, Mr. Wills concluded that the Mann building is adequate for the company's need.

In this next version, some of the information is subordinated, but not logically. The facts of real importance do not receive the emphasis they deserve. Logically, the points that should be emphasized are (1) the conclusion that the building is large enough and (2) the supporting evidence, showing that floor and storage space exceed the minimum requirements.

> Mr. George Wills, who inspected the Mann building on October 1, is a vice president of the company. His inspection, which supports the conclusion that the building is large enough for the proposed store, uncovered these facts. The store has 6,500 square feet of floor space and 2,400 square feet of storage space, which is more than the minimum requirements of 6,000 and 2,000 respectively, for floor and storage space.

The third illustration gives good emphasis to the pertinent points. The short, simple sentences placed for emphasis at the beginning present the conclusion. The supporting facts that the new building exceeds the minimum floor and storage space requirements receive main-clause emphasis. Incidentals, such as the identifying remarks about Mr. Wills, are relegated to subordinate roles.

> The Mann building is large enough for the new store. This conclusion, made by Vice President George Wills following his October 1 inspection of the building, is based on these facts. The building's 6,500 square feet of floor space is 500 more than the 6,000 set as a minimum. The 2,400 square feet of storage space is 400 more than the 2,000 minimum requirement.

The following sentences illustrate more specific violations of logical emphasis. The first shows how expressing an important idea as an appositional phrase weakens the idea. Notice the increased emphasis the improved position and construction give the same idea in the second sentence.

> *Weak emphasis:* Hamilton's typewriter, a machine that has been used daily for over 40 years, is in good condition.

Strong emphasis: Although Hamilton's typewriter has been used daily for 40 years, it is in good condition.

This next illustration shows how placement in a participial phrase subordinates an idea. The point receives greater emphasis as a dependent clause in the second version of the sentence.

Weak emphasis: Having paid the highest dividends in its history, the company anticipates a rise in the value of its stock.

Stronger emphasis: Because it paid the highest dividends in its history, the company anticipates a rise in the value of its stock.

☐ ARRANGE THE WORDS GRAMMATICALLY

In English, it is primarily the arrangement of words that indicates their relationship.

The English language is what is known as a noninflectional language. That is, it conveys the relationship among words in a sentence largely by position. (In contrast, an inflectional language, like Latin, conveys relationships through changes in suffixes.) Thus, there is a logic to a correctly written sentence: a clearly stated relationship among actor, action, and recipient of action (if that is the type of sentence we are dealing with) that includes all details about the participants and the circumstances as well.

The grammar of a sentence defines its logic.

The rules that help us define sentence logic are the grammar of the language. And grammar is neither arbitrary nor irrelevant. Every beginning writer's nemesis, the dangling modifier, is not a venial little error that only perfectionists need worry about. It is a major violation of logic. Consider this sentence: "After reaching an impasse, it was decided to consult an arbitrator." Who reached the impasse? We do not know. A misplaced modifier creates similar confusion. Study this statement: "After reaching an impasse, an arbitrator was called." Did the arbitrator reach the impasse? That does not make sense, but what else are we to think?

Follow the rules of grammar in your writing.

If you have had experience with computer languages, you know how unforgiving their "grammar" can be. Most such languages will not allow you to proceed until you have corrected all "syntax errors." Just because the English language is a little more flexible and less literal, however, does not mean you can ignore its rules, particularly not when you are writing for business. Therefore, place logically related words together and make sure their relationships are clear. Take care that all modifiers are appropriately assigned, all pronouns have clear antecedents, and subjects are clearly identified with their verbs. Finally, verify that each sentence you present is in fact a complete thought.

Consult Chapter 16 for a quick review of how to identify and correct the most common errors in grammar.

Chapter 16 offers a quick review of the most common grammatical errors. If you need detailed instruction in English grammar, you are well advised to consult one of literally hundreds of handbooks or to take a review course.

☐ PLACE RELATED WORDS CLOSE TOGETHER

Consider how alternative arrangements of words will affect the meaning of a sentence.

One very effective way to achieve clarity is to keep related words as close together as possible. The "as possible" is a necessary qualification, for frequently two or more words or even groups of words can be related to the same words. In deciding what to do in such cases, follow good logic and, of course, use correct grammar. Appraise the possible meanings conveyed by alternative arrangements and select the one arrangement that carries the meaning you intend.

The importance of placement in determining meaning is illustrated in the following series of sentences. In the series, the words are the same, but the orders change. The corresponding change in meaning is significant. Here is the first version:

If at the end of this quarter the workers vote to strike, the plant will close.

As the sentence stands, the phrase *at the end of this quarter* logically relates to the verb *vote*. In the following sentence, the shift of the phrase to a position between *workers* and *vote* produces confusion. The phrase could modify either word.

If the workers at the end of this quarter vote to strike, the plant will close.

Similar confusion is evident when the phrase comes between *vote* and *to strike*. Will the workers vote at the end of the quarter? Or will they strike at the end of the quarter? It is impossible to tell.

If the workers vote at the end of this quarter to strike, the plant will close.

By moving the phrase further down the sentence, you have similar confusion. At the end of this quarter, will the workers vote to strike? Or will they vote, at some unspecified time, to declare a strike, effective the end of this quarter? Again, we cannot tell.

If the workers vote to strike at the end of this quarter, the plant will close.

This next placement avoids confusion, but it changes the meaning of the initial statement. Here the phrase says when the plant will close. This version tells nothing of the timing of the strike or the vote, nor does it say which workers will be involved.

If the workers vote to strike, the plant will close at the end of this quarter.

It should be quite clear, then, that the position of words in a sentence can make a significant difference in what the sentence communicates. To avoid confusion in your own writing, keep related words together and edit carefully for possible misreadings.

CARE IN PARAGRAPH DESIGN

Effective paragraphing shows and emphasizes good organization.

Clear sentences alone do not assure clear writing. You need to carry the clarity standard the next step—to building clear paragraphs. Paragraphs need to be built logically and deliberately, and the process involves many of the same principles of order and emphasis that pertain to the construction of sentences. Here are a number of specific suggestions for effective paragraph design.

☐   GIVE THE PARAGRAPH UNITY

The contents of a paragraph should address just one topic or idea.

Consider what a paragraph is: a group of sentences developing a single thought. Unity is thus, by definition, the primary requirement of any paragraph. All sentences should contribute directly to the expression and development of just one topic or idea. The only exception is the transitional paragraph, which by its definition is allowed more than one topic.

Paragraph unity should not be defined too broadly. For example, all of a report may deal with a single topic and in this very broad sense be said to have unity. The same could be said of a major section of the report. But the unity of a paragraph deals with much smaller units of thought. In a report written in a detailed outline, a paragraph would develop the lowest level of subtopic, that part identified in the lowest outline captions—or even a part of that part. In any event, a good test of a paragraph is to reduce its content to a single topic statement. If that statement does not cover the paragraph content, the paragraph is probably not unified.

☐ KEEP PARAGRAPHS SHORT

Paragraphs generally should be short.

Consider your typical report readers and you will understand why short paragraphs are best. Typically, you are writing for busy staff people or executives who want to review your report quickly and perhaps study certain parts. They appreciate short paragraphs because they can readily see the beginnings and endings of items covered and identify points of emphasis. In addition, they appreciate the frequent breaks, so long as the breaks are not too frequent. Excessive interruptions cause a choppy effect that is both distracting and annoying.

Short paragraphs are inviting to read. Long paragraphs are intimidating.

The length of a paragraph can have a psychological effect as well. As a glance at Figure 10–1 will show, shorter paragraphs are more inviting than solid masses of words. Long paragraphs are intimidating. They look difficult to get through and impossible to master. Even if you assured your readers that the content of one 30-line paragraph was exactly the same as that of three 10-line paragraphs, they would probably balk at the longer version. Psychological differences are real.

Eight to 10 lines is a good length for a paragraph.

Just how long a paragraph should be, of course, depends on the topic. But, in general, an effective paragraph averages 8 to 10 lines. Of course, you can include a one-sentence paragraph now and then for emphasis, but it is not a good idea to go to the opposite extreme. In paragraphs 12 lines or longer, you can almost always find a place where it makes sense to interrupt, add a transitional word or phrase, and resume the discussion in a new paragraph.

☐ USE TOPIC SENTENCES EFFECTIVELY

A well-written paragraph has a topic sentence expressing the main point. Where you place the topic sentence depends upon your writing plan.

The topic sentence expresses the main idea of a well-written paragraph. Around the topic sentence, a writer builds the details that support or develop the main idea. How each paragraph is organized around its primary sentence depends upon what the content is and how the writer plans to cover it. But there are three basic designs from which to choose. In the first, called the deductive plan, the topic sentence is placed first; in the second, known as the inductive plan, the topic sentence comes last; and in the third, identified as the pivotal plan, the topic sentence appears somewhere near the middle.

You may place it first in the paragraph.

TOPIC SENTENCE FIRST   The deductive paragraph plan is the most widely used. The paragraph begins with the topic sentence, and supporting material follows in a logical order. Because the first sentence of a paragraph is the most emphatic, you can see why

FIGURE 10-1	Contrasting pages showing psychological effects of long and short paragraphs

 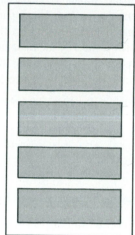

Heavy paragraphs make the
writing appear to be dull
and difficult.

Short paragraphs give well-
organized effect—invite the
reader to read.

this order is the most useful to report writers. As a matter of fact, some company writing manuals recommend that the topic-sentence-first plan be used almost exclusively.

The following paragraph illustrates an effective use of this format:

A majority of the economists consulted think business activity will drop during the first quarter of next year. Of the 185 economists interviewed, 13 percent look for continued increases in business activities; and 28 percent anticipate little or no change from the present high level. The remaining 59 percent look for a recession. Of this group, nearly all (87 percent) believe the downcurve will occur during the first quarter of the year.

You may place it last.   **TOPIC SENTENCE AT END**   Another logical arrangement places the topic sentence at the end, usually as a conclusion. The supporting details come first and in logical order build toward the topic sentence. The beginning sentence simply introduces the subject:

The significant role of inventories in the economic picture should not be overlooked. At present, inventories represent 3.8 months' supply. Their dollar value is the highest in history. If considered in relation to increased sales, however, they are not excessive. In fact, they are well within the range generally believed to be safe. *Thus, inventories are not likely to have a downward drag on the economy.*

Placing the topic sentence at the end sacrifices some emphasis, but not as much as you might suspect. If the paragraph is written well, the topic sentence becomes the culmination of the paragraph. It is the climax of the tension or interest the preceding sentences have built up.

TOPIC SENTENCE WITHIN THE PARAGRAPH   Some paragraphs are logically arranged with the topic sentence within. These paragraphs are not used much in report writing because they usually do not emphasize the key point of the paragraph as well as the other two forms. But if the key idea appears as the pivot of the paragraph, it can attract a great deal of attention. All previous sentences lead to it; all subsequent ones lead from it.

Or you may place it in the middle.

Placing the topic sentence in the middle works well in the following paragraph:

> Numerous materials have been used in manufacturing this part. And many have shown quite satisfactory results. *Material 329, however, is superior to them all.* Built with Material 329, the part is almost twice as strong as when built with the next best material. Also, it is 3 ounces lighter. Most important, it is cheaper than any of the other products.

☐ **MAKE THE PARAGRAPH MOVE FORWARD**

Each paragraph should move the reader another step toward the report goal.

Good report writing has a smooth, forward movement. At its best, effective writing is a continuous flow, easing the readers' progress through the report. To make your writing move is a challenging task. You need clear logic, skillful transitions, careful sentence design and word choice, and a writing style that has both a steady rhythm and an even tone. And all this starts at the paragraph level. If your readers feel at the end of each paragraph that they have made one sure step forward, they will have the incentive to move on to the next step and the step after that and so on until they reach their—and your—objective.

Although many arrangements can illustrate good paragraph movement, the following excerpt from a recommendation report demonstrates one method of making detailed material flow smoothly:

> Three major factors form the basis for the decision to relocate. First, the supply of building rock in the Crowton area is questionable. The failure of recent geological explorations in the area appears to confirm suspicions that the Crowton deposits are nearly exhausted. Second, distances from Crowton to major consumption areas make transportation costs unusually high. Obviously, any savings in transportation cost will add to company profits. Third, obsolescence of much of the equipment at the Crowton plant makes this an ideal time for relocation. New equipment could be moved directly to the new site, and obsolete equipment could be scrapped in the Crowton area.

A WORD OF CAUTION

Exercise good thinking in applying the principles of word selection, sentence construction, and

Like most elements of writing, the foregoing principles must be tempered with good judgment. If followed blindly to an extreme, they can produce writing that appears mechanical or that in some way calls attention to writing style rather than content. For example, slavish application of the rules for short sentences could produce a primer writing style. So could the rules stressing simple language. Such writing could offend

paragraph design. You can overdo them.

the more sophisticated reader. Your solution is to use the rules as general guides, but clear and logical thinking must guide you in applying them.

USE OF COMPUTERS TO IMPROVE WRITING

Software for improving writing has been developed.

Computer technology can complement the techniques of readable writing presented in this chapter. In recent years, computer software has been developed that checks writing for correctness as well as for certain principles of style. Thus, you can write a rough draft of a document using the computer's word processing function and then use it to test your rough draft. From these programs, you then receive analyses of your work with suggestions for improvement.

☐   SPELLING CHECKERS

Spelling checkers are available.

Among the most useful of these programs are spelling checkers. The early versions of the spelling checkers must be run separately; that is, they are not an integral part of the word processing program used to record the document. More recent spelling checkers, however, are an integral part of the word processing program. In fact, some of these programs even incorporate a thesaurus to help you choose words.

They check your words against their dictionaries.

Spelling checkers contain large numbers of correct word spellings (25,000, 50,000, and more). Each word in your document is tested against the dictionary. A word spelling that does not match the word in the dictionary is flagged on the screen. You then decide whether to make the correction. Some spelling checkers even suggest alternate spellings. Obviously, such programs cannot be 100 percent correct, because not all words you use will be in the spelling checker's dictionary. Also, a correctly spelled word may be used incorrectly. For example, both *there* and *their* are correctly spelled words. Use of one in place of the other, however, would be incorrect; yet the spelling checker would not catch the error. For such reasons, spelling checkers only call the possible errors to your attention; you must decide whether or not to change the spelling of a flagged word. Perhaps as artificial intelligence becomes more of a reality, human involvement may be lessened.

Another drawback to spelling checkers is their slowness. The early programs were tediously slow, but the more recent versions are faster. No doubt future programs will be much more efficient.

☐   PUNCTUATION AND GRAMMAR CHECKERS

Software has been developed for checking punctuation and grammar.

Several programs have been developed for checking documents for punctuation and grammar. Specifically, punctuation checkers test for missing marks, although they are limited in handling certain ones, such as commas. This is understandable. The use of commas depends on many factors, one being the writer's discretion. It would be difficult to codify all the rules of comma use.

Also, they check spacing, abbreviations, capitalization, and such.

These programs also are used to check a variety of mechanical elements. They can check spacing before and after punctuation marks, correctness of abbreviations, capitalization, balance of use of quotation marks, double words (unintentionally repeated), and incorrectly expressed numbers (such as $7,35.55).

☐ CLEAR-WRITING ANALYZERS

Some programs analyze readability.

A number of software programs can analyze your adherence to clear-writing principles. These programs are designed to measure the readability of your writing. They measure sentence length and determine percentages of long words. With this information, they calculate a quantitative measure of readability. (These measures have been developed by readability experts, such as Flesch and Gunning. The Gunning Fog formula is explained in Appendix D.) In addition, these programs search for other writing ingredients related to readability, such as the extent of personal and action words used.

Others analyze word choice and sentence patterns.

Some software programs also give feedback on various matters of word choice. For example, they flag erroneously used words, nominalizations (active verbs changed into nouns), redundancies, and trite expressions. Also, some programs can analyze your use of active and passive voice. Still others can give you an analysis of your sentence patterns, including your proportionate use of sentence types (simple, compound, complex). Typically, these programs only bring the incidence of usage to your attention. They leave changing them to your best judgment.

These programs are slow and limited in content.

Although these writing aid programs are useful, especially as teaching devices, they have some faults. They tend to be slow. Typically, you have to deal with each suggestion before going to the next, and this takes time. Also, they are limited in their content. The possibilities of usage are so great in each of the areas mentioned above that only a portion can be covered in the program. Another fault—one contributing to their slowness—is that the programs require too much human intervention. As improvements are made in the future, however, this limitation will be less a problem. The predictions are that as artificial intelligence is perfected, these programs can be structured to think like you and to make the decisions you would make.

☐ COMPUTER TOOLS FOR COLLABORATIVE WRITING

Computer tools help groups on a wide variety of tasks.

As noted in Chapter 3, you may sometimes be assigned to prepare a report with other people in a group. When group collaboration is the case, there are two useful sets of computer tools to support various aspects of the process. Asynchronous tools help groups when limited levels of participation are needed or possible. Synchronous tools assist groups when members need or want more participation.[3]

Asynchronous tools assist groups when minimum participation is needed.

ASYNCHRONOUS COMPUTER TOOLS   Asynchronous tools include word processing, conferencing systems, electronic mail systems, and group authoring systems. Word processing features useful in group writing include commenting, strikeouts, and redlining.

---

[3] Annette Easton, George Easton, Marie Flatley, and John Penrose, "Supporting Group Writing with Computer Software," *The Bulletin of the Association for Business Communication*, June 1990, 34.

Commenting allows you to insert comments in a document written by someone else. Strikeout and redlining allow you to identify text you would like to delete or insert. For example, a lead writer in a group might distribute a document draft to members of the group; these group members would use the features of their word processors and return the draft electronically to the leader. The leader would then review the documents and edit the original.

Computer conferencing is useful when time makes getting together difficult.

Computer conferencing, another group tool, is useful when groups have difficulty meeting due to location, time, or both. To begin the conference, a lead writer would enter the text. Others would then access the system, review the comments, and enter their own wording. All of the comments can be reviewed by the group. In some systems, group members have anonymity; but in others, audit trails are maintained so comments can be attributed to specific group members.

Electronic mail permits communicating to intended receivers only.

Electronic mail systems allow one writer to send a message to others in a group. Unlike conferencing, E-mail systems do not permit access to others' mailboxes. While you can distribute messages to a whole group, you do not have access to messages one member sends to someone else.

Group authoring systems help group work.

Group authoring systems are software programs designed specifically for group work. While different products have varied features, most are designed to allow document versions to be compared, to permit comments and suggestions to be entered at appropriate places, and to use common editing tools such as insert, delete, paragraph, stet, and such.

These asynchronous tools can improve both the speed and the quality of the final documents that groups with limited interaction produce. The planning, writing, and revising of the document occur in much the same way regardless of the interaction that may exist.

Synchronous tools are used when more interaction is possible.

SYNCHRONOUS COMPUTER TOOLS   Synchronous computer tools are used by all group members at the same time and same place. They allow multiple users to work on the document at the same time; they also allow users to view the comments of other users. These programs contain a variety of tools such as brainstorming, organizing, analyzing, and writing.

One member of a group may start the process with a question or a statement. Then, group members will comment on the statement anonymously. For example, one member may propose a statement of the report problem. The other members then may comment about it. After all group members comment, they would review the comments, assemble related ideas, rank order them, and write the final problem statement. This kind of group writing tool cuts meeting time significantly and produces better-quality documents. Research indicates that this electronic meeting technology improves group work by providing an equal opportunity for participation, discouraging behavior that negatively impacts meetings, enabling a large number of ideas to be managed effectively, and permitting the groups to use the tools as needed.[4]

---

[4] J. F. Nunamaker, Alan R. Dennis, Joseph S. Valacich, Douglas R. Vogel, and Joey F. George, "Electronic Meeting Systems to Support Group Work," *Communications of the ACM,* July 1991, 40.

You can definitely use technology to support collaborative writing. From simple PC disk-sharing programs to sophisticated network-based programs, computer support for group writing improves both the final report and the writing process used to complete it.

QUESTIONS

Instructions for Sentences 1 through 26: The following sentences are grouped by the principles they illustrate. Revise them to make them conform with the concepts discussed in the text.

☐ USING UNDERSTANDABLE WORDS

(Assume that these sentences are written for high-school-level readers.)

1. We must terminate all deficit financing.

2. The most operative assembly-line configuration is a unidirectional flow.

3. A proportionate tax consumes a determinate apportionment of one's monetary inflow.

4. Business has an inordinate influence on governmental operations.

5. It is imperative that the consumer be unrestrained in determining his or her preferences.

6. Mr. Casey terminated John's employment as a consequence of his ineffectual performance.

7. Our expectations are that there will be increments in commodity value.

8. This antiquated mechanism is ineffectual for an accelerated assembly-line operation.

9. The preponderance of business executives we consulted envision signs of improvement from the current siege of economic stagnation.

10. If liquidation becomes mandatory, we shall dispose of these assets first.

☐ SELECTING CONCRETE WORDS

11. We have found that young men are best for this work.

12. He makes good grades.

13. John lost a fortune in Las Vegas.

14. If we don't receive the goods soon, we will cancel.

15. Profits last year were exorbitant.

☐ LIMITING USE OF PASSIVE VOICE

16. Our action is based on the assumption that the competition will be taken by surprise.

17. It is believed by the typical union member that his or her welfare is not considered to be important by management.

18. We are serviced by the Bratton Company.

19. These reports are prepared by our research department every Friday.

20. You were directed by your supervisor to complete this assignment by noon.

☐ AVOIDING CAMOUFLAGED VERBS

21. It was my duty to make a determination of the damages.

22. Harold made a recommendation that we fire Mr. Shultz.

23. We will make her give an accounting of her activities.

24. We will ask him to bring about a change in his work routine.

25. This new equipment will result in a saving in maintenance.

26. Will you please make an adjustment for this defect?

☐ SELECTING PRECISE WORDS

Instructions for Sentences 27–38: Following is an exercise in word precision. Explain the differences in meaning for the word choices shown. Point out any words that are wrongly used.

27. Performance during the fourth quarter was (average) (mediocre).

28. This merchandise is (old) (antique) (secondhand) (used).

29. The machine ran (continually) (continuously).

30. The mechanic is a (woman) (lady) (female person).

31. His action (implies) (infers) that he accepts the criticism.

32. Her performance on the job was (good) (top-notch) (excellent) (superior).

33. On July 1, the company will (become bankrupt) (close its doors) (go under) (fail).

34. The staff (thinks) (understands) (knows) the results were satisfactory.

35. Before buying any material, we (compare) (contrast) it with competing products.

36. I cannot (resist) (oppose) her appointment.

37. Did you (verify) (confirm) these figures?

38. This is an (effective) (effectual) plan.

☐ CHOOSING CORRECT IDIOMS

Instructions for Sentences 39–48: These sentences use faulty and correct idioms. Make any changes you think are necessary.

39. The purchasing officer has gone in search for a substitute product.
40. Our office has become independent from the Dallas office.
41. The retooling period is over with.
42. This letter is equally as bad.
43. She is an authority about mutual funds.
44. When the sale is over with we will restock.
45. Our truck collided against the wall.
46. We have been in search for a qualified supervisor since August.
47. Murphy was equal to the task.
48. Apparently, the clock fell off the shelf.

☐ ELIMINATING DISCRIMINATORY LANGUAGE

Instructions for Sentences 49–58: Change these sentences to avoid discriminatory language.

49. Any worker who ignores this rule will have his salary reduced.
50. The typical postman rarely makes mistakes in delivering his mail.
51. A good executive plans his daily activities.
52. The committee consisted of a businessman, a lawyer, and a lady doctor.
53. A good secretary screens all telephone calls for her boss and arranges his schedule.
54. An efficient salesman organizes his calls and manages his time.
55. Our company was represented by two sales representatives, one Hispanic engineer, and one senior citizen.
56. Three people applied for the job, including two well-groomed black women.
57. Handicap parking spaces are strictly for use by the crippled.
58. He didn't act like a Mexican.

Instructions for Sentences 59–81: Revise to make these sentences conform with the concepts discussed in the text.

☐ KEEPING SENTENCES SHORT

59. Records were set by both the New York Stock Exchange industrial index, which closed at 191.27, up 1.65 points, topping its previous high of 189.62, set Wednes-

day, and Standard & Poor's industrial indicator, which finished at 297.61, up 2.20, smashing its all-time record of 295.41, also set in the prior session.

60. Dealers attributed the rate decline to several factors, including expectations that the U.S. Treasury will choose to pay off rather than refinance some $4 billion of government obligations that fall due next month, an action that would absorb even further the available supplies of short-term government securities, leaving more funds chasing skimpier stocks of the securities.

61. If you report your income on a fiscal-year basis ending in 1993, you may not take credit for any tax withheld on your calendar year 1993 earnings, inasmuch as your taxable year began in 1992, although you may include, as a part of your withholding tax credits against your fiscal 1994 tax liability, the amount of tax withheld during 1993.

62. The Consumer Education Committee is assigned the duties of keeping informed of the qualities of all consumer goods and services, especially of their strengths and shortcomings, of gathering all pertinent information on dealers' sales practices, with emphasis on practices involving honest and reasonable fairness, and of publicizing any of the information collected that may be helpful in educating the consumer.

63. The upswing in business activity that began in 1993 is expected to continue and possibly accelerate in 1994, and gross national product should rise by $65 billion, representing an 8 percent increase over 1993, which is significantly higher than the modest .5 percent increase of 1992.

64. As you will not get this part of Medicare automatically, even if you are covered by Social Security, you must sign up for it and pay $3 per month, which the government will match, if you want your physicians' bills to be covered.

65. Students with approved excused absences from any of the hour examinations have the option of taking a special makeup examination to be given during dead week or of using their average grade on examinations in the course as their grade for the work missed.

66. Although we have not definitely determined the causes for the decline in sales volume for the month, we know that during this period construction on the street adjacent to the store severely limited traffic flow and that because of resignations in the advertising department promotion efforts dropped well below normal.

☐ Using Words Economically

67. In view of the fact that we financed the experiment, we were entitled to some profit.

68. We will deliver the goods in the near future.

69. Mr. Watts outlined his development plans on the occasion of his acceptance of the presidency.

70. I will talk to him with regard to the new policy.

71. The candidates who had the most money won.

72. There are many obligations that we must meet.

73. We purchased coats that are lined with wolf fur.

74. Mary is of the conviction that service has improved.

75. Sales can be detected to have improved over last year.

76. It is essential that we take the actions that are necessary to correct the problem.

77. The chairperson is engaged in the activity of preparing the program.

78. Martin is engaged in the process of revising the application.

79. You should study all new innovations in your field.

80. In all probability, we are likely to suffer a loss this quarter.

81. The requirements for the job require a minimum of three years of experience.

☐ **CONSTRUCTING EFFECTIVE PARAGRAPHS**

Instructions for Paragraphs 82–85: Rewrite the following paragraphs in two ways to show different placement of the topic sentence and variations in emphasis of contents. Point out the differences in meaning in each of your paragraphs.

82. Jennifer has a good knowledge of office procedure. She works hard. She has performed her job well. She is pleasant most of the time; but she has a bad temper, which has led to many personal problems with the work group. Although I cannot recommend her for promotion, I approve a 10 percent raise for her.

83. Last year our sales increased 7 percent in California and 9 percent in Arizona. Nevada had the highest increase, with 14 percent. Although all states in the western region enjoyed increases, Oregon recorded only a 2 percent gain. Sales in Washington increased 3 percent.

84. Our records show that Penn motors cost more than Oslo motors. The Penns have less breakdown time. They cost more to repair. I recommend that we buy Penn motors the next time we replace worn-out motors. The longer working life offsets Penn's cost disadvantage. So does its better record for breakdown.

85. Recently, China ordered a large quantity of wheat from the United States. Likewise, Russia ordered a large quantity. Other countries continued to order heavily, resulting in a dramatic improvement in the outlook for wheat farming. Increased demand by Western European countries also contributed to the improved outlook.

Qualities of Effective Report Writing

Objectivity, coherence, and logical consistency in the use of time are additional factors that determine effectiveness.

Readability, as you saw in Chapter 10, is a critical factor in determining the effectiveness of a report. Adaptation, conciseness, concreteness, and liveliness in writing style all contribute to how well a report will read. As you might suspect, however, while effective report writing may start with writing readably, it does not end there. Other factors aid in communicating research results. They include presenting the results objectively, placing them logically and consistently in time, and structuring and relating them so they tell a coherent story. Add these elements to an interesting writing style, and you will indeed have an effective report.

THE ESSENTIAL QUALITY OF OBJECTIVITY

Good report writing is objective.

Objectivity is a matter of both substance and style. Your research should, of course, be factual. And your attitude in interpreting your research and in writing the results must be neutral, fair, and ethical. Not only do you have to approach the problem with an open mind and look at all sides of each question, but you also have to present the results in a writing style that allows your readers to make their own judgments about the data. Whatever bias or prejudice you may have about the problem has no place in any stage of the report, and certainly not in the final writing.

☐ OBJECTIVITY AS A BASIS FOR BELIEVABILITY

Objectivity guarantees the factual nature of your report and makes it believable.

Objectivity guarantees the factual nature of your report. It establishes your results as the culmination of thorough, balanced research and logical analysis—in short, as truth. It thus makes your report believable. Readers look at your documented evidence and valid reasoning and conclude, as a jury might, that "beyond a reasonable doubt," what you say is true.

Never underestimate the perception of that jury. They are neither gullible nor insensitive to how language and logic can be manipulated. Give them one suggestion of deceptive wording or of fraudulent reasoning, and they will be suspicious of the whole work. Therefore, painstaking objectivity is the only way to maintain your credibility.

☐ OBJECTIVITY AND THE QUESTION OF IMPERSONAL VERSUS PERSONAL WRITING

Some writers define objective writing as writing in the third person.

For some writers, objective writing means impersonal writing—that is, writing in the third person. The reasoning behind this definition is, first, that the third person eliminates the appearance of subjectivity by eliminating *I's, we's,* and *you's.* The second reason is the emphasis third person puts on fact. Writers using first or second person, the argument goes, may not be as thorough in testing a truth as they would if they were using third person. There is room for accommodating personal circumstances or for settling for opinion. For example, writers prefacing a conclusion with a phrase like "as you can see" or "we can conclude" may not be making the same commitment as they might were they obliged by the third person requirement to state, "the evidence shows" or "it can be concluded."

Advocates of personal writing disagree.

Advocates of personal writing take issue with these arguments. There is that chance of relaxing the standard for truthful statement, their defense goes, but that is all it is—a chance. Besides, third person does not guarantee truth. An argument specifically in favor of first- and second-person writing is the relationship it develops between reader and writer. The writing is more like conversing, with the writer very much in touch with the reader/listener. As a result, the style is direct and forceful with little need for passive voice.

Before you make any judgment of your own, review these longer samples of personal and impersonal writing.

Personal

After studying the advantages and disadvantages of using trading stamps, I conclude your company should not offer trading stamps to your customers. You would have to pay out money for them. And you would have to hire additional employees to handle the initial increase in sales volume.

Impersonal

A study of the advantages and disadvantages of using trading stamps leads to the conclusion that Mills Company should not offer trading stamps to its customers. The stamps would cost extra money. Furthermore, the initial increase in sales volume would require the hiring of additional employees.

As you can see, the styles do differ; but depending on the situation, either version of the conclusion could be effective. Note, too, that the impersonal writing is neither dull nor cumbersome. Good writing is good writing, regardless of what person is used.

Third-person writing is considered formal. First- and second-person is considered informal.

In deciding which style of writing to use, therefore, consider what your readers desire and expect. In addition, decide how much formality is called for. Third person is viewed as formal; first and second, informal. If you are writing for the usual business audience, more likely than not your readers will prefer third person.

However, if you are writing for a less traditional group or for an audience you know very well, then the personal style will be appropriate.

☐ AVOIDING DULLNESS AND AWKWARDNESS IN IMPERSONAL WRITING

Impersonal writing should never be dull.

Impersonal writing, as you have seen, does not have to be dull or awkward. When it is, the problem is usually an undue emphasis on passive voice or a contrived effort to avoid first-person references.

As far as the first issue is concerned, you can maintain the third person using active voice and taking full advantage of the forcefulness and liveliness direct action verbs provide (see the active-passive voice discussion in Chapter 10). As these two contrasting paragraphs illustrate, the difference in effect can be significant.

Impersonal Writing, Heavy Passive Voice

Sales in all outlets in the Southwest Region were observed to be 10 to 30 percent higher than last month. Outlets in the Dallas-Fort Worth district were found to have the lowest increase, averaging 13.7 percent. This low increase is believed to have been due in part to the fact that all construction in the area decreased significantly. The highest increase was determined to be in the Houston district, which averaged 25.3 percent. This high average was concluded to be a result of this area's sharp upswing in home construction.

Impersonal Writing, Emphasis on Active Voice

Sales of all Southwest Region outlets increased from 10 to 30 percent. Outlets in the Dallas-Fort Worth district increased least, averaging 13.7 percent. This low increase resulted from a general decline in construction in the area. Leading all districts, the Houston district averaged a 25.3 percent increase. A boom in home construction explains the increase.

And concerning the second problem, contriving a way to refer to yourself in your writing is not only awkward but usually unnecessary. The statements you write should be able to stand on their own. These contrasting sentences illustrate the point.

Awkward References

In the opinion of the writer this conclusion supports the need for additional research funding.

Because of the inconclusiveness of these findings, the author suggests additional research.

It is believed by the author that in view of the evidence sales will increase.

References Omitted

This conclusion supports the need for additional research funding.

The inconclusiveness of these findings calls for additional research.

The evidence indicates that sales will increase.

But again, remember: the impersonal-personal writing and active-passive voice issues are issues to be addressed on a case-by-case basis. Both styles have their appropriate place, as do both voice forms. What is important is that you understand what each of these options does and choose on the basis of which will produce the very best communication effect.

LOGICAL CONSISTENCY IN TIME VIEWPOINT

A basic issue in writing a report is deciding which tense to use.

Choosing the proper time viewpoint for presenting the information in a report is a problem for even seasoned writers. The issue is basically this: should you report survey findings as past or present? Should you write, "Twenty percent of Matson's women employees *were* college graduates"? Or should you write, "Twenty percent . . . *are* college graduates"? In defense of past tense, you could argue logically that the research has been completed—that the findings were current only at the time of the investigation. But you could also argue logically that in all likelihood the information is true at the time of the writing and thus can be reported in present tense.

What this debate illustrates is the matter of time viewpoint. By time viewpoint, we mean the place in time from which all the information in a report is viewed. That place may be either past or present. There is little consensus on which is the better. As you might suspect, you, the report writer, have to make your own decision. You select tense, like point of view, to fit the demands and expectations of a given situation.

Past time viewpoint views the research and the findings as past and presents them in past tense. Prevailing concepts and proven conclusions, however, are presented in present tense.

If you use the past time viewpoint, you treat the research findings and writings as past. Thus, you would report results from a recently completed survey this way: "Seven percent of the workers favored a change." And you would refer to another part of a report in words like these: "In Chapter 3, this conclusion was reached." Other similar information you would also view as being in the past, with two exceptions. One is universal truths, which are prevailing concepts or proven conclusions. For example, you could write, "Sales of ski equipment decline in the summer months." Or, "Relative humidity exceeding 90 percent increases the toxic effect of the fumes." The other exception is references to future happenings. You word these, logically, in future tense: "At this rate, the water supply will be exhausted by 2001," and "If the next 10 years are like the past 10 years, we will not be able to penetrate the market."

Present time viewpoint presents as current all that can be assumed to be current at the time of writing.

If you use the present time viewpoint, you place all information presented in its logical position in time at the moment of writing. Information that is current at the time of writing you write in present tense. Thus, if it is reasonable to assume that the survey results remain true, you could use these words to report a finding: "In Chapter 2 this conclusion is reached." For information clearly in the past or in the future, you would use past or future tense. For example, survey findings likely to be obsolete at the time of the writing you could word this way: "In 1969, this plan was favored by 44.2 percent of the managers." A predicted figure for the future you would report thus: "According to this projection, the value of these assets will exceed $32 million by 2002."

Note that a present time viewpoint does not mean every verb must be in the present tense. Nor does it mean placing a single event awkwardly in time. Again, all it requires is placing all facts in their logical place in time at the time of writing.

Which time viewpoint you use is a matter of preference—and convention. Writers in the sciences, for example, appear to prefer past time viewpoint. The important thing is consistency. Shifting arbitrarily from one to the other is illogical as well as confusing. Select one viewpoint—and stay with it throughout the report.

STRUCTURAL AID TO REPORT COHERENCE

Coherence enables the content of the report to flow smoothly.

Smoothness in the flow of information presented is an essential characteristic of good report writing. In a well-written report, each fact is in its logical place, and the relationship of each fact to other facts and to the plan of the report is clear to the reader. Thus, the parts of the report fit together, and the report reads as a unified composition. The writing quality that gives the report this smoothness is commonly called coherence.

Good organization is one source of coherence.

Perhaps the one best contributor to coherence is good organization—a topic discussed in detail in Chapter 6. Relating facts in a logical, natural sequence gives some degree of coherence to the writing. But logical arrangement of facts alone is not always enough, particularly in the long report, where the relationships of the parts are complex. In such reports, you need to make a special effort to structure the report so the relationships will be clear to your reader. Specifically, you can structure the report story by using concluding and summary paragraphs to mark the report's progress. You can use introductory and preview paragraphs to show major relationships. And you can use transitional sentences and words to show relationships between lesser parts.

☐ THE USE OF INTRODUCTORY, CONCLUDING, AND SUMMARIZING SECTIONS

Introductory, concluding, and summarizing sections help readers find their way through longer reports.

The extent to which you use introductory, concluding, and summarizing sections depends on the individual report. Perhaps the best rule to follow is to use such sections whenever you need them to relate the parts of the report or to move the report message along. In general, you are more likely to need these sections in longer reports, where you are also likely to follow a structural plan.

Such a plan, like the one illustrated in Figure 11–1, uses these special sections to tie together all the parts of the report. It keeps readers aware of where they have been, where they are, and where they are going. With such a plan, you can easily guide your readers through complex problems. The plan also helps casual readers to dip into the report at key places and quickly get their bearings.

As we note in Figure 11–1, there are three types of sections (usually a paragraph or more) you may use to structure the report. One is the introductory preview. Another is the section introduction. And still another is the conclusion or summary section, either for the major report parts or for the whole report.

Report introductions may include a section identifying the topics of the report and explaining the order of discussion.

For the longer reports, you may use a section of the report introduction (see Chapter 8) to tell the readers of the report's plan of organization. Generally, such a preview covers three things: the topics the report discusses, the order in which the report presents them, and the logic for this order. Informed of this plan, the readers are then able to understand quickly how each new subject they encounter in the following pages fits into the whole. They can make a connection between major report parts. The following paragraphs do a good job of previewing a report comparing four brands of automobiles for use by a sales organization.

> A comparison of data on cost, safety, and dependability serves as the basis for the decision as to which light car Allied should buy. The following analysis breaks down each of these factors into component parts and applies each part to the four brands considered.

FIGURE 11–1   **Diagram of the structural coherence plan of a long, formal report**

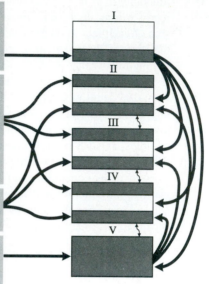

The first part of the structural coherence plan is the introduction preview. Here the readers are told how the report will unfold. Specifically, they are told what will be covered, in what order it will be covered, and the reasons for this order.

Because the report is long and involved, introductions are needed at the beginnings of the major sections to remind the readers where they are in the plan outlined in the preview. These parts introduce the topics to be discussed, point the way through the sections, and relate the topics of the sections to the overall plan of the report.

Conclusions and summaries help readers to gather their thoughts and to see the relationships of the report topics.

Completing the plan, a final conclusion or summary section brings the report to a head. Here, previously drawn section summaries and conclusions are brought together. From these a final conclusion may be drawn.

The cost section compares initial and trade-in values and operating costs as determined by gasoline mileage, oil usage, and repair expense. The section on car safety compares driver visibility, special safety features, brakes, steering quality, acceleration rate, and traction. The section on car dependability examines and compares repair records and time lost because of automobile breakdowns. The analysis ends with a weighting of the comparisons of the preceding three sections and a recommendation as to which brand is the best to buy.

Previews for each body section complement the introductory preview. They tell readers where they are in the report.

In addition to providing an introductory preview, you can help your readers identify relationships between the major report captions by placing introductory and summary sections at convenient spots throughout the report. You can also use these sections to remind readers of where they are in the progress of the report. Other possible uses are to elaborate on the relationships between report parts and in general give detailed connecting and introductory information. The following paragraph, for example, serves as an introduction to the final section of a report of an industrial survey. Note how the paragraph ties in with the preceding section, which covered industrial activity in three major geographic areas, and justifies covering secondary areas.

Although the state's industry is concentrated in three areas (Grand City, Milltown, and Port Starr), a thorough industrial survey needs to consider other areas of the state as well. In the rank of their current industrial potential, these areas are the Southeast, with Hartsburg as its center; the Central West, dominated by Parrington; and the North Central, where Pineview is the center of activities.

Summary-conclusion paragraphs end each report section and lead to the next.

The following summary-conclusion paragraph gives an appropriate ending to a major section. The paragraph brings to a head the findings presented in the section and points the way to the subject of the next section.

> These and the earlier findings all point to one obvious conclusion: when it comes to college coursework, small business executives are concerned primarily with subject matter that will aid them directly in their work. Still, they insist on some coverage of the liberal areas and indicate studying business administration is of some value. On most of these points, they are clearly out of tune with the majority of big business leaders and business administration professors who, in their answers to the survey, clearly rejected the extremely practical approach to business education. Nevertheless, small business executives are the primary consumers of the business education product, so their opinions should at least be considered. Their specific recommendations on courses, as reported in the following chapter, deserve careful review as well.

The final section of the report brings together the preceding information and applies it to the goal.

Completing the coherence plan is the final major section of the report. This is the section in which you achieve the report's goal. Here you recall from the preceding section summaries all the major findings and analyses. Then you apply them to the problem and make the conclusion. Thus, you complete the strategy explained in the introduction preview and recalled at strategic places throughout the report.

If you use paragraphs such as these properly, you will build a network of connections throughout the report. The longer the report, the more effective these connections are likely to be in assisting readers to understand how the various parts relate to each other and contribute to the whole.

☐   COMMUNICATION VALUE OF TRANSITION

Transitions connect sentences, paragraphs, or whole sections.

Transition, which literally means a bridging across, may be formed in many ways. In general, you make transitions by placing words or sentences in the writing to show relationships in the information presented. You may place transitions at the beginning of a discussion on a new topic to relate that topic to what has been discussed before; you may put them at the end of a discussion to provide a forward look; or you may include them internally as words or phrases that in various ways tend to facilitate the flow of subject matter.

Long reports require more transitional aids than short reports do.

Whether you should use a transition word or sentence depends upon the need for relating the parts concerned. A short report, because the relationship of parts is apparent in the logical sequence of presentation, is likely to need only a few transitional parts here and there. But a long report may require much more transitional help.

Never use transitions mechanically. Integrate them smoothly into your writing.

A WORD OF CAUTION   Transitions, like all other elements in a business report, have a clear and integral function. They are not, therefore, to be used mechanically. Include transitional words or sentences only when there is a need for them or when leaving them out would produce abruptness in the flow of report findings. Transitions should never appear to be stuck in; instead, they should blend naturally with surrounding writing. This is the type of transition you should avoid: "The last section has discussed topic X. In the next section topic Y will be analyzed."

Sentences sometimes function as transitional aids.

TRANSITIONAL SENTENCES   The connecting network throughout the report can be improved by the effective use of transitional sentences. Such transitions are especially useful in connecting secondary sections of the report. The following example illustrates clear transition between Sections B and C of a report. The first few lines draw a conclusion for Section B. Then, with a smooth tie-in, the next words introduce Section C and relate this topic to the report plan.

> **[Section B, concluded]**
>
> . . . Thus the data show only negligible difference in the cost for oil consumption [*subject of Section B*] for the three brands of cars. Even though costs of gasoline [*subject of Section A*] and oil [*subject of Section B*] are the more consistent factors of operation expense, the picture is not complete until the costs of repairs and maintenance [*subject of Section C*] are considered.

Here are additional examples of sentences designed to connect succeeding parts. By making a forward-looking reference, these sentences set up the material that follows. Thus, the shifts of subject matter appear both smooth and logical.

> These data show clearly that Edmond's machines are the most economical. Unquestionably, their operation by low-cost gas and their record for low-cost maintenance give them a decided edge over competing brands. *Before we reach a definite conclusion as to their merit, however, we should make one more vital comparison.*

The final sentence clearly sets up the discussion of an additional comparison. Now look at this transitional sentence.

> *At first glance the data appear to be convincing, but a closer observation reveals a number of discrepancies.*

Discussion of the discrepancies will logically follow.

Topic sentences have a transitional function, too.

Placing topic sentences at key points of emphasis is still another way you can use a sentence to improve the connecting network of the report. Usually the topic sentence is most effective at the paragraph beginning, where you can relate the subject matter very quickly to its spot in the organization plan as described in the introductory preview or the introduction to the section. Note in the following example how the topic sentences emphasize the key information. Note also how the topic sentences tie the paragraphs with the preview (not illustrated), which no doubt related the various parts of this organization plan.

> *Brand C accelerates faster than the other two brands, both on level road and on a 9 percent grade.* According to a test conducted by Consumption Research, Brand C attains a speed of 60 miles per hour in 13.2 seconds. To reach this same speed, Brand A requires 13.6 seconds, and Brand B requires 14.4 seconds. On a 9 percent grade, Brand C reaches the 60-miles-per-hour speed in 29.4 seconds and Brand A in 43.3 seconds. Brand B is unable to reach this speed.
>
> *Because it carries more weight on its rear wheels than the others, Brand C has the best traction of the three.* Traction, which means a minimum of sliding on wet or icy roads, is most important to safe driving, particularly during the winter months. Traction is directly related to the weight carried by the rear wheels. Thus a comparison of these weights gives some measure of the safety of the three cars. According to data released by the Automobile Bureau of Standards, Brand C carries 47 percent of its weight on its rear wheels. Brands B and A carry 44 percent and 42 percent, respectively.

Simple words and phrases join the smaller parts of the report.

TRANSITIONAL WORDS   Although the major transition problems involve making connections between sections of the report, there is also need for transition between lesser parts. If your writing is to flow smoothly, you will find frequent need to relate clause to clause, sentence to sentence, and paragraph to paragraph. Transitional words and phrases are effective in making these connections.

Here is a selection of common transitional words. Take note of how they explain the relationship between the items they connect.

We could not possibly list here all the transitional words and phrases you could use. But the following review gives a clear picture of what the most common of these words are and how you can use them. Use a little imagination to provide the context, and you can easily see how these words relate succeeding ideas. The classifications give you an idea of the relationships they show between preceding and ensuing discussions.

Relationship	Word Examples
Listing or enumeration of subjects	In addition First, second, etc. Besides Moreover
Contrast	On the contrary In spite of On the other hand In contrast However
Likeness	In a like manner Likewise Similarly
Cause-result	Thus Because of Therefore Consequently For this reason
Explanation or elaboration	For example To illustrate For instance Also Too

THE ROLE OF INTEREST IN REPORT COMMUNICATION

Good report writing should be interesting. Interest is essential for effective communication.

Like all forms of good writing, report writing should be interesting. Actually the quality of interest is as important as the facts of the report, for without interest, there is not likely to be any meaningful communication. If you do not maintain their interest, your readers will inevitably miss parts of the message. And it does not matter how motivated they are to read the report or how interested they are in the subject. The writing must sustain that motivation and maintain that interest. Just think of your own experiences studying for an examination. No matter how desperately you want to learn a subject, it is extremely difficult to force yourself through tedious reading.

Interesting writing is the result of careful word choices, rhythm, concreteness—in fact, all the good writing techniques.

Perhaps interesting writing is an art. But if it is, it is an art in which you can gain some proficiency by setting certain goals. Specifically, work at making your words build concrete pictures and your phrasings develop a rhythmic flow. Keep in mind that in back of every fact and figure there is some form of life—people doing things, machines operating, a commodity being marketed. The ultimate key to interesting writing is to bring that real life to the surface through concrete vocabulary and smooth, lively diction—all, of course, without using any more words than necessary.

But be careful. Writing should never divert the reader's attention from the information.

But, as a final word of caution, note that attempts to make writing style interesting can be overdone. Such is the case when the reader's attention focuses on how something is said rather than what is said. To be effective, good style simply presents information in a clear, concise, and interesting manner. You want your reader to say, "Here are some interesting facts," rather than, "Here is some beautiful writing." Consult Chapter 10 for specific suggestions for writing in an interesting way.

QUESTIONS

1. Discuss the need for objectivity in report writing.

2. Summarize the arguments on the question of using personal or impersonal writing in reports. What should determine the writer's decision to use personal or impersonal writing?

3. Explain how the question of impersonal versus personal writing involves the use of active and passive voice.

4. Explain and illustrate present and past time viewpoints.

5. What advice would you give a report writer on the matter of time viewpoint?

6. Using Figure 11–1 as a guide, summarize the coherence plan of the report.

7. Discuss how words, sentences, and paragraphs may be used to form transitions in reports.

8. Show your knowledge of transition by constructing three pairs of connecting sentences—one sentence in each pair ending a paragraph and one sentence beginning the following paragraph.

Techniques of Cross-Cultural Communication

Business is becoming more global.

With the recent technological advances in communication, travel, and transportation, business has become increasingly global. Indications are that this trend will continue in the foreseeable future. Thus, the chances that you will have to communicate with people from other cultures are good.

Cross-cultural communication involves understanding cultures and overcoming language problems.

In preparing to communicate with those from other cultures, you might well begin by reviewing the instructions given in Chapters 10 and 11. Most of them fit all people. But some do not. To determine which do not, you must study the cultures of the people involved, for cultural differences are at the root of the exceptions. In addition, you must look at our language for the special problems it presents to those who use it as a second language. It is around these two problem areas that this review of cross-cultural business communication is organized.

PROBLEMS OF CULTURAL DIFFERENCES

Culture is the way people in an area view human relationships.

Culture has been defined in many ways. The definition most useful in this discussion is one derived from anthropology: *Culture* is "a way of life of a group of people . . . the stereotyped patterns of learning behavior, which are handed down from one generation to the next through the means of language and imitation."[1] In other words, people living in different geographic areas have developed different ways of viewing human relationships. They have developed different values and different ways of relating to each other.

Culture differences affect communication in two major ways:

These differences are a major source of problems when people of different cultures try to communicate. Unfortunately, people tend to view the ways of their culture as normal and the ways of other cultures as bad, wrong, peculiar, or such. Specifically, these differences affect communication between people of different

---

[1] V. Barnouw, *Culture and Personality*, Chicago: The Dorsey Press, 1963, 4.

cultures in two major ways: (1) through visible body positions and actions and (2) through attitudes toward various factors of human relations (time, space, intimacy, and so on).

☐ BODY POSITIONS AND MOVEMENTS

(1) Body positions and movements differ by culture. For example, some people sit; some hunker.

On first thought, one might think the positions and movements of the body are much the same for all people. But such is not the case. Often they differ by culture, and the differences can affect communication. To illustrate, in our culture most people sit when they wish to remain in one place for a while. But in much of the world, people hunker, or squat. Because hunkering appears different to us, we tend to view it as primitive. Such views obviously affect our communication with people who hunker, for what we see when we communicate is a part of the message. But how correct are such perceptions? Actually, hunkering is a very normal human body position. Our children do it quite naturally—until they learn to sit from their elders. Who is to say that sitting is more advanced or better?

Manners of walking can differ.

As another example, people from our culture who visit certain Asian countries are likely to view the fast, short steps taken by the natives as peculiar or funny and to consider our longer strides as normal. And they may see these people bow as they meet and leave other people and interpret these actions as signs of subservience or weakness. Similarly, people from our culture see standing up as the appropriate thing to do on certain occasions (as when someone enters the room). People from some other cultures do not.

Communication with body parts (hands, arms, head, etc.) varies by culture.

Movements of certain body parts (especially the hands) are a vital form of human communication. Some of these movements have no definite meaning even within a culture. But some have clear meanings, and these meanings may differ by culture. To us, an up-and-down nodding of the head means yes; a side-to-side movement means no. These movements may mean nothing at all or something quite different to those from cultures in which thrusting the head forward, raising the eyebrows, jerking the head to one side, and lifting the chin are used to convey similar meanings.

A smile can be a sign of weakness; the left hand may be taboo.

In our culture, we view smiles as positive in most situations. In some cultures (notably African), a smile is a sign of weakness in certain situations (as in bargaining). Receiving a gift or touching with the left hand is a serious breach of etiquette among Moslems, for the left hand is viewed as unclean. We attach no such negative meaning to the left hand. And so it is with many other body movements—arching the eyebrows, positioning the fingers, raising the arms, and more. Every culture uses these movements in communicating, but people from other cultures do not understand them.

☐ ATTITUDES TOWARD FACTORS OF HUMAN RELATIONSHIPS

(2) Differing attitudes about certain relationship factors cause communication problems.

Probably causing even more miscommunication are the differing attitudes toward various factors of human relationships held by people of different cultures. Such attitude differences involve a wide range of relationships. For illustration purposes, we shall review five major ones: time, space, odors, frankness, and intimacy.

TIME   People from our culture tend to look on time as something that must be planned for the most efficient use. They strive to meet deadlines, to be punctual, to conduct business quickly, and to work on a schedule. People from some other cultures (especially from parts of Asia and the Middle East) view time in a more relaxed way. They see planning as unwise and unnecessary. Being late to a meeting, social function, or such is of little consequence to them. In fact, some hold the view that important people should be late to show that they are busy. In business negotiations, they move at a deliberately slow pace, using time for casual talk before getting to the main issue. It is easy to see how people from different cultures could have serious miscommunication problems because of their different views of time.

Views about time differ widely. Some stress punctuality; some do not.

SPACE   People from different cultures often vary in their attitudes about space. North Americans tend to prefer some distance between themselves and those with whom they speak—about two feet or so. In some cultures (some Arab and South American), the people stand closer. Not to follow this practice is impolite. North Americans view personal space as a right. They tend to respect this right of others; thus they stand in lines and wait their turns. People from some other cultures view personal space as belonging to all. Thus, they jostle for space when boarding trains, at ticket counters, in stores, and such. In the examples cited above, people in each culture would likely misinterpret the actions of people from another culture with a different attitude toward space.

Space is viewed differently. Some want to be far apart; some close.

ODORS   People from different cultures may have different attitudes about odors. Americans view body odors as bad. They work hard to neutralize them or cover them up. They view those with odors as dirty and unsanitary. But in some countries people view odors as a part of the human being—not to be hidden but to be experienced by friends. Some from these cultures feel that in conversation it is an act of friendship to "breathe the breath" of the other person and to feel his or her presence by smelling. Clearly, efforts to communicate by people with such widely differing attitudes could lead to serious miscommunication.

Some cultures view odors negatively; others view them as normal.

FRANKNESS   North Americans are relatively frank in their relationships with others. The British tend to be even more so. They tend to get to the point and may be blunt and sharp in doing so. Asians tend to be far more reticent and sometimes go to great lengths not to offend. Thus, to a North American, an Asian may appear evasive, roundabout, and indecisive. And to the Asian, the North American may appear harsh, impolite, and aggressive. An exception may exist in telephone customs, especially among the Chinese. They tend to end a telephone conversation abruptly after the purpose of the call has been completed. North Americans tend to move on to friendly talk and clearly prepare the listener for the end of the conversation.

Some cultures are more direct, more blunt than others.

INTIMACY OF RELATIONSHIP   Another area of differing cultural attitudes is in the intimacy of relationships. In many cultures, strict social classes exist; and one's class status determines how he or she is addressed and treated in communication. For this reason, one from this culture might quiz one from another culture to determine the person's class status. Questions might concern occupation, income, title, and such. People from

Intimacy between people varies by culture.

cultures that stress the equality of all people might take offense at such questioning and, in fact, to the attitude about class structure. This attitude is illustrated also by differences in familiarity of address. Some Americans are quick to get on a first-name basis and often seek to do so at a first meeting. The practice is offensive to some from other cultures, notably the English and Germans, who expect such intimate address only from long-standing acquaintances.

☐   **EFFECTS ON BUSINESS COMMUNICATION TECHNIQUES**

Cultural differences affect communication.

The foregoing examples illustrate only a few of the differences that exist between cultures. Books have been written on the subject. Our objective here is only to establish the points that cultures differ and that the differences affect communication between people of different cultures.

Some communication techniques do not work with all English-speaking people.

Moreover, we could even point out cultural differences among people using the same language. For example, even though England and the United States have a common language, the cultural differences between the two countries cause communication problems. This point is supported by an English writer in this comment about American business communication textbooks: "It is almost impossible to recommend them to students, for reasons other than academic interest because the 'cultural gap' is so great that, for example, the language and tone advocated are frequently inappropriate for an English reader."[2]

Overcome problems of cultural differences by learning cultures.

How cultural differences affect communication techniques presented in this book is difficult to say. You simply have to apply your knowledge of the culture involved to each technique. Because cultural differences can cause communication problems, you must become a student of culture—that is, you must learn the cultures of the people with whom you communicate. In doing so, you must take care not to overgeneralize or oversimplify for cultural differences are highly complex. There are many variations and exceptions within groups. Also, you must take care not to exaggerate the effects of cultural differences—that is, to go to the opposite extreme. Not all miscommunication between people of different cultures is the result of cultural differences. Obviously, the course you should take is not simple. You will never succeed completely in your effort to learn other cultures; but it is the only solution available.

PROBLEMS OF LANGUAGE

The many languages spoken cause communication problems.

People use many different languages—more than 3,000, according to authorities on the subject. Because few of us can learn many of them, problems of miscommunication are bound to occur in cross-cultural communication.

---

[2] Nicki Stanton, "Business Communication in England," in *International Business Communication,* ed. Herbert W. Hilderbrandt, Ann Arbor: Division of Research, Graduate School of Business Administration, University of Michigan, 1981, 16.

☐ LACK OF LANGUAGE EQUIVALENCY

Language differences make equivalent translations difficult.

Unfortunately, these languages differ widely in structure, making precisely equivalent translations difficult. Languages are based on the concepts, experiences, views, and such of the cultures that developed them. And all cultures do not have the same concepts, experiences, views, and such. For example, to us a *florist* is one conducting a business selling flowers and related items. In some cultures, however, flowers are not sold in stores but by street vendors, mainly women and children. Obviously, *florist* does not have a precise equivalent in the language of this culture. Similarly, *supermarket* has a clear meaning to us, but it has no equivalent in some languages. And so it is with words for many other objects, actions, concepts, and the like (*roundup, interview, strike, tough, monopoly, domestic, feminine, responsible, aloof*).

Grammar and syntax differences add to the difficulty.

Another explanation for the lack of equivalence in languages is their grammatical and syntactical differences. Some (Urdu, for example) have no gerunds, and some have no adverbs and/or adjectives. Not all languages deal with verb mood, voice, and tense in the same way. The obvious result is that often it becomes impossible to find literal equivalents, even for the best translators.

So do the multiple meanings of words.

Adding to these equivalency problems are the multiple meanings of words. Like English, other languages have more than one meaning for many words. Think, for example, how many meanings we have for the simple word *run* (to move fast, to compete for office, a score in baseball, a break in a stocking, a fading of colors, and more). Or consider the multiple meanings for words like *fast, cat, trip, gross, ring,* and *make.* Unless one knows a language well, it is difficult to know which of the meanings is intended.

Overcome these problems by knowing language, by questioning.

Overcoming such problems of language is difficult. The best way, of course, is to know both languages well; but the competency required is beyond the reach of most of us. Thus, your best course is first to be aware that these problems exist. Then ask questions—probe—to determine what the other person understands. For very important oral messages, documents, or such, you might consider using a procedure called **back translating.** It involves using two translators, one with first-language skills in one of the languages involved and one with similar skills in the other language. The first one translates the message into his or her language. Then the second one translates back to the original. If the translations are good, the last one matches the original.

Use back translating for important communications.

☐ DIFFICULTIES IN USING ENGLISH

English is the primary language of international business.

Fortunately for us, English is the primary language used in international business. This is not to say that other languages are not used, for they are. When business executives have a common language, whatever it may be, they are likely to use it. For example, a business executive from Iraq dealing with an executive from Saudi Arabia would communicate in Arabic, for Arabic is their common language. For the same reason, an executive from Venezuela would use Spanish in dealing with an executive from Mexico. The point is that when executives have no common language, they are likely to use English. Clearly, English is the leading international language, and its leadership continues to grow.

But many foreigners have problems using English.

Even though we can take comfort in knowing that ours is the most commonly used language in international business, we must keep in mind that it is not the primary language of many of those using it. Many of these users have had to learn English as a second language. They are not likely to use it as fluently as we. And they are likely to experience problems in understanding us. Some of their more troublesome problems are reviewed in the following pages.

Two-word verbs are hard for foreigners to understand,

TWO-WORD VERBS   One of the most difficult problems of nonnative speakers of English involves the use of two-word verbs. By two-word verbs, we mean a word consisting of (1) a verb and (2) a second element that, combined with the verb, produces a meaning that the verb alone does not have. For example, take the verb *break* and the word *up*. When combined they have a meaning quite different from the meanings the words have alone. And look how the meaning changes when the same verb is combined with other words: break away, break out, break in, break down. Dictionaries are of little help to nonnative speakers seeking the meanings of these word combinations.

as in these combinations.

There are many two-word verbs—so many, in fact, that a special dictionary of them has been compiled.[3] Following are a few of them arranged by the more common words that combine with the verbs:

Verb Plus "away"	Verb Plus "in"	Verb Plus "out"
give away	dig in	blow out
keep away	give in	clean out
lay away	run in	clear out
pass away	take in	crowd out
put away	throw in	cut out
throw away	**Verb Plus "off"**	die out
Verb Plus "down"	break off	dry out
calm down	brush off	even out
die down	buy off	figure out
hand down	check off	fill out
keep down	clear off	find out
let down	cool off	give out
lie down	cut off	hold out
mark down	finish off	lose out
pin down	let off	pull out
play down	mark off	rule out
put down	pay off	tire out
run down	run off	wear out
shut down	send off	work out
sit down	show off	**Verb Plus "up"**
wear down	shut off	blow up
Verb Plus "in"	sound off	build up
cash in	start off	call up
cave in	take off	catch up
close in	write off	cover up

---

[3] George A. Meyer, *The Two-Word Verb,* The Hague, Netherlands: Mouton and Company, 1975.

Verb Plus "up"	Verb Plus "back"	Verb Plus "over"
dig up	cut back	stop over
end up	feed back	take over
fill up	keep back	talk over
get up	play back	think over
hang up	read back	win over
hold up	take back	**Verb Plus Miscellaneous Words**
keep up	turn back	bring about
look up	win back	catch on
mix up	**Verb Plus "over"**	get across
pick up	check over	pass on
save up	do over	put across
shake up	hold over	put forth
shut up	pass over	set forth
slow up	put over	
split up	roll over	
wrap up	run over	

Use two-word verbs sparingly. Find substitutes, as shown here.

Of course, nonnatives studying English learn some of these word combinations, for they are a part of the English language. But many are not covered in language textbooks. Neither are they listed in dictionaries. It is apparent that we should use these word combinations sparingly when communicating with nonnative speakers of English. Whenever it is possible to do so, we should substitute for them words that appear in standard dictionaries. Following are some suggested substitutes:

Two-Word Verbs	Suggested Substitutes
give up	surrender
speed up, hurry up	accelerate
go on, keep on	continue
put off	defer
take off	depart, remove
come down	descend
go in, come in, get in	enter
go out, come out, get out	exit, leave
blow up	explode
think up	imagine
figure out	solve
take out, take away	remove
go back, get back, be back	return

Additional problems result from the fact that some of these two-word verbs have noun and adjective forms. They also tend to confuse nonnatives using English. Some examples of nouns are *breakthrough, cover-up, drive-in, hookup, show-off,* and *sit-in.* Adjective examples are *going-away* (a going-away gift), *cover-up* (cover-up tactics), *clean-up* (clean-up work), *turning-off* (turning-off place). Fortunately, some of these

Some have noun and adjective forms. Use them sparingly.

words are commonly used and appear in standard dictionaries (words such as *hook-up, feedback, breakthrough, lookout,* and *takeover*). In writing to nonnative readers, you will need to use sparingly such words that are not in standard dictionaries.

Culturally derived words cause problems, especially slang.

CULTURALLY DERIVED WORDS   Words that are derived from our culture also present problems. Most apparent are the slang expressions that continually come in and go out of use. Some of these catch on and find a place in our dictionaries (*brunch, hobo, blurb, bogus*). But most are with us for a little while and are gone. The "twenty-three skidoo" and "oh you kid" of the 1920s and the *ritzy, scram, natch, lousy, soused, all wet, hep, in the groove,* and *tops* of the following decade illustrate the point. More recent ones that are probably destined for the same fate are *nerd, wimp, earth pig, pig out, waldo, squid, grimbo,* and *dexter.*

So avoid slang.

Most of the slang words are not in dictionaries. Neither are they in the word lists nonnatives study to learn English. The obvious conclusion is that you should not use slang in cross-cultural communication.

Words derived from sports, social activities, and so on cause problems.

Similar to and in fact overlapping slang are the words and expressions we derive from our various activities—sports, social affairs, work, and the like. Sports especially have contributed such words, many of which are so widely used that they are a part of our everyday vocabulary. From football, we have *kick-off, goal-line stand,* and *over the top.* Baseball has given us *out in left field, strike out, touch base, off base, right off the bat, a steal, squeeze play, balk,* and *go to bat for.* From boxing, we have *knock out, down for the count, below the belt, answer the bell,* and *on the ropes.* From other sports and from sports in general, we have *jock, ace, par, stymie, from scratch, ball-park figure,* and *get the ball rolling.*

Colloquialisms also cause problems.

Similar to these words and expressions are the words developed within our culture (colloquialisms). Some of these have similar meanings to those from other cultures, but most are difficult for foreigners to understand. Following are some examples:

head for home	in the groove
have an itching palm	nuts (crazy)
on the lam	grand (thousand)
flat-footed	circle the wagons
on the beam	shoot from the hip
out to pasture	tuckered out
sitting duck	gumption
crying in his beer	tote (carry)
in orbit	in a rut
a honey	pump priming
a flop	make heads or tails of it
dope (crazy)	tear jerker
hood (gangster)	countdown
up the creek without a paddle	shortcut
a fish out of water	educated guess
a chicken with its head cut off	

We use these words in everyday communication. But avoid them in cross-cultural communication.

If you are like most of us, many of these words and expressions are a part of your vocabulary. You use them in your everyday communicating, which is all right. They are colorful, and they can communicate clearly to those who understand them. The point is, however, that nonnatives are not likely to understand them. So, in communicating with nonnatives you will need to eliminate such words and expressions. You will need to use the words that are clearly defined in the dictionaries nonnatives are likely to use in translating your message. Following are some examples:

Not This	But This
We were caught flat-footed.	We were surprised.
He frequently shoots from the hip.	He frequently acts before he thinks.
We would be up the creek without a paddle.	We would be in a helpless situation.
They couldn't make heads or tails of the report.	They couldn't understand the report.
The sales campaign was a flop.	The sales campaign was a failure.
I'll touch base with you on this problem in August.	I'll talk with you about this problem in August.
Take an educated guess on this question.	Answer this question to the best of your knowledge.
Your sales report put us in orbit.	Your sales report made us very pleased.
We will wind down manufacturing operations in November.	We will end manufacturing operations in November.
Your prediction was right on the beam.	Your prediction was correct.

☐   A CONCLUDING GENERAL SUGGESTION

Use simple, basic English.

In addition to the specific suggestions for improving your communication in English with nonnatives, you should follow one general suggestion: write (or talk) simply and clearly. In speaking, enunciate each word and talk slowly. Remember that most nonnative businesspeople learned English in school. They are acquainted mainly with primary dictionary meanings. They are not likely to understand slang words or shades of difference in meanings we give words. You can overcome these limitations by using simple, basic English.

QUESTIONS

1. "Just as our culture has advanced in technological development it has advanced in the sophistication of its body signals, gestures, and attitudes toward time, space, and such. Thus the ways of our culture are superior to those of most other cultures." Discuss this view.

2. What are the prevailing attitudes in your culture toward the following, and how can these attitudes affect your communication with nonnatives? Discuss.
   a.   Bargaining (selling) methods

    b.   Truth in advertising
    c.   Company-worker loyalty
    d.   Women's place in society

3. Think of English words (other than text examples) that would be likely not to have a precise equivalent in some other culture. Explain each and tell how you would attempt to define it to one from this culture.

4. Select a word with at least five meanings. List the meanings and tell how you would communicate each meaning to a nonnative.

5. From newspapers or magazines, find and bring to class 10 sentences that use words and expressions that nonnatives would not be likely to understand. Rewrite each for a nonnative reader.

Instructions, Numbers 6–15: Rewrite the following sentences for a nonnative reader.

6. Last year our laboratory made a major breakthrough in design, which really put sales in orbit.

7. You will need to pin down Mr. Wang to put across the need to tighten up expenses.

8. Recent losses have us on the ropes now, but we expect to get out of the hole by the end of the year.

9. We will kick off the advertising campaign in February, and in April we will bring out the new products.

10. Jamison gave us a ballpark figure on the project, but I think he is ready to back down from his estimate.

11. We will back up any of our products that are not up to par.

12. Mr. Maghrabi managed to straighten out and become our star salesperson.

13. Now that we have cut back on our advertising, we will have to build up our personal selling.

14. If you want to improve sales, you should stay with your prospects until they see the light.

15. We should be able to bring about a savings of about 8 or 10 grand.

Mechanics of Report Construction

PART 5

5

Physical Presentation of Reports

The appearance of reports forms impressions on readers.

When your readers look at your report, they see not only the message you have formed; they also see the overall appearance of your work. Like the words and illustrations, the appearance of your report becomes a part of the communication they receive and affects the messages formed in their minds.

Neat work equals favorable impressions; untidy work equals unfavorable impressions.

If, for example, they look at your work and see a neat, well-arranged document, a favorable impression is likely to form in their minds. Such favorable impressions probably will make them more receptive to the information in your message. Well-arranged reports give impressions of competency—of work professionally done. At the other extreme, if readers see an untidy, poorly arranged paper, they are likely to form a negative impression; and this will hurt their receptiveness to the information you seek to communicate. In other words, the impressions the appearance of your work forms in your readers' minds become a part of their filters' content. Thus, the physical appearance of reports serves to affect the meanings readers give to the information communicated.

Use the following guidelines for report presentations.

You can do much to ensure the communication success of your report by giving it the careful preparation and arrangement that will help in your communication effort. Hence, you should make good use of the following guides to the physical arrangement of reports.

GENERAL INFORMATION ON REPORT PRESENTATION

You will likely use a computer to produce your final report.

Your formal reports are most likely to be produced with some form of word processing equipment. In some cases, they might be typed on a memory or conventional typewriter. As technology continues to advance, however, the chances that you will use

227

typewriters become more and more remote. In any event, you will need to know the general mechanics of manuscript layout. Even if you do not prepare your own reports, you should know enough about the subject to ensure that the work is done right. You cannot be certain that your report is in good form unless you know good form.

☐ CHOICE OF COVER

Choose a cover that is appropriate for the occasion. Color and durability are key factors.

The first part of any report a reader sees is the cover. Thus, to make sure the first impression made by the report is favorable, select the cover carefully. There are any number of covers available commercially, and many of these are appropriate.

In selecting the right cover for a specific report, consider three basic features: the type of fastening used, the durability of the material, and the overall physical appearance. The fastening device must be able to hold the report pages firmly in place. As a rule, fasteners that hold through perforations in the pages do this job better than clamp type devices. Most types of covers provide sufficient protection for most reports, but for a report that will be handled a great deal you need something sturdy. Fabric covers or fabric-like plastic covers last longer than paper or clear plastic. They also look better and suggest quality. Color is something to consider, too. Darker colors are conservative, but bright colors stand out.

☐ CARE IN PAPER SELECTION

Paper is usually the best media choice for reports. E-mail and fax do not assure good appearance.

Today, paper is the top media choice for reports. But it is not the only choice, as there are less formal media. You could email a report. Except for certain short reports, however, this medium would be too informal for most reports. Or you could fax a report. Because you do not control the fax output, your report's appearance could suffer. By choosing paper as your medium, you can maintain maximum control over your report's physical appearance.

Paper content, color, and size communicate.

Contrary to what you might think, paper is not just paper. There are all sorts of variations of content, color, and size. And each combination potentially says something about the overall quality of your report.

Paper comes in two conventional sizes—8½ by 11 inches and 8½ by 14 inches. The first size is by far the more popular and is used in most printed reports. The long (8½ by 14 inch, sometimes called legal paper) is used principally for reports that require long tabular displays or illustrations.

In international business, paper is measured using the metric system, resulting in paper sized slightly narrower than 8½ inches and slightly longer than 11 and 14 inches.

You want to select a good grade of paper, one that will make the finished page stand out and will tolerate wear. A good-quality watermarked, rag-content bond is preferable to coated varieties. As a rule, a 20- or 16-pound weight is best, although quality paper of a lighter weight may be acceptable in certain circumstances.

White paper is used for most routine business reports and for all very formal reports. Some companies, however, use colored paper to identify work from certain departments or for special types of reports.

| FIGURE 13–1 | Different arrangements of 1:1 proportion of white space |

Double-spaced with long lines   Short lines with whitespace moved to margins

Unlike commercially printed matter, manuscript is usually printed on one side of the page. You would have to use opaque paper if your report specifications called for printing on both sides.

☐ **BASICS OF PAGE LAYOUT**

Layout means text and graphic arrangement on a page.

The layout of a printed page in a report refers to the arrangement of the text and graphics. Through careful attention to the elements that affect these page arrangements, you can achieve control over the results of your document layout. The major elements to which you need to attend are white space, spacing, margins, and justification.

External spacing is the white space around the text copy.

To make your document look its best, you must consider both external and internal spacing. External spacing is the white space that surrounds the copy—the space that some never consider. Just as volume of coverage denotes importance in writing, white space in document design emphasizes as well. Surrounding text or a graphic with white spaces sets it apart, emphasizing it to the reader. Used effectively, white space has also been shown to increase the readability of your documents, giving your readers' eyes a rest. Ideally, white space should be a careful part of the design of your document.

Consider a 1:1 ratio of white space to text.

A commonly accepted ratio of white space to text on a page is 1:1 for optimum readability. This means one-half of your page is devoted to text and the other one-half to white space. But there can be different arrangements of white space on the page. As shown in Figure 13–1, the proportion of white space to text is 1:1 in each page layout. The arrangement with the shorter lines and white space on the left is better for shorter reports; the one with long lines and double spacing is better for longer documents. You will need to consider balance and symmetry as you design the white space/text copy of your document.

FIGURE 13–2   Illustrations of different forms of justification

Left-justified   Right-justified   Fully justified

Internal spacing refers to vertical and horizontal spacing on a page. Use kerning to space between letters.

Internal spacing refers to both vertical and horizontal spacing between lines and letters on the page. Spacing between letters on a line of type is called kerning. With desktop publishing and some word processing software, you can adjust how close the letters are to each other. For example, the "T" can overhang the "h" in the word "The" using publishing software. A dot matrix printer would place the "h" after the overhang, appearing to leave more space between the "T" and "h" than between the "h" and "e." Thus, rather than using equal spacing between characters, you can stretch or squeeze text by tightening or loosening kerning or spacing between characters.

Leading controls space between vertical lines.

Another term, leading, is similar to kerning except that it refers to vertical spacing rather than horizontal. When your lines are too close together, modern-day software permits you to increase the leading to add more white space between vertical lines. The deciding factor in both cases—kerning and leading—is the typeface you choose to use. In any case, you need to make a conscious decision about the spacing aspects of the layout of your documents.

Margin settings determine white space too.

Margin settings, another element of layout, also control the proportion of white space in text copy. Ideally, your document should look like a framed picture with equal margins. Business preference and document length often call for fixed margins, however. In these cases, all margins will not be equal. It is still possible, though, to have vertical and horizontal balance.

Align type at left, right, or center of a page through justification.

Moreover, you can align type at the margins or in the center through justification. Left justification aligns every line at the left, right justification aligns every line at the right, and full justification aligns every line at both the left and right, as shown in Figure 13–2. Unless you are using a proportional font, full justification takes the extra spaces between the last word and the right margin and distributes them across the line. This extra white space may distract some readers' eyes a bit. Therefore, it is usually best to set a left-justified margin and ignore the resulting right margin. If the right margin is distracting, you may want to use the hyphenation feature. As shown in Figure 13–3, you can divide words at the end of the line and smooth the uneven appearance of the unjustified right margin.

□ CONVENTIONAL PAGE LAYOUT

Recommended dimensions for layout of a conventional page are 1-inch top and side margins for double spacing and 1¼ to 1½ inches for single spacing. Bottom margins are 1⅓ times the side margins.

For the typical report text page, a conventional layout is one that appears to fit the page like a picture in a frame (see Figure 13–4). This eye-pleasing layout, however, is arranged to fit the page space not covered by the report's binding. Thus, you must allow an extra half-inch or so on the left margins of the pages of a left-bound report and at the top of the pages of a top-bound report. In centering headings and numbers, you will have to exclude the left-hand margin; otherwise, your headings and numbers will look off balance when you bind a report on the left.

As a general rule, top, left, and right margins should be equal and uniform. For double-spaced manuscripts, about one inch is recommended. From 1¼ to 1½ inches is considered ideal for single-spaced work (see Figure 13–5). Bottom margins customarily are made slightly larger than top ones—about half again as much. The left margin, of course, is easily defined by the characters that begin the line. The right margin is formed by the average lengths of the full lines. When you use word processing equipment with right margin justification capability, the right margin will be uniformly straight.

□ SPECIAL PAGE LAYOUTS

Pages displaying major titles may require special layouts.

Certain text pages may require individual layouts. Pages displaying major titles (first pages of chapters, tables of contents, executive summary, etc.) conventionally have an extra half-inch or so of space at the top (see Figure 13–6). This technique has long been followed by book publishers.

The letter of transmittal also may have an individual layout. It is arranged in any conventional letter form. In more formal reports, it may be arranged so as to have the same general shape as the space on which it appears (see Figure 13–12 on page 244).

□ CHOICE OF FORM

Both double and single spacing are acceptable.

It is conventional to double-space the finished report. This procedure stems from the old practice of double spacing to make typed manuscripts more easily readable for the proofreader and printer. The practice has been carried over into work that is not to be further reproduced. Advocates of double spacing claim that it is easy to read, as the reader is unlikely to lose line place.

In recent years, the use of single spacing has gained in popularity. The general practice is to single-space paragraphs, double-space between paragraphs, and triple-space above all centered heads. Supporters of single spacing contend it saves space and enables fast reading, since it is like the printing to which most people are accustomed. Single spacing also is becoming more accepted as word processing and desktop publishing increase in availability.

FIGURE 13-3   Examples illustrating the use of the hyphenation feature

Without hyphen feature

Computers, Human Intellect, and Organizational Nervous Systems

An executive provides vision and direction, makes decisions, diagnoses and solves problems, negotiates, convinces, and selects and coaches people. All these actions depend on the executive's ability to think creatively and communicate clearly; clear communication and creative thinking can be enhanced by the use of computers.

Unfortunately, most people don't realize this. The computer's role as a valuable thinking tool seems to be a secret. Instead, many intelligent people, even today, believe that computers are best suited to clerical and administrative tasks. They see the computer as only a convenience or an operational necessity. I see the computer as an extension of the human brain.

An understanding of the connection between the evolution of the human mind and computers takes us back in time.

With hyphen feature

Computers, Human Intellect, and Organizational Nervous Systems

An executive provides vision and direction, makes decisions, diagnoses and solves problems, negotiates, convinces, and selects and coaches people. All these actions depend on the executive's ability to think creatively and communicate clearly; clear communication and creative thinking can be enhanced by the use of computers.

Unfortunately, most people don't realize this. The computer's role as a valuable thinking tool seems to be a secret. Instead, many intelligent people, even today, believe that computers are best suited to clerical and administrative tasks. They see the computer as only a convenience or an operational necessity. I see the computer as an extension of the human brain.

An understanding of the connection between the evolution of the human mind and computers takes us back in time.

FIGURE 13-4   **Recommended layout for normal double-spaced page**

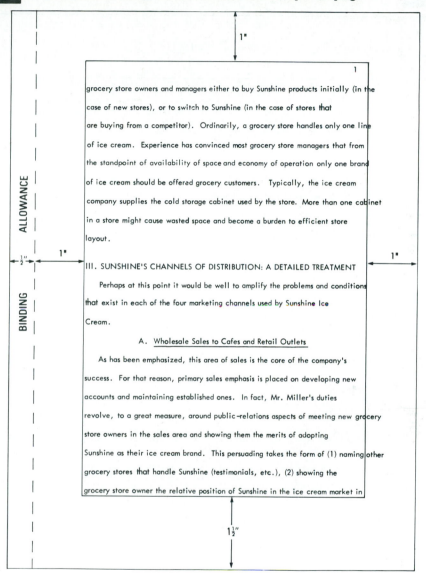

FIGURE 13-5   Recommended layout for a normal single-spaced page

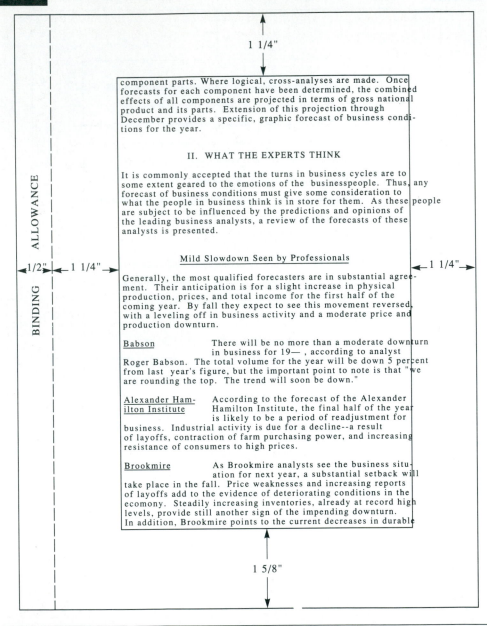

FIGURE 13–6   **Recommended layout for double-spaced page with title displayed**

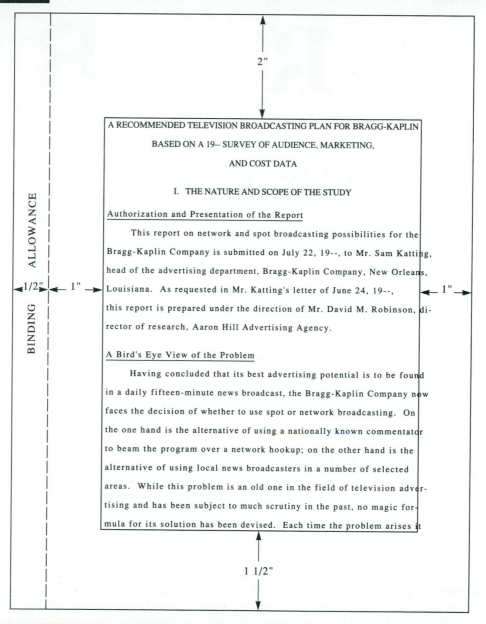

A RECOMMENDED TELEVISION BROADCASTING PLAN FOR BRAGG-KAPLIN

BASED ON A 19-- SURVEY OF AUDIENCE, MARKETING,

AND COST DATA

I.   THE NATURE AND SCOPE OF THE STUDY

Authorization and Presentation of the Report

    This report on network and spot broadcasting possibilities for the Bragg-Kaplin Company is submitted on July 22, 19--, to Mr. Sam Katting, head of the advertising department, Bragg-Kaplin Company, New Orleans, Louisiana. As requested in Mr. Katting's letter of June 24, 19--, this report is prepared under the direction of Mr. David M. Robinson, director of research, Aaron Hill Advertising Agency.

A Bird's Eye View of the Problem

    Having concluded that its best advertising potential is to be found in a daily fifteen-minute news broadcast, the Bragg-Kaplin Company now faces the decision of whether to use spot or network broadcasting. On the one hand is the alternative of using a nationally known commentator to beam the program over a network hookup; on the other hand is the alternative of using local news broadcasters in a number of selected areas. While this problem is an old one in the field of television advertising and has been subject to much scrutiny in the past, no magic formula for its solution has been devised. Each time the problem arises it

FIGURE 13–7   Examples of serif and sans serif typefaces

R   R

Times Roman (Serif)   Helvetica (Sans Serif)

☐ PATTERNS OF INDENTATION

Indent double-spaced text; block single-spaced text.

You should indent double-spaced page formats to show paragraph beginnings. In contrast, you should block single-spaced pages, because paragraphs are clearly marked by extra line spacing.

The number of indentation spaces is optional, but be consistent.

No generally accepted number of indentation spaces exists. Some sources suggest 4 spaces, some 5, some 8, and still others 10 or more. The decision as to the best number of spaces to use is up to you, although you would do well to follow the practice established in the office, group, or school for which you are writing the report. Whatever your selection, it is important to be consistent.

☐ POSSIBILITIES IN FONT SELECTION

Computer word processing offers you a wide variety of font selections.

Computer word processing offers a variety of options for printing the final report—more options than were ever available on typewriters. Through font selection, you can create many different character appearances on the finished pages you print. For example, you can select a typeface (Times Roman, Gothic, etc.), a weight (bold or italic), and a point size (10 or 12 point, etc.) for each font.

Use serif type for text; sans serif for headings.

In general, typefaces are classified as serif and sans serif. As shown in Figure 13–7, serif typefaces have feet (cross-lines at the end of main strokes) whereas sans serif do not. Since readers usually use the visual cues they receive from feet to form words in their minds, they probably will find text of documents easier to read if a serif type is used. Sans serif typefaces are good for headings where clear, distinct letters are important. You can use 9–14 point type size for report text and 15 point or larger for headings.

Laser printers give the most selections. Impact printers allow fewer ones. You can do good work on both.

Also, there are cartridges and other sources for you to add even more font possibilities to your printer's capability. If you are using a laser printer, the possibilities are almost endless for you to select a finished page format that will enhance the physical attractiveness of your report. If you are using impact printers, there are fewer selections; but you can still produce professional work.

A word of caution is in order, however. As with most technological developments, you may become so fascinated with font selection possibilities that you create more clutter on a printed page than physically attractive copy. Thus, you must be cautious

Do not become overly fascinated with technology. Your goal is to produce an attractive report.

about using too many fonts on one page and throughout the report just because they look interesting. Remember that your goal in font selection is to produce a physically attractive, professional report. It is not your goal to demonstrate the versatility of your printer.

☐ USE OF DESKTOP PUBLISHING

Desktop publishing produces reports similar to those prepared by commercial printers.

One way you can create professional looking reports is through *desktop publishing*. Desktop publishing allows you to produce documents similar to those produced with typesetting used by commercial printers. In other words, from your own desktop you can put together words and graphic aids to form a physically attractive business report (and other business documents as well). All you need for this task is a microcomputer, desktop publishing software, a laser printer, and a high-resolution CRT screen.

You can design professional reports with many features at low cost. Physically attractive reports communicate better.

With desktop publishing, you can select page layouts, type fonts, type sizes, line heights, multiple columns, right-hand justification, hyphenations, and character spacings. In making these selections, you can design a report that has a finished appearance beyond dot matrix and letter quality production—and without having to pay the cost associated with commercial printing (see Figure 13–8). Desktop publishing adds to the effectiveness of reports by increasing their physical attractiveness.

☐ NEATNESS IN THE FINISHED REPORT

Neatness is essential.

As mistakes, misspellings, and other signs of sloppy work will reflect on your reports, you should work for a neat end product. With sophisticated electronic word processing equipment, you can reach this goal easily. There should be no errors in your printed report. You will be able to correct your errors in the document file before printing the final copy. If you are using a conventional typewriter, however, you can still turn out acceptable work if you are careful.

The appearance of your report reflects your work philosophy.

The need for neat, correct work cannot be overemphasized. The physical appearance of your report reflects on you and your work philosophy. Regardless of its content, a report with mistakes and with an untidy appearance will be doomed to failure.

☐ NUMBERING OF PAGES

Number prefatory pages in small roman numerals and text pages in arabic numerals.

Two systems of numbers are used in numbering the pages of the written report. Arabic numerals are conventional for the text portion, normally beginning with the first page of the introduction and continuing through the appendix. Small roman numerals are standard for the prefatory pages. Although all of the prefatory pages are counted in the numbering sequence, the numbers generally do not appear on the pages preceding the table of contents.

For top-bound reports, place numbers at the bottom.

Placement of the numbers on the page depends on the binding used for the report. With reports bound at the top, you should center all page numbers at the bottom of the page, a double or triple space below the page layout.

FIGURE 13–8   Illustration of format arrangement using desktop publishing

Our Company
BUSINESS REPORT

VOLUME 1: No. 1   June 6, 1990

CEO Sets Record for Industry

We recently announced our highest-performance, easy to use, full-function page composition software apllication-Deskware Publisher.

"We're happy to provide an integrated group of products for personal publishing with the addition of Deskware Publisher to our family of applications," said our chief Executive Officer. "Users now have a full function, and easier-to-use way to combine text and graphics than ever before. In addition, the user will appreciate hte outstanding price/performance offered by our product.

Flexibility is a key feature of this software product. The user can define a location anywhere in a document and automatically place text or graphics at this location.

Continued on page 3

We Increase Our Share of the Market

Employees Using Own Desktop Publishing Software

Projected Market Shares

"It's one of the best things that ever happened to personal computers," says desktop publishing expert, Stacey C. Sawyer about desktop publishing, in the May issue of Use Your Computer.

Desktop publishing, the latest development in microcomputers, offers the user the ability to combine text and graphics to create professional quality brochures, newsletters, fliers, sales reports, marketing briefs, books, manuals, forms, and other publications on their own computer. And as Stewart Alsop says in the February edition of *PC Magazine*, "Ever since Guttenberg, publishers have been looking for a better, cheaper, faster way to get words and pictures on paper."

Experts say that desktop publishing lets users compose text in a manner that comes close to the requirements of typesetting, including well-designed and proportionally spaced characters, multiple fonts, sizes, and so on.

The system should allow users to perform typesetting and composition tasks in a manner that is considerably less code-intensive than that which characterizes trade computer typesetting. This includes the feature of WYSIWYG, (What You See Is What You Get) which lets you point to the effects desired rather than requiring that you describe them by some sort of command language. Software programs that are "code-intensive" and require considerable user experience should not be included in the desktop publishing category.

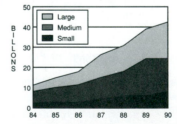

Growth Revenues for U.S. Suppliers

For left-bound reports, place numbers in the upper right corners.

With left-side binding, you should place the numbers in the upper right corner, a double or triple space above the top line and in line with the right margin. Exception to this placement customarily is made for special-layout pages that have major titles and an additional amount of space displayed at the top. Included in this group may be the first page of the report text, the executive summary, the table of contents, and, in very long and formal works, the first page of each major division or chapter. Numbers for these pages are centered a double or triple space below the imaginary line marking the bottom of the layout. Centering would necessitate excluding the left-hand binding allowance.

☐   **DISPLAY OF HEADINGS**

Headings (captions) are titles to the report parts. They are the outline parts and are designed to lead the reader through the report. To do this, they must show the reader at a glance the importance of the information they cover.

Use type and position to distinguish headings from text printing.

You can show the importance of headings with two mechanical devices: type and position. You can use any logical combination of the two. But you should use no type or position for a heading that is higher in importance than the types or positions you use for higher-ranking headings.

Position choices are (1) centered, (2) marginal, and (3) run in.

In showing heading importance by position, you have three main choices. As shown in Figure 13–9, the most important position is that of centered between left and right margins. Next comes the marginal heading on a line by itself. Third is the run-in heading (also called *paragraph heading*). It runs into the line and is distinguished from the text by underscoring or, if you are using a word processor, varying the type size relative to that of the text.

If you are using word processing equipment that is limited to capital and lower-case letters, you can show four levels of importance by using the underscore:

Type choices are these four.

SOLID CAPITALS UNDERSCORED

SOLID CAPITALS

Capitals and Lowercase Underscored

Capitals and Lowercase

Use any logical combination of type and position.

If your word processing equipment has a variety of type sizes and faces available, you can select other progressions to fit your needs. You can also use boldface or double striking to create additional levels of importance. Your goal, of course, should be to select type styles that will show rankings at first glance—much like this book.

You can use any combination of type and position that clearly shows the headings' relative importance. The predominant rule to follow in considering heading types and positions is that no heading may have a higher-ranking type or position than any of the higher-level headings. But you can use the same type for two successive levels of headings as long as the positions vary. Also, you can use the same position for two successive levels as long as the types vary. Finally, you can skip over any of the steps in the progression of type or position.

FIGURE 13-9   Heading positions in order of importance

MECHANICS AND FORMAT OF THE REPORT PARTS

Following is a part-by-part review of the construction of a formal report.

The foregoing notes on physical appearance generally apply to all parts of the report. But for the individual construction of the specific report pages, additional special notes are needed. To enable you to understand these special notes, a part-by-part review of the physical construction of the formal report follows.

☐ TITLE FLY

The title fly contains only the report title. In constructing the page, place the title slightly above the vertical center of the page in an eye-pleasing arrangement. Center all lines with respect to left and right margins. Give it the highest-ranking type used in

The title fly contains only the title, centered and relatively high on the page.

the report (usually solid capitals underscored), and double-space it if you need more than one line.

□ Title Page

The title page typically contains three elements. First is the report title.

The title page normally contains three main areas of identification (Figure 13–10), although some forms present the same information in four or five spots on the page (Figure 13–11). In the typical three-spot title page, the first item covered is the report title. You should give it the highest-ranking type used in the report, usually solid capitals underscored. Center it and, if you require more than one line, break the lines between thought units and center the lines. Double-space the lines.

Second is authorizer identification.

The second area of identification names the individual or group for whom the report is being prepared. Precede it with an identifying phrase, such as "Prepared for" or "Submitted to"—words that indicate the authorizer's role in the report. In addition to the name, include identification by title or role, company, and address, particularly if you and your recipient are from different companies. If the information below the identifying phrase requires three or more lines of type, single-space it. If you have fewer than three lines, double-space them. But regardless of how you space this information, the identifying phrase best appears set off from the facts below it with a double space.

Third is writer identification. You may also include the date.

The third area of information identifies you, the writer of the report. It too is preceded by an identifying phrase. You may use "Prepared by," "Written by," or any such wording describing your role in the report. You may also give your title or role, company, and address. The final part of this group of information is the date of publication. You should single-space this identification information if four lines are required and double-space for three lines or fewer. Likewise, you should set off the identifying phrase with a double space. Preferably double-space the date line from the information preceding it, regardless of previous spacing. Placement of the three spots of information on the page should form an eye-pleasing arrangement.

One such arrangement begins the title about 1¼ inches from the top of the page. The final spot of information ends about 2 inches from the page bottom. The center spot of information appears so as to split the space between the top and bottom units in a 2:3 ratio, the bottom space being the larger. Line lengths of the information units usually are governed by the data they contain. But for best appearance, you may need to combine or split units.

□ Letters of Authorization and Transmittal

Include the original letter of authorization. Type the letter of transmittal in an acceptable form.

As their names imply, the letters of authorization and transmittal are actual letters. You may include the letter of authorization (or memo) in the report, but it must be the original. You should type or print the letter of transmittal in an acceptable letter form. Because the report is important, you should give the letter an ideal layout. "Ideal" layout means one that fits the letter into a rectangle of the same shape as the space in which it is typed or printed (see Figure 13–12). This rectangle is marked by the dateline at the top, the initial type characters at the left, the average of the line lengths

FIGURE 13–10   Good layout for the three-spot title page

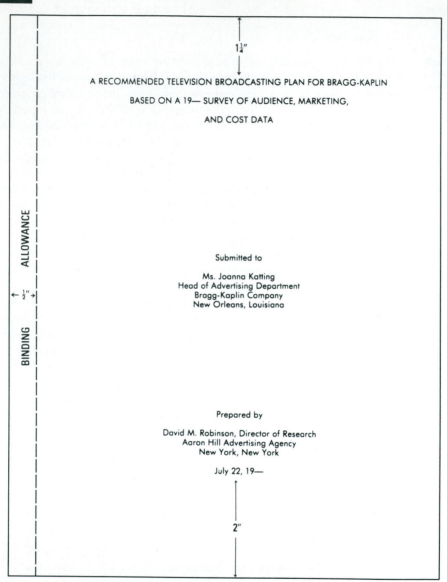

FIGURE 13–11   **Good layout for the four-spot title page**

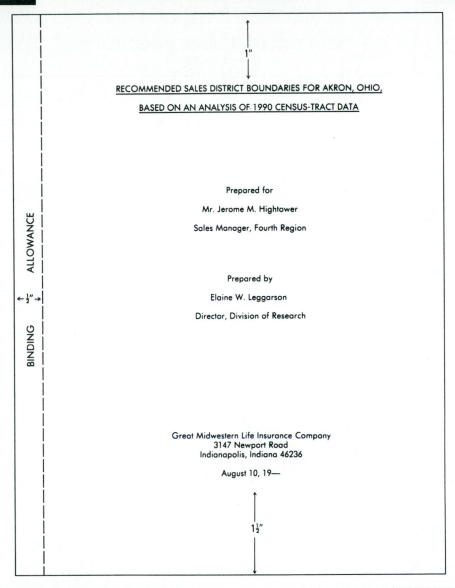

FIGURE 13–12   **Letter of transmittal fitted to the shape of the space in which formatted**

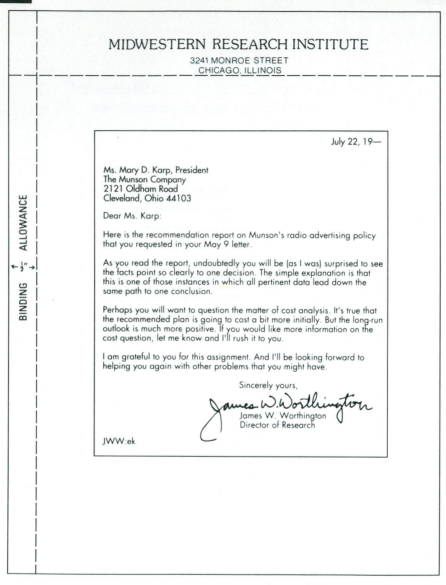

at the right, and the last line in the signature at the bottom. For the best optical effect, the rectangle should ride a little high in the space available for it. The ratio of top to bottom margin should be about 2:3.

☐ ACKNOWLEDGMENTS

Include a special page for acknowledgments when you are indebted for help.

When you are indebted to the assistance of others, it is fitting that you acknowledge them somewhere in the report. If the number of individuals is small, you may acknowledge them in the report's introduction or in the letter of transmittal. In the rare case of numerous acknowledgments, you may construct a special section for this purpose. This section is headed with the simple title "Acknowledgments" and is formatted with the same layout as any other text page that has a displayed title.

☐ TABLE OF CONTENTS

The table of contents displays the report outline with page numbers.

Set up the headings in a column to the left and page numbers in a column to the right.

The table of contents is the report outline in its polished, finished form. It lists the major report headings with the page numbers on which they appear. Although not all reports require a table of contents, one should be a part of any report long enough for a guide to be helpful to the readers.

The page is appropriately headed by the caption "Contents" or "Table of Contents," as shown in Figure 13–13. The page layout is that used for any report page with a displayed title. Below the title, you should set up two columns. One contains the headings, generally beginning with the first report part following the table of contents. You have the option to include or leave out the outline letters and numbers. If you use numbers, arrange them so that their last digits are aligned. In the other column, which is brought over to the right margin and headed by the caption "Page," place the page numbers on which the captions appear. Align these numbers on their right digits. Connect the two columns by leaders (lines of periods), preferably with intervening spaces, and align the leaders vertically.

A good rule to follow is to double-space above and below all headings of the highest level of division. Headings below this level should be uniformly single spaced or double spaced, depending on their overall lengths. If the headings are long, covering most of the line or extending to a second line, use uniform double spacing between them. Short headings appear bulky in consistently single-spaced form. Some authorities, however, prefer double-spacing all of the contents entries when double spacing is used in the text.

In the table of contents, as in the report body, you may vary the type to distinguish different levels of headings. But the type variations of the table of contents need not be the same as those used in the report text. Usually, the highest-level headings are distinguished from the other levels, and sometimes second-level headings are distinguished from lower-level headings with type differences. It is also acceptable to show no distinction by using plain capitals and lowercases for all levels of headings.

FIGURE 13–13   Good layout and mechanics in the first page of table of contents

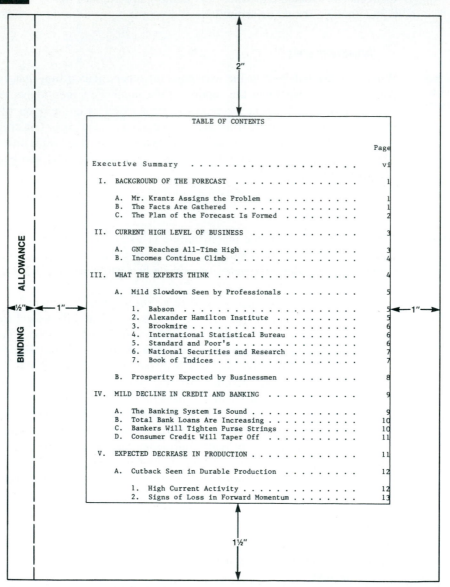

Labels on figure: 2″   ALLOWANCE   BINDING   ½″   1″   1″   1½″

☐ **TABLE OF ILLUSTRATIONS**

A table of illustrations may be a part of the table of contents.

The table of illustrations may be either a continuation of the table of contents or a separate table. This table, shown in Figure 13–14, lists the graphic aids presented in the report in much the same way that the report parts are listed in the table of contents.

In constructing this table, head it with an appropriately descriptive title, such as "Table of Charts and Illustrations," "List of Tables and Figures," or "Table of Figures." If you place the table on a separate page, the page layout is the same as that for any other text page with title displayed. If you place it as a continuation of the table of contents, you should begin it four or more lines below the last contents entry.

The table consists of two columns—one for the graphic-aid title and the other for the page on which it appears. Head the second column "Page" and connect the two columns with leaders. Line spacing in the table is optional, again depending on the line lengths of the entries. Place each entry's number before its title. If the numbers are roman, two or more digits, or otherwise require more than one character, align the last characters. If your report contains two or more illustration types (tables, charts, maps, etc.) and you have given each its own numbering sequence, you may list the entries successively by type.

VARIATIONS IN FORMS OF REPORTS

Short reports have many of the same form requirements. Use those that are appropriate for the type of report or occasion.

So far in this chapter we have been reviewing the presentation requirements of the long, formal report. However, most of the reports written in business are much shorter and considerably less formal (see Chapter 9). Even so, they use many of the same form requirements for the parts they do have in common. That is, they have balanced margins, use captions, pay attention to neatness, and so forth. The report identified as the short report usually uses a title page as well.

Letter reports are set up much as the letter of transmittal in the long report is. The first page includes the appropriate headings, salutations, and, if it is a one-page report, closings and notations, too. And all are contained within an imaginary picture frame. If the report is more than one page long, each ensuing page begins with an identification of the addressee, the page number, and the date, the three distributed proportionately across the first line (see Figure 9–2).

Memorandum reports usually begin with *Date, To, From,* and *Subject* and move on to an informal but well-organized presentation of facts (see Figure 13–15). There are other forms of memorandum reports that are organized like surveys with lists of items or topics to check off or respond to. And there are still others that are handwritten on standard interoffice communication forms.

QUESTIONS

1. "Business readers want facts. They could care less about the form in which the facts are presented." Comment on the logic of this evaluation.

2. Explain what a report writer should know about page layout and design. Why are these concepts important?

FIGURE 13–14   Good layout and mechanics in the last page of the table of contents showing the table of illustrations attached

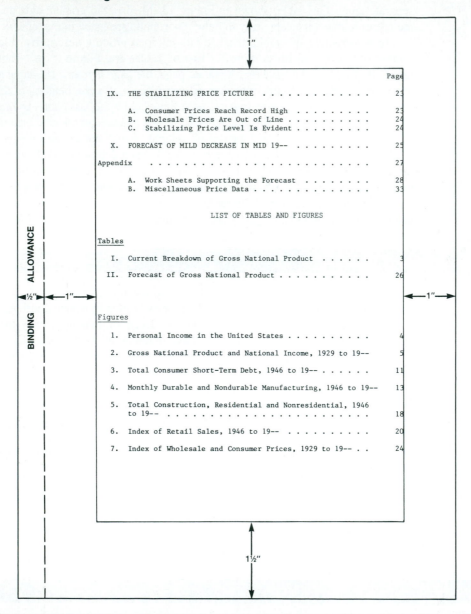

FIGURE 13–15   Good form for a memorandum report

Campus Correspondence

LOUISIANA STATE UNIVERSITY

TO: Faculty, College of   DATE: December 15, 19—
               Business Administration

FROM: Committee on Courses and Curricula *JWH*
               J. William Hughes, Chairperson

SUBJECT: Report of progress and plans on the study of the business
               administration curricula

Progress for the Period October 1 to December 15

On October 10 the Committee mailed questionnaires (copy attached) to the deans
of 24 selected colleges of business administration. To date, 21 of the deans have
returned questionnaires.

Professors Byrd, Calhoun, and Creznik have tabulated the replies received and
are now analyzing the findings.

Future Plans

Professors Byrd, Calhoun, and Creznik will present their analyses to the Committee
at its February 4th meeting. At this time, the Committee expects to study these
analyses and to make final recommendations.

Professor Byrd will record the Committee's recommendations in a written report.
The Committee will distribute copies of this report to all voting members of the
faculty at least one week before the faculty meeting scheduled for May 9.

3. Describe the layout of an ideal conventional page in a report. How does this differ from the layout of a special page?

4. Summarize the arguments on the question of whether to single or double space the report.

5. Describe the page numbering procedure of a formal report, beginning with the title fly and ending with the last page of the appended parts.

6. Discuss the two basic ways of giving emphasis to the captions in a report.

7. Work up two schemes of caption emphasis that are different from those illustrated in the text. Evaluate them critically.

8. Discuss the content and layout considerations of a title page.

9. Describe the form of the letter of transmittal.

10. In what ways may acknowledgments be handled?

11. Summarize the layout and mechanics of the table of contents.

12. Describe the structure of a letter report. Do the same for a memo report.

Documentation and the Bibliography

Information developed through secondary research must be footnoted and the sources listed in a bibliography.

In the course of developing information about your report problem, you are very likely to use material you have not developed yourself. Your sources may include published information—books, periodicals, brochures, other reports, and the like. They may include correspondence, interviews, lectures, and similar sources as well. When you write your report, you have to identify these sources both individually in the text of your report and in summary fashion in a bibliography. The traditional reason for this requirement is, of course, your legal and ethical obligation to give credit where credit is due.

Besides giving credit where it is due, documenting and listing secondary sources provide valuable information to your readers.

But there is a second reason that is equally important: you have the obligation to give your readers as complete a body of information as you can. Your readers need to be able to distinguish your original research from other information you present. They should be able to verify the data you cite or to see them in full context. They also need the full record of your research, both for its own sake and for the opportunities it provides for their continuing the investigation of the problem. The bibliography is, after all, a key to your approach to the research problem. And when it is completed, it becomes one of the prepared bibliographies you yourself may have found so helpful in the early stages of your own research.

Therefore, if you keep in mind both reasons for including complete documentation and a representative bibliography, you will avoid the confusion often associated with this aspect of report writing. Deciding what to footnote, what to include in the bibliography, where to place footnotes, how to organize the list of works cited, even what style of documentation to use, thus becomes a matter of what is fair to your sources and is helpful to your readers.

HOW TO QUOTE AND PARAPHRASE

You may quote directly from a secondary source or paraphrase the material you select. Make the decision on a case-by-case basis.

When you use information from other sources, you may either quote directly or paraphrase—that is, restate the information in your own words. The choice should be made on a case-by-case basis. You should paraphrase when you can convey information more efficiently or effectively than it is conveyed in the original. You should quote directly when the wording is distinctive or when using the source's own words will add credibility to the information you are presenting.

Be sure to integrate the secondary material smoothly into the text of your writing.

Whether paraphrasing or quoting, integrate the secondary material carefully. Splice the various segments together, much as you would splice together segments of a tape or a film, so the reader/audience will move smoothly from one writing "voice" to another. Transition words help in this splicing process. Editorial adjustments to verb tense, singulars and plurals, and pronoun references help to integrate paraphrased material. However, you must not alter the original meaning of the material.

Paraphrased material, though it is acknowledged, is not differentiated from the text. However, quoted material, which also is acknowledged, is distinguished from the text either by quotation marks or indentation, depending on the length.

Place paraphrased information within the text and footnote it. Distinguish quotes from text in one of two ways, depending on length. If four lines or less, place in quotation marks. If five lines or more, single-space and block without marks.

The conventional rule for distinguishing quoted material from the text is simple. If the quoted passage is four lines or less in length, it is typed within the report text and distinguished from the normal text by quotation marks. If a longer quotation (five lines or more) is used, the conventional practice is to set it in from both left and right margins (about five spaces) but without quotation marks. If the text is double spaced, the quoted passage is further distinguished from the main text with single spacing.

Use ellipses or a line of periods to show omissions.

Thus, quoted material can vary from one key word or phrase to five or more consecutive lines; and it can be reproduced verbatim or with unnecessary words edited out, using ellipses (. . .). If omissions appear at the end of a sentence, you must use four periods (. . . .)—one for the final sentence punctuation plus the ellipses. In long quotations, it is conventional to show omission of one or more paragraphs with a full line of periods, usually typed with intervening spaces.

To review these possibilities, consider the following examples. For these illustrations, we are using the traditional footnote superscript.

Paraphrase: Logan Wilson criticized academicians for being scientific in their approach to every area of inquiry but their own. Lacking exact qualitative measures, administrators tend to rely upon rather inexact quantitative measures, he says.[1]

Key phrase quotation: Logan Wilson characterizes as a "curious paradox" what he sees as the failure of academics to be scientific in their approach to every area of inquiry but their own.[1]

Verbatim quotation: Logan Wilson makes this penetrating observation: "Lacking precise qualitative criteria, administrators are prone to fall back upon rather crude quantitative measures as a partial substitute."[1]

Partial quotation: According to Logan Wilson, ". . . academicians display a scientific attitude toward every universe except that which comprises their own profession."[1]

Extended quotation: Of those opposing the issue, Logan Wilson makes this penetrating observation:

It is a curious paradox that academicians display a scientific attitude toward every universe of inquiry except that which comprises their own profession. . . . Lacking precise qualitative criteria, administrators are prone to fall back upon rather crude quantitative measures as a partial substitute.[1]

These logical, straightforward, and simple arguments of the proponents of teacher evaluation appear to be irrefutable.

WHEN TO ACKNOWLEDGE

Always acknowledge a quotation. Acknowledge paraphrased material when it is not general knowledge.

As stated above, you must acknowledge a source on the bases both of giving credit where credit is due and of providing the full component of information the readers need to understand the source and your use of it. If you are quoting the words of another, you must give credit. If you are paraphrasing, you should give credit unless the material covered is general knowledge.

HOW TO ACKNOWLEDGE

Select a reference system.

Acknowledge sources by citing them in the text, using one of a number of reference systems. Three of the most commonly used systems are the Chicago (*The Chicago Manual of Style*), MLA (Modern Language Association), and APA (American Psychological Association). Although all are similar, they differ somewhat in format, as you will see in the following pages. Because the Chicago system is the most widely used in business books and journals, we will review it first. Then we will illustrate the MLA and APA systems to note primary differences.

Use (1) parenthetic or (2) footnote references.

After you have selected a system, you must choose a method of acknowledgment. Two methods are commonly used in business: (1) parenthetic author-date references within the text, and (2) footnote references. A third method, endnote references, is sometimes used, although it appears to be losing favor. Only the first two are discussed here.

☐   THE PARENTHETIC AUTHOR-DATE METHOD

Author-date method: Last name and year in parentheses after material cited.

In recent years, the author-date method has become the most popular reference method in business. It involves placing the author's last name and year of publication in parentheses immediately following the material cited:

(Calahan 1994)

Specific page numbers can follow date.

The reference is keyed to a list of all publications cited (a bibliography), which appears at the end of the report (see discussion of the bibliography in a following section.) If specific page numbers are needed, they follow the date:

(Calahan 1994, 117–18)

Cite last names for multiple authors.

The last names are listed of works with two or three authors:

(Smith, Corley, and Doran 1993, 31)

Use *et al.* if more than three.

For works with more than three authors, "et al." is used:

(Clovis et al. 1991)

Use an organization's name as author for unsigned publications.

When no author is listed, as in unsigned publications issued by a company, government agency, labor union, or such, the author's name is the organization name:

(U.S. Department of Labor 1994)

(American Federation of Labor 1993, 31)

References in a report are keyed to the bibliography at end of the report.

As noted earlier, these references are keyed to a bibliography that appears at the end of the report. To find the details of the reference, the reader turns to the bibliography and traces the reference through the alphabetical listing. For the reference "(Sanders 1994)," for example, the reader would find Sanders in its alphabetical place. If more than one publication by Sanders is listed, the reader would refer to the one written in 1994.

☐   THE FOOTNOTE METHOD

Place footnotes at the bottom of the page and key them to the text with superscripts.

The traditional method of acknowledging sources is by footnotes; that is, the references are placed at the bottom of the page and are keyed with the text material by superscripts (raised arabic numbers). The numbering sequence of the superscripts is consecutive, by page, by chapter, or by the whole work. The footnotes are placed inside the page layout, are single-spaced, and are indented or blocked just as the text is formatted.

There are two form variations: (1) abbreviated and (2) complete.

Although footnote form varies from one source to another, one generally accepted procedure is presented here. It permits two structures: an abbreviated reference that is used with a bibliography in the report and a complete reference when no bibliography is present.

Abbreviated form gives author's surname, title of publication, page.

In the abbreviated form (not accepted by everyone), the footnote reference needs to contain only these parts: (1) author's surname; (2) title of the article, bulletin, or book; and (3) page number.

[3]Wilson, *The Report Writer's Guide,* 44 (book reference).

[4]Allison, "Making Routine Reports Talk," 71 (periodical reference).

The complete form gives more complete identification. Study requirements for each publication type.

For the complete reference (usually preferred) the descriptive points are listed in the order mentioned below. Capitals are used only with proper nouns, and abbreviations are acceptable if consistently used.

In these lists, all of the items that could be placed in each type of entry are named in the order of the arrangement. Those items not available or not important should be passed over. In other words, the following list gives all possible contents in order. But many of the items listed should be used as needed.

Book Entry

1. *Superscript.* Arabic numeral keyed to the text reference and placed before the first part of the entry without spacing.

2. *Name of the author, in normal order.* If two or more authors are involved, all may be presented. If the number of authors is too great to list, the first author followed by the Latin *et al.* may be used.

3. *Capacity of the author.* Needed only when contribution to the publication is not truly that of the author, such as *editor* or *compiler.*

4. *Chapter name.* Necessary only in rare instances when the chapter title helps the reader to find the source.

5. *Book title.* Book names are placed in italics. In typewritten work, italics are indicated by underscoring or by solid caps.

6. *Edition.*

7. *Publishing company.*

8. *Location of publisher.* If there is more than one city listed on the title page, the one listed first should be used. If the population exceeds 500,000, the name of the city is sufficient; otherwise the city and state (or province) are best given.

9. *Date.* Year of publication. If revised, year of latest revision.

10. *Page or pages.* Specific page or inclusive pages on which the cited material is found.

The following are examples of book entries.

A Typical Book

[1]Cindy Burford, Aline Culberson, and Peter Dykus, *Writing for Results,* 4th ed., New York: Charles Storm Publishing Company, 1990, 17–18.

A Book Written by a Staff of Writers under the Direction of an Editor   (chapter title is considered helpful)

[2]W. C. Butte and Ann Buchannan, editors, "Direct Mail Advertising," *An Encyclopedia of Advertising,* New York: Binton Publishing Company, 1993, 99.

A Book Written by a Number of Coauthors

[3]E. Butler Cannais *et al., Anthology of Public Relations,* New York: Warner-Bragg, Inc., 1994, 137.

Periodical Entry

1. *Superscript.*

2. *Author's name.* Frequently, no author is given. In such cases the entry may be skipped; or if it is definitely known to be anonymous, the word *anonymous* may be placed in the entry.

3. *Article title.* Typed within quotation marks.

4. *Periodical title.* Set in italics, which are indicated in typewriting by underscoring.

5. *Publication identification.* Volume number in arabic numerals followed by specific date of publication (month and year or season and year). Volume number is not needed if complete (day, month, year) date is given.

6. *Page or pages.*

Examples of periodical entries are shown below:

[1]Mildred C. Kinning, "A New Look at Retirement," *Modern Business,* July 31, 1994, 31–32.

[2]William O. Schultz, "How One Company Improved Morale," *Business Leader,* August 31, 1992, 17.

[3]Mary Mitchell, "Report Writing Aids," *ABC Bulletin,* October 1991, 13.

NEWSPAPER ARTICLE

1. *Superscript.*

2. *Source of description.* If article is signed, give author's name. Otherwise, give description of article, such as "United Press dispatch" or "Editorial."

3. *Main head of article.* Subheads not needed.

4. *Newspaper title.* City and state (province) names inserted in brackets if place names do not appear in newspaper title. State (province) names not needed in case of very large cities, such as New York, Toronto, and Los Angeles.

5. *Date of publication.*

6. *Page* (p.) and *column* (col.) are optional.

The following are typical newspaper article entries:

[1]United Press dispatch, "Rival Unions Sign Pact," *Morning Advocate* [Baton Rouge, Louisiana], September 3, 1993.

[2]Editorial, "The North Moves South," *Austin* [Texas] *American,* February 3, 1992, p. 2–A, col. 3.

LETTERS OR DOCUMENTS

1. *Nature of communication.*

2. *Name of writer.*

3. *Name of recipient.*   [With identification by title and organization where helpful.]

4. *Date of writing.*

5. *Where filed.*

An example of an entry citing a letter is given below:

[1]Letter from J. W. Wells, president, Wells Equipment Co., to James Mattoch, secretary-treasurer, Southern Industrialists, Inc., June 10, 1992, filed among Mr. Mattoch's personal records.

Material from a Computer Service

1. The publication information as provided by the service.

2. The name of the vendor (BRS or DIALOG, for example).

3. The access or identification number of the item.

An example of an entry citing an item developed from a computer service is thus as follows:

[1]K. E. Weick, "Stress in Accounting Systems," *Accounting Review*, 58, April 1991, 350–69, DIALOG file 75, item 249762 ACR83DKO350.

For unique footnotes, consult a detailed stylebook. If no model is available, use your best judgment.

The types of entries discussed in the preceding paragraphs are those most likely to be used. Yet, unusual types of publications may occasionally come up, as may involved applications of the basic books and periodical formats. In such circumstances, consult a detailed handbook or style manual. If you find no model entry, construct one according to the entry form used by a similar source. Use your best judgment in selecting and arranging the information your reader needs to know.

Standard Reference Forms

Here is a list of traditional footnote notations. Though you may not use them yourself, you will need them to follow the documentation in older sources.

Certain traditional forms are sometimes used in conjunction with the footnote method to handle repeated references. Although the increasing use of parenthetical documentation and the short form of footnoting have made these notations largely superfluous, you will find it helpful to know them just the same. If you do not use them yourself, you can understand what they mean when you come across them in other reports and in secondary research materials.

Ibid. refers to the preceding entry but a different page.

1. Ibid.   Literally, **ibid.** means "in the same place." It is used to refer the reader to the preceding footnote. The entry consists of the superscript, *ibid.,* and the page number if the page number is different, as shown in these entries:

[1]Janice Smith, *How to Write the Annual Report,* Chicago: Small-Boch, Inc., 1993, 173.

[2]*Ibid.,* 143 (refers to Smith's book but to a different page).

Use a short reference form (author's last name, date) to refer to other entries rather than op. cit. and loc. cit.

2. Op. Cit.   ("in the work cited") and **loc. cit.** ("in the place cited") also can refer to references cited previously; but they are rarely used today. It is better to use in their place a short reference form (author's last name, date).

3. OTHER   Other abbreviations used in footnote entries are as follows:

Abbreviation	Meaning
cf.	Compare (direct reader's attention to another passage)
cf. ante	Compare above
cf. post	Compare below
ed.	Edition
e.g.	For example
et al.	And others
et passim	And at intervals throughout the work
et seq.	And the following
i.e.	That is
infra	Below
l., ll.	Line, lines
MS, MSS	Manuscript, manuscripts
n.d.	No date
n.n.	No name
n.p.	No place
p., pp.,	Page, pages
f., ff.,	Following page, following pages
supra	Above
vol., vols.	Volume, volumes

DISCUSSION FOOTNOTES

Discussion footnotes explain and cross-reference without interrupting the text.

In sharp contrast with source footnotes are the discussion footnotes. Through the use of discussion footnotes the writer strives to explain a part of the text, to amplify discussion on a phase of the presentation, to make cross-references to other parts of the report, and the like. The following examples illustrate some possibilities of this footnote type.

CROSS-REFERENCE

[1]See the principle of focal points on page 72.

AMPLIFICATION OF DISCUSSION AND CROSS-REFERENCES

[2]Lyman Bryson says the same thing: "Every communication is different for every receiver even in the same context. No one can estimate the variation of understanding that there may be among receivers of the same message conveyed in the

same vehicle when the receivers are separated in either space or time." See *Communication of Ideas,* 5.

COMPARISON

[3]Compare with the principle of the objective: Before starting any activity, one should make a clear, complete statement of the objective in view.

THE BIBLIOGRAPHY

A bibliography is an orderly list of sources.

A bibliography is an orderly list of material on a particular subject. In a formal paper, the list covers references on the paper's subject. The entries in this list closely resemble source footnotes, but the two must not be confused.

It is placed after the appendix, grouped by publication, and alphabetized by group.

The bibliography normally appears as an appended part of a formal paper and is placed after the appendix. It may be preceded by a fly page containing the one word *Bibliography.* The page that begins the list is headed by the main caption *Bibliography,* usually formatted in solid capital letters. Below this title the publications are presented by broad categories and in alphabetical order within the categories. Such groupings as *Books, Periodicals,* and *Bulletins* may be used. But the determination of groups should be based solely on the types of publications collected in each bibliography. If, for example, a bibliography includes a large number of periodicals and government publications plus a wide assortment of diverse publication types, the bibliography could be divided into three parts: *Periodicals, Government Publications,* and *Miscellaneous Publications.*

Bibliographic entries are similar to source footnotes with four exceptions.

As with footnotes, variations in bibliographical style are numerous. A simplified form recommended for business use follows the same procedure as described above for source footnotes, with four major exceptions:

(1) Reversed author's name (surname first), for alphabetizing.

1. The author's name is listed in reverse order—surname first—for the purpose of alphabetizing. If coauthors are involved, however, only the first name is reversed.

(2) Hanging indention form.

2. The entry is generally formatted in hanging-indention form. That is, the second and following lines of an entry begin some uniform distance (usually about five spaces) to the right of the beginning point of the first line. The purpose of this indented pattern is to make the alphabetized first line stand out.

(3) Inclusive pages for articles, but not for books.

3. The bibliography entry gives the inclusive pages of articles, but not for books, and does not refer to any one page or passage.

(4) Uniform line for subsequent references by same author.

4. Second and subsequent references to publications of the same author are indicated by a uniform line (see bibliography illustration). In typed manuscripts, this line might be formed by the underscore struck 10 consecutive times. But this line may be used only if the entire authorship is the same in the consecutive publications. For example, the line could not be used in a situation in which consecutive entries have one common author but different coauthors.

Following is an example of a bibliography:

BIBLIOGRAPHY

Books

Burton, Helen. *The City Fights Back.* New York: Citadel Press, 1992.

Caperton, Hudson D. *The Business of Government.* Boston: Sherman-Kaufman Company, 1967.

Chapman, Kenneth W., Harvey H. Heinz, and Robert V. Martinez. *The Basics of Marketing.* 4th ed. New York: Barrow-Dore, Inc., 1937.

Kernan, Gladys M. *Retailers Manual of Taxes and Regulation.* 12th ed. New York: Institute of Distribution, Inc., 1993.

Surrey, N. M. M. *The Commerce of Louisiana During the French Regime, 1699–1763.* New York: Columbia University Press, 1916.

Government Publications

United States Bureau of the Census. "Characteristics of the Population." *Nineteenth Census of the United States: Census of Population,* Vol. 2, Part 18. Washington, D.C.: United States Government Printing Office, 1991.

———, *Statistical Abstract of the United States.* Washington, D.C.: United States Government Printing Office, 1990.

United States Department of Commerce, *Business Statistics: 1985.* Washington, D.C.: United States Government Printing Office, 1991.

———, *Survey of Current Business: 1995 Supplement.* Washington, D.C.: United States Government Printing Office, 1995.

Periodicals

Montgomery, Donald E. "Consumer Standards and Marketing." *Annals of the American Academy of Political and Social Science* 7 (May 1993). 141–49.

Phillips, Emily F. "Some Studies Needed in Marketing," *Journal of Marketing* 9 (July 1978). 16–25.

———. "Major Areas of Marketing Research." *Journal of Marketing* 28 (July 1994). 21–26.

Miscellaneous Publications

Bradford, Ernest S. *Survey and Directory, Marketing Research Agencies in the United States.* New York: Bureau of Business Research, College of the City of New York, 1991.

Reference Sources on Chain Stores. New York: Institute of Distribution, Inc., 1991.

Smith, T. Lynn. *Farm Trade Centers in Louisiana, 1901 to 1986.* Louisiana Bulletin No. 234. Baton Rouge: Louisiana State University, 1987.

THE ANNOTATED BIBLIOGRAPHY

An annotated bibliography features a brief comment on the content of each entry.

Frequently, in scholarly writing each bibliography entry is followed by a brief comment on the value and content of the entry. That is, the bibliography is annotated. Form and content of annotated bibliographies are shown in these entries:

Donald, W. T., ed. *Handbook of Business Administration.* New York: Shannon-Dale Book Co., Inc., 1993.

Contains a summary of the activities in each major area of business. Written by foremost authorities in each field. Particularly useful to the business specialist who wants a quick review of the whole of business.

Braden, Shelby M., and Lillian Como, eds. *Business Leader's Handbook.* 4th ed. New York: Mercer and Sons, Inc., 1994.

Provides answers to most routine executive problems in explicit manner and with good examples. Contains good material on correspondence and sales letters.

DIFFERENCES IN CHICAGO, APA, AND MLA FORMATS

As noted previously, the APA and MLA systems differ somewhat from that of the Chicago system presented in preceding pages. The primary differences are evident from the following illustrations.

☐ PARENTHETIC REFERENCES

Chicago and MLA:

(Burton 1929)

APA:

(Burton, 1919)

☐ FOOTNOTES

BOOKS
Chicago:

²Helen Burton, *The City Fights Back,* New York: Citadel Press, 1994, 17.

MLA:

²Helen Burton, *The City Fights Back,* (New York: Citadel Press, 1994), 17.

APA: Does not use footnotes.

PERIODICALS
Chicago:

³Donald E. Montgomery, "Consumer Standards and Marketing," *Journal of Distribution,* May 1993, 144.

MLA:

³Donald E. Montgomery, "Consumer Standards and Marketing," *Journal of Distribution,* May 1993: 144.

APA: Does not use footnotes.

□ BIBLIOGRAPHY

BOOKS
Chicago:

> Burton, Helen. *The City Fights Back.* New York: Citadel Press, 1994.

MLA:

> Burton, Helen. *The City Fights Back.* New York: Citadel Press, 1994.

APA:

> Burton, H. (1994). *The city fights back.* New York: Citadel Press.

PERIODICALS
Chicago:

> Montgomery, Donald E. "Consumer Standards and Marketing." *Journal of Distribution,* (May 1994). 141–49.

MLA:

> Montgomery, Donald E. "Consumer Standards and Marketing." *Journal of Distribution,* (May 1994): 141–49.

APA:

> Montgomery, D. E. (1994). Consumer standards and marketing. *Journal of Distribution,* 15(5), 141–149.

In place of the specific date of publication, APA style uses volume and number—in this example 15(5).

Any of these systems are appropriate in business. Of course, you should use only one in a paper.

QUESTIONS

1. In what two ways may quoted material be placed within the text of a report?

2. Distinguish between paraphrased and verbatim use of secondary information.

3. Explain the use of the ellipsis. Illustrate its use at the beginning of a passage, at the end of a passage, and within a passage.

4. How are omissions of a paragraph or more conventionally indicated?

5. What is the major determinant of when a source footnote is needed?

6. Distinguish between the need for footnotes for paraphrased material and for quoted material.

7. Describe the mechanical arrangement of the footnote on the page.

8. From the garbled information presented below, construct *(a)* a series of footnote entries for material with a bibliography and *(b)* a series of entries for a paper without a bibliography. The entries are all within the space of three consecutive pages. Assume you are using the footnote method.

First entry: reference to page 132 of a book written by Lloyd Peabody, James Melton, and William Byrd; published by Jones Publishing Company, Atlanta, Georgia; entitled *Advanced Personnel Management;* 4th edition; published 1992.

Second entry: reference to page 71; a magazine article appearing in *Management News;* October 7, 1993, "An Experiment with Incentive Plans"; written by Kirk Tobin; Volume 71.

Third entry: second reference to Peabody's book, this time to page 33.

Fourth entry: another reference to page 33 of Peabody's book.

Fifth entry: a second reference to page 71 of Tobin's article.

9. Construct bibliography entries for the textbooks you are using.

10. Construct bibliography entries for five magazine articles in your major field of study.

11. Find and construct the bibliography entries for five sources you believe involve unusual problems in footnoting. (Publications other than books or periodicals are most likely to meet this requirement.)

12. Distinguish between the discussion footnote and the source footnote.

13. Using hypothetical information, construct discussion footnotes used *(a)* to make a cross-reference, *(b)* to amplify discussion, and *(c)* to make a comparison.

14. Define the annotated bibliography. What is its purpose?

15. From the information below, make the entry as it would appear
    a. In a bibliography.
    b. As a footnote (No. 2) referring to page 374 (no bibliography).
    c. As a footnote that is No. 4 in a series in which No. 2 referred to the same book and the same page.
    d. As a footnote that is No. 5 in the same series, but reference is to another page (p. 411).
        Book title—*A History of Modern Business.*
        Author—James W. Gordon.
        Date of publication—1994.
        Edition—1st.
        Total pages—567.
        Publisher—Maybery Publishing Company, Boston.

Graphic Aids for Reports

Words need help in conveying meaning to readers.

Perhaps Confucius was not precisely correct when he said, "A picture is worth a thousand words." But we can quarrel only with the number in the statement. Study of the communication process (see Chapter 2) shows us that words are imprecise conveyors of meaning. We must make a limited number of words cover an infinite number of variations in reality. At best, words fit reality only loosely. Thus, it is little wonder that we frequently have difficulty communicating through words.

Pictures help words communicate information in reports.

Because many of your reports must communicate complex, voluminous information, you are likely to have difficulty making words do the job. In a statistical analysis, for example, you will probably get your reader lost in a maze of data if you tell the report's story in words. In a technical report, you will likely have difficulty using words to describe a process or a procedure. In many such cases, you will need to use pictures of some kind to help communicate your information.

Graphic aids (pictures) are any form of illustration. They supplement words, present minor details, emphasize key points, and improve the report's appearance.

Pictures, or *graphic aids,* as we call them in report writing, are an essential part of many reports. Graphic aids are any form of illustration designed to supplement the text: charts, pictures, diagrams, maps, and such. Except in summary-type reports, they rarely take the place of words, for words are essential for communicating the information in most reports. Their role is more a supplementary one—of helping the words to communicate the report content. In addition, graphic aids serve to present minor supporting details not covered in words. They help give emphasis to the key points of coverage. Also, they serve to improve the report's physical appearance, making the report more inviting and readable. With computer-generated graphic packages and desktop publishing systems, you can help give your graphic aids a distinctive and professional flavor.

FORESIGHT IN PLANNING

You should plan the use of graphic aids early in the report-writing process.

You should plan the graphic aids for a report soon after you determine and organize your findings. As you approach the task of planning your graphic aids, you should keep in mind your fundamental purpose of communicating. Thus, you should never select some random number of illustrations, nor should you judge the completeness of graphic presentation in a report by the number of illustrations used. Instead, you should plan each graphic aid to serve a specific communication purpose. Each one should help present your report information. Each one should be included because it is needed. Only if it is needed to help convey the report purpose more clearly can you justify including it in your report.

RELATIONSHIP OF NEED TO THE PLAN

Use graphic aids in two ways: (1) to emphasize and supplement and (2) to present findings in summary reports.

Just which graphic aids you will need to communicate a report's story is not easy to determine. Much depends on your overall plan. If you plan to cover the subject in detail, the graphic aids should emphasize and supplement. Specifically, they should point up the major facts discussed and present the detailed data not covered in the text. On the other hand, if you plan to present the facts in summary form, you may use the graphic aids to work more closely with your text.

The first is conventional; the second is used in summary reports for the general public and for executives. Sometimes reports use both.

The first arrangement—complete text supplemented with graphic aids—is the more conventional and is best for all studies that require completeness. The second plan—summary text closely aligned with graphic aids—is gaining importance. It is especially used in popular types of reports, such as those addressed to the general public. As Figure 15–1 illustrates, this plan produces fast-moving, light reading—the kind the public likes. Many top executives also prefer this plan. With increasing demands on their time, they want reports to give them the facts quickly and easily. Short summary reports, helped with an abundance of clear graphic aids, do this job best. Because of the need for a complete report for future reference and for presentation of summary information to top executives, both kinds of reports frequently are written for the same problem.

PREFERRED PLACEMENT WITHIN THE REPORT

Place the graphic aids as close to the related text as you can.

For the best communication effect, you should place graphic aids as close to the related text as possible. In such positions, they will likely be seen when they need to be seen. Exactly where on the page to place each illustration depends on its size. If the graphic aid is small (less than a page), you should surround it with the associated text. If it requires a full page for display, you should place it immediately following the page on which it is discussed. When the discussion covers several pages, however, the full-page illustration is best placed on the page following the first reference to its content.

FIGURE 15-1   **Page from a popular report illustrating use of a summary text closely aligned with graphic aids**

Long Industry Lead Times

In considering measures to ease the energy supply situation (section VI), the importance of long lead times cannot be overemphasized. In some activities a sufficient concentration of brains and money can solve problems through "crash" action. In the oil industry, however, as the diagram below shows, planners must think in terms of several years, not months. An understanding of the time factor in oil operations is fundamental.

CHART 15

Lead Times in Oil Industry Developments

Geophysical work
to find commercial field
1-3 years

Offshore drilling
1-2 years to drill wells
6-18 months to set
platforms
2-3 years in development

Refinery Construction
3 years to obtain site, to
design, and to get permits
2-4 years for construction

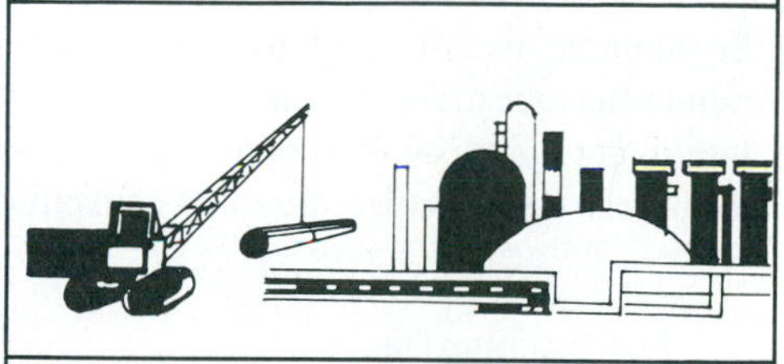

Marine Terminals
3 years upwards

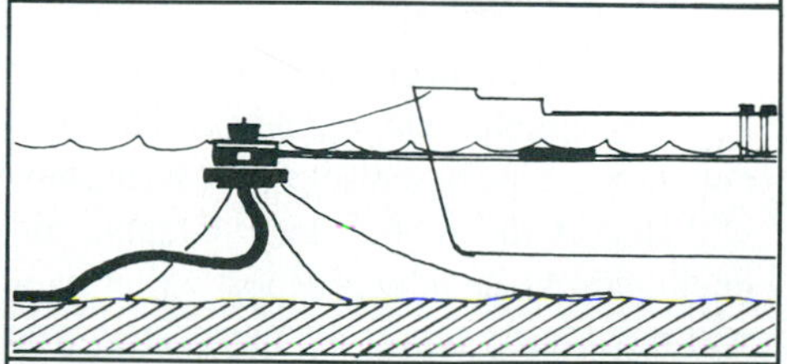

Tanker construction
2-3 years

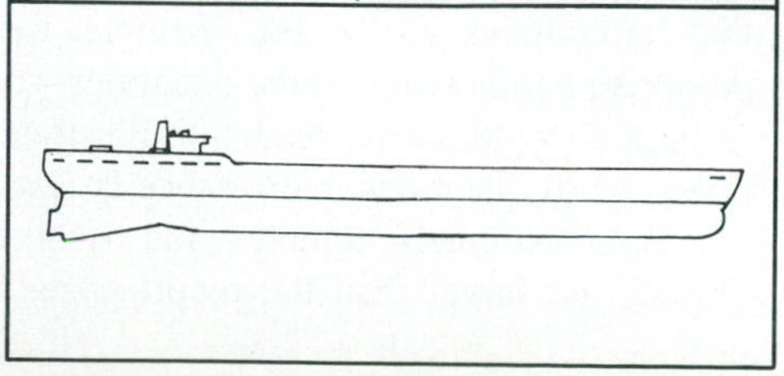

Graphic aids at the end of the report do not help the reader.

Some report writers place all of the illustrations in the appendix. Aside from being easier for the writer, little can be said for this practice. Certainly, it does not work for the convenience of the readers, who must flip through several pages each time they wish to see the graphic presentation of a part of the text.

Graphic aids not discussed in the report belong in the appendix.

If you want to include graphic aids that do not relate to a specific part of the report story, place them in the appendix. Included in this group are all graphic aids that belong within the report for completeness yet have no specific point of relevance within the main text. As a rule, this group is composed of long, complex tables that may cover large areas of information. Such tables may even cover the data displayed in a number of charts and other, more graphic devices that generally are constructed to illustrate very specific spots within the report.

Incidentally invite the reader to look at the graphic aids at the appropriate place.

Whether you place the illustrations within or at the end of the text, you should key them to the text portions they cover by means of references. In other words, you should call the reader's attention to illustrations that cover the topic under discussion. Such references are best made as incidental remarks in sentences that contain significant comments on the data shown in the illustration. Such incidental wordings include the following:

. . . , as shown in Figure 4. . . .
. . . , indicated in Figure 4. . . .
. . . , as a glance at Figure 4 reveals. . . .
. . . (see Figure 4). . . .

GENERAL MECHANICS OF CONSTRUCTION

Following are some general points about constructing graphic aids.

In planning the illustrations—and in actually constructing them—you will confront numerous questions of mechanics. Many of these issues you must solve through intelligent appraisal of the conditions at hand. The mechanics fall into certain general groups. We summarize the most conventional in the following paragraphs.

☐ SIZE DETERMINATION

Make each graphic aid the size its contents justify.

One of the first decisions involved in constructing a graphic aid is determining how large the graphic aid should be. The answer to this question should not be arbitrary, nor should it be based solely on your convenience. A too large or too small graphic aid will distort the report story. Graphic aids that are deliberately made too large are unethical. As an ethical report writer, you should make each graphic aid the size that will most fairly report the facts. Thus, you should seek to give the illustration the size that its contents justify. For example, for an illustration that is relatively simple—comprising only two or three quantities—a quarter page might be adequate; certainly a full page would not be needed to illustrate the data. But if a graphic aid consists of a dozen or so quantities, more space is justified—possibly even a full page.

With extremely complex and involved data, it may be necessary to make the graphic aid larger than the report page. Such long presentations must be carefully

Graphic aids larger than a page are justified if they contain enough information.

inserted and folded within the report so they will open easily. The fold selected will, of course, vary with the size of the page; so there is no best fold we recommend. You will have to experiment until you find a convenient fold.

☐ LAYOUT ARRANGEMENT

Size and content determine the shape of graphic aids.

You should determine the layout (shape) of the graphic aid by size and content requirements. Sometimes a tall, narrow rectangle is the answer. Other times it might be a short, wide rectangle or a full-page rectangle. You simply consider the logical possibilities and select the one that appears best. You should keep the graphic aid within the normal page layout as much as possible.

☐ RULES AND BORDERS

Use rules and borders when they will enhance appearance.

You should arrange rules and borders in any form of graphic presentation to help display and clarify the data presented. Thus, you should determine their use chiefly through careful planning. As a general practice, however, you should set off graphic aids of less than a page from the text with a lined border that completely encloses the illustration and its caption. You may use this arrangement for full-page illustrations as well, although the border does not serve as practical a purpose. You should not extend the borders beyond the normal page margins. An exception to this rule is, of course, the unusual instance in which the volume of data to be illustrated simply will not fit into the space of the normal page layout.

☐ COLOR AND CROSS-HATCHING

Color and cross-hatching can improve graphic aids.

When appropriately used, color and cross-hatching help the reader to see the comparisons and distinctions. In addition, they give the report a boost in physical attractiveness. Color is especially valuable for this purpose, and you should use it whenever practical.

☐ NUMBERING

Number graphic aids consecutively by type.

Except for minor tabular displays that are actually a part of the text, you should number all illustrations in the report. Many numbering schemes are available to you depending on the makeup of the graphic aids.

If you have many graphic aids that fall into two or more categories, the preferred practice is to number each category consecutively. For example, if your report is illustrated with six tables, five charts, and six maps, you may number these graphic aids "Table 1," "Table 2," . . . "Table 6"; "Chart 1," "Chart 2," . . . "Chart 5"; and "Map 1," "Map 2," . . . "Map 6."

But if the illustrations used are a wide mixture of types, preferably number them in two groups: tables and figures. To illustrate, consider a report containing three tables, two maps, three charts, one diagram, and one photograph. You could group these graphic aids and number them "Table I," "Table II," and "Table III" and

"Figure 1," "Figure 2," . . . "Figure 7." By convention, tables are never grouped with other forms of presentation. *Figures* represent a somewhat miscellaneous grouping, which may include all illustration types other than tables. It would not be wrong to group and number as figures all graphic aids, other than tables, even if the group contained sufficient subgroups (charts, maps, and so on) to warrant separate numbering of each subgroup.

Figures are a miscellaneous grouping of types. Number tables separately.

□ CONSTRUCTION OF TITLE CAPTIONS

The title should describe content clearly. Consider the five Ws—who, what, where, when, and why.

Every graphic aid should have a title caption that adequately describes its contents. Like the captions used in other parts of the report, the title to a graphic aid has the objective of concisely covering the contents. As a check of content coverage, you might well use the journalist's five Ws—who, what, where, when, and why. Sometimes you might include *how* (the classification principle). But as conciseness of expression is also desired, it is not always necessary to include all of the Ws in the caption. A title of a chart comparing annual sales volume of Texas and Louisiana stores of the Brill Company for the 19x0–19x1 period might be constructed as follows:

Who: Brill Company

What: Annual sales

Where: Texas and Louisiana

When: 19x0–19x1

Why: For comparison

The caption might read, "Comparative Annual Sales of Texas and Louisiana Branches of the Brill Company, 19x0–19x1."

□ PLACEMENT OF TITLES

Place titles consistently above or below graphic aids. Most go at the top.

The most common practice nowadays is to place all titles above the information displayed. Historically, however, the convention was to place table titles at the top and titles of all other forms at the bottom. Either practice is correct if followed consistently.

□ FOOTNOTES AND ACKNOWLEDGMENTS

Use footnotes to explain or elaborate.

Occasionally, parts of a graphic aid require special explanation or elaboration. When these conditions arise—just as when similar explanations are required within the report text—you should use footnotes. Such footnotes are nothing more than concise explanations placed below the illustration and keyed to the part explained by means of a superscript (raised number) or asterisk. Sometimes a raised lowercase letter of the alphabet (a, b, c, etc.) is used so as not to cause confusion with quantitative data. Footnotes for graphic aids are best placed immediately below the information presented.

Usually, a source acknowledgment is the bottom entry on the page. By *source acknowledgment,* we mean a reference to the person or entity that deserves the credit for gathering the data used in the illustration. The entry consists simply of the word *source* followed by a colon and the source name. A source note for data based on information gathered by the U.S. Department of Agriculture might read like this:

Acknowledge source of information with note below the graphic aid.

Source: U.S. Department of Agriculture.

If you or your staff collected the data, you may follow one of two procedures. You may give the source as "primary," in which case the source note would read:

"Source: Primary" is the proper note for information you gathered yourself.

Source: Primary.

Alternatively, you may omit the source note altogether.

CONSTRUCTION OF TABLES

A table is an orderly arrangement of information.

A *table* is any systematic arrangement of quantitative information in rows and columns. Although tables are not graphic in the literal meaning of the word, they are instrumental in communicating information. Therefore, you may appropriately consider them a part of the graphic-aids planning of your report, although you probably will not want to use them exclusively. The purpose of a table is to present a broad area of information in convenient and orderly fashion. Such an arrangement simplifies the information and facilitates comparison and analysis.

You may use general-purpose tables (those with broad information).

Two basic types of tables are available to you—the general-purpose table and the special-purpose table. *General-purpose tables* contain a broad area of information. They are repositories of detailed statistical data and have no special analytical purpose. As a rule, general-purpose tables belong in the report appendix.

You may also use special-purpose tables (those containing specific areas of information).

Special-purpose tables, as their name implies, are prepared for a special purpose—to help to illustrate a particular phase of the report. Usually, they consist of information carefully drawn from the general-purpose tables. Only those data pertinent to the analysis are selected, and sometimes they are rearranged or regrouped to better illustrate their purposes. Such tables belong within the text near the discussion of their contents.

See Figure 15–2 for details of table arrangement.

Besides the title, footnotes, and source designation previously discussed, the table consists of stubs, captions, and columns and rows of data, as shown in Figure 15–2. *Stubs* are the titles to the rows of data and *captions* are the titles to the columns. The captions, however, may be divided into subcaptions—or column heads, as they are sometimes called.

Because the text tables should be specially planned, their construction is largely influenced by their illustration purpose. Nevertheless, a few general construction rules apply:

1. If rows tend to be long, the stubs may be repeated at the right.

2. A dash (—) or the abbreviation "n.a.," but not a zero, is used to indicate data "not available."

3. Footnote references to numbers in the table should be keyed with asterisks, daggers, double daggers, and such. Numbers followed by footnote reference numbers may cause confusion.

FIGURE 15–2   **Good arrangement of the parts of a typical table**

	TABLE NO. TITLE OF TABLE			
Stub head	**Spanner head**			
	Column head	Column head	Column head	Column head
Stub	X X X	X X X	X X X	X X X
Stub	X X X	X X X	X X X	X X X
Stub	X X X	X X X	X X X	X X X
Stub	X X X	X X X	X X X	X X X
"	"	"	"	"
"	"	"	"	"
"	"	"	"	"
"	"	"	"	"
"	"	"	"	"
"	"	"	"	"
TOTAL	X X X	X X X	X X X	X X X
Footnotes				
Source:				

4. Totals and subtotals should appear wherever they help the purpose of the table. The totals may be for each column and sometimes for each row. Usually, row totals are made at the right; but when the totals need emphasis, they may be placed at the left. Likewise, column totals generally appear at the bottom but may be placed at the top of the column when the writer wants to emphasize them. A ruled line (usually a double one) separates the totals from their data.

5. Units in which the data are recorded must be clear. Unit descriptions (bushels, acres, pounds, etc.) appropriately appear above the columns as part of the captions or subcaptions. If the data are in dollars, however, a dollar sign ($) placed before the first entry in each column is sufficient.

Tabulated information need not always be presented in formal tables. In fact, short arrangements of data may be presented more effectively as parts of the text. Such arrangements generally are made in three ways: as leaderwork, as text tabulations, or as bullet lists.

Tabular information can also be presented as (1) leaderwork,

Leaderwork is the presentation of tabular material in the text without titles or rules. (Leaders are a string of dots.) Typically, a colon precedes the tabulation, as in this illustration:

August sales for representatives of the Western Region were as follows:

Charles B. Brown	$13,517
Thomas Capp	19,703
Bill E. Knauth	18,198

(2) text tabulations, or

Text tabulations are simple tables, usually with headings and some rules. But they are not numbered, and they have no titles. They are made to read with the text, as in this example:

August sales for the representatives in the Western Region increased sharply from the preceding month, as these figures show:

Representative	July Sales	August Sales	Increase
Charles B. Brown	$12,819	$13,517	$698
Thomas Capp	17,225	19,703	2,478
Bill E. Knauth	16,838	18,198	1,360

(3) bullet lists.

Bullet lists are listings of points arranged with bullets (•) to set them off. These lists can have a title that covers all points, or they can appear without titles, as they appear at various places in this book. When you use this arrangement, make the points grammatically parallel. If the points have subparts, use sub-bullets for them. Make the sub-bullets different by color, size, or weight. The filled circle is commonly used for the primary bullets and darts, check mark, squares, or triangles for the secondary ones.

VISUAL TYPES OF ILLUSTRATIONS

A review of *visual* illustrations follows.

The truly visual types of graphic aids include a variety of forms. Of the many available to you, the following forms are the most widely used.

☐ THE SIMPLE BAR CHART

Simple bar charts compare differences in quantities by varying bar lengths.

Simple *bar charts* compare differences in quantities by the length of the bars representing each quantity. You should use them to show quantity changes over time or over geographic distance.

As Figure 15–3 shows, the main parts of the bar chart are the bars and grid (the field on which the bars are placed). The bars should be of equal width, and they may be arranged horizontally or vertically. You should identify each bar, usually with a caption at the left or beneath. The grid shows the magnitude of the bars, and the scale caption below identifies the units (dollars, pounds, miles, etc.).

FIGURE 15-3   Good arrangement of a simple bar chart

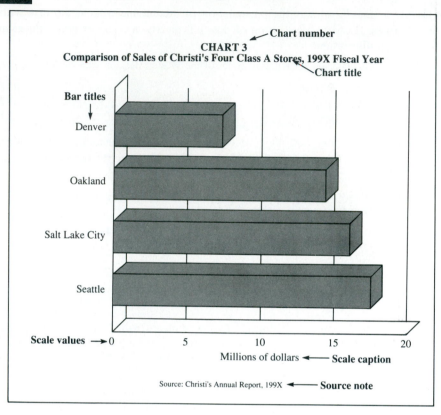

CHART 3

Comparison of Sales of Christi's Four Class A Stores, 199X Fiscal Year

VARIATIONS OF THE BAR CHART

In addition to the simple bar chart just described, you may use a number of other types of bar charts in presenting a report. The more commonly used variants are the multiple bar chart, the bilateral bar chart, and the subdivided or component-part bar chart.

Multiple bar charts are useful for comparing two or three kinds of quantities.

MULTIPLE BAR CHARTS   Comparisons of two or three variables within a single bar chart are made possible by the use of multiple bars distinguished by cross-hatching, shading, or color. In other words, the bars representing each of the variables being compared are distinguished by these mechanical means, as Figure 15–4 illustrates. The key to the variables is given in a legend, which may be placed within the illustration or below it, depending on where space is available. Generally, it is confusing and, therefore, inadvisable to make multiple comparisons of this type for more than three variables.

BILATERAL BAR CHARTS   When you must show plus or minus deviations, you may use bilateral bar charts. The bars of these charts begin at a central point of reference and may go either up or down, as illustrated in Figure 15–5 on page 276. Bar titles may

FIGURE 15–4   **Multiple bar chart**

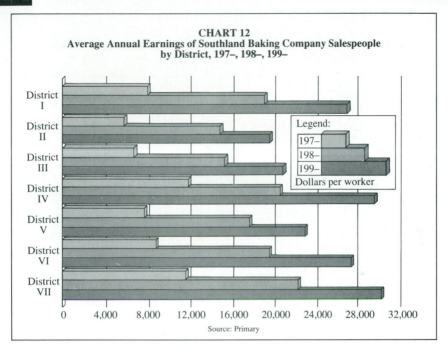

CHART 12
Average Annual Earnings of Southland Baking Company Salespeople
by District, 197–, 198–, 199–

Legend:
197–
198–
199–
Dollars per worker

Source: Primary

When you need to show plus and minus differences, bilateral bar charts are useful.

appear either within, above, or below the bars, depending on which placement best fits the illustration. Bilateral bar charts are especially good for showing percentage changes, but you may use them for any series in which minus quantities are present.

SUBDIVIDED BAR CHARTS   If you need to compare subdivisions of the bars, you may use subdivided bar charts. In this form of chart, you first assign cross-hatchings, shadings, or colors to each part to be shown; then you mark off the bars into their component parts, as Figure 15–6 on page 277 illustrates. As in all cases that use cross-hatching or color, a legend guides the reader.

To show subdivisions of the bars, use a subdivided bar chart.

You also can use this form of chart for comparing subdivisions of percentages.

Another form of the subdivided bar chart frequently is used to compare the subdivision of percentages. This type of chart differs from the typical bar chart mainly because the bar lengths are meaningless in comparisons. All the bars are of equal length, and only their components vary. As Figure 15–7 on page 278 depicts, the component parts may be labeled; but they may also be explained in a legend.

☐   **PIE CHART CONSTRUCTION**

Also of primary importance in comparing the subdivisions of a whole is the pie chart (see Figure 15–8 on page 279). As the name implies, the *pie chart* shows the whole of the information being studied as a pie (circle) and the parts as slices. The slices may be

FIGURE 15-5   Bilateral bar chart

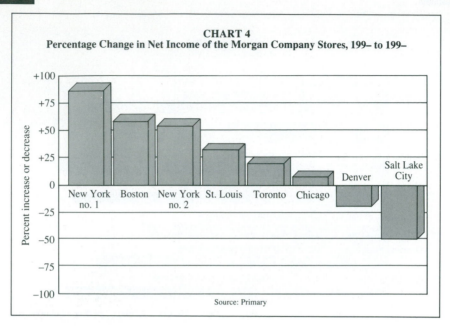

CHART 4
Percentage Change in Net Income of the Morgan Company Stores, 199– to 199–

Source: Primary

Pie charts show subdivisions of a whole.	distinguished by color, cross-hatching, or both. Because it is difficult to judge the value of the slices with the naked eye, it is wise to include the percentage values within each slice. A good rule to follow is to begin slicing the pie at the 12 o'clock position and move around clockwise. It is also advisable to arrange the slices in descending order from largest to smallest.
But do not vary the sizes of the pies.	You should never use pie charts to compare two or more wholes by varying the sizes of the pies. Such comparisons are almost meaningless. The human eye simply cannot judge the sizes of the circles accurately.

☐ ARRANGEMENT OF THE LINE CHART

Line charts show changes over time.	*Line charts* are useful for showing changes in information over time. They are especially helpful for showing changes in prices, sales totals, and employment. You may plot line charts on an arithmetic, semilogarithmic, or logarithmic grid. Since the arithmetic plot is most common in business reports, it is described here.
The line appears on a grid (a scaled area) and is continuous.	In constructing a line chart, you should draw the information to be illustrated as a continuous line on a grid. The *grid* is the area in which the line is displayed. On the grid, you should plot time on the horizontal axis (*X* axis) and quantity changes on the vertical axis (*Y* axis). You should clearly mark the scale values and time periods on the axis lines, as shown in Figure 15–9 on page 280.

FIGURE 15–6   **Subdivided bar chart with bars of unequal length**

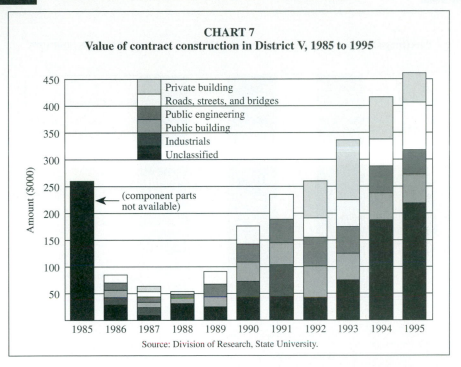

CHART 7
Value of contract construction in District V, 1985 to 1995

Legend:
Private building
Roads, streets, and bridges
Public engineering
Public building
Industrials
Unclassified

(component parts not available)

Amount ($000)

Source: Division of Research, State University.

Two or more lines may appear on one chart.

Component-part line charts show the makeup of a series.

But avoid the following errors: (1) Failure to start at zero (you can show scale breaks).

You can also compare two or more series on the same line chart (see Figure 15–10 on page 281). In such a comparison, you should clearly distinguish the lines by color or form (dots, dashes, etc.). You should clearly label them with a legend somewhere in the chart. But the number of series that you may compare on one chart is limited. As a practical rule, four or five series should be a maximum.

It is also possible to show component parts of a series by using a line chart. This arrangement is sometimes called a *belt chart*. Such an illustration, however, can show only one series. As Figure 15–11 on page 282 shows, you construct this type of chart with a top line representing the total of the series. Then, starting from the base, you cumulate the parts, beginning with the largest and ending with the smallest. You can use cross-hatching or coloring to distinguish the parts.

Even though the line graph is simple to construct, you should be aware of three common pitfalls. First is the error of violating the zero beginning of the series. The *Y* scale (vertical axis) should begin at zero even if the points to be plotted are relatively high in value. If most of the points to be plotted are relatively high in value, you may facilitate the comparison by breaking the scale somewhere between zero and the level of the lowest plotted value. Of the numerous means of showing scale breaks, these two techniques are recommended:

FIGURE 15–7   **Subdivided bar chart with bars of equal length**

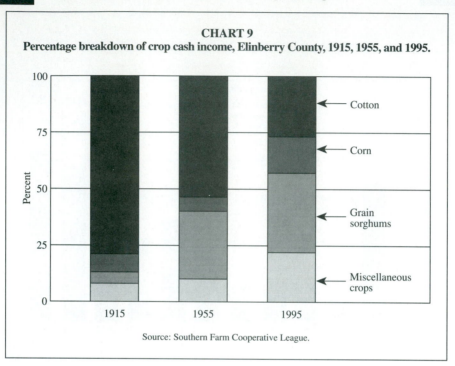

CHART 9
Percentage breakdown of crop cash income, Elinberry County, 1915, 1955, and 1995.

Source: Southern Farm Cooperative League.

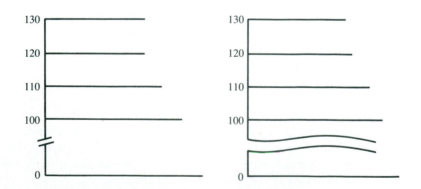

(2) Failure to keep scales uniform.

Second, equal magnitudes on both X and Y scales should be represented on the grid by equal distances. For instance, all dimensions from left to right (X axis) should be equal, as should all dimensions from bottom to top (Y axis). Any deviation from this rule would present the information incorrectly, thereby deceiving the reader.

A third common violation of good line chart construction concerns determining proportions on the grid. Obviously, expanding one scale and contracting the other will

FIGURE 15–8   **Pie chart**

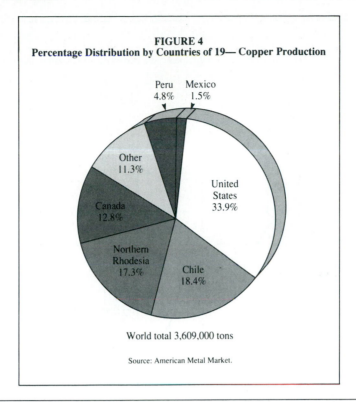

FIGURE 4
Percentage Distribution by Countries of 19— Copper Production

World total 3,609,000 tons

Source: American Metal Market.

(3) Failure to use a grid that shows a true picture.

create impressions of extreme deviation. For example, data plotted on a line chart with time intervals one sixteenth of an inch apart will certainly appear to show more violent fluctuations than the same data plotted with time intervals one-half inch apart. Only by applying good judgment can you prevent this violation. The grid distances selected must present the data realistically.

□ **DESIGN OF THE STATISTICAL MAP**

You can show quantitative information for geographic areas in a statistical map.

You may also use maps to help communicate quantitative information. Maps are useful primarily when quantitative information is to be compared by geographic area. On such maps, the geographic areas are clearly outlined, and the differences between them are shown by some graphic technique. Of the numerous possible techniques, four are most common:

Here are some specific instructions for statistical maps.

1. Possibly the most popular technique is that of showing quantitative differences of areas by color, shading, or cross-hatching (Figure 15–12 on page 283). Such maps, of course, must have a legend to explain the quantitative meanings of the various colors, cross-hatchings, and so forth.

FIGURE 15–9   **A line chart with one series**

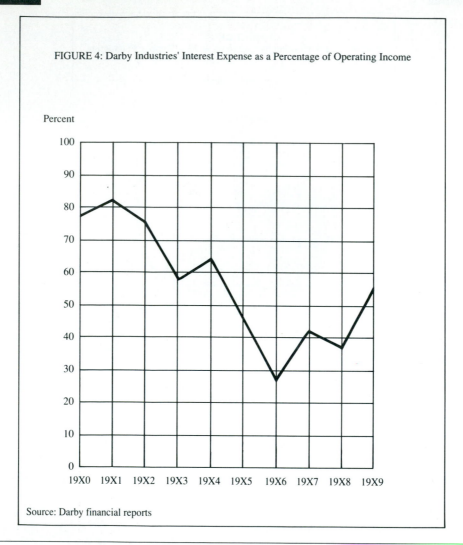

FIGURE 4: Darby Industries' Interest Expense as a Percentage of Operating Income

Source: Darby financial reports

2. Some form of chart may be placed within each geographic area to depict the quantities that represent it, as Figure 15–13 on page 284 illustrates. Bar charts and pie charts are commonly used in such illustrations.

3. Placing the quantities in numerical form within each geographic area, as shown in Figure 15–14 on page 285, is another widely used technique.

4. Dots, each representing a definite quantity (Figure 15–15 on page 286), can be placed within the geographic areas in proportion to the quantities to be illustrated for each area.

FIGURE 15–10   Line chart comparing more than one series

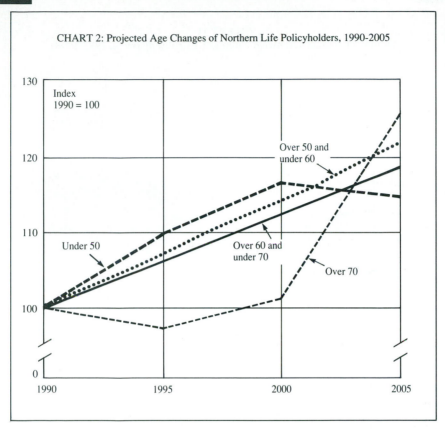

CHART 2: Projected Age Changes of Northern Life Policyholders, 1990-2005

☐   **CONSTRUCTION OF THE PICTOGRAM**

Pictograms are bar charts made with pictures.

A *pictogram* is a bar chart that uses bars made of pictures. The pictures typically are drawings of the items being compared. For example, a company seeking to graphically depict its profits from sales could use a simple bar chart for the purpose. Or it could use a column of coins equal in length to the bars. Coins might be selected because they depict the information to be illustrated. The resulting graphic form, as illustrated in Figure 15–16 on page 287, is the pictogram.

In constructing pictograms, follow the procedure for making bar charts.

When constructing a pictogram, you should follow the procedure you used in constructing bar charts. In addition, you should follow two special rules. First, you must make all of the picture units of equal size; that is, you must make the comparisons on the sole basis of the number of illustrations used and never by varying the areas of the individual pictures. The reason for this rule is obvious. The human eye is grossly inequipped to compare areas of geometric designs. Second, you should select pictures or symbols that fit the information to be illustrated. A comparison of the navies of the world, for example, might use miniature ship drawings. Cotton produc-

FIGURE 15–11   **Component-part line chart**

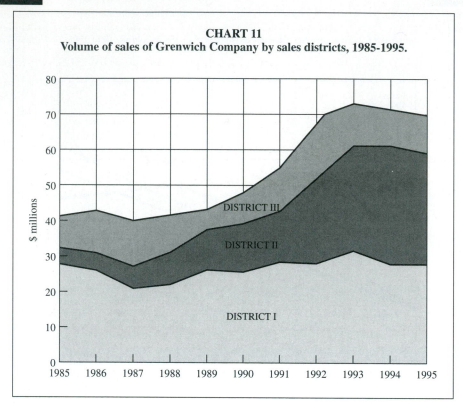

CHART 11
Volume of sales of Grenwich Company by sales districts, 1985-1995.

DISTRICT III

DISTRICT II

DISTRICT I

tion might be shown by bales of cotton. Obviously, the drawings used must be immediately interpretable by the reader.

☐ MISCELLANEOUS GRAPHICS

Other graphic aids available to you are diagrams, drawings, and photographs.

The graphics discussed thus far are those most commonly used. Others are sometimes helpful. Photographs and drawings may serve a useful communication purpose. Diagrams (Figure 15–17 on page 288) and drawings (Figure 15–18 on page 289) may help simplify a complicated explanation or description, particularly when technological procedures are being communicated. For all practical purposes, any form of graphic design is acceptable as long as it helps communicate the true story. The possibilities are almost unlimited.

COMPUTER GRAPHICS

If you have access to the appropriate computer, printer, and software, you can use them to prepare graphics quickly and easily. Unlike the earlier versions, today's com-

FIGURE 15–12   **Statistical map showing quantitative differences of areas by cross-hatching**

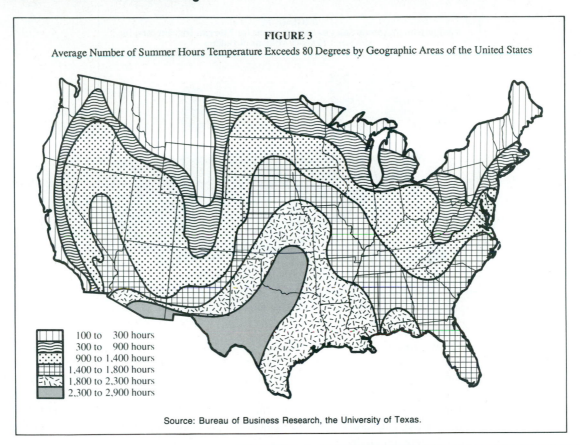

FIGURE 3

Average Number of Summer Hours Temperature Exceeds 80 Degrees by Geographic Areas of the United States

100 to   300 hours
300 to   900 hours
900 to 1,400 hours
1,400 to 1,800 hours
1,800 to 2,300 hours
2,300 to 2,900 hours

Source: Bureau of Business Research, the University of Texas.

Easy-to-use computer graphics are available.

puter graphics software programs are simple and easy to use. With some of them, you need only choose the form of graph you want and then, using simple English instructions, supply the information that the program requests. For example, when using one popular program to construct a bar chart, you simply respond "Bar" to the initial request for chart type. Then you supply plain English answers to a series of questions covering number of bars, names of bars, values of bars, and the like. As you supply the answers, the results appear on the screen. After producing the bar chart on the screen, you can manipulate its design until it meets your ideal requirements. When you are satisfied with the design you see on the screen, you print the chart in black and white or in color, depending on your equipment.

But do not overuse them.

Because computer graphics are easy to make and can be exciting and colorful, you may be tempted to overuse them. Keep in mind that the one requirement for including a graphic in a report is usefulness in communicating the report message. Too many charts can clutter the report and cause confusion.

FIGURE 15–13   **Statistical map showing comparisons by charts within geographic areas**

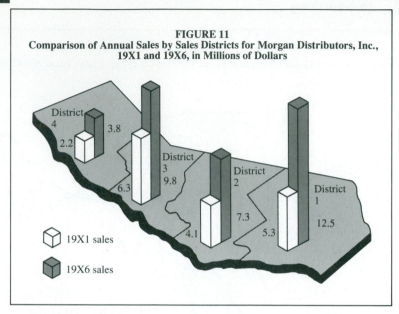

FIGURE 11
**Comparison of Annual Sales by Sales Districts for Morgan Distributors, Inc.,
19X1 and 19X6, in Millions of Dollars**

Make sure the graphics you use help to communicate.

Also keep in mind that clarity is a major requirement of graphics and that even computer-generated graphics can be unclear. The possibilities for changing and enhancing graphics can lead to interesting, beautiful, exciting, but confusing results. Thus, the purpose of graphics—to communicate instantly clear messages—is defeated. Even though the software package will do much of the planning and thinking for you, you should take care to follow the guidelines presented in this chapter as you construct graphics by computer.

QUESTIONS

1. For the past 20 years, Professor Kupenheimer has required his students to include five graphic aids in the long, formal report he has them prepare. Evaluate this requirement.

2. Because it is easier to do, a report writer prepared all her graphic aids on separate pages. Each one took up a full page. Some of the graphic aids were extremely complex; others were very simple. Comment on this policy.

3. "I have placed all charts near the places I write about them. The reader can see them without any *additional* help from me. It just doesn't make sense to direct attention to these charts with words." Evaluate this comment.

FIGURE 15-14   **Statistical map showing quantitative differences by numbers placed within geographic areas**

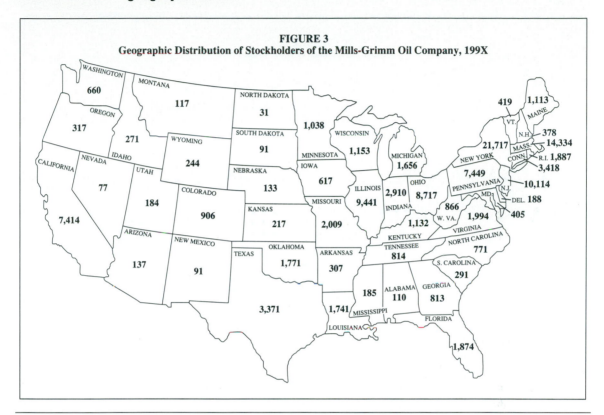

FIGURE 3
Geographic Distribution of Stockholders of the Mills-Grimm Oil Company, 199X

4. A report has five maps, four tables, one chart, one diagram, and one photograph. How would you number these graphic aids?

5. How would you number this composition of graphic aids in a report: seven tables, six charts, and nine maps?

6. Construct a complete, concise title for a bar chart that shows annual attendance at home football games at your school from 1980 to the present.

7. The chart prepared in Question 6 requires an explanation for the years 1988 to the present, in which one extra home game was played. Explain how you would do this.

8. For each of the following areas of information, which form of graphic aid would you use? Explain your decision.
   a.   Record of annual sales for the Kenyon Company for the past 20 years.
   b.   Comparison of Kenyon Company sales by product for this year and last year.
   c.   Monthly production in units for the automobile industry.

FIGURE 15–15   **Statistical map using dots to show quantitative differences by geographic area**

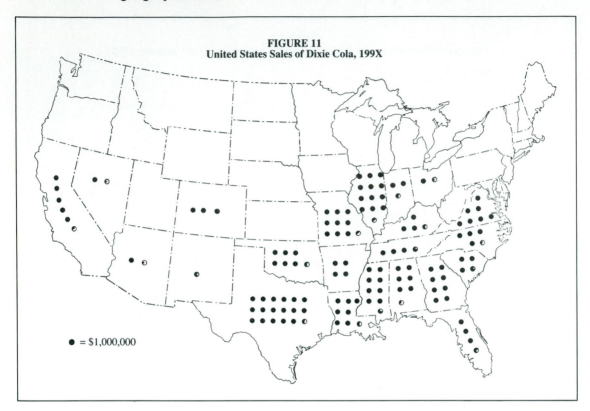

FIGURE 11
United States Sales of Dixie Cola, 199X

● = $1,000,000

    d. Breakdown of how the average middle-income family in your state disposes of its income dollar.

    e. Comparison of how middle-income families spend their income dollars with similar expenditures of low-income families.

    f. Comparison of sales for the past two years for each of the B&B Company's 14 sales districts. The districts cover all 50 states and Puerto Rico.

    g. National production of automobiles from 1945 to the present, broken down by manufacturer.

9. Discuss the logic of showing scale breaks in a chart.

10. Discuss the dangers of using illogical proportions in constructing a grid for a chart.

11. Discuss the techniques you may use to show quantitative differences by area on a statistical map.

12. Select some data that are ideally suited for presentation in a pictogram. Explain why a pictogram is good for this case.

FIGURE 15-16   **Pictogram**

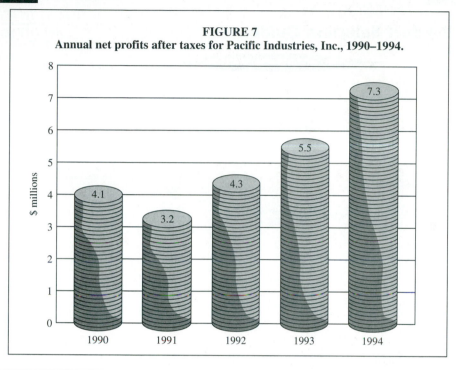

FIGURE 7
Annual net profits after taxes for Pacific Industries, Inc., 1990–1994.

13. Discuss the dangers of using a pictogram.
14. For each of the following sets of facts, (*a*) determine the graphic aid(s) that would be best, (*b*) defend your choice, and (*c*) construct the graphic aid.

(1) Average (mean) amount of life insurance owned by Fidelity Life Insurance Company policyholders, classified by annual income

Income	Average Life Insurance
Under $10,000	$ 5,245
10,000–14,999	14,460
15,000–19,999	26,680
20,000–24,999	39,875
25,000–29,999	51,440
30,000 and over	76,390

FIGURE 15–17   Illustration of a diagram

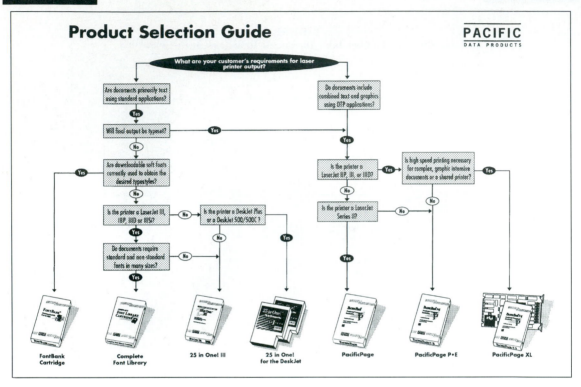

(2) Profits and losses for D and H Food Stores, by store, 1990–1994, in dollars

Year	Able City	Baker	Charleston	Total
1990	13,421	3,241	9,766	26,428
1991	12,911	−1,173	11,847	23,585
1992	13,843	−2,241	11,606	23,208
1993	12,673	2,865	13,551	29,089
1994	13,008	7,145	15,482	35,635

FIGURE 15–18   Illustration of a drawing

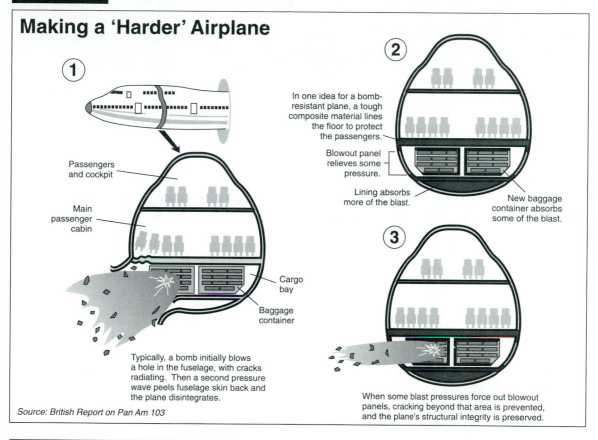

Making a 'Harder' Airplane

①

Passengers and cockpit

Main passenger cabin

Cargo bay

Baggage container

Typically, a bomb initially blows a hole in the fuselage, with cracks radiating. Then a second pressure wave peels fuselage skin back and the plane disintegrates.

Source: British Report on Pan Am 103

②

In one idea for a bomb-resistant plane, a tough composite material lines the floor to protect the passengers.

Blowout panel relieves some pressure.

Lining absorbs more of the blast.

New baggage container absorbs some of the blast.

③

When some blast pressures force out blowout panels, cracking beyond that area is prevented, and the plane's structural integrity is preserved.

(3) Share of real estate tax payments by ward for Bigg City, 1990 and 1995, in thousands of dollars

	1990	1995
Ward 1	17.1	21.3
Ward 2	10.2	31.8
Ward 3	19.5	21.1
Ward 4	7.8	18.2
City total	54.6	92.4

(4) Percentage change in sales by salesperson, 1989–90, District IV, Abbot, Inc.

Salesperson	Percentage Change
Joan Abraham	+7.3
Wilson Calmes	+2.1
Todd Musso	−7.5
Mary Nevers	+41.6
Wilson Platt	+7.4
Carry Ruiz	+11.5
David Schlimmer	−4.8
Helen Dirks	−3.6

(5) Net income from operations of seven largest U.S. banks, with percentage of profit derived from foreign operations, 1993–1994

Bank	1993 Operations Net (millions)	Foreign (percent)	1994 Operations Net (millions)	Foreign (percent)
BankAmerica	$178.4	25%	$166.5	20%
1st Nat'l City	168.2	42	145.1	38
Chase Manhattan	147.7	20	139.3	15
J. P. Morgan	109.1	30	102.0	25
Mfgrs. Hanover	77.9	28	85.2	24
Chemical	72.5	15	77.4	10

Correctness of Communication in Report Writing

Correctness of communication is as important to effective report writing as careful planning, logical organization, readable style, and objective perspective. Yet it is an area that many report writers mistakenly overlook—or take for granted. As you will see, how well you follow the standards of the language determines how your report will be received and whether it will be understood. Your respect for the rules also determines how credible you will be to an audience that expects and depends on accurate communication.

THE NEED FOR CORRECTNESS

Correct grammar and punctuation are essential to clear and accurate communication.

Correctness of communication in report writing is primarily a matter of following the accepted standards of grammar and punctuation. Grammar and punctuation are, after all, the foundation of written language. That is why you begin the study of both in the earliest years of your schooling and review basic principles periodically as you advance in your education and career. Correctness is obviously important for its own sake. You need correct grammar in order to define relationships among words and to convey the logic of thoughts, actions, and events. You need correct punctuation in order to group words meaningfully and to refine or emphasize the logic. Punctuation does for the written word what pauses and inflections do for the spoken word.

Correctness enhances your credibility as a report writer.

Correctness is also important because of what it says about you as a writer. As you present your research in written form, you are assumed to have a basic knowledge of both grammar and punctuation and to know how to edit your work for careless errors. To write without that knowledge, or to leave obvious errors uncorrected, is to undermine your credibility as a business reporter. Business is very traditional in its attitudes and expects the highest standards of writing. As a result, your expertise as a report writer will be judged largely on the correctness of your presentation. Attention to the details of grammar and punctuation shows readers that you are thorough, informed, interested in and proud of your research effort, and respectful of your reader. Lack of attention suggests just the opposite and in extreme cases marks you as unintelligent, illiterate, uninformed, or rude.

THE NEED FOR CLARITY

Like words, grammar and punctuation convey meaning. Correctness thus requires that you use grammatical constructions and punctuation that communicate what you intend.

However, even when you have taken great care in your writing, there will be times when grammar and punctuation that look correct may be incorrect for what you want to say. If you read carefully the following set of sentences, you will see the confusion misplaced punctuation or inaccurate grammar can cause. For example, you may mean this:

I left the union leaders, convinced we had a contract.

That is, *you* were convinced you and they had a contract. But look at what you are saying when you write:

I left the union leaders convinced we had a contract.

Here it is *they* who are convinced you and they have a contract. Your position on the matter is not clear.

Similarly, you may mean this:

Every company, I know, will object to the tax proposal.

But that is not what you are saying when you write this:

Every company I know will object to the tax proposal.

And you may mean to write this:

The receptionist was instructed to stand by the door and call the trustees' names.

However, imagine the confusion that will result when you write this:

The receptionist was instructed to stand by the door and call the trustees names.

There is confusion in a sentence like this, too:

Mr. Emery told Mr. Johnson he was responsible for the error.

Who is responsible? It is not possible to tell. And look at the problems a sentence like this may cause:

The company that called back its stock to avoid a takeover issued long term bonds.

Which strategy did the company use to avoid a takeover? Did it call back its stock or did it issue long term bonds? Again, it is not possible to tell.

The following review covers the major standards. The standards are coded for your convenience.

Because the standards of correctness are important to your report writing, this chapter presents a review. Although not complete due to space limitations, the review covers the most common points. For your convenience, the standards are coded with symbols (letters and numbers) for identification. Your instructor should find them useful as grading marks for identifying errors in your writing.

STANDARDS FOR PUNCTUATION

The following list covers the most important standards for correctness in punctuation. For purposes of accuracy, the explanations use some technical words. Even so, the illustrations should make the standards clear.

☐ APOSTROPHE: APOS

Use the apostrophe to show possession.

APOS 1 Use the apostrophe to show the possessive case of nouns and indefinite pronouns. If the word does not end in *s,* add an apostrophe and an *s.* If the word ends in *s,* add only an apostrophe.

Nominative Form	Possessive Form
company	company's
employee	employee's
companies	companies'
employees	employees'

Proper names and singular nouns ending in *s* sounds are exceptions. To such words you may add either the apostrophe and the *s* or just the apostrophe. Add only an apostrophe to the nominative plural.

Nominative Form	Possessive Form
Texas (singular)	Texas', Texas's
Jones (singular)	Jones', Jones's
Joneses (plural)	Joneses'
countess (singular)	countess', countess's

Mark omissions in contractions with the apostrophe.

APOS 2 Use an apostrophe to mark the place in a contraction where letters are omitted.

has not	hasn't
cannot	can't
it is	it's

☐ BRACKETS: BKTS

Use brackets to set off your own words within a quotation.

Set off in brackets words that you wish to insert within a quotation.

"Possibly the use of this type of supervisor [the trained correspondence expert] is still on the increase."

"At least direct supervision has gained in importance in the past decade [the report was written in 1983], during which time 43 percent of the reporting business firms that started programs have used this technique."

☐ COLON: CLN

Use the colon to introduce formal statements.

CLN 1   Use the colon to introduce a statement of explanation, an enumeration, or a formal quotation.

> *Statement of explanation:* At this time, the company was pioneering a new marketing idea: It was attempting to sell its products direct to consumers by means of vending machines.

> *Enumeration:* There are four classes of machinists working in this department: apprentice machinist, journeyman machinist, machinist, and first-class machinist.

> *Formal quotation:* President Hartung had this to say about the proposal: "Any such movement that fails to have the support of the rank-and-file worker in this plant fails to get my support."

Do not use a colon when it breaks the thought flow.

CLN 2   Do not use the colon when the thought of the sentence should continue without interruption. If you are introducing a list with a colon, precede it with a word that the list explains or identifies.

> *Below standard:* Cities in which new sales offices are in operation are: Fort Smith, Texarkana, Lake Charles, Jackson, and Biloxi.

> *Acceptable:* Cities in which new sales offices are in operation are Fort Smith, Texarkana, Lake Charles, Jackson, and Biloxi.

> *Acceptable:* Cities in which new sales offices are in operation are as follows: Fort Smith, Texarkana, Lake Charles, Jackson, and Biloxi.

☐ COMMA: CMA

Use the comma to separate clauses connected by *and, but, or, nor,* and *for.*

CMA 1   Use a comma to separate principal clauses connected by a coordinating conjunction—that is, *and, but, or, nor,* and *for.* (A *principal clause* has a subject and a verb, and it stands by itself. A *coordinating conjunction* connects words or phrases of equal rank.)

> Only two of the components of the index declined, and these two account for only 12 percent of the total weight of the index.

> New automobiles are moving at record volumes, but used-car sales are lagging well behind the record pace set two years ago.

Exceptions to this rule may be made, however, in the case of compound sentences consisting of short and closely connected clauses.

> We sold and the price dropped.

> Sometimes we profit and sometimes we lose.

Use the comma to separate items in a series.

CMA 2.1   Separate the elements listed in series by commas. In order to avoid misinterpretation in the rare instances in which some of the elements listed have compound constructions, it is advisable to place the comma between the last two items (before the final conjunction).

> Good copy must cover fact with accuracy, sincerity, honesty, and conviction.

Direct advertising can be used to introduce salespeople, fill in between salespeople's calls, cover territory where salespeople cannot be maintained, and keep pertinent reference material in the hands of prospects.

A survey conducted at the 1988 automobile show indicated that black and cream, blue and grey, dark maroon, and black cars were favored by the public. [Note how this example illustrates the need for a comma before the final conjunction.]

Use the comma between adjectives in a series.

CMA 2.2   Separate coordinate adjectives in a series by commas when they modify the same noun and if there is no *and* connecting them. A good test for determining whether adjectives are coordinate is to insert an *and* between the words. If the *and* does not change the expression's meaning, the words are coordinate.

Ms. Pratt has been a reliable, faithful, efficient employee for 20 years.

We guarantee that this is a good, clean car.

Light green office furniture is Mr. Orr's recommendation for the stenographic pool. [If *and* were placed between *light* and *green,* the word meaning would be changed.]

A big Dawson wrench proved to be best for the task. [The *and* won't fit between *big* and *Dawson.*]

Use the comma to set off nonrestrictive modifiers (those that can be left out without changing the sentence's basic meaning).

CMA 3   Set off nonrestrictive modifiers from the sentence by commas. By a *nonrestrictive modifier,* we mean a modifier that can be omitted from the sentence without changing its meaning. *Restrictive modifiers* (those that restrict the words they modify to a particular object) are not set off by commas. A restrictive modifier cannot be left out of the sentence without changing the sentence's meaning.

Restrictive: The salesperson who sells the most will get a bonus. [*"Who sells the most"* restricts the meaning to one particular salesperson.]

Nonrestrictive: James Smithers, who was the company's top salesperson for the year, was awarded a bonus. [If the clause "who was the company's top salesperson for the year" is omitted, the statement is not changed.]

Restrictive: J. Ward & Company is the firm that employs most of the physically handicapped in this area.

Nonrestrictive: J. Ward & Company, the firm that employs most of the physically handicapped in this area, has gained the admiration of the community.

Notice how some modifiers can be either restrictive or nonrestrictive, depending on the meaning intended.

Restrictive: All of the suits that were damaged in the fire were sold at a discount. [Implies that a part of the stock was not damaged]

Nonrestrictive: All of the suits, which were damaged by the fire, were sold at a discount. [Implies that all the stock was damaged]

Use commas to set off the following: (1) parenthetic expressions (comments that are "stuck in").

CMA 4.1   Use commas to set off parenthetic expressions. A *parenthetic expression* consists of words that interrupt the normal flow of the sentence. In a sense, they appear to be "stuck in." For example, the sentence "A full-page, black-and-white advertisement was run in the *Daily Bulletin*" contains a parenthetic expression when the word order is altered: "An advertisement, full-page and in black and white, was run in the *Daily Bulletin.*"

This practice, it is believed, will lead to ruin.

The Johnston Oil Company, so the rumor goes, has cut back sharply its exploration activity.

Although you may use dashes and parentheses for similar reasons, the three marks differ as to the degree to which they separate the enclosed words from the rest of the sentence. The comma is the weakest of the three, and it is best used when the material set off is closely related to the surrounding words. Dashes are stronger marks than commas and are used when the words set off tend to be long or contain internal punctuation marks. Parentheses, the strongest of the three, are used primarily to enclose material that helps explain or supplement the main words of the sentence.

(2) Apposition words (words explaining another word).

CMA 4.2   Use commas to set off an *appositive* (a noun or a noun and its modifiers inserted to explain another noun) from the rest of the sentence. In a sense, appositives are forms of parenthetic expressions, for they interrupt the normal flow of the sentence.

The Baron Corporation, our machine-parts supplier, is negotiating a new contract.

St. Louis, home office of our Midwest district, will be the permanent site of our annual sales meeting.

President Carthwright, a self-educated woman, is the leading advocate of our night school for employees.

But appositives that identify very closely are not set off by commas.

The word *liabilities* is not understood by most laborers.

Our next shipment will come on the steamship *Alberta.*

(3) Certain parenthetical words (*therefore, however*).

CMA 4.3   Set off parenthetic words such as *therefore, however, in fact, of course, for example,* and *consequently* with commas.

It is apparent, therefore, that the buyers' resistance has been brought about by an overvigorous sales campaign.

After the first experiment, for example, the traffic flow increased 10 percent.

The company will, however, be forced to abandon the old pricing system.

Included in this group of introductory words may be interjections (*oh, alas*) and responsive expressions (*yes, no, surely, indeed, well,* etc.). But if the words are strongly exclamatory or are not closely connected with the rest of the sentence, they may be punctuated as a sentence (*No. Yes. Indeed.*).

Yes, the decision to increase production has been made.

Oh, contribute whatever you think is adequate.

(4) Units in a date.

CMA 4.4   When more than one unit appears in a date or an address, set off the units by commas.

One unit: December 30 is the date of our annual inventory.

One unit: The company has one outlet in Ohio.

More than one unit: December 30, 1906, is the date the Johnston Company first opened its doors.

More than one unit: Richmond, Virginia, is the headquarters of the new sales district.

Use the comma after subordinate clauses.

CMA 5.1   Use commas to separate subordinate clauses preceding main clauses:

Although it is durable, this package does not have eye appeal.

Since there was little store traffic on Aisle 13, the area was converted into office space.

Use commas after introductory verbal phrases.

CMA 5.2   Place commas after introductory verbal phrases. A *verbal phrase* is one that contains some verb derivative—a gerund, a participle, or an infinitive.

Participial phrase: Realizing his mistake, the foreman instructed his workers to keep a record of all salvaged equipment.

Gerund phrase: After gaining the advantage, we failed to press on to victory.

Infinitive phrase: To increase our turnover of automobile accessories, we must first improve our display area.

Do not use commas without good reason, such as between subject and verb.

CMA 6.1   Use the comma only for a good reason. It is not a mark to be inserted indiscriminately at your whim. As a rule, you should always justify use of commas with one of the standard practices previously noted.

CMA 6.1.1   Do not be tripped into putting a comma between subject and verb.

The thought that he could not afford to fail spurred him on. [No comma after *fail.*]

Use commas wherever they enhance clarity.

CMA 6.2   Make an exception to the preceding standards whenever insertion of a comma will help clarity of expression.

Not clear: From the beginning inventory methods of Hill Company have been haphazard.

Clear: From the beginning, inventory methods of Hill Company have been haphazard.

Not clear: When you are eating your hands should be clean.

Clear: When you are eating, your hands should be clean.

☐   **DASH: DSH**

Use the dash to show interruption or emphasis.

Use the dash to set off an element for emphasis or to show interrupted thought. Use it particularly with long parenthetic expressions or those containing internal punctuation (see Cma 4.1). With the typewriter and most word processors, make the dash by striking the hyphen twice, without spacing before or after.

Budgets for some past years—1990, for example—were prepared without consulting the department heads.

The test proved that the new process is simple, effective, accurate—and more expensive.

Only one person—the supervisor in charge—has authority to issue such an order.

If you want a voice in the government—vote.

☐ EXCLAMATION MARK: EX

Use exclamation marks to show strong feeling.

Use the exclamation mark at the end of a sentence or an exclamatory fragment to show strong emotion. But use this mark sparingly; never use it with trivial ideas.

We've done it again!

No! It can't be!

☐ HYPHEN: HPN

Mark word divisions with hyphens.

HPN 1   Indicate division of a word at the end of a line by the hyphen. You must divide between syllables. It is generally impractical to leave a one-letter syllable at the end of a line (*a-bove*) or to carry over a two-letter syllable to the next line (*expens-es*).

Place hyphens between compound words.

HPN 2   Place hyphens between the parts of some compound words. Generally, the hyphen is used whenever its absence would confuse the meaning of the words.

Compound nouns: brother-in-law, cure-all, city-state

Compound numbers twenty-one through ninety-nine: thirty-one, fifty-five, seventy-seven

Compound adjectives (two or more words used before a noun as a single adjective): *long-term* contract, *50-gallon* drum, *door-to-door* selling, *end-of-month* clearance

Prefixes (where omission would confuse meaning or form a peculiar word): co-worker, ex-chairperson, re-creation, anti-labor

Do not place hyphens between proper names.

HPN 2.1   A proper name used as a compound adjective needs no hyphen or hyphens to hold it together as a visual unit for the reader. The capitals perform that function.

Correct: A Lamar High School student

Correct: A United Airlines pilot

Do not use hyphens between words that only follow each other.

HPN 2.2   Two or more modifiers in normal grammatical form and order need no hyphens. Particularly, a phrase consisting of an unmistakable adverb (one ending in *ly*) modifying an adjective or participle that in turn modifies a noun shows normal grammatical order and is readily grasped by the reader without the aid of the hyphen. But an adverb not ending in *ly* should be joined to its adjective or participle by the hyphen.

No hyphen needed: A poorly drawn chart

Hyphen needed: A well-prepared chart

☐ ITALICS: ITAL

Use italics for publication titles.

ITAL 1   For the use of italics for book titles, see QM 4. Note that italics are also used for titles of periodicals, works of art or music, and names of naval vessels and aircraft.

Italicize foreign words and abbreviations.

ITAL 2   Italicize rarely used foreign words—if you must use them (*pro bono publico, raison d'État, ich dien*). Once a foreign word is widely accepted, however, it need not be italicized (bon voyage, pizza, rancho). A current dictionary is a good source for this information.

Italicize a word used as its own name.

ITAL 3   Italicize a word, letter, or figure used as its own name. Without this device, we could not write this set of rules. Note the use of italics throughout this book to label name words.

> The little word *sell* is still in the dictionary.

> The pronoun *which* should always have a noun as a clear antecedent. [Try reading that one without the italics; it becomes a fragment ending in midair!]

☐ PARENTHESES: PARENS

Set off parenthetic words with parentheses.

Use parentheses to set off words that are parenthetic or are inserted to explain or supplement the principal message (see Cma 4.1).

> Dr. Samuel Goppard's phenomenal prediction (*Business Week,* June 20, 1990) has made some business forecasters revise their techniques.

> Smith was elected chairperson (the vote was almost 2 to 1), and immediately he introduced his plan for reorganization.

☐ PERIOD: PD

End a declarative sentence with a period. Use periods in abbreviations.

PD 1   Use the period to indicate the end of a declarative sentence.

PD 2   Use periods after abbreviations or initials:

> Ph.D., Co., Inc., A.M., A.D.

Use a series of periods to show omissions.

PD 3   Use ellipses (a series of periods) to indicate the omission of words from a quoted passage. If the omitted part consists of something less than a sentence, place three periods at the point of omission (add a fourth period if the omission is a sentence or more). If the omitted part is a paragraph or more, however, use a full line of periods. In either case, the periods are appropriately typed with intervening spaces.

> Logical explanations, however, have been given by authorities in the field. Some attribute the decline . . . to the changing economy in the state during recent years. . . .
>
> . . . .
>
> Added to the labor factor is the high cost of raw material, which has tended to eliminate many marginal producers. Also, the rising cost of electrical power in recent years may have shifted many of the industry leaders' attention to other forms of production.

☐ QUESTION MARK: Q

End direct questions with the question mark.

Place question marks at the ends of sentences that are direct questions.

> What are the latest quotations on Ewing-Bell common stock?

Will this campaign help sell Dunnco products?

But do not use the question mark with indirect questions:

The president was asked whether this campaign will help sell Dunnco products.

He asked me what the latest quotations on Ewing-Bell common stock were.

☐ QUOTATION MARKS: QM

Use quotation marks to enclose a speaker's exact words.

QM 1   Use quotation marks to enclose the exact words of a speaker or, if the quotation is short, the writer's exact words. By "short written quotations," we mean something four lines or less. Longer quoted passages are best displayed without quotation marks and with additional right and left margins (see Chapter 14).

Short written passage: H. G. McVoy sums up his presentation with this statement: "All signs indicate that automation will be evolutionary, not revolutionary."

Verbal quotations: "This really should bring on a production slowdown," said Ms. Kuntz.

If the quoted words are broken by explanation or reference words, each quoted part is enclosed in quotation marks.

"Will you be specific," he asked, "in recommending a course of action?"

Use single quotation marks for a quotation within a quotation.

QM 2   Enclose a quotation within a quotation with single quotation marks.

President Carver said, "It has been a long time since I have heard an employee say, 'Boss, I'm going to beat my quota today.' "

Periods and commas go inside quotation marks; semicolons and colons go outside; question marks and exclamation points go inside when they apply to the quoted part and outside when they apply to the sentence.

QM 3   Always place periods and commas inside quotation marks. Place semicolons and colons outside. Place question marks and exclamation points inside if they apply only to the quoted passage and outside if they apply to the whole sentence.

"If we are patient," he said, "prosperity will some day arrive." [The comma is within the quotes; the period is also within the quotes.]

"Is there a quorum?" he asked. [The question mark belongs to the quoted passage.]

Which of you said, "I know where the error lies"? [The question mark applies to the entire sentence.]

I conclude only this from the union's promise to "force the hand of management": Violence will be their trump card. [Here the colon is not part of the quotation.]

Use quotation marks to enclose titles of parts of a publication.

QM 4   Enclose in quotation marks the titles of the parts of a publication (articles in a magazine, chapters in a book). Place titles of whole publications, however, in italics. Use underscoring or solid caps to show italics in typewritten material.

The third chapter of the book *Elementary Statistical Procedures* is entitled "Concepts of Sampling."

Joan Glasgow's most recent article, "A Union Boss Views Automation," appears in the current issue of *Fortune*. [Typewritten as <u>Fortune</u>]

☐ SEMICOLON: SC

Use the semicolon to separate independent clauses not connected by a conjunction.

SC 1   Separate with a semicolon independent clauses that are not connected by a conjunction.

Cork or asbestos sheeting must be hand-cut; polyurethane may be poured into a mold.

The new contract provides substantial wage increases; the original contract emphasized shorter hours.

Covered by this standard are clauses connected by conjunctive adverbs, such as *however, nevertheless, therefore, then, moreover,* and *besides.*

The survey findings indicated a need to revise the policy; nevertheless, the president vetoed the amendment.

Small-town buyers favor the old models; therefore, the board concluded that both models should be manufactured.

You may choose to separate independent clauses joined by a conjunction with a semicolon.

SC 2   You may separate with a semicolon independent clauses joined by *and, but, or, for,* and *nor* (coordinating conjunctions) if the clauses are long or contain other punctuation. You also may use the semicolon in this situation for special emphasis.

The FTU and IFL, rivals from the beginning of the new industry, have shared almost equally in the growth of membership; but the FTU predominates among workers in the petroleum-products crafts, including pipeline construction and operation, and the IFL leads in memberships of chemical workers.

The market price was $4; but we paid $7.

Use the semicolon to separate items in a list when the items contain commas.

SC 3   Separate with semicolons the parts in a list when the parts contain commas.

The following gains were made in the February year-to-year comparison: Fort Worth, 7,300; Dallas, 4,705; Lubbock, 2,610; San Antonio, 2,350; Waco, 2,240; Port Arthur, 2,170; and Corpus Christi, 1,420.

Elected for the new term were Anna T. Zelnak, attorney from Cincinnati; Wilbur T. Hoffmeister, stockbroker and president of Hoffmeister Associates of Baltimore; and William P. Peabody, a member of the faculty of the University of Georgia.

Use semicolons only between equal units.

SC 4   Use the semicolon between equal (coordinate) units only. Do not use it to attach a dependent clause or phrase to an independent clause.

Below standard: The flood damaged much of the equipment in Building 113; making it necessary for management to stop production and lay off all production workers.

Acceptable: The flood damaged much of the equipment in Building 113, making it necessary for management to stop production and lay off all production workers.

Acceptable: The flood damaged much of the equipment in Building 113; thus, it was necessary for management to stop production and lay off all production workers.

STANDARDS FOR GRAMMAR

Like the review of punctuation standards, the following summary of grammatical standards is not intended to be a complete handbook on the subject. Instead, it is a summary of the major trouble spots most report writers encounter. If you will learn these grammatical principles, you should at least be able to write with the correctness businesspeople expect.

☐ ADJECTIVE-ADVERB CONFUSION: AA

Do not use adjectives for adverbs.

Do not use adjectives for adverbs or adverbs for adjectives. Adjectives modify only nouns and pronouns, while adverbs modify verbs, adjectives, or other adverbs.

Possibly the chief source of this confusion occurs in statements in which the modifier follows the verb. If the modifier refers to the subject, you should use an adjective. If it limits the verb, you need an adverb.

Below standard: She filed the records *quick.*

Acceptable: She filed the records *quickly.* [Refers to the verb]

Below standard: John doesn't feel *badly.*

Acceptable: John doesn't feel *bad.* [Refers to the noun]

Below standard: The new cars look *beautifully.*

Acceptable: The new cars look *beautiful.* [Refers to the noun]

Note that many words are both adjectives and adverbs (*little, well, fast, much*). Also, some adverbs have two forms. One form is the same as the adjective; the other adds *ly* (*slow* and *slowly, cheap* and *cheaply, quick* and *quickly*).

Acceptable: All of our drivers are instructed to drive *slow.*

Acceptable: All of our drivers are instructed to drive *slowly.*

☐ SUBJECT-VERB AGREEMENT: AGMT SV

Verbs must agree in number with their subjects.

Nouns and their verbs must agree in number. A plural noun must have a plural verb form and a singular noun a singular verb.

Below standard: Expenditures for miscellaneous equipment *was* expected to decline. [*Expenditures* is plural, so its verb must be plural.]

Acceptable: Expenditures for miscellaneous equipment *were* expected to decline.

Below standard: The *president,* as well as his staff, *were* not able to attend. [*President* is the subject, and the number is not changed by the modifying phrase.]

Acceptable: The *president,* as well as his staff, *was* not able to attend.

Compound subjects require plural verbs.

Compound subjects (two or more nouns joined by *and*) require plural verbs.

Below standard: The *welders* and their *foreman is* in favor of the proposal. [*Welders* and *foreman* are compound subjects of the verb, but *is* is singular.]

Acceptable: The *welders* and their *foreman are* in favor of the proposal.

Below standard: Received in the morning delivery *was* a *computer* and two *reams* of letterhead paper. [*Computer* and *reams* are the subjects; the verb must be plural.]

Acceptable: Received in the morning delivery *were* a *computer* and two *reams* of letterhead paper.

Collective nouns may be singular or plural.

Collective nouns may be either singular or plural, depending on the intended meaning.

Acceptable: The *committee have* carefully *studied* the proposal. [*Committee* is thought of as separate individuals.]

Acceptable: The *committee has* carefully *studied* the proposal. [The *committee* is considered as a unit.]

The pronouns listed here are singular.

As a rule, the pronouns *anybody, anyone, each, either, everyone, everybody, neither, nobody, somebody,* and *someone* take a singular verb. The word *none* may be either singular or plural, depending on whether it is used to refer to one unit or to more than one unit.

Acceptable: Either of the advertising campaigns *is* costly.

Acceptable: Nobody who watches the clock *is* successful.

Acceptable: None of the boys *understands his* assignment.

Acceptable: None of the boys *understand their* assignments.

☐ ADVERBIAL NOUN CLAUSE: AN

Do not use an adverbial clause as a noun clause.

Do not use an adverbial clause as a noun clause. Clauses beginning with *because, when, where, if,* and similar adverbial connectives are not properly used as subjects, objects, or complements of verbs.

Not this: He did not know *if* he could go or not.

But this: He did not know *whether* he could go or not.

Not this: The reason was *because* he did not submit a report.

But this: The reason was *that* he did not submit a report.

Not this: A time-series graph is *where* [or *when*] changes in an index such as wholesale prices are indicated.

But this: A time-series graph is the picturing of . . . .

☐ AWKWARD: AWK

Avoid awkward writing.

Avoid awkward writing. By "awkward writing" we mean word arrangements that are unconventional, uneconomical, or simply not conducive to quick understanding.

☐ DANGLING MODIFIERS: DNG

Avoid dangling modifiers (those that do not clearly modify a specific word).

Avoid the use of modifiers that do not logically modify a word in the sentence. Such modifiers are said to *dangle.* They are both illogical and confusing. Usually, you can correct sentences containing dangling constructions in either of two ways: You can insert the noun or pronoun that the modifier describes, or you can change the dangling part to a complete clause.

Below standard: Believing that credit customers should have advance notice of the sale, special letters were mailed to them.

Acceptable: Believing that credit customers should have advance notice of the sale, we mailed special letters to them. [Improvement is made by inserting the noun being modified.]

Acceptable: Because we believed that credit customers should have advance notice of the sale, special letters were mailed to them. [Improvement is made by changing the dangling element to a complete clause.]

Dangling modifiers are of four principal types: participial phrases, elliptical clauses, gerund phrases, and infinitive phrases.

Below standard: Believing that District 7 was not being thoroughly covered, an additional salesperson was assigned to the area. [Dangling participial phrase]

Acceptable: Believing that District 7 was not being thoroughly covered, the sales manager assigned an additional salesperson to the area.

Below standard: By working hard, your goal can be reached. [Dangling gerund phrase]

Acceptable: By working hard, you can reach your goal.

Below standard: To succeed at this job, long hours and hard work must not be shunned. [Dangling infinitive phrase]

Acceptable: To succeed at this job, one must not shun long hours and hard work.

Below standard: While waiting on a customer, the radio was stolen. [Dangling elliptical clause—a clause without noun or verb]

Acceptable: While the salesperson was waiting on a customer, the radio was stolen.

Some introductory phrases are permitted to dangle.

A few generally accepted introductory phrases, however, are permitted to dangle. Included in this group are "generally speaking," "confidentially speaking," "taking all things into consideration," and expressions such as "in boxing," "in welding," and "in farming."

Acceptable: Generally speaking, business activity is at an all-time high.

Acceptable: In farming, the land must be prepared long before planting time.

Acceptable: Taking all things into consideration, this applicant is the best for the job.

☐ SENTENCE FRAGMENT: FRAG

Avoid sentence fragments (words that cannot stand alone as a complete thought).

Avoid sentence fragments. Although sometimes a sentence fragment may be used to good effect, as in sales writing, it is best omitted by all but the most skilled writers. A *sentence fragment* consists of any group of words that cannot stand alone as a complete, independent statement. Probably the most frequent violation of this rule results from the use of a subordinate clause as a sentence.

Below standard: Believing that you will want an analysis of sales for November. We have sent you the figures.

Acceptable: Believing that you will want an analysis of sales for November, we have sent you the figures.

Below standard: He declared that such a procedure would not be practical. And that it would be too expensive in the long run.

Acceptable: He declared that such a procedure would not be practical and that it would be too expensive in the long run.

☐ **PRONOUNS: PN**

Pronouns should clearly refer to a preceding word.

PN 1   Make certain that the word to which each pronoun refers (its antecedent) is clear. Failure to conform to this standard causes confusion, particularly in sentences in which two or more nouns are possible antecedents or the antecedent is far away from the pronoun.

Below standard: When the president objected to Mr. Carter, he told him to mind his own business. [Who told whom?]

Acceptable: When the president objected to Mr. Carter, Mr. Carter told him to mind his own business.

Below standard: The mixture should not be allowed to boil; so when you do it, watch the temperature gauge. [*It* doesn't have an antecedent.]

Acceptable: The mixture should not be allowed to boil; so when conducting the experiment, watch the temperature gauge.

Below standard: The model V is being introduced this year. Ads in *Time, People Weekly,* and big-city newspapers over the country are designed to get sales off to a good start. It is especially designed for the novice boater who is not willing to pay a big price.

Acceptable: The model V is being introduced this year. Ads in *Time, People Weekly,* and big-city newspapers over the country are designed to get sales off to a good start. The new model is especially designed for the novice boater who is not willing to pay a big price.

Confusion may sometimes result from using a pronoun with an implied antecedent.

Below standard: Because of the disastrous freeze in the Citrus Belt, it is necessary that most of them be replanted.

Acceptable: Because of the disastrous freeze in the Citrus Belt, it is necessary that most of the citrus orchards be replanted.

As a rule, avoid using *which, that,* and *this* to refer to broad ideas.

Except when their reference is perfectly clear, it is wise to avoid using the pronouns *which, that,* and *this* to refer to the whole idea of a preceding clause. Often you can make the sentence clear by using a clarifying noun after the pronoun.

Below standard (following a detailed presentation of the writer's suggestion for improving the company suggestion-box plan): This should be put into effect without delay.

Acceptable: This suggestion-box plan should be put into effect right away.

The number of a pronoun should be the same as that for the word to which the pronoun refers.

PN 2   The number of the pronoun should agree with the number of its antecedent (the word it stands for). If the antecedent is singular, its pronoun must be singular. If the antecedent is plural, its pronoun must be plural.

Below standard: Taxes and insurance are necessary evils in any business, and it must be considered carefully in anticipating profits.

Acceptable: Taxes and insurance are necessary evils in any business, and they must be considered carefully in anticipating profits.

Below standard: Everybody should make plans for their retirement. [Words like *everyone, everybody,* and *anybody* are singular.]

Acceptable: Everybody should make plans for his or her retirement.

Use the correct case of pronoun.

PN 3   Take care to use the correct case of the pronoun. If the pronoun serves as the subject of the verb or if it follows a form of the infinitive *to be,* use a pronoun in the nominative case. (Nominative cases of the personal pronouns are *I, you, he, she, it, we,* and *they*.)

Acceptable: He will record the minutes of the meeting.

Acceptable: I think that it will be he.

If the pronoun is the object of a preposition or a verb, or if it is the subject of an infinitive, use the objective case. (Objective cases for the personal pronouns are *me, you, him, her, it, us,* and *them*.)

Below standard: This transaction is between you and *he.* [*He* is nominative and cannot be the object of the preposition *between.*]

Acceptable: This transaction is between you and *him.*

Below standard: Because the investigator praised Ms. Smith and *I,* we were promoted.

Acceptable: Because the investigator praised Ms. Smith and *me,* we were promoted.

The case of relative pronouns (*who, whom*) is determined by the pronoun's use in the clause it introduces. One good way to determine which case to use is to substitute the personal pronoun for the relative pronoun. If the case of the personal pronoun that fits is nominative, use *who.* If it is objective, use *whom.*

Acceptable: George Cutler is the salesperson *who* won the award. [*He* (nominative) could be substituted for the relative pronoun; therefore, the nominative *who* should be used.]

Acceptable: George Cutler is the salesperson *whom* you recommended. [Objective case *him* would substitute. Thus, objective case *whom* is used.]

Usually the possessive case is used with substantives that immediately precede a gerund (verbal noun ending in *ing*).

Acceptable: Our selling of the stock frightened some of the conservative members of the board.

Acceptable: Her accepting the money ended her legal claim to the property.

☐ PARALLELISM: PRL

Express equal thoughts in a parallel (equal) grammatical form.

Parts of a sentence that express equal thoughts should be parallel (the same) in grammatical form. Parallel constructions are logically connected by the coordinating conjunctions *and, but,* and *or.* Take care to ensure that the sentence elements connected by these conjunctions are of the same grammatical type. In other words, if one of the parts is a noun, the other parts should be nouns; if one of the parts is an infinitive phrase, the other parts should be infinitive phrases.

Below standard: The company objectives for the coming year are to match last year's production, higher sales, and improving consumer relations.

Acceptable: The company objectives for the coming year are to match last year's production, to increase sales, and to improve consumer relations.

Below standard: Writing copy may be more valuable experience than to make layouts.

Acceptable: Writing copy may be more valuable experience than making layouts.

Below standard: The questionnaire asks for this information: number of employees, what is our union status, and how much do we pay.

Acceptable: The questionnaire asks for this information: number of employees, union affiliation, and pay scale.

☐   TENSE: TNS

The tense of each verb should show the logical time of happening.

The tense of each verb, infinitive, and participle used should reflect the logical time of happening of the statement. Every statement has its place in time. In order to precisely communicate this place in time, you must be careful of your selection of tense.

Use present tense for current happenings.

TNS 1   Use present tense for statements of fact that are true at the time of writing.

Below standard: Boston was not selected as a site for the aircraft plant because it *was* too near the coast. [Boston is still near the coast, isn't it?]

Acceptable: Boston was not selected as a site for the aircraft plant because it *is* too near the coast.

Use past tense for past happenings.

TNS 2   Use past tense in statements covering a definite past event or action.

Below standard: Mr. Burns *says* to me, "Bill, you'll never make an auditor."

Acceptable: Mr. Burns *said* to me, "Bill, you'll never make an auditor."

The past participle (*having been* . . .) indicates happenings earlier than the present participle (*being* . . .).

TNS 3   The time period reflected by the past participle (*having been* . . .) is earlier than that of its governing verb. For the present participle (*being* . . .), the time period reflected is the same as that of the governing verb.

Below standard: These debentures are among the oldest on record, *being* issued in early 1937.

Acceptable: These debentures are among the oldest on record, *having been* issued in early 1937.

Below standard: Ms. Sloan, *having been* the top salesperson on the force, was made sales manager. [Possible but illogical]

Acceptable: Ms. Sloan, *being* the top salesperson on the force, was made sales manager.

Verbs in principal clauses govern those in subordinate clauses.

TNS 4   Verbs in subordinate clauses are governed by the verb in the principal clause. When the main verb is in the past tense, usually you should place the subordinate verb in the past tense (past, present perfect, or past perfect). Thus, if the time context of the subordinate clause is the same as that of the main verb, use past tense.

Acceptable: I *noticed* [past tense] the discrepancy, and then I *remembered* [same time context as main verb] the incidents that *caused* it.

If the time context of the subordinate clause is previous to that of the main verb in the past tense, use the past perfect tense for the subordinate verb.

Below standard: In early July we *noticed* [past] that he *exceeded* [logically should be previous to main verb] his quota three times.

Acceptable: In early July we *noticed* that he *had exceeded* his quota three times.

The present perfect tense is used for the subordinate clause when the time context of this clause is subsequent to that of the main verb.

Below standard: Before the war we *contributed* [past] generously, but lately we *forget* [should be time context subsequent to that of main verb] our duties.

Acceptable: Before the war we *contributed* generously, but lately we *have forgotten* our duties.

Present perfect tense (*have . . .*) refers to the indefinite past.

TNS 5   The present perfect tense does not logically refer to a definite time in the past. Instead, it indicates time somewhere in the indefinite past.

Below standard: We *have audited* your records on July 31 of 1993 and 1992.

Acceptable: We *audited* your records on July 31 of 1993 and 1992.

Acceptable: We *have audited* your records twice in the past.

☐   WORD USE: WU

Use words correctly.

Misused words call attention to themselves and detract from the writing. Although the possibilities of error in word use are infinite, the following list contains a few of the most common ones:

Don't Use	Use
a long ways	a long way
and etc.	etc.
anywheres	anywhere
different than	different from
have got to	must
in back of	behind
in hopes of	in hope of
in regards to	in regard to
inside of	within
kind of satisfied	somewhat satisfied
nowhere near	not nearly
nowheres	nowhere
off of	off
over with	over
seldom ever	seldom
try and come	try to come

STANDARDS FOR THE USE OF NUMBERS: NO

Quantities may be either spelled out or expressed in numerical form. Whether to use one form or the other is often a perplexing question. It is especially confusing to report writers, for much of their work is with quantitative subjects.

Spell out numbers nine and under; and use figures for higher numbers, except as follows.

No 1   Although authorities do not agree on number usage, report writers would do well to follow the "rule of nine." By this rule, you spell out numbers nine and below and use figures for numbers above nine.

> *Correct:* The auditor found 13 discrepancies in the stock records.

> *Correct:* The auditor found nine discrepancies in the stock records.

Spell out numbers that begin a sentence.

No 2   Make an exception to the rule of nine when a number begins a sentence. Spell out all numbers in this position.

> *Correct:* Seventy-three bonds and six debentures were destroyed.

> *Correct:* Eighty-nine men picketed the north entrance.

Keep all numbers in comparisons in the same form.

No 3   In comparisons, keep all numbers in the same form. The form should be the one that according to the rule of nine occurs most often in the series.

> *Correct:* We managed to salvage three lathes, one drill, and thirteen welding machines.

> *Correct:* Sales increases over last year were 9 percent on automotive parts, 14 percent on hardware, and 23 percent on appliances.

When two series are in a sentence, use words for one and numerals for the other.

No 4   When two series of numbers appear in one sentence, spell out one (preferably the smaller) and present the other in numerical form.

> *Correct:* Three salespersons exceeded $1,500, fourteen exceeded $1,000, and thirty-one exceeded $500.

Use figures for days of the month when the month precedes the day.

No 5   Present days of the month in numerical form when the month precedes the day.

> *Correct:* July 3, 1994

When they appear alone or precede the month, the days of the month may be either spelled out or in numerical form according to the rule of nine.

> *Correct:* I shall be there on the 13th.

> *Correct:* The union scheduled the strike vote for the eighth.

> *Correct:* Ms. Millican signed the contract on the seventh of July.

> *Correct:* Sales have declined since the 14th of August.

SPELLING AND CAPITALIZATION

The following rules for spelling and capitalization should help as you prepare your reports. They, too, are important in ensuring the quality, accuracy, and overall professionalism of your writing.

| **FIGURE 16-1** | Eighty of the most frequently misspelled words |

absence	despair	leisure	receive
accessible	development	license	recommend
accommodate	disappear	misspelling	repetition
achieve	disappoint	necessary	ridiculous
analyze	discriminate	newsstand	seize
argument	drunkenness	noticeable	separate
assistant	embarrassment	occurrence	sergeant
balloon	exceed	panicky	sheriff
benefited	existence	paralyze	stationary (standing)
category	forty	parallel	stationery (paper)
cede	grammar	pastime	succeed
changeable	grievous	persistent	suddenness
committee	holiday	possesses	superintendent
comparative	incidentally	predictable	supersede
conscience	indispensable	principal	surprise
conscious	insistent	privilege	truly
coolly	irrelevant	proceed	until
definitely	irresistible	professor	vacuum
description	irritable	pronunciation	vicious
desirable	judgment	pursue	weird

☐ **SPELLING: SP**

Spell words correctly. Use the dictionary.

Probably misspelling is the most frequently made error in writing. It is also the least excusable, because all one need do to eliminate the error is use a dictionary. Remember, too, that computer programs with spelling checkers (see Chapter 10) can help you.

Study Figure 16–1 for the 80 most commonly misspelled words.

Unfortunately, we must memorize in order to spell. Thus, becoming a good speller involves long, hard work. Even so, you can improve your spelling significantly with relatively little effort. Studies show that fewer than 100 words account for most spelling errors. Thus, if you will learn how to spell these most troublesome words, you will go a long way toward solving your spelling problems. Eighty of these words appear in Figure 16–1.

Although English spelling follows little rhyme or reason, a few helpful rules exist. You would do well to learn and use them.

☐ **RULES FOR WORD PLURALS**

These three rules cover plurals for most words.

1.   To form the plurals of most words, add *s:*

cat, cats
dog, dogs

2.   To form the plurals of words ending in *s, sh, ch,* and *x,* usually add *es* to the singular:

glass, glasses   dish, dishes
bunch, bunches   ax, axes

3. To form the plural of words ending in *y*, if a consonant precedes the *y* drop the *y* and add *ies.* But if the *y* is preceded by a vowel, add *s:*

pony, ponies
chimney, chimneys

☐ OTHER SPELLING RULES

These rules cover four other trouble areas of spelling.

1. Words ending in *ce* or *ge* do not drop the *e* when adding *ous* or *able:*

charge, chargeable
change, changeable
notice, noticeable
service, serviceable

2. Words ending in *l* do not drop the *l* when adding *ly:*

final, finally
principal, principally

3. Words ending in silent *e* usually drop the *e* when adding a suffix beginning with a vowel:

love, lovable
dive, diving
time, timing

4. Place *i* before *e* except after *c:*

relieve   conceive
believe   receive

Exception: when the word is sounded as a long *a:*

neighbor   weigh

Other exceptions:

either	Fahrenheit	height
seize	surfeit	efficient
sufficient	neither	foreign
leisure	ancient	seizure
weird	financier	codeine
forfeit	seismograph	sovereign
deficient	science	counterfeit

☐ CAPITALIZATION: CAP

Capitalize all proper names and the beginning words of sentences.

Use capitals for the first letters of all proper names. Common examples are these:

Streets: 317 East Boyd Avenue

Geographic places: Chicago, Indiana, Finland

Companies: Berkowitz Manufacturing Company, Inc.

Titles preceding names: President Watkins

Titles of books, articles, poems: *Report Writing for Business*

First words of sentences and of complimentary closes

The word number (or its abbreviation) when used with a figure to identify something

As noted earlier, other standards are useful in clear communication. But those covered in the preceding pages will help you through most of your report-writing problems. Most certainly, by using them you can give your writing the precision good communication requires.

EXERCISE IN CORRECTNESS

Correct any punctuation or grammar errors you can find in the following sentences. Explain your corrections.

1. Janice E. Baskin the new member of the advisory committee has been an employee for seven years.

2. The auditor asked us, "If all members of the work group had access to the petty cash fund?"

3. Our January order consisted of the following items; two dozen Norwood desk calendars, note size, one dozen desk blotters, 20 by 32 inches, and one dozen bottles of ink, permanent black.

4. The truth of the matter is, that the union representative had not informed the workers of the decision.

5. Sales for the first quarter were the highest in history, profits declined for the period.

6. We suggest that you use a mild soap for best results but detergents will not harm the product.

7. Employment for October totaled 12,741 an increase of 3.1 percent over September.

8. It would not be fair however to consider only this point.

9. It is the only water-repellent snag-proof and inexpensive material available.

10. Henry Thatcher a supervisor in our company is accused of the crime.

11. Ms. Goodman made this statement, "Contrary to our expectations, Smith and Company will lose money this year."

12. I bought and he sold.

13. Soon we saw George Sweeny who is the auditor for the company.

14. Manufactured in light medium and heavy weights this razor has been widely accepted.

15. Because of a common belief that profits are too high we will have to cut our prices on most items.

16. Such has been the growth of the cities most prestigious firm, H. E. Klauss and Company.

17. In 1990, we were advised in fact we were instructed to accept this five year contract.

18. Henrys playing around has got him into trouble.

19. Denise B. Henshaw who was our leading salesperson last month is the leading candidate for the position.

20. The worker who completes the most units will receive a bonus.

21. The word phone which is short for telephone should be avoided in formal writing.

22. In last months issue of Modern Business appeared Johnson's latest article What Systems Theory Means to You.

23. Yes he replied this is exactly what we mean.

24. Why did she say John it's too late?

25. Place your order today, it is not too late.

26. We make our plans on a day to day basis.

27. There is little accuracy in the 60 day forecast.

28. The pre Christmas sale will extend over twenty six days.

29. We cannot tolerate any worker's failure to do their duty.

30. An assortment of guns, bombs, burglar tools, and ammunition were found in the cellar.

31. If we can be certain that we have the facts we can make our decision soon.

32. This one is easy to make. If one reads the instructions carefully.

33. This is the gift he received from you and I.

34. A collection of short articles on the subject were printed.

35. If we can detect only a tenth of the errors it will make us realize the truth.

36. He takes shorthand good.

37. There was plenty of surprises at the meeting.

38. It don't appear that we have made much progress.

39. The surface of these products are smooth.

40. Everybody is expected to do their best.

41. The brochures were delivered to John and I early Sunday morning.

42. Who did he recommend for the job.

43. We were given considerable money for the study.

44. She seen what could happen when administration breaks down.

45. One of his conclusions is that the climate of the region was not desirable for our purposes.

46. Smith and Rogers plans to buy the Bridgeport plant.

47. The committee feels that no action should be taken.

48. Neither of the workers found their money.

49. While observing the workers, the assembly line was operating at peak perfection.

50. The new building is three stories high, fifteen years old, solid brick construction, and occupies a corner lot.

51. They had promised to have completed the job by noon.

52. Jones has been employed by the Sampson Company for twenty years.

53. Wilson and myself will handle the job.

54. Each man and woman are expected to abide by this rule.

55. The boiler has been inspected on April 1 and May 3.

56. To find problems and correcting them takes up most of my work time.

57. The carton of canned goods were distributed to the workers.

58. The motor ran uneven.

59. All are expected except John and she.

60. Everyone here has more ability than him.

Oral Reporting

CHAPTER 17
Communicating through Oral Reports

Communicating through Oral Reports

Many business occasions call for an oral presentation rather than a written report.

Since most business reports are presented in writing to colleagues, clients, officials, and other audiences, our focus thus far has been on written business reports. However, there are many occasions in business when an oral presentation is both appropriate and effective.

In some cases, it is timing that determines whether a report will be delivered orally rather than in writing. Rapid developments in a highly competitive market, for example, might not allow time for writing, copying, and distributing the research and analyses critical for decision making. In other cases, oral presentation may be a matter of style. Companies that have developed an informal style of conducting business, for instance, may find written presentations out of character. And in still other cases, the decision to present material orally is determined by the nature of the business problem itself. Corporate officers may want to explain a controversial decision directly to shareholders. Similarly, a sales manager may want to demonstrate an exciting new sales campaign to the company directors.

Oral reports, like written reports, require setting objectives, planning research, and determining report order. They also demand the same high standard of objectivity written reports do.

Oral reports, as you will see, share with written reports the basic principles of defining objectives, planning research, and determining the report order. They also demand the same high standard of objectivity in analysis. As a result, you can apply much of what you have learned about written reports directly to oral reports. What this chapter does, therefore, is highlight the differences between the two media and identify several of the challenges—and opportunities—posed by the spoken word.

DIFFERENCES BETWEEN ORAL AND WRITTEN REPORTS

Oral reports differ from written reports in three ways:

As written reports have been covered thoroughly in preceding chapters, let us look at the differences between written and oral reports. Three in particular stand out.

☐ VISUAL ADVANTAGES OF THE WRITTEN WORD

(1) writing and speaking are different, and each has its advantages and disadvantages;

The first major difference between oral and written reports is that writing permits greater use of visual cues than speaking does. With writing, you can use paragraphing to show the reader the structure of the message and to make the thought units stand out. In addition, by writing your message, you can use punctuation to relate, subordinate, and qualify the various parts of your report. The result of these techniques is to improve the communication effect of the entire message.

On the other hand, when you make an oral presentation, you can use none of these techniques. However, you can use others—techniques peculiar to oral communication. For example, you can use inflection, pauses, volume emphasis, and changes in rate of delivery. Both oral and written presentations, therefore, have techniques that are effective in aiding communication. The point is to appreciate what each medium can do and to make sure your cues to your listeners are as clear as those you are accustomed to giving your readers.

☐ READER CONTROL OF WRITTEN PRESENTATION

(2) the speaker controls the pace of an oral report, and the reader controls the pace of a written report; and

A second difference between oral and written reporting is that in a written report your readers control the pace of the communication. They can pause, reread, change their rate of reading, or stop as they choose. As a result, you can communicate even when your writing is difficult. In an oral report, on the other hand, you control the pace. The audience has to grasp your meaning as you present it—or miss your point. It is important, therefore, that you keep your oral report relatively simple.

☐ EMPHASIS ON CORRECTNESS IN WRITING

(3) written reports have more stress on correctness.

A third difference between oral and written reporting is the degree of correctness stressed in each. Because your written work is likely to be inspected carefully, you will want to work for a high degree of correctness. That is, you will probably be very careful to follow the recognized rules of grammar, punctuation, sentence structure, and so on. The standards for oral communication are considerably more flexible. Of course, you should still follow the basic rules of grammar, give attention to effective phrasing, and use words correctly. Nevertheless, depending on the formality of the situation, you can adopt a more conversational style, adapt sentence structure to the rhythm of speech, and include colloquial expressions.

Other differences exist, of course, but these three are the most significant. They serve as foundations from which to explain the techniques of oral reporting.

PLANNING THE ORAL REPORT

Planning is the first step in preparing oral reports.

As in a written report, it is probable that you will want to do some planning work before beginning on the actual body of your oral report. For the short, informal report, of course, planning may be minimal. But for the more formal presentations, particularly those involving audiences of more than one, proper planning is likely to be as involved as that for a comparable written report.

☐ DETERMINATION OF REPORT OBJECTIVE

First, determine the goal and how to reach it.

Logically, your first step in planning an oral report is to determine your objective. This step is similar to what we described for the written report in Chapter 3: You should clearly state the report goal in clear, concise language. Then you should clearly state the factors involved in achieving this goal. These steps will give you a clear guide to the information you must gather and to the framework around which you will build your presentation.

In the process of determining your goal, you must be aware of your general objective. That is, you must decide on your general purpose in making the presentation. Is it to persuade? To inform? To recommend? Your conclusion here will have a major influence on how you develop your material for presentation and perhaps even on the presentation itself.

☐ ORGANIZATION OF CONTENT

Next, organize content. Either the indirect or direct order is all right,

Your procedure for organizing oral reports is similar to that for written reports. You have the choice of using either the direct or the indirect order. Even so, the same information presented orally and in writing is not necessarily presented in the same way. Time pressure, for example, may justify direct presentation for an oral report. The same report problem presented in writing might be best arranged in the indirect order. A reader in a hurry can always skip to the conclusion or ending of the report. The listener does not have this choice.

but the indirect order is more common.

Although oral reports may use either the direct or the indirect order, the indirect is by far the more widely used order as well as the more logical. Because your audience is not likely to know the problem well, some introductory comments are needed to prepare them to receive the message. In addition, you may need introductory words to arouse interest, stimulate curiosity, or impress the audience with the importance of the subject. The main goal of the introductory remarks is to state the purpose, define unfamiliar terms, explain limitations, describe scope, and generally cover all the necessary introductory subjects (see discussion of introduction, Chapter 8).

Organization for oral and written reports is much the same, except oral reports usually have a closing summary.

In the body of the oral report, you should develop the goals you have set. Here, also, there is much similarity with the written report. Division of subject matter into comparable parts, logical order, introductory paragraphs, concluding paragraphs, and such are equally important to both forms.

The major difference in organization of the written and oral report is in the ending. Both forms may end with a summary, a conclusion, a recommendation, or a combination of the three. But the oral report is likely to have a final summary tacked on, regardless of whether it has a conclusion or a recommendation. In a sense, this final summary serves the purpose of an executive summary by bringing together all the really important information, analyses, conclusions, and recommendations in the report. It also emphasizes the points that should stand out and thus helps your audience recall what you have said.

CONSIDERATION OF PERSONAL ASPECTS

A logical first step in preparing a speech is to analyze yourself. You are a part of the message.

A preliminary step to effective oral reporting is to analyze yourself as a speaker. In oral presentations you, the speaker, are in a very real sense a part of the message. Your audience takes in not only the words you communicate, but also what they see in you. And what they see in you can have a most significant effect on the meanings that develop in their minds. Thus, you should carefully evaluate your personal effect on the message you present. You should do whatever you can to detect and overcome shortcomings and to sharpen any strengths you might have.

You should seek the following four characteristics:

Although the following summary of such characteristics may prove to be useful, probably you know them from experience. The chances are you can easily recognize the good qualities and the bad. To some extent, the problem is recognizing these characteristics, or the lack of them, in yourself. To a greater extent, it is doing something about improving your bad characteristics when you recognize them. The following review should help you pinpoint these problem areas and should give you some practical suggestions on how to overcome them.

☐ CONFIDENCE

(1) *Confidence* in yourself is important. So is having the confidence of your audience.

A primary characteristic of effective oral reporting is confidence. This confidence should include confidence in yourself as well as confidence of the audience in you, the speaker. Actually, the two are complementary, for your confidence in yourself tends to produce an image that gives your audience confidence in you. Similarly, your audience's confidence in you can give you a sense of security, thereby making you more confident of your ability.

Confidence of your audience in you must be earned. Project the right image, and talk in a strong, clear voice.

Confidence of your audience in you typically is earned over periods of association. But there are things you can do to project an image that invites confidence. For example, you can prepare your presentation diligently, and you can practice it thoroughly. Such careful preliminary work gives you confidence in yourself. Having confidence leads to more effective communication, which in turn builds confidence in your listener's mind. Another thing you can do to gain confidence is to check your physical appearance carefully. Unfair and illogical as it may be, certain manners of dress and certain hairstyles create strong images in people's minds ranging from one extreme to the other. Thus, if you want to communicate effectively, you should analyze the audience you seek to reach. And you should work to develop the physical appearance that projects an image in which your audience can have confidence. Yet another suggestion for being confident is simply to talk in strong, clear tones. Such tones do much to project an image of confidence. Although most people can do little to change their natural voices, they can try to add sufficient volume.

☐ SINCERITY

Your listeners are quick to detect insincerity in you. And when they detect it, they are likely to give little weight to what you say. On the other hand, sincerity is a valuable aid to conviction, especially if the audience has confidence in your ability. As to what

(2) *Sincerity* is vital. You get an image of sincerity by being sincere.

you can do to project an image of sincerity, the answer is clear and simple: You must *be* sincere. Pretense of sincerity rarely is successful.

☐ THOROUGHNESS

(3) *Thoroughness*— giving the listeners all they need—helps your image.

When you are thorough in your presentation, generally your message is better received than when your coverage is scanty or hurried. Thorough coverage gives the impression that time and care have been taken, and such an impression tends to make the message believable. But you can overdo thoroughness. If you present the information in too much detail, your listeners may become lost in a sea of information. The secret is to select the important information and to leave out the unimportant. To do this, of course, requires that you use good judgment. You must put yourself in your listeners' place and ask yourself just what the listeners need to know and what they do not need to know.

☐ FRIENDLINESS

(4) *Friendliness* projected by you aids your communication effort.

A speaker who projects an image of friendliness has a significant advantage in communicating. People simply like people who are friendly, and they are more receptive to what friendly people say. Like sincerity, friendliness is difficult to feign. It must be honest if it is to be effective. But with most people, friendliness is honest, for most people want to be friendly. Some just are not able to project the friendly image they would like to project. With a little self-analysis, a little mirror-watching as you practice speaking, you can find ways of improving the friendliness of your image.

These are but some of the characteristics that should aid you as a speaker. There are others, such as *interest, enthusiasm, originality,* and *flexibility*. But the characteristics described are the most significant and the ones most speakers need to work on. Through self-analysis and dedicated effort to improve the personal aspects of oral reporting, you can improve your speaking ability.

AUDIENCE ANALYSIS

You should know your audience.

One requirement of effective oral reporting is to know your audience. You should study your audience before and during the presentation.

☐ PRELIMINARY ANALYSIS

Size up the audience in advance.

Analyzing your audience before the report requires that you size up the group—that you search for any characteristics that could have some effect on how you should present your speech.

For example, size of audience is likely to influence how formal or informal you make your speech. (As a rule, large audiences require more formality.) The personal characteristics of the audience can also affect how you make your speech. Characteristics such as age, sex, education, experience, and knowledge of subject matter can determine how you present your message. They determine the words you use, the need for illustration, and the level of detail required. Just as in writing, you should adapt your speeches to your audiences. And knowing your audience is a first step in adaptation.

Look for characteristics that will affect your speech—for example, things like audience size, sex, age, education, knowledge.

☐ ANALYSIS DURING PRESENTATION

Your audience analysis should continue as you make your report. Called *feedback,* this phase of audience analysis gives you information about how your listeners are receiving your words. With this information, you can adjust your presentation to improve the communication result.

Continue analyzing the audience during the speech. Consider *feedback.*

Facial expressions, movements, noises give feedback information that helps you adapt to the audience.

Your eyes and ears will give feedback information. For example, facial expressions will tell you how your listeners are reacting to your message. From smiles, blank stares, and movements you get an indication of whether they understand, agree with, or accept your message. You can detect from sounds coming (or not coming) from the audience whether they are listening. If questions are in order, you can learn directly how your message is coming across. By being alert, you can thus learn much from your audience; and what you learn can help you make a more effective presentation.

APPEARANCE AND BODILY ACTIONS

As your listeners hear your words, they are looking at you. What they see is a part of the message, and it can have a very real effect on the success of your report. What your audience sees, of course, is you. And they see that which surrounds you. Thus, in your efforts to improve the effects of your oral presentations, you should understand thoroughly the communication effects of what your listeners see.

Your audience forms impressions from these six factors:

The following review of what your audience sees should help you analyze how your environment, appearance, and delivery affect your presentation. What will help even more, however, is rehearsing a presentation, or better yet, videotaping a rehearsal and reviewing the tape. Only when you can see yourself as others see you can you accurately assess the strengths and weaknesses of your oral reporting techniques.

☐ THE COMMUNICATION ENVIRONMENT

(1) all that surrounds you (stage, lighting and such),

Much of what your audience sees is all that surrounds you as you speak—all that tends to form a general impression. This includes the physical things—the stage, lighting, background, and such. Although not visual, a related influence here would be outside noises. For the best communication results, the factors in your communication environment should not detract from your message. Rather, they should contribute to good communication. Your own experience as a listener will tell you what is important.

☐   PERSONAL APPEARANCE

(2) your personal
appearance,

Your personal appearance is a part of the message your audience receives. Of course, you have to accept the physical properties you have, but not many of us need be at a disadvantage in appearance. All that is necessary is that you use what you have appropriately. Specifically, you should dress appropriately for the audience and the occasion. Use facial expressions and bodily movements to your advantage, too. Just how you go about using your facial expressions and bodily movements is described in following paragraphs.

☐   POSTURE

(3) your posture,

Posture is likely to be the most obvious personal characteristic that your audience will see. Even if listeners cannot be close enough to detect facial expressions and eye movements, they can see the general form the body makes.

You probably think no one needs to tell you what good posture is. You know it when you see it. The trouble is that you are not likely to see it in yourself. One solution is to have others tell you whether your posture needs improvement. Another is to practice speaking before a mirror or again to videotape a presentation and review the results.

In your efforts to improve your posture, keep in mind what must go on within your body to form a good posture. Your body weight must be distributed in a comfortable and poised way consistent with the impression you want to make. You should stand up straight without appearing stiff and look comfortable without appearing limp. Your bearing should be self-poised, alert, communicative, and, above all, natural. The great danger of being conscious about your posture is that you will appear artificial.

☐   WALKING

(4) your manner of
walking,

The way you walk before your audience also makes an impression on your listeners. A strong, sure walk to the speaker's position gives an impression of confidence. Hesitant, awkward steps give the opposite impression. Walking during the presentation can be effective or ineffective, depending on how you do it. Some speakers use steps forward and to the side as a form of bodily gesture, especially to emphasize points. Too much walking, however, attracts attention and detracts from the message. You would be wise to hold your walking to a minimum and use it as a technique only when you are reasonably sure of its effect.

☐   FACIAL EXPRESSIONS

(5) facial expressions
(smiles, frowns), and

Probably the most apparent and communicative bodily movements are facial expressions. The problem is, however, that you may unconsciously use facial expressions that convey meanings not intended. For example, a frightened speaker may tighten the jaw unconsciously and begin to grin. The effect may be an ambiguous image that detracts from the entire communication effort. A smile, a grimace, a puzzled frown, all convey clear messages. Without question, they are effective communication devices; and you should use them.

Equally important in considering facial expressions is the matter of eye contact. The eyes have long been considered "mirrors of the soul" and provide most observers with information about your sincerity, goodwill, and flexibility. Some listeners tend to shun speakers who refuse to look at them. Also, discriminate eye contact tends to show that you have a genuine interest in your audience.

☐ GESTURES

(6) gestures.

Gestures, like posture, add to the message you communicate. Just what they add, however, is hard to say, for they have no definite or clear-cut meanings. A clenched fist, for example, certainly adds emphasis to a strong point. But it also can be used to show defiance, to make a threat, or to signify respect for a cause. And so it is with other gestures. They register vague meanings.

Gestures have vague meanings, but they communicate.

Even though they have vague meanings, gestures are strong. They are natural aids to speaking. It appears natural, for example, to emphasize a plea with palms up and to show disagreement with palms down. Raising first one hand and then the other reinforces a division of points. Slicing the air with the hand shows several divisions. Although such gestures as these generally are clear, we do not all use them exactly alike.

In summary, your bodily movements aid your speaking.

In summary, it should be clear that you can use bodily movements effectively to help your speaking. Just which movements you should use, however, is hard to say. They are related to personality, physical makeup, and the size and nature of the audience. A speaker appearing before a formal group generally should use relatively few bodily actions. A speaker appearing before an informal audience should use more. What you should use on a given occasion is a matter for your best judgment.

USE OF VOICE

Good voice is a requirement for good speaking. Four faults affect voice:

Good voice is an obvious requirement of a good oral presentation. Like bodily movements, the voice should not hinder the listener's concentration on the message. More specifically, the voice should not call attention away from the message. Voices that cause such difficulties fall generally into four areas of fault: (1) lack of pitch, (2) lack of variety in speaking speed, (3) lack of emphasis by variation in volume, and (4) unpleasantness in voice quality.

☐ LACK OF PITCH VARIATION

(1) lack of variation in pitch (usually a matter of habit),

Speakers who talk in monotones are not likely to hold the interest of their listeners for long. As most voices are capable of wide variations in pitch, usually the problem can be corrected. Most often the failure to vary pitch is a matter of habit—of voice patterns developed over years of talking without being aware of effect.

☐ LACK OF VARIATION IN SPEAKING SPEED

(2) lack of variation in speed (cover the simple quickly, the hard slowly),

Determining how fast to talk is a major problem. As a general rule, you should present the easy parts of the message at a fairly fast rate. You should present hard-to-understand information at a slower rate. The reason for varying the speed of presentation should be apparent. Easy information presented slowly is irritating; hard information presented fast may be difficult to understand.

A problem related to the pace of speaking is the incorrect use of pauses. Of course, pauses used at the appropriate time and place are effective. When properly used, they emphasize the upcoming subject matter and are effective means of gaining attention. But frequent pauses for no reason are irritating and break the listener's concentration. The error becomes worse when the speaker fills in the pauses with *uh's* and meaningless *you know's* and *OK's.*

☐ LACK OF VOCAL EMPHASIS

(3) lack of vocal emphasis (gain emphasis by varying pitch, pace, and volume), and

One secret of effective oral reporting is to give the words the emphasis due them by varying the manner of speaking. You can do this by (1) varying the pitch of your voice, (2) varying the pace of your presentation, and (3) varying the volume of your voice. As the first two techniques have been discussed, only the use of voice volume requires comment.

You must talk loudly enough for all of your audience to hear, but not too loudly. (Thus, the loudness—voice force—for a large group should be more than that for a small group.) Regardless of group size, however, variety in force is good for interest and emphasis. It produces contrast, which is one way of emphasizing the subject matter. Some speakers incorrectly believe that the only way to gain emphasis is to get louder and louder. But you can show emphasis also by going from loud to soft. The contrast with what has gone on before provides the emphasis. Again, variety is the key to making the voice more effective.

☐ UNPLEASANT VOICE QUALITY

(4) unpleasant voice (most can be improved).

It is a hard fact of communication that some voices are more pleasing than others. Fortunately, most voices are reasonably pleasant. But some are raspy, nasal, or in some other way unpleasant. Although therapy often can improve such voices, some speakers must live with what they have. But by concentrating on variations in pitch, speed of delivery, and volume, one can make even the most unpleasant voice effective.

☐ IMPROVEMENT THROUGH SELF-ANALYSIS

You can correct the foregoing faults through self-analysis and work.

You can overcome any of the foregoing voice problems through self-analysis. In this day of tape recorders, it is easy to hear yourself talk. Since you know good speaking when you hear it, you should be able to improve your presentation.

USE OF VISUAL (GRAPHIC) AIDS

As spoken words have limitations, sometimes visual aids can help them.

The spoken word is severely limited in communicating. Sound is here a brief moment and then it is gone. If the listener misses the message, there may be no chance to hear it again. Because of this limitation, speeches often need strong visual support—charts, tables, chalkboards, film, and such. Visual (graphic) aids may be as vital to the success of an oral report as the words themselves.

☐ PROPER USE OF DESIGN

Use visual aids for the hard parts of the message.

Effective visual aids are those drawn from the message. They should fit the one speech and the one audience.

In selecting visual aids, you should search through the presentation for topics that appear vague or confusing. Whenever a picture or other form of visual aid will help clear up vagueness, you should use one. Visual aids are truly a part of your message, and you should look upon them as such.

Use the form (chart, diagram, picture) that communicates the information best.

After you have decided that a topic deserves visual help, you determine the form the help should take. That is, should it be a chart, a diagram, a picture, or what? You should base your decision primarily on the question of which form communicates best. As simple and obvious as this point may appear, people violate it all too often. They select visual aids more for appearance and dramatic effect than for communication effect.

☐ FORMS TO CONSIDER

Because no one form is best for all occasions, you should have a flexible attitude toward visual aids. You should know the good and bad qualities of each, and you should know how to use each effectively.

Select from the various types available, as described in Chapter 15.

In selecting visual aids, you should keep in mind the types available. Primarily, you will consider the various forms of photographed or drawn illustrations—charts, graphs, tables, diagrams, and pictures. Each of these forms has its special strengths and weaknesses, as described in Chapter 15. Each may be displayed in various ways—by slide, overhead, or opaque projector; by flip chart; by easel display; on a chalkboard; on a felt board; or in other ways. And each of these display forms has its strengths and weaknesses. In addition, visual aids may take the form of motion pictures, models, samples, demonstrations, and the like. Remember, too, that desktop publishing allows you to design inviting and distinctive presentation graphics.

☐ TECHNIQUES IN USING VISUAL AIDS

Make the visual aids points of interest in the presentation.

Visual aids usually carry key parts of the message. Thus, they are points of emphasis in your presentation. You blend them in with your words to communicate the message. How you do this is to some extent an individual matter, for techniques vary. They vary so much, in fact, that it would be hard to present a meaningful summary of them. It is more meaningful to present a list of do's and don't's. Such a list follows:

Here is a list of specific suggestions for using graphic aids.

1. Make certain everyone in the audience can see the visual aids. Too many or too light lines on a chart, for example, can be hard to see. Too small an illustration can be meaningless to people far from the speaker.

2. Explain the visual aid if there is any likelihood that it will be misunderstood.

3. Organize the visual aids as a part of the presentation. Fit them into the plan.

4. Emphasize the visual aids. Point to them with bodily action and with words.

5. Talk to the audience—not to the visual aids. Look at the visual aids only when the audience should look at them.

6. Avoid blocking the listener's view of the visual aids. Make certain that lecterns, pillars, chairs, and such do not block anyone's view. Take care not to stand in anyone's line of vision.

USE OF COMPUTER TECHNOLOGY IN ORAL REPORTING

Computer technology can help oral reporting.

Computer technologies exist that can help and extend the process of oral reporting. Two of them that combine oral and video communication effectively are teleconferencing and videodisc systems. While these technologies have existed for some time, new developments in optical fibers, satellite transmissions, and software and chip refinements may push them into even higher favor with business professionals. Also, costs of the technologies are being lowered.

Teleconferencing links people who are in different locations.

Teleconferencing uses technology to link people together electronically to conduct a meeting when group members are located in different places. Quite elaborate systems exist to transmit oral messages to others, primarily through television. Most systems also have the advantage of enhancing visuals and providing for feedback. As you can see, teleconferencing saves time, travel expense, and scheduling conflicts.

Videodiscs store pictures, audio, and written words.

Videodisc technology, which stores pictures, audio, and written words, has great potential for business in general and oral reporting in particular. To date, however, its applications have been limited to training and education. As hypertext is developed, videodisc technology may see more extensive application to business. Hypertext allows readers to link pictures, audio, and written words in any order they prefer.

Both use oral and visual communication.

Both of these technologies—teleconferencing and videodisc—enable a report writer to use oral and visual communication. As these and other technologies develop, there will likely be other applications to oral reporting as well.

A SUMMARY LIST OF SPEAKING PRACTICES

This review has covered the high points of speaking.

The foregoing review of business speaking is selective, for the subject is broad. In fact, entire books are devoted to the subject. But this review has covered the high points, especially those that you can transfer into practice easily. Perhaps even more practical is the following list of what to do and not to do while speaking.

This summary checklist of good and bad speaking practices should prove helpful.

1. Organize the speech so it leads the hearer's thoughts logically to the conclusion.

2. Move surely and quickly to the conclusion. Do not leave a conclusion dangling, repeat unnecessarily, or appear unable to close.

3. Use language specifically adapted to the audience.

4. Articulate clearly, pleasantly, and with proper emphasis. Avoid mumbling and the overuse of *ah, er, uh,* and so forth.

5. Speak correctly, using accepted grammar and pronunciation.

6. Maintain an attitude of alertness, displaying appropriate enthusiasm and confidence.

7. Employ body language to best advantage. Use it to emphasize points and to assist in communicating concepts and ideas.

8. Avoid stiffness or rigidity of bodily action.

9. Look the audience in the eye and talk directly to them.

10. Avoid excessive movements, fidgeting, and other signs of nervousness.

11. Punctuate the presentation with reference to visual aids. Make them a part of the report story.

12. Even when faced with unfair opposition, keep your temper. To lose your temper is to lose control of the presentation.

QUESTIONS

1. Explain the principal differences between written and oral reports.

2. Compare the typical organization plans of oral and written reports. Note the major difference between the two plans.

3. Explain how one's personal aspects influence the meanings of one's spoken words.

4. A reporter presented an oral report to an audience of 27 middle and upper level administrators. Then he presented the same information to an audience consisting of the three top executives in the company. Note some of the differences that probably took place in these two presentations.

5. What is meant by the language style of an oral report? What advice would you give to one trying to achieve good style?

6. Explain the role of feedback in oral reporting.

7. Discuss how the general impression one receives of a reporter has an effect on the message received.

8. By description (or perhaps by example), identify good and bad postures and walking practices for speaking.

9. Explain how facial expressions can miscommunicate.

10. Give some illustrations of gestures that can be used for multiple meanings. Demonstrate them.

11. "We are born with voices—some good, some bad, and some in between. We have no choice but to accept what we have been given." Comment.

12. What should be the determining factor in the use of a visual aid?

13. Discuss (or demonstrate) some good and bad techniques of using visual aids.

14. In presenting an oral report to a group made up of her peers as well as a few of her superiors, a speaker is harassed by the questions of one of her peers. Apparently, this person is just trying to embarrass the reporter. What advice would you give this reporter? Would your advice be different if the critic were one of her superiors? What if it were one under her in position?

Oral reporting problems are included at the end of Appendix A.

Report Problems

SHORT LENGTH: MEMORANDUM AND LETTER REPORTS

1. **Investigating a problem in the shipping department.** Today Marci McDougal, the vice president for sales for the Drake-Meeks Carpet Company, received a telephone call from an angry retailer, Cyrus O'Keefe, in Beacon City. Mr. O'Keefe reported that he had made a large order of Durabilt carpeting by telephone. He said he was assured the carpeting was in stock and would be delivered within five days. On the fifth day (today), he received a notice that the carpeting is out of stock and will not be delivered for at least two weeks. To make matters worse, Mr. O'Keefe had advertised the carpeting for his store's annual super sale, which began today. The conversation ended with Mr. O'Keefe canceling the order and promising not to do business with Drake-Meeks again.

Following her conversation with Mr. O'Keefe, Ms. McDougal called you (her assistant) into her office. After explaining Mr. O'Keefe's problem, she asked you to look into the matter for her. "I want to know precisely what happened," she instructed. "Find out who, if anyone, is responsible. And I want to know what we should do to prevent problems like this from occurring in the future."

You begin your investigation by interviewing Sylvester O. Timm, the person who handles mailorder and telephone sales. His explanation was as follows: "I remember the order. I checked with Nicole Gratz in shipping. She said they had a limited supply, but enough to fill this order. So I told her to mark it sold, and I gave her the shipping information."

Next, you talked with Nicole Gratz. "Yes, Mr. Timm called and I did what he told me. We were ready to send the carpeting when the boss (David Copus, manager of the shipping department) came in and stopped it. He said he had already promised Sheri Kaufman (an outside salesperson) the carpeting for one of her good customers. I just follow orders."

David Copus was your next interviewee. "I had no choice," he explained. "Sherri had called me earlier that day asking how much of this carpeting we had in stock. She said she had it all sold and asked me to hold it for her customer. I said I would, and I did. I told Nicole to inform O'Keefe that we have to backorder his carpeting."

With the preceding information in mind, you are ready to write your memorandum report to Ms. McDougal. You will put together the testimony to determine what happened. And you will recommend some procedural changes that will prevent such problems from occurring.

2. **Reporting storm damage to the home office.** For this assignment, you are the manager of the Millville warehouse of the Forshee-Pierce Wholesale Furniture Company. Last night a severe storm came through the area, causing damage to one of your storage buildings. You will have to prepare a report of the damage for the home office.

With notepad in hand, you inspected the damage. When you finished, your notepad contained this information:

Building: corrugated metal roof blown off—completely destroyed (bent and twisted). Other damage to building minimal—some damage to overhead lights (apparently hit by roof fragments). Outside door blown loose from hinges, but not otherwise damaged.

Contents: Sofas and chairs stored in building—all suffered water damage—upholstery soaked by rains—faded and fit only for salvage. Fortunately, building not full. Damaged contents as follows: 7 Dubary sofas, Stock No. 7173; 13 Dubary easy chairs, Stock No. 7181; 19 Haggerton sofas, Stock No. 7073; 3 Weideman sofas, Stock No. 7113; 15 Weideman recliner chairs, Stock No. 8173. No current orders to fill any of these items.

After surveying the building, Scott A. Michel, a local contractor specializing in repairs and remodeling, proposed to repair the building for $12,200. He could start right away and could finish the job in five working days. He has worked for Forshee-Pierce before and proved to be reputable and competent. No doubt the company has insurance that covers the damage, but that information is kept at headquarters. You will only report and wait for instructions.

Write the report in memorandum form. You will fax it to Mark O. Ferguson, who is the president.

3. **Recommending dismissal of a subordinate.** You will have to recommend that Erik Kuykendall be fired. He leaves you no choice.

Mr. Kuykendall joined your sales force at the Victoria office of Technology Unlimited six months ago. Your boss, Monica I. Schaefer, selected him. Ms. Schaefer, who is the national sales manager, makes all the hiring and firing decisions for the sales force.

Mr. Kuykendall came to the job with no sales experience. Apparently, Ms. Schaefer thought that his work as director of the computer center at Darden University and his sparkling personality overcame his lack of sales experience.

For the first month you worked closely with Mr. Kuykendall, and all went well. In fact, your evaluation report on him at that time was very positive. He demonstrated good potential. He proved to you that he was knowledgeable and that he had the aggressive and personable qualities needed for success with Technology Unlimited.

After the first month, you put Mr. Kuykendall on his own. At first, his sales were good. Then, after five weeks something happened. His sales became erratic—high some days, low other days. Overall, his sales continued to decline. On the four-month anniversary of his hiring, you called Kuykendall in for a conference. The man appeared to be genuinely embarrassed, and he apologized for his weak record. He explained his problem as "a lack of experience." The meeting ended with assurances from Kuykendall that his sales would improve.

In the following weeks Kuykendall's sales did not improve. In fact, they got progressively worse. So you decided to visit the man in the field. To your surprise, he did not show up at any of the businesses he was scheduled to call on that day. And a check of businesses he was scheduled to call the day before showed that he had seen none of these.

Next, you went to Mr. Kuykendall's home. From his wife you learned that she and Erik had separated. "Erik has a drinking problem," she told you. "That's why he left the university. Actually, they let him go, but they gave him the opportunity of resigning." Mrs. Kuykendall gave you her husband's current address, so you went to see him.

When confronted with the information you had obtained, Mr. Kuykendall admitted his problem. "But I am getting my life back together," he said. "I've spent the last three days drying out. I've had my last drink. I plan to go back to work tomorrow. You just watch me."

You believed the man, probably because you wanted to. You left with the feeling that things would be better. They were for a few days, but then the old pattern returned. You visited him a second time. As before, you found him at home and not at work. He was inebriated and unable to carry on a conversation. You informed him that you would have to recommend his dismissal, but you are not certain he understood.

Now back in your office, you will write the report that will recommend dismissal. You may bring in any specific details that are vital to your report, but they must be consistent with the information given. You will fax this memorandum report to Ms. Schaefer.

4. **Comparing your computer store's sales with national norms.** You are assistant to Dustin O. Dabney, president of Compumart, a new and rapidly growing chain of computer specialty stores. Today, Mr. Dabney called you into his office and showed you a brief article in *Computer Marketing*. In the article appeared a table that caught Mr. Dabney's attention.

"This table shows a breakdown of sales by customer types for computer specialty stores nationwide," Mr. Dabney explained to you. "It also shows the average size of the first purchase and the add-on sales for the following 12 months. I'd like to know how our sales compare with these national figures. Also, the article says that the future emphasis on stores like ours will be in the business, professional, and industry markets—that these are the markets we should stress if we are to survive. I'd especially like to know how we are doing in these markets.

TABLE 1	(Problem 4) **National and Compumart sales by customer type with average initial sale price and 12-month add-ons**

Customer Type	Percent of Sales		Initial Sale Price		12-month Add-ons	
	N*	CM*	N*	CM*	N*	CM*
Business	26.4	23.9	$9,760	$8,970	$1,792	$1,232
Industrial	16.9	6.7	6,935	7,133	1,532	971
Home	20.4	32.3	2,780	2,087	951	582
Education	19.4	28.6	4,237	3,974	910	637
Professional	16.9	8.5	8,120	9,270	1,439	903

* N = national averages
CM = Compumart averages

Please get the comparable sales data from our records. Then compare them with the data in the table. Analyze what you find, and present your findings and analyses to me in a concise report."

Your next step was to gather the information from sales records. Time did not permit anything more than a sampling, for company sales records are voluminous. But you feel you got a good sample—enough to give you reasonably accurate figures.

Now you will make the comparisons and analyses Mr. Dabney requested and present them in a memorandum report. (The table from *Computer Marketing* and the information you have gathered are combined in Table 1.)

5. **Presenting beach-litter information to a plastics manufacturer.** Chem-Tech is a manufacturer of a variety of plastic products, primarily bags, caps and lids, cups, and beverage bottles. Recently, the company has been the target of environmentalists who claim that plastic products are polluting the earth—especially the seashores. The environmentalists have backed their claims with photographs showing litter on otherwise beautiful stretches of sandy beach. Most of the litter shown is made of plastic.

Chem-Tech management is concerned about the problem, although they feel the environmentalists are exaggerating the case. So management will seek more specific information. They have assigned you, a newly hired management trainee, to get this information.

Following the advice of one of your superiors, you began work on the assignment by going to White Sands City and visiting the director of the White Sands Cleanup Association. WSCA is a volunteer organization dedicated to keeping the area beaches clean. For the past 11 months, its volunteers have walked the area beaches daily, picking up litter. Perhaps most significant for you, WSCA has kept a record of the types of litter picked up. "After a full year, we intend to use this information to publicize the problem," the director told you. "But I'll share the information with you, if you'll promise to keep it confidential until we release it to the public." You promised, and the director gave you the following summary:

Item	Number Picked Up
1. Plastic pieces	4,044
2. Plastic cups, lids	2,943
3. Glass pieces	2,231
4. Small foam plastic pieces	2,063
5. Plastic trash bags	1,906
6. Glass beverage bottles	1,863
7. Plastic rope (2 ft. or less)	1,853
8. Plastic cups, spoons, forks, straws	1,693
9. Miscellaneous plastic bags	1,532
10. Foam plastic cups	1,378
11. Paper pieces	1,213
12. Plastic rope (longer than 2 ft.)	1,190

Now you must report and interpret these findings. You will do this in a memorandum report addressed to Dee K. Tuttle, President.

6. **Evaluating effects of a promotion on your department's sales.** You are manager of the sporting goods department of the Metro City branch of Mason's, a major chain of department stores. Every July the Metro City store conducts a major promotion. As in past years, you were asked to select five items to emphasize in the store's advertisements in local newspapers. The idea was to select items that would appeal to a wide range of customers, get them into the store, and sell to them.

Now that the promotion is over, Earl O. Richter, store manager, is assessing results. He has asked each department manager to gather the information on sales of the products advertised as well as on overall sales. Specifically, he wants to know how good the selections of advertised products were—that is, how much did their sales increase as a result of the promotion. Also, since customers brought in by the advertising often buy other products, Mr. Richter wants a comparison of total sales volume for the department during the week of the promotion with past weekly sales volume totals.

Your computations for this report produce the following information concerning sales of the products advertised:

Advertised Products	Average Number Sold Weekly, Preceding Weeks	Number Sold during Promotion
Airborne joggers	11	63
Riteflex casting rods	7	23
Ace tennis racquets	2	4
Hi-Fli golf balls (doz.)	7	89
Mountaineer backpack	1	3

Sales for the department for the week of the promotion totaled $17,544. The weekly sales average during the preceding four weeks was $6,772.

Now present this information with your interpretations in a memorandum report addressed to Mr. Richter. You may supply price data for the five products advertised if you feel they are needed.

7. **Justifying termination of a probationary employee.** Six months ago, you hired Crystal Stedman as manager of the cafeteria at the Prairie City plant of the H. W. Nicholson Manufacturing Company. You are the plant's director of employee services, and the cafeteria is under your control.

Ms. Stedman came to you with nine years of related experience, working first as a cook for five years and later as owner-manager of her own small restaurant for four years. After her restaurant failed (because of a major plant closing in the area, she explained), Ms. Stedman sought employment. She saw your advertisement and responded to it. You hired her.

From the beginning, you could see that Ms. Stedman had some skills in restaurant operations. The quality of the food was excellent—better than ever before according to a survey of employees. You thought you made an excellent choice until you saw the accounting report for the first month. The cafeteria lost $2,753. You assumed much of the loss was due to Ms. Stedman's newness on the job; so you did nothing for a month. Again, the account report showed a loss—this time for $3,022.

You decided it was time to talk with Ms. Stedman, so you did. You explained that while the cafeteria was not supposed to make money serving the employees, it was not supposed to lose money. She promised to watch costs closely, and the meeting ended.

Soon after the meeting, Ms. Stedman increased prices on all items served on the average of 20 percent. The employees protested vigorously. In fact, a delegation of them visited you in your office. They asked for an explanation. The increases could not be justified by increased food costs, they argued, and you had to agree with them. You then went back to Ms. Stedman to discuss the problem further.

At this meeting, you got into the specifics of her operation. A review of her purchases showed that she bought unusually expensive foods—in some cases, gourmet foods. Some of the foods she sold below cost; others she sold above cost. There was little logic to her pricing. Apparently, she had little ability to determine appropriate prices. Also, you found that she had increased the kitchen staff by one. You could not justify this addition, for there had been no increase in customers served. After pointing out these shortcomings to Ms. Stedman you left her, thinking she would change her manner of operation.

The third month was somewhat better, for the loss was only $517. Ms. Stedman did cut back on her kitchen help, and she responded to the employees' complaints by eliminating the price increases she had made. It appeared to you that she really was trying. At the end of the fourth month the loss was $1,031. Again, you visited Ms. Stedman.

This time you became more convinced than ever that Ms. Stedman did not understand the economics of running a food operation. She had continued to buy exceedingly expensive foods. She had made other expensive purchases—for example, flowers for the tables totaling $290 for the month. You explained to her that the company could not continue this losing operation—that she could not be retained unless she turned things around. She responded by saying that she took pride in serving quality food. "I'll try to cut expenses," she commented, "but I won't sacrifice quality." The next month the cafeteria lost $2,317.

Now in the sixth month, losses appear to be continuing, although you do not have a specific figure. Following company policy, after six months of probationary service, new employees must be reevaluated for retention. Thus, you must reevaluate Ms. Stedman. You will have to let her go. To do this, you must write a memorandum to the personnel department conveying your decision and explaining and justifying it. Personnel will inform Ms. Stedman of the decision, so you will be spared that unpleasant task. Address the memorandum to Jessica Manley, who is the personnel director.

8. **Assessing results of a program to combat gang violence.** Assume the role of administrative assistant to the city manager of Metroville. Like most large cities, Metroville has suffered in recent years from problems related to gang violence. The problems became so bad that five months ago the city council decided to take remedial steps. They developed a comprehensive plan consisting of the establishment of neighborhood youth centers and police-sponsored athletic clubs. In addition, they provided additional funds for increased police patrols in problem areas.

Perhaps it is too early to assess the value of the program. Even so, the council has asked for a first report on results. You were assigned the task of reporting.

You began by going to the Metroville Police Department and extracting the pertinent information from their files. Specifically, for each of the past four months you got the actual numbers of gang-related offenses, arrests of juveniles, drive-by shootings, and total arrests. You can't be certain that all drive-by shootings are gang related, but past evidence suggests that almost all are. And you got the total of all arrests to give you a basis for comparing gang-related crime with the total of all crime in the city. In summary form, your findings are as follows:

	4 Months Ago	3 Months Ago	2 Months Ago	Last Month
Gang-related offenses	97	122	81	74
Arrests of gang members	52	52	31	27
Drive-by shootings	7	7	4	2
Total of all arrests	239	277	266	277

Now you must present this information to the council in a memorandum report.

9. **Reporting supervisors' viewpoints on AIDS to management.** The main topic of discussion at last month's meeting of the executive staff of EZ Electronics, Inc., was the question of how to deal with employees who have AIDS. As viewpoints were mixed, no consensus was reached. The group concluded that they needed more information before continuing.

They asked you, administrative assistant to the plant manager, to get some of the information they think they need. Specifically, they want the viewpoints of the company's supervisors. Such information, they believe, should be considered in working out any comprehensive policy on the matter. After all, the supervisors are the ones who will have to implement whatever policies are worked out.

You began your task by going directly to the supervisors with the basic question of how a supervisor should react upon learning that an employee has AIDS. You got their reactions to eight likely responses. You were able to interview all but five of EZ's 62 supervisors. (These five were unavailable for various reasons.) Following is a summary of the responses obtained:

Basic question: How should a supervisor respond to the knowledge that an employee has AIDS?

Responses	Yes	No	Don't know
Dismiss employee	5	24	28
Educate yourself on AIDS	35	5	17
Provide support to the victim	37	3	17
Encourage victim to resign	8	15	34
Provide victim with AIDS information	36	6	15
Inform the co-workers	29	10	18
Meet with experts to answer employee questions	23	13	21
Keep AIDS worker from contact with others	16	8	33

Now you will present this information to the staff in a memorandum report. The report will not merely present the facts, but will include implications for any policies on the matter devised by the staff.

10. **Determining the meaning of sexual harassment for a committee.** You are an administrative assistant to the director of human resources at Gifford-Belino Manufacturing Company, Inc. Your boss has been assigned to a committee charged with developing guidelines that will crystallize company policies on sexual harassment. At its first meeting, the committee members found that they could not agree on just what defines sexual harassment. They decided to get the answer from those directly involved—the women workers. And your boss volunteered you for the assignment.

To get the information you need, you designed a simple survey. You randomly selected 100 female workers, and you asked them to either agree or disagree on whether eight specific types of attention constituted sexual harassment. You inquired further as to whether they had actually experienced each of these types of attention. The answers should provide a practical answer to the committee's question.

Now the information is before you in the form of the following simple table. Analyze these results and present your findings to the committee in a memorandum report.

Types of Sexual Attention	Considered Sexual Harassment	Personally Experienced
Staring	7	57
Flirting	8	71
Suggestive gestures	46	27
Sexual remarks	51	61
Touching, grabbing, brushing	69	41
Sexual propositions	81	26
Sexual relations	46	8
Other	3	4

11. **Reporting an errant subordinate for good reason.** As much as you dislike doing such things, today you must report Roger A. Tucker for improper conduct and neglect of duty.

Mr. Tucker joined your sales force about 8 months ago after over 18 years of sales experience with your rival company, Temple Brothers, Inc. At first, Tucker did a reasonably good job for you, making his quotas each of the first five months. Since that time, however, sales have dropped. In fact last month he sold only 44 percent of quota, as compared with 68 percent the month earlier, and 76 percent the preceding month.

About six weeks ago, you learned from an old customer in Tucker's territory that this customer had apparently been dropped from Tucker's route without explanation. Further investigation revealed that at least five other customers were also dropped, apparently without cause.

You called in Tucker, talked with him, and learned that marital trouble was to blame. Tucker admitted not making many of his regular calls, and promised to do better, saying his troubles were behind him.

In following weeks, he showed no improvement. In fact, his work deteriorated further. Three additional talks with the man produced only promises for improvement, but improvement never occurred. His sales continued to drop, and you continued to hear about lost and dissatisfied customers.

You really do not know just how many customers have been lost or the exact extent of the damage done. But you know that something has to be done soon. So you will recommend that Tucker be relieved of his sales duties. As basically he is a capable man with problems, you will recommend that the company keep him in some other capacity—if he is willing.

Using standard memorandum form, write a report, stating your recommendation and backing it up with supportable reasoning. Use your imagination to supply details not given.

12. **Helping Protecto Inc.'s Clients Control Their Shoplifting Problem.** Today's assignment finds you as assistant manager of Protecto, Inc., a service company that assists retailers in keeping their merchandise secure. Originally founded as a security patrol business, Protecto has expanded its product mix to include laser surveillance, crime prevention, and loss detection. It is in this last area of

service—loss detection—that you have your writing assignment for the moment.

Several months ago, you were talking with one of your store manager clients when the subject of shoplifting arose. The client mentioned she believed losses from shoplifting had risen in the last year. She didn't know exactly how to approach the problem or its solution. She did know, however, that missing merchandise—unaccounted for in her inventory control system—was eating away at her already low profit margin. In other words, her problem was causing her losses at the bank.

Informally, you checked out the shoplifting problem with several other clients and they confirmed its existence, although the magnitude of the problem varied. All of the clients you contacted, however, indicated that the problem was real and that it did create significant losses.

With these informal contacts in mind, you decided to determine in more detail the extent of the shoplifting problem in retail establishments. You designed a short questionnaire that emphasized the who, when, and how of the problem. Specifically, you emphasized the how of the problem because of the practical and preventative nature of the services you offer to customers. After you designed and pretested the questionnaire, you sent it to 100 retailers in the trading area that you serve. You stratified your sample to include supermarkets, drug stores, and discount stores, because these outlets represent 70 percent of your clients and because you believe that shoplifting occurs more frequently in these types of marketing institutions.

Today, four weeks after your initial mailing of the questionnaire, you have received 65 usable responses. After tallying them, you determine some definite patterns of the trading area shoplifting problem. First, Fridays and Saturdays are more common for shoplifting than other days of the week. Second, more shoplifting seems to occur between 4:00 and 7:00 P.M. than at other times. Third, the methods used by shoplifters vary by type of outlet as follows:

Methods Used to Shoplift	Drug Store	Supermarket	Discount Store
Pocket	28.2%	25.4%	28.3%
Under clothing	28.3	24.3	20.9
Purse	23.1	28.8	27.7
Shopping bag	3.1	2.7	2.9
Label switching	2.1	0.9	1.8
Accomplice	3.0	3.8	3.1
Other bag	4.3	4.9	2.8
Other method	7.9	9.2	12.5

It's this last area of information that you think will benefit your customers the most. So you will use it as the basis of a memo you will prepare for all store managers served by Protecto, Inc.

In the memo, you will present and interpret the findings—specifically the ways used by shoplifters to steal—to the store managers. Perhaps they can use these findings to alert their employees to detect those who might be likely suspects—especially at key times of the day and week. In time, you might develop your own training program for store managers on the subject. But for now your purpose is to help your existing clientele with a problem that affects them.

Write the memo to the store managers to give them your findings, tell them what the findings mean, and help them solve one of their merchandising problems.

13. **Using Survey Results to Increase Compumart's Sales.** As assistant manager of Compumart, a chain of computer retail stores, you have an interesting and important assignment for the moment. Your boss, Mr. Warren Bottoroff, tells you this way: "It's always been my philosophy that we compete best on service not price. We do our best job when we relate our product knowledge to an individual customer's needs. So send these facts to our store managers and tell them how to use them. It will mean increased sales for all of them, I'm sure."

The "facts" that Mr. Bottoroff refers to are those you collected from sales prospects of Compumart stores across the country. You designed a short questionnaire listing possible ways people could use a personal computer. You sent the questionnaire to all Compumart store managers and asked them to make it available to people who entered their businesses—whether they purchased anything or not. A postage paid return envelope was provided.

Although you did not control for demographics or seasonal factors, you feel that the number of returns you have received gives you reasonably reliable results. Also, the percentages by category appear to have stabilized as you have tallied the results. Thus, you are confident that the results are not random and show a certain preference/profile for using a personal computer. The results are as follows:

Uses for a Personal Computer	% Response*
Budgeting/paying bills	28.2
Keeping books/household records/rent/utility bills/taxes	18.8
Schooling/help with school work/homework	17.5
Finances/checkbook balancing/bank statements	16.9
Entertainment/games	14.5
Business	10.4
Writing	9.6
Math	6.4
Store addresses/phone numbers/special events	5.8
Real estate purchases	2.1
Set up office at home	2.1
Hook up to a bank	0.8
Resumes	0.8
Communication purposes	0.8
Other	0.8
No use/no need for one	2.9

*Totals are more than 100% because of multiple responses.

Your job now is to send this information to Compumart store managers. For this purpose, you will use your standard E-mail format. As your boss has instructed you, however, you will need to do more than present the facts. You will need to comment on them, showing how floor sales personnel can use them to increase sales. Thus, you will need to relate the facts to the sales work of the employees—and that's a process of interpretation.

Write the E-mail memo report for the Compumart store managers.

14. **Developing a Nonsmoking Campaign at Avant Gentry.** Avant Gentry, a large office supply company, is considering banning smoking at work. To implement such a policy successfully, the company will need to be strategic in its efforts to establish the behavior change program. As assistant to the owner, you have been selected to help with the nonsmoking program.

Susan Scallan, the owner of Avant Gentry, reasons that a nonsmoking personnel policy is best for the company at this stage of its growth for several reasons. First, it will reflect society's values about good health. In fact, Avant Gentry may even be behind the times, as most companies have already banned smoking from company premises. Second, the company will save in insurance claims and premiums. For both these reasons and perhaps others, it makes good sense for Avant Gentry to pursue its nonsmoking program.

And this is where you enter the picture. Ms. Scallan gives you the problem in this manner: "We'll need to approach this nonsmoking problem systematically and scientifically. Before we do anything, I need to know the attitudes of our people. Find out what our workers think about this smoking issue. Then we can accurately diagnose the problem and design an effective strategy."

With these words still ringing in your ears, you return to your desk, trying to clear your thoughts about how you can collect the data Ms. Scallan wants. You conclude generally that a survey would be best. Using your own logic and the ideas of several colleagues, you derive reasons for quitting and not quitting smoking. Then you arrange them on paper for easy checking by respondents. This instrument will be the one you use to collect the facts.

Next, you duplicate the form and distribute it through paycheck envelopes and paycheck receipts (for those who use electronic transfers to financial institutions) to all employees. The questionnaire asks for several demographics—age, gender, smoker vs. nonsmoker, and such; but it does not ask for the names of the respondents. Today you have received 225 returns—135 who are smokers and 90 who are not. Thus, you believe the results below represent reliably the sentiments of your employees.

Reasons for Quitting Smoking	Yes	No
Fear of losing job	23%	77%
Peer pressure	16	84
Information provided in a quit-smoking program	17	83
Pressure from family members	38	62
Personal concern for health	86	14
Increased restriction on smoking in public	21	79
Pressure from clients	1	99
Increased social view of smoking as a dirty habit	43	57

Reasons against Quitting Smoking

Enjoy smoking	93%	7%
Unable to quit even through quit-smoking program	30	70
Do not want my employer to tell me to quit smoking	77	23
Many of clients smoke	66	34
People in household smoke	55	45
Friends smoke	52	48
Under too much stress	75	25

You must now present these facts in a memo report to Ms. Scallan. In that report, you will point out any information that will help in planning the nonsmoking campaign. Put differently, you will have to do more than merely list the facts. You will need to analyze them and relate them to the smoking policy change at Avant Gentry.

Prepare the report that will help Ms. Scallan plan her smokeless campaign at Avant Gentry.

15. **Redesigning the company recruiting brochure.** As special assistant to the vice president of human resources at Sunbelt Realtors, you have an interesting assignment to deal with today. Your boss, Danielle Brentz, wants to redesign the company recruiting brochure to make it more up-to-date. But she doesn't know exactly what points to emphasize in the newly structured promotional piece. Thus, she lays it on the line to you with these instructions: "Find out what college students today want to know about us. We'll need to determine that before we can decide anything about how we promote the company in the employment market this year."

Ms. Brentz goes on to say that your printers will decide on the physical format of the brochure; so you won't be concerned with such things as paper, color, format, design, and such. You will concern yourself with the contents of the brochure and the proportion and emphasis that the contents receive.

To get the data you need to answer Ms. Brentz's questions, you think first of constructing a questionnaire and sending it to a selected sample of college students at universities where you recruit heavily. But getting results this way is costly; so before you design such a study, you decide to check with sources that might collect such data in the course of their normal operations. The College Placement Service Bureau is one organization that you determine might provide the information you need.

A quick call to their central headquarters reveals that they do indeed collect information from graduating seniors each year—and rather extensively. The secretary to whom you talk agrees to fax you their most recent report (15 pages of tables) based on a random sample of 1,500 students throughout the United States and Canada. As you sift through the faxed pages you received, you notice the following data:

Types of information most preferred from company brochures

What day-to-day job will entail	56%
Starting salary	45
Where company is located	43
Training policy	36
Promotion opportunities	28
Degree/discipline required	25
Long-term pay and benefits	23
How much responsibility/how early given	17
Overseas work/foreign travel	10
Site of organization	8
History of organization	8

To be sure, the facts are ideal for your use. And you will use them to form the basis of a memo report that you will write to Ms. Brentz.

The facts, however, are only part of the report story. You will need to analyze the facts (tell what they mean) as well before you derive conclusions to give to Ms. Brentz. Because she is interested in the answers to her questions, you will write the memo in the direct order. Prepare the report that will give Ms. Brentz the information she wants about the content of Sunbelt Realtors' recruitment brochure.

16. **Writing an evaluation report on Russell Snyder.** You are sales manager for Capital Investment, Inc.'s Region 6. It is time to write annual evaluation reports on your subordinates.

Capital Investment's evaluation reports are narrative. And they are not the sugar-coated types written at many companies. They are honest and objective. They praise when praise is deserved. They condemn when condemnation is justified. Their goal is to be constructive. These evaluation reports become a part of each person's permanent personnel file. In addition, the subordinates who are evaluated receive copies of them.

Presently, you are working on the report for Russell Snyder, your newest salesperson. Your garbled notes on him are as follows:

More concerned with sales volume than service. Excellent personality—pleasant mannerisms, good conversational skills, outgoing. Have received some reports that he is too aggressive. (Reports investigated and appear to be valid.) A hardworking and diligent performer. Sales volume for year was $210,000 ($18,000 above quota). Productive customer accounts increased from 73 to 82. Even so, he appears to go after the high-volume orders and big-ticket items. His calls on smaller accounts are irregular compared to those on larger accounts. He could improve his manner of dress to reflect the conservative, businesslike image of the company (add details to support this point).

Now, you will organize these items into an orderly and meaningful report. You will use the company's standard memorandum. (If you have access to it, assume the report will be prepared and transmitted through company E-mail.) Address the report to Mr. Snyder. And identify the subject as "Annual Performance Evaluation of Russell Snyder."

17. **Investigating a personnel problem in department 5–B.** Today's assignment in your role as special assistant to Dean Polanski, director of employment relations of Magnum Travels, takes you to department 5–B. Your objective is to investigate charges brought to you by Carlos Rozario, the union steward who represents the people of this department. According to Rozario, union members in department 5–B have been discriminated against in the awarding of overtime work. Nonunion workers have been getting the lion's share of overtime.

On arriving at the department, you discuss the matter with the department's supervisor, Sylvia DeWitt. DeWitt's version of the story goes like this: Of the eight workers in the department, five are members of the union and three are not. The three nonunion people have had more overtime than the others, but they deserve it. DeWitt claims that she gives overtime on the basis of seniority and productivity—nothing else. This policy, she points out, is permitted in the contract with the union. If the nonunion people got most of the overtime, DeWitt says, it is because they have seniority and are better workers.

After talking to DeWitt, you go to the files that contain the department's records. Here you find data that should prove or disprove DeWitt's claim and, in fact, should point to the solution of the whole problem. After an hour or more or poring over these records of the past six months, your summary notes look like this:

Employee and Union Status	Hours of Overtime Work	Years Employed	Productivity (Average Daily Units Performed)	Percent Rejection (Not Meeting Inspection)
James Addison (U)	0	14	30	0.08
Cynthia Webb (U)	0	1	21	0.09
Kenneth Harvey (U)	10	3	32	0.07
Willie Wolcott (U)	60	8	26	0.01
Maria Shulman (U)	60	7	30	0.03
Ramona Gomez (NU)	40	35	26	0.02
Tim Sheppard (NU)	70	17	35	0.03
David Bates (NU)	90	12	43	0.03

*U, union; NU, nonunion

Now your task is to analyze these data and to present your finding to Mr. Polanski in the form of the standardized memorandum report used by the company. In addition to analyzing the data, you will recommend a course of action on the problem.

18. **Writing an inspection report on the cleanliness of a service station.** (Requires research) Assume that you are a management trainee for International Oil Company. Today, you are assigned to work with Nicole Wilensky, director of customer services. Wilensky's job is mainly that of trying to get managers of the company's service stations to be more customer oriented. Especially has she been working to

get the managers to keep up the physical appearance of these stations. In fact, for the past month, she has been conducting a "clean station" campaign. It is your belief that a neat, attractive physical facility will mean that customers are treated more courteously as well.

So far, the campaign has produced good results. Customer opinion reports (forms placed in restrooms and on checkout counters to be filled out and mailed in by customers) have been most complimentary on this point. But as might be expected, a few negative reports have come in. Wilensky assigns you the task of checking them out.

Specifically, your task is to go to select stations, posing as a customer. While there, you will inspect the whole operation for its neatness and cleanliness. Then, you will write a memorandum report on each station summarizing your findings. (For this assignment, select a station in your locale and inspect it. Prepare a report that summarizes your observations.)

Note: This assignment can be adapted to other establishments such as hotels/motels, fast-food operations, convenience stores, and such.

19. Recommending an equipment purchase for Worldwide Travel's home office. (Requires research) As office manager in charge of a staff of 16 at the home offices of Worldwide Travels, you have just had a visit from Vice President Judith Carreras, your boss. Ms. Carreras reported that funds have been made available for purchasing _____ (copiers, computers, office furnishings—your instructor will specify the products). She wants you to collect information on the major brands available and to recommend the brand to be purchased.

Your procedure will be to collect all pertinent information on what you think to be the three best buys. Then, you will set up what you believe to be the logical bases of comparison for the products. After that, you will compare the different brands on the bases you select. Lastly, you will arrive at your recommendation. You will present your evaluation and recommendation to Ms. Carreras in Worldwide Travel's standard memorandum form. Because you believe Ms. Carreras will accept your recommendation without question, you will place it at the first of the report. You will still need to present the facts and their analysis to support your beginning recommendation.

20. Selecting the best laundry service for De De's Cafeterias. Today, you are in the position of a management consultant hired by De De's Cafeterias of Chicago. There are five locations throughout the greater Chicago area. One of the many problems you have been asked to investigate (and solve!) for De De's is how the company should handle its linen and laundry. Specifically, the company wants to know whether they should own their own cloth equipment and have it laundered. Or should they rent the cloth equipment?

To answer these questions, you gather data to support both sides of the argument. First, De De's management will need about $6,000 worth of cloth equipment as an initial investment and its life expectancy is about two years. The laundry rate for this equipment is $120 per month, including pickup and delivery.

On the other hand, weekly costs of renting the comparable equipment needed are as follows:

540	54″ tablecloths	@$ .24 each
2,100	napkins	@$3.50 per 100
175	aprons	@$ .30 each
84	dresses	@$1.00 each
60	coats (waiters)	@$ .90 each
140	dish towels	@$ .06 each

Now that you have the data collected, your task is to analyze them, compare alternatives, and select one to recommend to President Michael Eubanks. Do all of these things in a memorandum using the direct order of presentation.

21. **Selecting a site for a Jimmy Jack store.** As assistant to the president of Jimmy Jack, Inc., a national chain of drive-in convenience stores featuring gasoline, groceries, and fast-food items, you must select a site for the location of a new store in Metro City. You have collected the following information on three locations that are suitable.

STEMMONS FREEWAY
AND NORTHWOOD DRIVE

Commercial area. Lot 150 × 100 feet. Corner location. Cost: $65,000. Traffic count per day (7 A.M. to 9 P.M.): 4,200 cars. Distance from nearest company store: 3.1 miles.

120 BELTLINE ROAD

Commercial area. Lot 200 × 100 feet. Noncorner location. Cost: $55,000. Traffic count per day: 9,000 cars. Distance from nearest company store: 3.9 miles.

PRESTON ROAD
AND MAPLE BOULEVARD

Commercial area. Lot 150 × 150 feet. Corner location. Cost: $75,000. Traffic count per day: 6,500 cars. Distance from nearest company store: 2.1 miles.

Your job is to evaluate these sites and to recommend one of them to the company president, Peter Gianetti. You will present your recommendations and analyses in a direct-order memorandum report.

INTERMEDIATE-LENGTH REPORTS

22. **Comparing lease and purchase data for three automobiles.** For reasons of economy, E. A. Chenault and Company (a major pharmaceutical manufacturer and distributor) has decided to stop furnishing automobiles to its salespeople. Instead, it will pay them $.28 per mile for company travel in their personal automobiles. This amount, company management believes, is sufficient to cover the costs of ownership and operation.

| TABLE 2 | (Problem 22) **Comparison of lease and purchase data for three automobiles** |

	Automobile A		Automobile B		Automobile C	
	36-Mo. Lease	36-Mo. Purchase	36-Mo. Lease	36-Mo. Purchase	36-Mo. Lease	36-Mo. Purchase
Purchase price		$16,305		$11,361		$19,557
Monthly payment	$ 270	$ 448*	$ 158	$ 280*	$ 316	$ 600*
Cash down payment	$ 3,000	$ 3,000	$ 2,500	$ 2,500	$ 1,700	$ 1,700
Security payment*	$ 300	NA	$ 175	NA	$ 325	NA
Total cash at inception	$ 3,541	$ 3,448	$ 2,833	$ 2,500	$ 3,024	$ 1,700
Total amount payments	$ 9,734	$16,131	$ 5,689	$10,069	$16,395	$24,589
End-of-lease purchase option	$ 6,853	NA	$ 4,112	NA	$ 8,050	NA
Total mileage allowed**	45,000	NA	45,000	NA	60,000	NA
Excess mileage charge	$.10 mi.	NA	$.10 mi.	NA	$.11 mi.	NA

*12.5% interest.
**Company average is 21,000 miles per year.

As might be expected, the announcement was not well received by some of the salespeople. In fact, a group of them visited the office of Charlotte Bates, the vice president for sales, to voice their displeasure. Soon after this visit, Ms. Bates (you are her assistant) called you into her office and assigned you a task relating to the problem. She explained her assignment in these words:

"No doubt you know that some of our salespeople aren't happy about losing their company cars and getting their own. Can't blame them. But we can't reverse the decision. We must cut expenses, and I am convinced this is one way to do it.

"What we can do, though, is help the salespeople by giving them useful information. Some of them have raised the question of whether they should buy or lease. As you may know, many dealers are pushing leasing now, and some claim it beats buying. I want you to get information that will help the salespeople decide. Select three or so cars—cars varying in price level because we don't know how much our people will want to pay. It's their decision. For these cars, find out the costs of leasing and of buying. Analyze the information. Then come up with a recommendation—or recommendations.

"Write up your work in report form and address it to the salespeople. We'll distribute it to them. Make the report easy to understand and as helpful as you can make it. Maybe some visuals will help."

Following the meeting, you selected three automobiles for analysis. Then you went to dealerships handling them and got cost information for buying and leasing. Your information is summarized in Table 2. (The automobile brands are not identified, but you may choose to use realistic brand names.)

In addition to this specific information, your investigation turned up other matters the salespeople should consider, especially in leasing. One is insurance. Another is tax considerations. You won't get into these matters in your report.

Suggestions that the salespeople check with knowledgeable people (insurance agents, tax advisers) should be sufficient. Also, there is the matter of ownership at the end of the purchase or lease period. The purchaser owns; the leaseholder doesn't. You'll make certain that you cover this point adequately, for it makes a big difference at the end of the 36–month period.

Now write the report.

23. **Evaluating changes in hospitalization payments relating to "high-risk factors."** The Dependable Insurance Company is a major supplier of health-care insurance for business organizations. Two years ago the company began a hard-hitting campaign to educate its policyholders on the so-called "high-risk factors" related to hospitalization expense (smoking, alcohol, seat belt use, hypertension, and diet). The objective was to make these people more conscious of these dangers to their health and to get them to take corrective actions. The end result would be healthier policyholders and lower hospitalization expenditures.

Now at the end of the second year, Dependable management feels good about the campaign. As Alexander P. Percy (the president) explained to you (his assistant), "All the reports I have heard are positive, but these are primarily reports based on impressions. I have seen nothing definite—no supporting facts and figures. I want you to look into this matter for me. Find the facts—actual payouts of claims. Compare the year just completed with the year before we started the campaign. Analyze what you find, and give me the information in a report."

Mr. Percy continued his instructions with these words of caution: "Now, we can't take credit for all the improvements, if we find any. Other forces have been at work. For example, a massive national movement toward exercising and improving diet habits has been going on. But we've been a part of it. I am not so much concerned about who gets the credit as I am about whether people are beginning to take steps to improve their health. Address the report to me, but keep in mind that others will read it. We'll probably duplicate it for distribution to all senior administrators."

Following Mr. Percy's instructions, you got the payment records from the claims department (Table 3). Now you must interpret them. As you do, keep in mind Mr. Percy's precautionary instructions. Because this is a report that will get good exposure for you throughout the company, you'll give it your very best effort. You will use visuals wherever they support your major findings. And you'll give the report a makeup appropriate for its importance.

24. **Reporting city employees' viewpoints to council members.** Assume that your college work is behind you and you have been hired as a human resources specialist for the city government of Bigg City. Soon after being hired, you learned that conditions are not ideal among city employees. They have not had a raise in four years, and prospects for getting a raise now are not good. In fact, some members of the city council have stated publicly that some layoffs might be needed to balance the budget for the coming year.

| TABLE 3 | (Problem 23) **Hospitalization costs associated with high-risk factors per 100,000 insured last year and two years ago** |

Risk Factor	Last Year	Two Years Ago*
Smoking		
Respiratory system cancer	$ 897,806	$ 919,477
Lip, oral cavity, and pharynx cancers	105,580	121,490
Bladder cancer	42,741	37,219
Chronic lung disease	527,833	593,778
Ischemic heart disease	1,504,627	1,478,878
	3,078,587	3,150,843
Alcohol		
Cirrhosis	77,840	79,431
Injuries, alcohol-related accidents	561,277	603,778
	639,117	683,209
Seat Belt Use		
Injuries sustained from seat belts not in use	591,162	627,383
Hypertension		
Ischemic heart disease	1,516,321	1,637,411
Essential and secondary hypertension	110,218	121,394
	1,626,539	1,758,805
Diet		
Colo-rectal cancer	46,558	58,217
Breast cancer	62,187	70,919
Ischemic heart diseases, cholesterol related	397,391	413,307
	506,136	542,443
Total all costs from high-risk factors	$6,441,541	$6,762,683

*Adjusted for inflation.

Not all council members have taken this view, however. Today, three of them came into the human resources director's office to express an opposing position and seek some information. As one of them put it, "We are aware of your situation and want to help. We know that you people are doing a good job under trying circumstances. If you will help us get some supporting information, we think we can work this thing out."

In the discussion that followed, the council members explained that it would be helpful if the department conducted a survey of city government workers. The survey would gather information that could be used to support the government workers' case. As the council members explained it, a survey could get information on matters such as the adequacy of resources with which the workers work, job satisfaction, and viewpoints about the pay increase.

You were selected to conduct the survey. Following the meeting you met with Alice Timmons, who appeared to be the leader of the council members,

TABLE 4	(Problem 24) **Responses of Bigg City Workers to a survey on employment viewpoint**

How would you rate the amount of resources allocated to your department to perform its services?

24.1% Very inadequate to provide needed service level

42.4% Slightly inadequate to provide needed service level

25.5% Adequate to provide needed service level

2.3% A little in excess of what is needed

0.8% Considerably in excess of what is needed

4.8% Other*

Do you believe your department makes efficient use of its resources?

71.8% Yes

24.8% No

3.4% Other

What is the issue which most concerns you? (number of respondents, not percent)

Pay raise	410
Job security	149
Merit increases	126
Pay equity	43
Health insurance	42
Improved working conditions	33
To have a say	29
Employee parking	24
Health & safety	24
Performance/evaluation	21
Personnel policies	11
Retirement	9
Leave policies	4
Other	18
Responses not ranked	55

Do you believe an across-the-board (cost-of-living) pay raise is needed and justified for city employees next year?

94% Yes

4.1% No

1.9% Other*

Do you support a pay raise even if existing positions in government must be eliminated in order to pay for the raises?

53.2% Yes

36.9% No

9.9% Other*

What level of pay raise do you most support?

0.8% Less than 2%

12 % 2%–4%

53.7% 4%–6%

27.2% More than 6%

6.3% Other*

Are you proud to be an employee of Bigg City?

81.9% Yes

10.1% No

8 % Other*

How long have you been a City employee?

28.2% Less than 2 years

29.8% 2–5 years

25.5% 5–10 years

14.8% More than 10 years

1.6% Other (omitted)

What is your annual salary?

14.3% Less than $15,000 a year

56.1% $15,000–$25,000 a year

19.4% $25,000–$35,000 a year

8 % More than $35,000 a year

2.2% Omitted question

*Omitted or other answer.

and worked out a simple questionnaire. You sent the questionnaire to all 2,399 city employees. A week later, when you had to cut off responses, 1,002 (41.8 percent) had responded. Next, you tabulated the answers by the questions asked (see Table 4).

Your next task is to interpret your findings. That is, you will give them meaning as they relate to the city's current problem. Then, you will present your findings and your interpretations in a report that you will address to Ms. Timmons and the other two council members (Woodrow Wardlow and Maxine A. Shannon). Although you must give the report rush treatment, you will not sacrifice quality. You will give it the makeup the situation requires. And you will use graphics wherever they will help to communicate the report information. Possibly the three council members will duplicate the report for the benefit of the other leaders at city hall.

25. **Investigating charges of sex discrimination in job pay.** As a personnel specialist for the D. E. Jeffrey Manufacturing Company, you have been assigned the task of investigating charges of sex-biased pay discrimination. The charges were made by ERA (Equal Rights for All), an association dedicated to the goals its name identifies. Although you cannot be certain, probably some of your employees have brought the matter to ERA's attention. In fact, some Jeffrey employees are known to be among the local chapter's leaders.

Jeffrey management was deeply disturbed by the charges. In the words of Alan O. Pilich, president of Jeffrey, "We have been working on this problem for the past decade. We have made good progress. We don't deserve this criticism." In spite of Mr. Pilich's words, he authorized an inquiry into the matter. You got the job.

Following suggestions of Naomi Boies, director of personnel, you began by getting pay data for the most common jobs in the five basic pay categories at Jeffrey. Then, you organized this information by sex and calculated the average pay for each sex in each pay category. Because you believe that the workers' abilities could have some effect on salaries, you included the average evaluation scores received by the workers in each group. (Jeffrey evaluates on a scale of 1 to 10, with 10 being the highest.) Also, because length of time in a pay grade could indicate a sex-biased unwillingness to increase salaries, you computed averages of time spent in each pay grade.

Now you must analyze these data (summarized in Table 5) to determine whether they give evidence of sex discrimination. You will take extra precautions to be objective, for Jeffrey management wants only the truth. If discrimination is present, management will address the matter. After your analysis, you will reach a conclusion. You are not expected to recommend specific actions, but your conclusions will indicate where actions need to be taken.

You will present the information in a report form appropriate for the situation (a report addressed to the president).

26. **Determining ways to improve recycling.** (Requires research) When recycling first started in your offices, everyone was so enthusiastic. However, Don Anderson, president of the company, has noticed a decline over the past year in both the enthusiasm and in the actual amount of material being recycled. He keeps statistics on the amount of recycling done in order to show the public the company's interest in improving the environment. Therefore, he ran a questionnaire in the last company newsletter asking employees to explain why they think the figures are down.

TABLE 5   (Problem 25) **Distribution of employees by sex, in pay grades, with pay averages, months in grade, and evaluations**

Pay Grade & Job Title	Number		Average Hourly Pay		Months in Pay Grade		Average Evaluation	
	Male	Female	Male	Female	Male	Female	Male	Female
PG-1								
Assembler, light	23	137	8.92	8.47	11.3	15.5	7.1	8.0
Janitor	13	3	8.83	8.21	20.5	19.4	6.9	6.9
Material handler	17	8	8.91	8.40	19.3	27.9	6.9	7.3
PG-2								
Assembler, heavy	113	13	9.55	8.90	11.3	21.2	7.4	6.9
Drill press operator	22	20	9.66	9.23	18.7	22.3	6.9	6.9
Inspector	13	22	9.08	9.13	13.6	19.5	6.8	7.4
PG-3								
Press operator	19	4	10.04	9.65	25.4	25.7	6.9	7.0
Maintenance painter	9	5	10.34	9.77	24.3	26.1	6.8	7.5
PG-4								
Press setup worker	10	0	11.77	—	24.6	—	6.9	—
Maintenance mechanic	17	0	12.54	—	32.4	—	7.4	—
PG-5								
Maintenance electrician	10	2	13.45	12.50	29.4	38.8	8.3	8.4
Pipefitter	7	0	14.08	—	31.4	—	8.4	—

He was impressed to discover that nearly two thirds of your employees reported they would recycle more if it were made easier. Here are the biggest problems they identified:

Problem	Percent Identifying as a Problem
Lack of storage	57
Insect infestation	43
Bad smells	31
Difficult to separate trash	15
Bins too small	15

He asked you to gather both primary and secondary information on these five problems and recommend solutions for eliminating the problems in order to make it even easier for employees to recycle. Along with your recommendations, give cost estimates for each of your recommendations.

Submit the report to your boss and to Michael Murphy, Director of Public Relations.

27. **Present survey results on a convention center to council members.** Two years ago, the Metroville Convention Center opened its doors. At the time, enthusiasm

for this costly structure ran high, especially with the mayor and the other civic leaders who were instrumental in promoting the project. In short time, however, the enthusiasm waned. Operational problems cropped up, and patrons increasingly voiced discontent with the center.

In fact, concerns about the center and its operations became so great that after 15 months of operation, the council fired the convention center manager and hired a new one. After a few months of operation under the new manager, however, complaints again surfaced. They increased steadily until they appeared to be as negative as before. They had become so negative the council placed the matter on the agenda for its first meeting this month.

At this meeting, the subject was thoroughly discussed. Accusations and strong statements flowed freely, and tempers flared. After two hours of heated discussion, council member Albert J. Cobb suggested that much of what had been said was more rumor and opinion than fact. He further suggested that the council get first-hand information from the users of the convention facilities. "These are the ones who count," Cobb said. "They are the ones who will determine the success of the center. Why not conduct a survey of them? Ask them the pertinent questions. Then we'll have something substantive to work with."

The council members quickly bought Cobb's suggestion. They agreed to ask city manager Otis A. Patton to conduct a survey of convention users. Since you are Patton's assistant, in turn you got the assignment. Of course, you will do the bulk of the work, but Patton will look over your shoulder and will be designated as coauthor of the report (if he approves your work).

After the meeting, you began the task by designing a comprehensive but simple questionnaire covering all of the problem areas discussed at the meeting. It simply asked the respondents to rank on a 1-to-5 scale their views on the various facilities and activities at the center. Next, using attendance rolls from a variety of conventions held at the center, you built a sample of people to be interviewed. Because many on the list are out-of-towners, you elected to mail the questionnaires, with return-postage-paid envelopes. (For class purposes, you may create any other specific methodology information you may need.)

Now you have your returns, and you have computed scale averages for each question (Table 6). Next you must review these findings to see what they tell you about the center—and perhaps more important, what they tell you about how to improve things. With your analyses done, you will then organize your information in the best possible order for presentation. Then you will supply the words that will convey your message in a fast-moving, readable report.

Probably you will use conventional short-report form (title page and text). Since the council members will want the highlights fast, you will begin with a summary. You may use graphics—wherever they help tell the report story. Address the report to the city council, listing all seven of its members.

28. Reporting on employee viewpoints about stealing from their employer. For this problem, assume the role of executive trainee in the Human Resources De-

TABLE 6	(Problem 27) **Satisfaction of respondents with Metroville Convention Center facilities and operations***

	All events	Events held before management change	Events held on or after management change	One-day events	Two-day events	Three-day events	Longer than three-day events	Less than 1,000 attendees	1,000 to 10,000 attendees	More than 10,000 attendees
Overall experience at center	2.16	2.50	1.93	2.40	2.33	1.90	2.00	2.22	2.33	2.33
Functionality of meeting space	1.79	1.86	1.75	1.87	1.83	1.50	2.33	1.83	2.08	1.00
Functionality of loading area	2.39	2.40	2.39	3.50	2.71	1.83	1.67	2.80	2.42	2.25
Functionality of overall building	2.06	2.00	2.10	1.92	2.43	1.92	2.25	1.91	2.25	2.25
Cooperation of sales staff	1.61	1.65	1.57	1.73	1.57	1.58	1.25	1.75	1.58	1.50
Honesty and integrity of center staff	1.61	1.71	1.52	1.93	1.86	1.25	1.00	1.58	1.67	1.25
Cooperation of center staff during the event	1.47	1.59	1.38	1.60	1.57	1.42	1.00	1.42	1.42	1.75
Cooperation of center top management	1.87	2.00	1.75	2.17	2.00	1.58	1.67	1.78	1.73	2.25
Fairness of overall price	2.50	2.41	2.57	2.67	2.86	2.25	2.00	2.58	2.33	3.00
Quality of food	2.61	2.41	2.79	1.93	3.43	2.75	3.33	1.90	2.92	3.25
Affordability of food	3.00	2.69	3.29	2.75	3.50	2.92	3.33	3.00	3.08	3.50
Availability of parking	4.13	4.06	4.19	4.13	4.29	4.00	4.25	4.17	4.33	4.00
Building location	2.65	2.50	2.76	2.71	2.86	2.33	3.00	2.55	3.25	2.25
Availability of hotel space	2.18	1.86	2.33	2.50	2.50	1.80	2.50	2.00	2.36	1.00
Quality of hotel space	2.00	1.86	2.07	2.25	1.83	1.90	2.50	1.75	2.27	1.00
Proximity of hotels	2.09	1.75	2.27	2.00	2.17	1.90	3.00	2.00	2.27	1.00
Assistance from City Convention and Visitors Bureau	2.24	1.83	2.40	3.00	2.20	1.90	2.50	3.00	1.90	1.00

*Ranking System   1: excellent   2: good   3: average   4: bad   5: very poor

partment of Electronco, Inc., a major manufacturer of electronic products. Today, you were called into the office of the director, Helen O. Cortez. Ms. Cortez explained to you that at the staff meeting she attended earlier in the day the discussion centered on employee theft. Apparently, the various executives believe that some of their workers are stealing and they support their views with evidence such as inventory records, personal observations, and employee admissions.

As Ms. Cortez explained it, some of the pilferage involves little things like paper and pencils; but much of it concerns big items like work tools, manufac-

TABLE 7	(Problem 28) **Tabulations of questions involving yes-no responses**

	Employees Admitting Stealing (96)			Employees Denying Stealing (116)		
Question	Yes	No	No Response	Yes	No	No Response
Would you report a fellow worker whom you saw stealing?	16	76	4	44	52	20
Should your employer provide an incentive for reporting stealing?	8	81	7	31	69	8

TABLE 8	(Problem 28) **Responses to question on why employee thinks other employees steal from their employer***

Explanation	Employees Admitting Stealing (96)	Employees Denying Stealing (116)
Believe underpaid	24	11
Has grudge against employer	21	6
Easy to do	9	36
Doesn't see it as stealing	67	38
Thinks he/she can get away with it	11	39
Thinks he/she deserves it	36	5
Personal or financial problems	6	4
Other	21	19

*Responses exceed number interviewed because some respondents gave more than one explanation.

tured products in inventory, and telephone answering machines. In fact, one department has discovered that one of its computers has disappeared.

The staff agreed to begin work on policy changes designed to reduce the stealing. But so the administrators will fully understand the problem they face, they have asked your department to conduct a survey of company employees. The objective of this survey will be generally to get a measure of employee opinions toward stealing—who steals, what they think about stealing, what should be done about the matter, and such. Ms. Cortez assigned you the task of conducting this survey.

You began the task by designing a questionnaire that will get the information the administrative staff needs. You included what you believe to be all the questions necessary. You concluded that you would like to report the views separately of those who have stolen and those who have not; so you took elaborate pains to make the responses anonymous. Then you conducted the survey (for class purposes, you may create any additional logical information about methodology you may need).

After conducting the survey, you first tabulated responses to the question concerning whether the employee ever had stolen from his or her employer. Surprisingly, of the 212 responses you received, 96 admitted having stolen and 116 denied stealing. Because you suspect these two groups differ in their views on the subject, you tabulated the responses to the other questions separately. (Tables 7 and 8.)

Now you have completed the tabulations and have begun to analyze findings. You will present your analyses and the data uncovered to the administrative staff in conventional short report form (title page plus text). Whether you will use graphics will depend on the need for them. Probably you will begin with a quick summary of highlights.

29. **Comparing retail data of selected cities for the RMA.** In your capacity as research associate for the Ableburg Retail Merchants Association, you have been assigned the task of comparing the retailing activity of your city with five other cities. As explained by Eva Barton, chair of the Association's board, you are to present a current report on just how Ableburg ranks with comparable cities in other areas. Ms. Barton's instructions were both simple and clear: "We'd like to know how our market compares with others of about the same size. And most important, we want to know how we're performing relative to these markets."

Ms. Barton didn't say more. She didn't even suggest which other cities to use in the comparisons. Apparently, she trusts your good judgment on this important matter.

So you began your assignment by carefully selecting the five cities. Your choices come from all major regions of the country; and although they are not precisely comparable (no cities are), they appear to serve your purposes well. Next, from the most recent *National Research Bureau Shopping Directory*, you gathered the pertinent data. First, you gathered the data that generally present a market overview of the cities—data such as population, number of households, income, and shopping centers (Table 9). Then you got the sales data. These data you recorded by general category of retail operations—food, furniture, apparel, and such (Table 10).

Now you are ready to organize your findings and present them to the Association. For the most part, your presentation will be informational—an orderly and clear presentation of data. But you will make conclusions concerning Ableburg's ranking with the other cities. Perhaps you will be able to make an overall conclusion about Ableburg's relative status.

You will present the report in conventional short report form (title page and text). And you will use graphics wherever they help to tell the report story. Probably, you will begin with a brief summary. Eventually, the report information will be distributed to the membership in the form of a newsletter, but the current report will be addressed to the Board of Directors, Ableburg Retail Merchants Association, Eva Barton, Chair.

TABLE 9	(Problem 29) **Market overview of cities used in study**

Market Overview

Market Overview	Metropolitan areas					
	Ableburg	**Bakerville**	**Charleston**	**Danfield**	**Eaton**	**Fall City**
Population	909,600	974,400	913,400	1.04 million	970,000	1.54 million
Median age	30 years	31.5 years	32.3 years	31.7 years	34.1 years	32.3 years
Number of households	351,800	347,400	359,500	377,400	372,000	525,900
Median household pre-tax incomes	$32,487	$35,546	$35,493	$31,379	$33,662	$50,296
Number of shopping centers*	216	47	168	180	153	234
Leasable shopping center space per capita	21.4 sq. ft.	7.79 sq. ft.	25.18 sq. ft.	22.2 sq. ft.	20.3 sq. ft.	17.6 sq. ft.

*Shopping centers are defined as buildings that contain at least three retail stores. Single-standing retail locations are not reflected in these figures.

TABLE 10	(Problem 29) **Retail spending for cities used in study**

Retail Spending	Metropolitan areas					
	Ableburg	**Bakerville**	**Charleston**	**Danfield**	**Eaton**	**Fall City**
Total retail sales	$7.48 billion	$7.6 billion	$7.7 billion	$7.7 billion	$7.51 billion	$13 billion
Total food store sales	$1.59 billion	$1.1 billion	$1.41 billion	$1.48 billion	$1.25 billion	$1.9 billion
General merchandise sales	$877 million	$1.28 billion	$788 million	$1.2 billion	$1.26 billion	$1.75 billion
Furniture, appliances sales	$480 million	$446 million	$463 million	$478 million	$319 million	$1.16 billion
Automotive sales	$1.54 billion	$1.87 billion	$1.6 billion	$1.7 billion	$1.87 billion	$2.62 billion
Apparel sales	$411 million	$366 million	$369 million	$363 million	$234 million	$946 million

30. **Analyzing Sales Data for Chock-O-Let.** Today's report writing assignment casts you into the role of assistant to the executive vice president of the Chock-O-Let Company. Your job is to prepare the annual report on sales for your boss, Thomas H. Mongan. As in the past, you will present sales data for your company and compare them with the two leading competitors, showing changes from the preceding year.

The sales data assembled in Tables 11 and 12 will provide the facts for your report. Your report will show the progress made (if any) for Chock-O-Let's major candy. Also, it will present a picture of sales for the major sales seasons for candy (Easter, Halloween, Christmas, and Valentine's Day), as shown in Table 12.

The report will be informational to some extent, but it will need to include an analysis of any changes observed. The company is especially sensitive to its competitive position even though it might be slight. Thus, you will need to be alert to major patterns as well as minor variations in sales that could affect the company's position. You will submit the report in the typical short report format—title page and report proper in direct order; and you will need to include graphics to tell the sales story to Mr. Mongan. You will word the report without personal references.

TABLE 11   (Problem 30) **Top-selling candy in past 52 weeks (regular-sized items)**

Product Name	Manufacturer	Sales $ (Millions)	% Change from Last Year
Sniders	Chock-O-Let	$62.4	11.3%
Russell's Peanut Butter Cups	Russell's	42.2	9.3
Chip Chat	Russell's	37.5	15.9
O & A's Plain	Chock-O-Let	32.4	−1.3
Magnabar	Haven	31.5	15.7
O & A's Peanut	Chock-O-Let	29.3	−2.6
Munch	Haven	27.0	9.0
Russell's Milk Chocolate	Russell's	24.5	16.4
Russell's Almond	Russell's	23.0	12.3
Anchors Away	Chock-O-Let	19.9	7.8

TABLE 12   (Problem 30) **Seasonal candy sales**

Season and Product	Sales $ (Millions)	% Change from Last Year	Share of Seasonal Category Sales
Easter Candy	$477.2	31.5%	100.0%
Russell's	121.3	30.4	26.9
Chock-O-Let	56.3	24.6	12.4
Haven	14.6	88.1	3.5
Halloween Candy	420.5	14.6	100.0
Russell's	127.6	7.8	32.2
Chock-O-Let	133.8	14.5	33.7
Haven	62.1	16.9	13.6
Christmas Candy	370.2	13.4	100.0
Russell's	133.3	9.4	36.1
Chock-O-Let	74.5	8.6	19.3
Haven	5.5	67.7	1.7
Valentine's Day Candy	195.3	17.9	100.0
Russell's	27.7	48.9	13.1
Chock-O-Let	23.9	55.3	12.2
Haven	8.4	4.6	3.7

31. Examining Topic Issues for Next Year's CEO Symposium. You are the Executive Secretary of the CEO Symposium, which is conducted at Crescent View University. This two-day conference focuses on issues of concern to chief executives each year. It draws key executives from all types of industries throughout the United States and Canada.

You have recently completed the current year's annual conference and it was total success—in attendance and in the eyes of the executives who attended and participated. But your experience tells you that you must begin now to plan for a successful conference for next year. In fact, the CEO Symposium Board of Directors instructed you to determine the most pressing executive issues that currently exist. These issues will be the topics for coverage and discussion at next year's symposium.

To determine what these issues are, you asked three groups—executives, professors, and executives of small business organizations—to give you their perceptions of the most pressing business issues. You surveyed by mail 1,100 professors, 1,025 executives, and 675 executives of small business organizations. (You may assume whatever research design details you prefer as long as they are in keeping with standards of sound research methodology.) Today, two months after your initial mailing, you have the returns tallied as shown in Table 13. Now you will present them to the directors for their review.

You will use the short report form (title page plus text) for your report. Because it is an internal document, you will use a four-spot title page as the only prefatory element. The report proper will begin with recommendations based on the facts you have assembled. You will do more than present the facts in the report body, however. You will need to analyze the facts, comparing responses among the groups, before a final picture emerges. It's likely, too, that you will need graphics to help your analysis as well.

Construct the report that will present and discuss the significant business issues for next year's CEO Symposium.

32. **Evaluating Selection Criteria for Store Managers at Electronic Super Stores.** Electronic Super Stores, a major chain of computer hardware and software, believes that the key to its future is leadership. Toward that end, top management is committed to attracting and selecting good leadership talent—especially at the store manager level. This is where your report situation begins.

In order to remain competitive and to be a significant player in the market, ESS management must select and retain talented store managers for the 125 stores it owns. To do that, management hired you—a human resource consultant—to develop criteria to use in selecting store managers.

Accordingly, you interviewed 100 successful high-tech store managers to determine their views on desirable characteristics for effective leadership in computer sales and service at the retail level. As shown in Table 14, you asked the 100 managers to rate 19 characteristics of a store manager as detrimental, irrelevant, and necessary for the work of managing store operation. Because you needed more specificity in the "necessary" category, you had the 100 respondents further differentiate these characteristics as below average, average, above average, and highly developed.

Now, you must analyze these responses and report them to ESS. Your final report will include recommendations, as well as facts and analyses. Prepare the formally worded report (in short report form—indirect with three-spot title page)

| TABLE 13 | (Problem 31) **Significant business issues as viewed by professors, executives, and executives of small business organizations** |

Groups and Issues	Number	Percent
Professors		
Competing globally	157	29.35%
Productivity	61	11.40
Quality products/services	47	8.79
Incorporating new technology	46	8.60
Short-term/long-term	45	8.41
LBOs	44	8.22
Managing better	43	8.04
R & D/innovation	34	6.36
Motivating employees	31	5.79
Change	27	5.04
Total	535	100.00
Executives		
Regulations and paper work	118	21.85
Competing globally	88	16.30
Motivating employees	46	8.52
Attracting quality workers	46	8.52
Quality products/services	40	7.41
Taxes/tax laws	40	7.41
Education of the workforce	36	6.67
Short-term/long-term	34	6.30
Productivity	32	5.93
Budget deficit	30	5.56
Cost of health insurance/care	30	5.56
Total	540	100.00
E/SBOs		
Regulation and paperwork	76	20.11
Competing globally	54	14.29
Attracting quality workers	32	8.47
Taxes/tax laws	32	8.47
Motivating employees	30	7.94
Education of the workforce	26	6.88
Quality products/services	26	6.88
Mandated benefits	22	5.82
Cost control	20	5.29
Cost of health insurance/care	20	5.29
Short-term/long-term	20	5.29
Productivity	20	5.29
Total	378	100.00

TABLE 14	(Problem 32) **Evaluation of characteristics of store managers in computer retail sales and service**

Characteristic	Detrimental	Irrelevant	Necessary			
			Below Average	Average	Above Average	Highly Developed
High achievement motivation (i.e. strong desire to succeed)	0%	0%	0%	8%	37%	55%
Enthusiastic about product and business	0	1	0	11	39	49
Persevering	0	0	2	17	36	45
Creative	0	1	4	9	45	41
Highly competitive	4	8	1	15	50	22
Unable to work well with others	92	6	1	0	0	1
Does not freely communicate information ("plays cards close to chest")	75	11	2	8	2	2
Disruptive	73	9	9	7	2	0
Does not delegate well	67	21	4	6	2	0
Obstinate	66	14	4	13	3	0
Strong ego	6	22	5	15	43	9
Personal charisma	0	20	5	43	25	7
Makes decisions rapidly	12	17	5	33	30	3
Makes decisions intuitively	23	20	10	16	25	6
A good organization person	12	29	12	33	7	7
Willing to take large but calculated risks	3	4	5	31	39	18
Compulsive	61	17	1	11	7	3
Physically strong	1	50	6	27	10	6
A zealot	41	21	6	13	19	0

for the ESS top management team. You will need to include graphics to help the words tell the story of the successful store manager at ESS.

33. **Controlling air travel costs at Urban Developers.** Today's assignment takes you to the office of Jason Aguilar, President of Urban Developers. Mr. Aguilar has just reviewed the latest budget figures, and he's most concerned about one line item—travel expenditures. For the first six months of the fiscal year, travel costs have increased 15 percent over last year. And presently, travel costs account for 12 percent of the total budget. Mr. Aguilar believes this figure is much, much too high.

Recognizing a problem and doing something about it are two different things, however. That's where you enter the picture. Mr. Aguilar wants you to look into the matter further, as he charges you with these words: "Find out what we can do

TABLE 15   (Problem 33)   **Actions to control air travel costs**

Action	Number Taking Action	Overall (239 firms)	Big Users* (163)	Small Users† (76)
Use of lowest available airfare, when feasible	190	79	95%	92%
Require employees turn in frequent-flier benefits for company use	30	12	23	16
Require that employees use specified travel agencies so company can obtain rebate	148	62	85	61
Reduced air travel	95	40	32	54
In-house company travel agency	142	60	35	67
Request that employees use frequent-flier points earned on business trips for company travel purposes	48	20	41	31
Review employee travel plans in advance	122	51	48	61
Agreements with airlines for corporate discounts	115	48	85	23
Establish independent group for auditing travel expenses	69	28	44	27
Require that employees use airlines that give frequent-flier benefits to businesses as well as individuals	35	14	22	12

*Big users have total annual travel costs of at least $12 million.
†Small users spend less than $12 million annually.

to reduce these travel costs. You might want to see what other companies are doing to control their costs.''

To respond to his assignment, you decide to conduct a survey of what actions organizations are taking to control travel costs. First, you call several companies and talk with their key executive personnel to determine their policies. From these conversations, you identify 10 actions that appear to be central to controlling travel costs in industry. To determine the extent of use of these actions and their effectiveness, you next design a questionnaire that you send to a large sample of companies. One part of the questionnaire asks respondents to indicate whether they take the actions that you list in their companies (a simple yes/no format is used). Another part asks respondents to rate the effectiveness of the actions to control costs—that is, whether the actions have a small, moderate, or substantial impact. As a further measure of good research design, you ask for the amount spent on travel annually so you can divide the companies into large and small users.

It has now been six weeks since you mailed the 490 questionnaires, and you have received 239 back—a much greater return rate than you expected. You tally the data in two tables (Tables 15 and 16), and they now become the

TABLE 16	(Problem 33) **Effectiveness of actions to control air travel costs (action had "substantial impact")**

Action	Overall	Big Users	Small Users
Reduced air travel	40	57%	37%
In-house company travel agency	85	73	62
Use of lowest available fares, when feasible	62	64	61
Review employee travel plans in advance	48	12	36
Require that employees use specified travel agencies so company can obtain rebate	65	51	49
Establish independent group for auditing travel expenses	33	32	36
Require employees to turn in frequent-flier benefits for company use	18	12	15
Request that employees use frequent-flier points earned on business trips for company travel purposes	19	18	16
Require that employees use airlines that give frequent-flier benefits to businesses as well as individuals	10	13	17
Agreements with airlines for corporate discounts	30	29	27

basis for a report you will prepare for President Aguilar in answer to the questions he posed.

Because of the nature of the situation, you will write the report on the formal side—without personal references. You will need to interpret the facts as well, because Mr. Aguilar expects you to give him the benefit of your best thinking on the matter. No doubt, you will find good use for graphics to help explain your interpretations, too. Use the short-report format and begin it with your conclusions (don't use recommendations because you know Mr. Aguilar likes to make his own decisions).

34. **Designing a course for recruitment and selection.** As a member of the training and development staff at Synergy Management Consultants, you've been asked to help in the design of a new course for the company's personnel entitled "Recruitment and Selection." Part of the course will involve labor market structures, laws governing recruiting and selecting, and such. Another part will deal with the recruiting and selecting techniques. This is where you draw your report writing assignment.

It is your boss's belief—and a logical one—that the course needs to be built on solid evidence about current practices in the marketplace. One of the more important topics that you will want to include in the training classes is résumés and how to evaluate them. Based on your own experience, you know that there is little empirical evidence on which to base any decision about what to look for in job market résumés. To be sure, there are good standards to follow. But these standards, you feel, need to be backed by factual support.

In order to get this factual support, you decide to conduct a survey on the subject of what experts in the employment market feel are important content items to be included in job-seeking résumés. From the national headquarters of the International Human Resources Association, you purchase a mailing list of key personnel officials (those who have hiring authority and those who are campus recruiters) in North America. From the list (which totals 5,684), you draw a random sample of 20 percent each for the two groups you want to be included—that is, 568 for hirers and 568 for recruiters.

To these two samples, you send a list of content items that could be included in a résumé. In total, you have compiled a list (which, incidentally, you sent to 17 human resource managers as a pretest) of 62 such items. You ask that respondents rank order the list and return their rankings to you.

As of today, you have received 251 (44.2 percent) and 237 (41.7 percent) returns from the hirers and recruiters, respectively. (You attribute the high return rate to the interest in the topic and the quality of the persuasive letter that accompanied the questionnaire.) You have arranged the results in two tables (Tables 17 and 18). Table 17 shows the most important content items as ranked by the two groups. Table 18 shows the content items that received lower rankings.

Because you believe these facts have importance beyond just the design of the recruitment and selection training course, you are going to write up the results of your work in a medium-length report with some formality. You will have a three-spot title page, and you will word the report without personal pronouns. On the one hand, you will interpret the results of your survey primarily for the course you are structuring. On the other, you will interpret the results in terms of what recruiters and executives look for in new college graduates. Several of your human resource executives give speeches to college groups, and you believe they could find good use for your results.

Be sure to use graphics in the report. Write it for Victor Frerichs, vice president of human resources, Synergy Management Consultants.

35. Diagnosing a communication problem. (Requires research) Today's report assignment casts you in the role of director of communication at _____ (a business in your locale). In addition to providing financial data to investors, you also do many other things. One of these activities is to diagnose any actual or potential communication problem that the company might have. At the moment, you are concerned about _____, (writing apprehension, telephone apprehension, oral reporting practices, interpersonal styles, listening behavior, etc.—your instructor will specify the problem). To properly solve the problem, you will have to do four things.

First, you will have to research the nature of the problem. This step will take you to your library to do background research on it. After you are thoroughly familiar with the problem, you will proceed to the next phase in the problem-solving process. The second step will involve selecting a measuring instrument for the problem that you have researched. You should only use one that presently

TABLE 17	(Problem 34) **Résumé content ranked important by 50 percent or more of hiring officials**

Résumé Content Items in Order of Importance	Hiring Officials	College Recruiters
1. Name	99.6%	99.0%
2. Degree	99.5	98.3
3. Name of college	99.1	98.1
4. Employing company	98.7	97.1
5. Job held (title)	98.6	99.5
6. Telephone number	98.4	97.3
7. Dates of employment	98.3	98.6
8. Address	97.1	99.0
9. Duties—work experience	96.2	98.3
10. Major	96.0	95.9
11. Special aptitudes/skills	94.5	90.7
12. Achievements—work experience	93.1	91.9
13. Previous employers—references	91.4	90.2
14. Date of graduation—college	90.4	95.8
15. Job objective	91.5	87.8
16. Career objective	89.8	90.0
17. Years attended—college	89.3	92.6
18. Summary of qualifications	86.4	83.9
19. Awards, honors	85.6	85.7
20. Willingness to relocate	84.2	81.2
21. Combined job and career objective	80.8	79.9
22. Professional organizations—extracurricular activities	79.3	93.3
23. Grade-point average	77.6	90.5
24. Minor	77.2	94.9
25. References supplied on request	76.2	84.9
26. Military experience	75.9	77.8
27. Current organization memberships	71.0	83.4
28. Professors—references	70.0	79.7
29. Reasons for leaving job	69.9	67.8
30. Scholarships—college achievements	67.1	84.8
31. Student government activities	66.0	87.4
32. Work supervisor names	62.2	61.2
33. References—completeness of data	61.5	59.6
34. Name of high school	60.3	57.3
35. Publications	59.9	58.7
36. Résumé title	58.7	45.6
37. Community involvement	58.2	63.1
38. Date of graduation—high school	53.0	36.1
39. Salaries received for jobs	51.6	39.5
40. Diploma—high school	51.3	43.2

TABLE 18   (Problem 34) **Résumé content ranked important by 25 to 50 percent of hiring officials**

Résumé Content Items in Order of Importance	Hiring Officials	College Recruiters
1. Hobbies/interest	48.8%	54.6%
2. Health	48.2	29.8
3. Personal references	47.2	60.2
4. Yearbook editor, etc.—college	47.1	73.5
5. Social organizations—college	46.0	81.3
6. Years attended—high school	45.4	45.8
7. Athletic involvement—college	43.3	62.3
8. Social security number	43.1	28.9
9. Band, choral group, etc.—college	39.8	54.3
10. Awards, honors—high school	38.7	41.2
11. Grade average—high school	38.4	40.0
12. Professional organizations—high school	30.4	44.5
13. List of college courses taken	27.1	75.8

exists in the literature and is well established. You will not concern yourself with the preparation of a new measuring instrument. Remember, too, that some instruments require that you get author permission to use them. You will need to do this to legally and ethically administer the instrument.

The third step will require that you administer the instrument in an ongoing organization that your instructor selects. In addition, you will need to tally the results in an orderly fashion so that they can be used in the last step.

The fourth step will require that you write your results in a medium-length report with some formality requirements. You will use graphic aids, and you will write without personal references. The report will have a four-spot title page and you will address it to the president of the company.

Write the report that results from this problem situation.

(Note: This report problem can be repeated for as many communication problems and measuring instruments as can be identified.)

PROPOSALS

36. **Proposing an environmental "offensive" for a company.** For this problem, you are the director of public relations for _____ (a manufacturing plant in your area or a place designated by your instructor). Today at the weekly staff meeting, Scott Corley, the company's president, opened with some words about the company's deteriorating image in the community. As he put it, "We are seen as major polluters. As you know, we have reduced emissions over half, and we'll reduce

them more by the end of the year. We've publicized all this as much as we can through newspaper and television advertising. Even so, the public remembers us as we were. We've got to do something to change our image.''

After some discussion of what could be done, you expressed your ideas. You made the point that the company should take steps to become the community leader in environmental concerns. "We should take the offensive," as you expressed it.

When you were asked to give specific examples of what you were suggesting, you were not at a loss for words. You said there were many things the company could do. For example, it could become a depository for recycling newspapers, glass, and aluminum cans. You pointed out that currently the community has only limited facilities for collecting materials for recycling. You explained how the company could set up bins at the plant entrance for people to deposit the items for recycling. You even suggested that it could establish and service collection points throughout the community.

Next you gave the example of how the company could launch a campaign against highway litter. It could organize teams of its own employees as well as induce service organizations, student groups, and such to clean up the roads and neighborhoods. You also said that the company could organize similar activities to clean up area lakes and streams.

You were ready to make additional suggestions when Mr. Corley stopped you. "I like your suggestions," he said. "No doubt you have other ideas. I'd like for you to think through the matter, develop a plan, and write it up in proposal form. Make copies for all of us. We'll discuss it next week."

Additional discussion followed. Much of it concerned how much the program would cost. Even though most of what you propose would be absorbed by your department's budget, you would incur some additional costs. Now you must do as your president instructed: "Think through the matter, develop a plan, and write it in proposal form."

37. **Presenting a course in sound business management for ASB members.** As president of Business Training and Consulting Associates, you are looking over an invitation from the executive secretary of the Association for Small Businesses to submit a proposal for a course. (ASB is an organization of owners and administrators of small businesses.) Concerned about the high rate of failure among its smaller members, ASB wishes to offer them a comprehensive course on the essentials of sound business operations. The plan is to initially offer the course in a major metropolitan area. Then, if the course proves to be successful, it would be offered in other areas. A successful course, the invitation states, could be offered indefinitely—as long as demand exists. And ASB's survey of its membership shows high interest in such a course.

As described in the invitation, the course would be limited to 25 students paying $400 each. ASB would publicize the course, and take care of registration, money collecting, and such. The length of the course has not been decided, and would be determined by the proposal accepted. As stated in the announcement, the total hours of instruction should be structured to fit into the $10,000 in revenues the course will bring in. As for times for the instruction, the invitation specified either evenings or weekends. Concerning frequency and length of the sessions, the invitation suggested that the groups submitting proposals "use their best professional judgment based on experience." The invitation also noted that the matter of what to teach was left to the judgment of those submitting proposals. It did, however, suggest that the curriculum include "whatever an ongoing small-business person needs to know."

You are excited about the prospects of getting this contract. Business has not been good for your small company in recent months. A contract such as the one ASB offers might well be the difference between success and failure. So you will submit a proposal, making sure that it gives ASB what it needs. As you plan the course, keep in mind that your four teacher-consultant employees are experts in the basic fields of marketing, finance, accounting, and management. If you need additional specialization, you can employ professors from a local university. You charge $125 an hour for your employees' services, which includes a reasonable profit for the company.

Since the invitation did not specify a form for the proposal, you will develop your own. Make certain that it includes all vital information—curriculum, times, methods of instruction, instructors' credentials, supplies needed, and such.

38. **Proposing peer review be included as part of employee performance evaluations.** Your company has been through a lot in recent years. Not only did it go through a major restructuring, but also the employees are now major shareholders in the company. How well the workers next to you perform seems to mean more now, since it is directly related to your pocketbook. Therefore, you would like some say in those workers' pay and promotion decisions.

You have decided to propose to management that peer reviews be implemented as a major part of regular performance evaluations. Since the restructuring, you are working mostly as self-directed teams. It only makes sense that those closest to the work have some part in its evaluation. You think that if 80 percent of your team agrees on a particular action, management should heed it. Co-workers should get the opportunity to determine who gets raises and advances. In your proposal, give as many reader-benefit reasons for implementing this proposal as you can think of. Encourage management to implement this proposal as soon as possible.

39. **Proposing child care be added to employee benefits list.** As the director of corporate benefits at your company, write a proposal to top management for adding child care to your employee benefits list. Not only will this help you in recruiting some of the best new employees, it will help in keeping the best.

Let your management know what has happened at some of the other companies which have already instituted some form of child-care benefits. For instance, Travelers, which pays between 10 and 30 percent of child-care costs, has seen reduced turnover. Mutual Insurance claims child care has been a good recruiting tool. One company, Stride Rite Corporation, has even extended its child-care facilities to include eldercare. These intergenerational daycare centers are costly, but valued by employees.

Support your proposal with other facts such as companies or businesses in your town that offer day-care benefits for employees. Include primary information when appropriate. Be sure your call for action is clear.

40. Preparing a proposal for a company considering Centaur Hotels as a convention site. You've only been in your job as assistant sales manager of Centaur Hotel in San Diego, California, for six months. That's been enough time, however, for you to realize that you need to attract the high volume of business Centaur Hotel needs to keep operating consistently and profitably in the future. In fact, a good part of your job involves putting together different costs and prices for your boss, Howard Carmichael, who in turn submits them to individuals and groups who are considering Centaur Hotels for various functions and activities. But the assignment that Mr. Carmichael gives you today is one that will allow you to pull a number of isolated items together in "one big job."

As Mr. Carmichael explains it, "I have a number of organizations who call me and request proposals, as you know. Most of the bigger accounts I deal with myself. But I believe I need help in servicing some of the others. I received a call today from Corporate Marketing Systems. They are considering our hotel as a convention site next year. Work up a proposal for them. I'll need it right away— by day after tomorrow—to send to them. I'm sure they're considering other locations as well."

Back in your office, you begin thinking about the items to include in the proposal. Room rates and room blocks are some things, for sure. And there are cancellation clauses, catering functions, and meeting room descriptions, too. No doubt there are other categories you will want to cover once you get into the project. Corporate Marketing Systems is not a large organization. Based on last year's convention in Denver, Colorado, they had 405 people attend. And the Tourist Bureau in Colorado reports they used 200, 315, and 235 rooms for the three days of the convention.

Think through this situation carefully and then prepare a proposal for Mr. Carmichael. Of course, Mr. Carmichael will have to approve your work. Make it good, though, because if Mr. Carmichael is pleased, you'll get other opportunities to show your stuff—which means raises and promotions.

(Note: You may want to contact a hotel to determine what areas they usually include in proposals for convention groups.)

41. Purchasing an analyzer computer package. As office manager for Turnkey Consultants, you are excited about the opportunity your boss gave you today. David Romano, president of Turnkey Consultants, told you that he is quite satisfied with the results of the business writing training sessions you arranged six months ago. You can take much of the credit for the success of the program because your input resulted in most of the design of the training. Each employee in the headquarters staff received 20 hours of classroom-type training from Dr. Erika Sortini, a professor of business communication at Central State University. In addition, Dr. Sortini spent another week at the company in a consultant's role reviewing correspondence files and providing tutorial, one-on-one help to anyone wanting follow-up support for the classroom-type training. Of course, the text that Dr. Sortini used as her source of reference was *Basic Business Communication*, 6th edition.

But Mr. Romano wants to reinforce that training even more. He would now like to have a common style-analyzer computer package available to all employees in the company. But he doesn't know which one to purchase. So he turns to you for advice. Says he: "Examine four or five of the most popular style-analyzing packages and submit the best one to me. Consider this a proposal because I will likely purchase the package you select."

To begin the proposal that Mr. Romano wants, you will first have to study the most popular packages currently available on the market. A trip to the library should give you the information you need for the first stage of the proposal preparation process. (Or you might want to contact various vendors for information.) From whatever sources you use, you will decide on the "best" package available. Next, you will need to present this best style-analyzing package to Mr. Romano in the form of a written proposal. Deciding on the content of the proposal is important; most likely, at a minimum you will include cost, features of the package, compatibility with hardware capabilities, and unique characteristics. No doubt there are other topics you will include to make your proposal complete and distinct.

Prepare the proposal for Mr. Romano. You will dress it up physically and word it formally.

(Note: This assignment could be repeated for computer graphics and statistical packages as well.)

42. **Proposing that your company begin an education-support program.** As the new training director for _____ (your choice of a major company in your area), you had an interesting visit with the company president today. You presented your ideas of what you proposed to do on your job, and the president appeared to like them. The president especially liked your suggestion that the company begin a program of support to those employees who desire to further their education.

Basically, your idea is for the company to pay tuition, supplies, and fees for those who take approved courses at local colleges and trade schools. Your office would administer the program. As you see it, both the company and the employees would benefit—if the program is designed right. It would have to be restricted to course work that would increase the employee's value to the company. And, of course, satisfactory work would be required. Probably your office would have to handle course approvals and would generally police the work.

The president's final words to you were: "Write it up in the form of a proposal so I can bring it up with my staff. See if you can sell them like you sold me." So now you will have to write the proposal. Think through the idea and develop the information that will convince the staff your idea has merit. Use your imagination, but keep it logical and orderly. Organize the proposal so that the major points stand out clearly. As well as you can, use real facts concerning the appropriate schools in your area.

REPORT PROBLEMS: LONG

43. **Determine the need for a sporting goods store in your area.** (Requires research) The Athlete's Warehouse, a large chain of sporting goods stores, is considering locating a store in your community. It has hired you and your independent research organization to analyze the need for such a store and to recommend the appropriate decision.

   The Athlete's Warehouse sells a broad range of merchandise for the sports-minded consumer. Included in each store's inventory are all the sports equipment popular in the community served. Also, the stores carry a large assortment of sports clothing. The Athlete's Warehouse stores are truly first class. In addition, their prices are highly competitive. In fact, the company promotes its stores as being "discount outlets."

   From you, the Athlete's Warehouse management wants a recommendation on the question of whether to locate in your area. In reaching your recommendation, you will thoroughly review the existing sporting goods outlets. You will evaluate each on the following criteria: service, prices, and convenience.

   The "service" criterion includes the question of whether the stores take care of the total needs of the community—the completeness and depth of the goods offered, choices available, and such. Quality of personal service provided by store employees also is a part of this consideration, but time does not permit you to conduct a survey of consumers, which would be the ideal way of getting this information. Perhaps you can report information you can pick up from knowledgeable people in the community. As such information is not based on scientific investigation, be careful in reporting it.

   Your investigation of "prices" can be more scientific, for you can get quantitative comparisons here. Probably you will select a cross section sample of products—volume sellers in each major sports category. Then you will get prices for these products. You will compare these prices with those for the Athlete's Warehouse, which the company has given you. (For class purposes, you may assume that the Athlete's Warehouse prices are lower than the lowest prices you find in the community on 80 percent of the items.)

   Your study of "convenience" will be an analysis of the geographic area served and how accessible the stores are. Ease of parking, hours of operation, store arrangement, display of merchandise, and such also are parts of this factor.

As you make your evaluations, keep in mind the words the Athlete's Warehouse president left with you: "Unless the competition is firmly entrenched and is already providing super service and low prices, we can come in and succeed. Our merchandise, service, and prices are second to none. We don't mind a little competition."

After you have gathered the information you need and have analyzed it, you will present your findings in an appropriate report form. As you view the situation, it is somewhat formal; and the report will be longer than most you write. Although the information you will assemble is not heavily quantitative, you hope to use some graphics. Probably, you will construct some form of map showing locations of existing stores. And perhaps the price data will lend to a graphic presentation. Address the report to Mr. Wade O. Borg, president.

44. **Reporting on the desirability of holding an association's annual meeting in a city.** (Requires research) You are the executive director of the International Association of Public Relations Administrators. At its last meeting, the organization's board of directors tentatively selected _____ (a city of your instructor's choice) for its annual meeting two years from now. The board asked you to visit the city, look it over, and report on its desirability as a meeting site. The board will make its final decision on the site at its next meeting, scheduled for the coming month.

Following your visit to the city, you returned to your office. There you reviewed the information you had collected. As you viewed your assignment, the board's decision should be based on these primary considerations:

(a) availability of adequate hotels—accommodations for the 450 people expected to attend; meeting rooms—8 small (50-person capacity) and 1 large (for an assembly of all attending);

(b) transportation, both to and from the city and within the city; distance between airport and hotels, hotels and shopping areas, etc.;

(c) attractions—entertainment, shopping, cultural attractions, restaurants, and such. (The delegates expect to play as well as attend meetings.)

After you have completed your analysis, you will write the report. You will select a form appropriate for this fairly long and formal report. Address it to Cindy DeMaris, president.

45. **Reporting survey results to the board of a country club.** The board of directors of the Deer Creek Country Club is considering these projects for improving their facilities:

(a) expanding the golf course from 18 to 27 holes.

(b) repairing and resurfacing the swimming pool.

(c) building a new tennis clubhouse.

(d) resurfacing the five tennis courts and installing lights.

(e) purchasing adjacent land for future expansion.

The golf course expansion would be on land already owned by the club. Thus, this proposal is not related to the last proposal. The land being considered for purchase is viewed by proponents as a site for an additional nine holes of golf some years in the future. The land is available for purchase now and may not be available if and when the club needs it in the future.

Unfortunately, these improvements will require that the club borrow the money needed, either from a bank or by selling bonds to its members. The additional indebtedness would require an increase in membership dues of $40 per month if all improvements are made—less if only some are made.

At their last meeting, the directors discussed the matter thoroughly. Some of them opposed all the projects. Some favored all of them. And some favored certain proposals and opposed others. The discussions brought out differing viewpoints concerning what the club should be. One group felt strongly that golf and social activities should be the sole emphasis. Others expressed broader and varying views. After long and heated debate, the directors concluded that they should take the matter to the membership. They asked you, the club manager, to prepare an appropriate questionnaire, mail it to the members, record and analyze the results, and report your findings to them. They want the report before next month's meeting.

As instructed, you prepared a questionnaire. It was a simple one consisting of four basic questions. The cover letter explained the proposed expenditures and the effect they would have on dues and the club's indebtedness. Since the board is concerned with individual preferences, you sent the questionnaire to every member over 21 (thus a husband and wife with joint membership each received a questionnaire).

The club has three classes of membership: senior, corporate, and junior. For purposes of the survey, you combined the corporate and senior members, for both typically are families. However, you did separate the junior members from the seniors. The juniors are young adults (under 30). They pay the same dues as senior members, but they pay substantially less for the initial cost of membership. What they pay for membership can be applied to a senior membership when they reach age 30. As this group represents the future of the club, the board members are interested in their viewpoints separately.

Two weeks after mailing the questionnaires, you concluded that you would have to cut off the returns and determine your findings. At this point, your returns by membership type and by sex were as follows:

Membership Type	Number Mailed	Number Returned	Percent Returned
Senior, male	1,125	877	80.0
Senior, female	981	609	62.1
Junior, male	381	169	44.1
Junior, female	133	51	38.3
Total	2,620	1,706	61.1

TABLE 19	(Problem 43) **Members' responses about what club emphasis should be, in percentages and number of responses (in parentheses)**

Membership Type	A	B	C	D
Senior, male	34.4%	5.4%	0.8%	59.4%
	(302)	(47)	(7)	(521)
Senior, female	24.4%	3.4%	0.5%	71.6%
	(149)	(21)	(3)	(436)
Junior, male	24.2%	3.0%	1.8%	71.0%
	(41)	(5)	(3)	(120)
Junior, female	15.7%	3.9%	0	80.4%
	(8)	(2)	(0)	(41)
Total	29.3%	4.4%	.8%	65.5%
	(500)	(75)	(13)	(1,118)

The emphasis of the club should be on
A—golf and social activities only
B—golf, tennis, and social activities
C—golf, swimming, and social activities
D—golf, swimming, tennis, and social activities

TABLE 20	(Problem 43) **Willingness of members to pay dues increase, by membership type, in percentages and numbers responding (in parentheses)**

Membership Type	No Increase; No Improvement	Some Increase; Some Improvements	Pay $40 Mo.; All Improvements
Senior, male	33.0%	53.0%	14.0%
	(289)	(465)	(123)
Senior, female	26.3%	55.2%	18.5%
	(160)	(336)	(113)
Junior, male	18.3%	37.3%	44.4%
	(31)	(63)	(75)
Junior, female	15.7%	31.4%	52.9%
	(8)	(16)	(27)
Total	28.6%	51.6%	19.8%
	(488)	(880)	(338)

Then you began tabulating your responses. You started with the basic question of what the members think the club should be—that is, what activities it should provide. Your summary of responses to this question appears in Table 19. Then you tabulated responses to the second question, which asked the members their willingness to pay additional dues to cover all, some, or none of the costs of the improvement (Table 20).

Next you tabulated the responses to the third question, which asked whether the respondents favor or oppose each of the proposed projects (Table 21). Finally,

TABLE 21   (Problem 43) **Members approving proposed projects in percentages and number of responses (in parentheses)**

Membership type	9 Holes Golf	Swimming Pool	Tennis Clubhouse	Tennis Courts, Lights	Land Purchase
Senior, male	53.7% (471)	27.7% (243)	24.5% (215)	22.9% (201)	11.5% (101)
Senior, female	42.4% (258)	40.6% (247)	31.5% (192)	29.0% (171)	8.9% (54)
Junior, male	64.5% (109)	61.5% (104)	59.8% (101)	43.8% (74)	16.0% (27)
Junior, female	62.7% (32)	70.5% (36)	64.7% (33)	41.1% (21)	11.8% (6)
Total	51.0% (870)	36.9% (630)	31.7% (541)	27.4% (467)	11.0% (188)

TABLE 22   (Problem 43) **Respondents participating in golf, tennis, and swimming at club in past year, in percentages and number of responses (in parentheses)**

Membership Type	Golf	Tennis	Swimming
Senior, male	79.0% (693)	9.0% (79)	7.7% (68)
Senior, female	22.5% (137)	16.9% (103)	9.5% (58)
Junior, male	75.1% (127)	15.4% (26)	31.3% (53)
Junior, female	60.8% (31)	35.3% (18)	33.3% (17)
Total	57.9% (908)	13.2% (226)	11.5% (196)

you tabulated responses to your question about the respondents' use of club facilities in the past year (Table 22). Designed to find out how the members use the club, this question might well produce information that explains how the members answered the third question. But it also shows the size of the major interest groups (tennis, golf, and swimming) in the club. The board members feel that they should take care of all significantly large interest groups among the membership.

With these tables before you, you are ready to begin interpreting and analyzing them. You will present your work to the board in a clear and helpful report. Wherever the report will benefit from graphics, you will use them. Address the report to the board. Follow the address reference to the board with a list of the 12 board members. Show Ms. Patricia A. Arnold as president.

46. **Comparing prices of Prairie City's discount stores.** U-Save is a chain of general discount stores operating in your area. "We meet or beat all prices of the competition" is the company's motto, and company management has conscientiously worked to make this motto a reality. In fact, department heads (who are responsible for the prices of their merchandise) have been instructed to continually monitor prices and make certain theirs are lowest. Of course, it is to be expected that occasional exceptions will occur, as when a competitor conducts a special promotion. But U-Save intends to be the price leader as a general rule.

Today's mail brought U-Save's corporate headquarters evidence that the company's price objectives are not being met in the Prairie City area. From a stockholder came a clipping of a feature story in the *Prairie City Chronicle* reporting a shopping basket comparison of prices in the area's discount stores. The message of the story is clearly summarized in the headline: "Study Shows Lo-Mart Prices Lowest." The study was made by Alex O. Hawkins, a business reporter for the *Chronicle*. Mr. Hawkins made a list of 20 items commonly purchased and got their prices at the three discount stores in Prairie City (Lo-Mart, U-Save, and Bonus) and reported his findings. He found that Lo-Mart held a slight lead over the other stores, although prices tended to be close. In the story, Mr. Hawkins took a verbal slap at U-Save's motto: "The U-Save claim of lowest prices proved to be just a claim. The evidence does not support it."

U-Save's president, Lisa A. Mattingly, was highly upset about the article, and she wants something done about it. So she called you, her assistant, into her office. Her words explain her thinking: "My first reaction to this study was that it is unfair—a low blow. The items selected are not representative of our store's merchandise. Obviously, the study was done by a reporter who knows little about business—especially about survey techniques. Even so, the publicity is damaging. And there just might be some truth to the findings. I want you to look into the situation. Get some price comparisons from the three discount stores in Prairie City. Use a sufficiently broad selection of items to give a good indication of overall prices. I am not interested in just refuting the story. I want the truth. Are we or aren't we the price leaders?"

Following Ms. Mattingly's general instructions, you began work on the project. You selected eight departments that you thought were representative of U-Save's operation and that were comparable to departments in the two competing stores. Then you selected 12 items in each department. You took care that these were branded items that could be precisely identified (no private labels, for example) and were sold at all three stores. Then you got the prices for the items at all three stores. In doing so, you made certain that the items were not currently being promoted—that you were getting, normal, day-to-day prices. When you finished this task, you assembled your findings neatly in tabular form (Table 23).

Now you are ready to analyze and report. Your analysis, of course, should lead to an overall conclusion about U-Save's prices relative to those of its competition. You will also point out how the U-Save store pricing compares by department with the competition; and in doing so, you will note where corrective actions

TABLE 23

(Problem 46) **Prices by departments of selected items at three discount stores in Prairie City**

Departments and Items	Prices		
	U-Save	Lo-Mart	Bonus
Health and Beauty Aids			
Advil, 200 mg., 100 tablets	$ 6.99	$ 6.49	$ 6.79
Gillette Trac II cartridges, 12-pk.	5.19	4.79	4.89
Conair curling iron, 1/2 or 3/4 in.	17.49	16.19	18.09
Visine eye drops, 1/2 oz.	2.19	2.29	2.29
Colgate toothpaste, 8.2 oz.	1.79	1.88	1.99
Mabelline mascara	2.98	3.09	3.19
Ten-O-Six skin lotion	4.09	4.69	4.57
Jergens hand lotion, 10-oz.	2.39	2.59	2.45
Clairmist hair spray, 8-oz.	1.47	1.49	1.59
Mennen Speed Stick deodorant, 2¼ oz.	1.99	2.19	2.19
Head & Shoulders shampoo, 15 oz.	3.49	3.77	3.69
Ultra Slim-Fast, 15 oz.	4.99	4.89	5.09
Housewares			
Black & Decker Spacemaker can opener	27.99	27.49	29.47
Rubbermaid cleanup caddy	5.39	5.19	5.49
Anchor Hocking wine glasses, 4 pk.	9.99	10.49	10.89
Wearever cookware, 7-piece set	42.99	39.99	40.99
Old Homestead knife set, 7 piece	33.99	30.99	34.49
Roughneck trash container, 32 gal.	10.49	9.99	10.29
Hamilton Beach blender, 7 speed	19.29	18.88	19.99
Dirt Devil hand vacuum	37.49	36.99	40.29
Roll-O-Matic sponge mop	6.99	7.29	7.69
Duracell batteries, AA, 4 pk.	2.29	2.49	2.59
Proctor-Silex coffeemaker, 12 cup	15.19	14.99	15.47
Black & Decker self-cleaning iron, F-520	33.49	31.99	32.39
Hardware			
Arrow T-50 staple gun	21.39	18.99	20.97
Black & Decker drill, 3/8 in.	31.88	38.96	35.98
GE Miser Circlite, 44 watt	19.97	17.69	20.49
Stanley Workmaster hammer, 16 oz.	13.49	14.59	15.99
First Alert smoke alarm	13.97	15.49	26.89
Black & Decker scrub brusher	39.99	43.49	43.79
Skil drill, 3/8-in. cordless, 7.2 v.	131.99	129.99	130.49
Teledyne shower massage, hand-held	34.79	34.99	32.99
GM180 glue gun	4.69	4.49	4.67
Stanley screwdriver set, #64-457	4.99	4.27	4.49
Formby's tung oil, 16 oz.	7.19	6.97	7.27
Duro Tub 'n Sink Jelly, 8 oz.	2.69	2.57	2.67
Apparel			
Fruit of the Loom boys' briefs, 3 pk.	4.98	4.47	4.89
Underalls pantyhose, style 320	2.47	2.29	2.09

TABLE 23   (Problem 46)   *continued*

Departments and Items	Prices		
	U-Save	**Lo-Mart**	**Bonus**
Apparel *continued*			
Lee jeans, ladies, pepperwashed	$ 19.99	$ 19.99	$ 20.99
Levi's polo shirts, cotton-poly, men's	15.99	15.49	15.99
London Fog windbreaker, children's	15.79	16.09	15.99
Hanes tube socks, boys, 6 pr.	4.19	4.19	3.97
Greatland socks, women's, 3 pr.	4.89	4.67	4.49
Playmate panties, bikini, nylon, 3 pr.	7.19	7.47	7.29
Dappi diaper pants	5.29	5.98	5.39
Happy Kids jumpers, corduroy, 1 pc.	9.47	8.97	8.99
Henley knit tops, ladies, cotton-poly	12.47	12.95	11.99
Pretty Miss fleece jacket, cotton-poly	19.99	19.99	29.49
Automotive			
Prestone antifreeze-coolant, 1 gal.	4.99	4.89	4.99
Champion spark plugs, 8 pk., RBL 12-6	12.47	11.98	12.19
STP gas treatment, 15 oz.	1.49	1.39	1.33
Armorall car wash, 40 oz.	4.19	3.99	4.29
Schauer battery charger, 8 amp.	30.88	29.99	32.49
NuFinish liquid car polish, 16 oz.	4.89	4.29	4.49
Mobil motor oil, 10W-30, qt.	1.19	.99	.99
Fram air filter, CA 357	3.29	2.99	3.09
Monroe Gas Matic shocks	18.99	19.49	19.99
Ultra Spark plug wires, 6 cyl.	16.19	16.49	15.99
Dupont freon, R-12, 12 oz.	3.69	3.49	2.99
Scotchgard upholstery protector	6.29	6.29	5.99
Domestics			
Stevens Ultra Touch sheets, queen	29.97	28.49	28.79
Dundee Centennial towels, 27 × 54 in.	10.49	9.99	10.29
Cannon lid cover, 100% cotton	6.99	6.97	6.89
Spring Performance quilted bedspread	29.99	33.49	31.99
Crown Crafts comforter sets, full	69.99	64.99	66.99
Heirloom pillows, quilted, goose feathers, standard	20.49	20.99	21.39
Crystal bath rug, nylon, 21 × 34 in.	5.99	6.79	6.19
Lady Pepperell sheets, cotton-poly, full	7.99	8.79	7.99
American Country Classics mitt	2.79	2.97	3.09
Cannon Monticello bath towels	6.99	7.29	6.49
Spring Rain shower curtain, 70 × 72 in., vinyl lined	22.99	24.49	23.99
Tahiti mini blinds, aluminum, 23 × 42 in.	15.29	16.49	25.99
Sporting Goods			
Mountain Trek Organizer day pack	12.49	13.29	13.99
California Pro racerline skates	69.99	74.99	77.49
Atlantic Dive mask	20.49	19.99	20.49
Prince Pro tennis racquet	39.99	44.49	43.99
Wilson Tour Le driver	59.99	69.99	64.49

TABLE 23   (Problem 46)   *continued*

| | Prices | | |
Departments and Items	U-Save	Lo-Mart	Bonus
Sporting Goods *continued*			
Remington 870 12-gauge shotgun	$199.99	$212.99	$209.99
Daiwa Black Widow casting rod	17.99	20.49	20.99
Everlast polyester-cotton gym shorts	16.99	18.39	17.99
Nike gym shorts, nylon print, women's	25.47	24.99	25.99
Adidas Primo soccer ball	30.49	29.99	30.19
Ektelon Controller racquetball glove	8.99	9.99	9.79
Wilson TDJ football, youth	34.97	36.29	35.29
Photography-Electronics			
Bell South cordless telephone, #688	94.99	89.99	92.99
GE Compact Stereo, #11-2012	109.99	99.99	111.99
Magnavox VHS VCR, #VR9020	207.99	199.99	209.99
Maxell XL II blank cassette, 90 min.	9.29	8.49	8.99
Fuji 3.5 MF2HD floppy disks, 10	13.19	12.99	13.49
Casio #FX991 calculator	15.99	16.99	16.49
Sony Walkman, #WM-F2081	82.99	79.99	74.99
35-mm. color processing, 24 exp.	4.49	4.19	4.49
GE micro-cassette recorder, #3-53705	28.49	27.99	29.49
Kodak Gold Film, 35 mm., 24 exp.	3.49	3.59	3.49
Sony T-120 videotape, 2 pk.	7.17	6.88	7.09
GE microcassette answering system	39.99	41.59	40.99

need to be taken. You will use graphics wherever they are useful in communicating the important parts of your message. You will present your report in a form suitable for the occasion (a report to the president with copies for all members of the board of directors). The matter is on the agenda for the meeting of the board next month. Perhaps the board will want similar studies made in other cities.

47. Reporting community viewpoints relating to a company's policy on same-sex partners. For the past week, the citizens of Flat Rock City have been in an uproar over a decision made by their city council. For some months, Starr Computer Company, Inc., has been negotiating with the council for a tax break as an inducement to locate a major customer service center in the city. The center would employ 800 initially. In time, the number would increase to 1,700—quite an addition to a community of less than 100,000 population.

All appeared to be going well for Starr until a week ago when the matter came up for a vote. The council voted "no"—with two members supporting and three opposing. The reason: Starr's policy of extending insurance and other benefits to same-sex domestic partners. In the words of one of the council members opposing Starr, "To have voted otherwise would have been tantamount to endorsing immoral behavior." Following the vote, Starr officials announced that they would locate elsewhere unless the council reconsidered its stand.

Immediately following Starr's announcement, loud cries of protest were heard throughout the community. The local newspaper was especially critical, and some of the local politicians loudly took the city council to task. But strong support for the council's decision also were heard. Led by a coalition of local ministers, the supporters vigorously defended the council action as a "move that would preserve the morality of our community." Quickly, the citizens took sides, with neighbors against neighbors and friends against friends.

In the wake of this controversy, the city council called an emergency meeting. "Maybe we made a mistake," said Sam P. Wasson, leader of the council members opposing Starr. "Maybe we misjudged community attitudes. But I don't want to just give in to the extremists who are making most of the noise. I think we should find out what the community really thinks. Why not have a survey done on the matter. And we should do more than just find out what the majority want. We need to know where the opposition comes from—their ages, sex, incomes—even their political leanings. Their religious commitments are significant, too. I thought I knew our citizens, but with so many new families moving in, maybe things have changed."

Wasson's suggestion was quickly accepted by the other members, and in short order you, the assistant to the city manager, were given the task of conducting the survey. "You have all the city government resources at your disposal," they told you. "But work fast. You may have to sacrifice scientific correctness because of the time problem. But get for us information that will help us do the thing that is right for our community. We've told Starr that we will reconsider our decision. We have promised them a final decision by Friday of next week."

Quickly, you constructed a simple questionnaire, building it around five basic questions that appear to be the keys to the problem. To bring in information about just who thinks what, you worked in the demographics Wasson suggested (age, politics, income, etc.). Then, using personnel from the city manager's office, you conducted a telephone survey of voters. You randomly selected the people to be interviewed and think your final sample is fairly representative of the citizens of Flat Rock City. (For class purposes, you may create any additional information about methodology you may need.)

Now you have tabulated the responses and have them neatly arranged before you (Table 24). You will present them as objectively as you can even though you may have your own bias on the matter. You will present your findings and analyses in appropriate form, which means that you will include all the trappings of formality the situation justifies. Wherever it will help in communicating the report message, you will use graphics. Address the report to the city council, listing the five members by name.

48. Reporting information on how to organize and operate a recycling program to a city manager. As a research associate for Probst-Stecher Research, Inc., you have been given an interesting assignment by one of the leaders of your city. That

TABLE 24 (Problem 47) Responses to questions relating to city council's decision to deny tax abatement to Starr Computer

Responses shown by various categories of demographics: political party affiliation, church attendance, age, income and residence of respondents. (For complete wording of question, see table footnote.) All figures in percent.

| | Question 1 | | | | Question 2 | | | | |
	Approve	Mixed Feelings	Disapprove	Don't Know/ No Opinion	Oppose Tax Abatements	Oppose Domestic Partners	Oppose Both	Other Reason	Don't Know
All respondents	37	5	50	7	15	57	23	3	1
Political party identification									
Republican	47	8	39	6	12	64	17	3	2
Democrat	23	5	65	7	28	52	16	0	4
Independent/other	39	3	51	8	13	52	32	3	0
Church attendance									
Regular	45	4	43	8	10	62	24	2	1
Occasional	32	8	55	5	20	53	23	0	3
Rarely	25	3	64	8	25	50	12	6	0
Not at all	35	0	53	12	27	47	20	7	0
Sex									
Male	42	4	46	9	15	51	28	4	1
Female	33	6	55	6	16	64	16	1	1
Age									
18 to 34	27	4	56	13	16	74	11	0	0
35 to 44	37	5	53	6	15	51	23	6	4
45 to 64	39	4	49	8	15	56	25	2	0
65 and older	43	9	42	6	18	57	25	0	0
Years in Flat Rock City									
Less than 5	20	2	60	18	11	67	0	11	11
5 to 9	42	3	53	2	12	63	20	5	0
10 to 19	32	8	52	7	16	58	22	2	2
20 or more	48	3	40	9	18	49	31	0	0
Household income									
Less than $30,000	38	5	44	14	15	58	21	6	0
$30-40,000	44	9	40	7	10	71	19	0	0
$40-50,000	39	2	55	4	9	73	14	0	5
More than $50,000	30	6	57	7	26	38	26	5	2

Questions asked:

1. Do you approve or disapprove of the City Council's decision to deny tax abatements to Starr Computer Company, Inc., because Starr has a policy of extending benefits to domestic partners of their employees?

2. (If approve:) Do you approve that decision because you oppose tax abatements or because you oppose policies that recognize domestic partners?

Question 3				Question 4					Question 5				
Yes	Maybe/ Depends	No	Don't Know/No Opinion	Approve	Disapprove	No Strong Feelings	Depends	Don't Know/No Opinion	Approve	Disapprove	No Strong Feelings	Depends	Don't Know/No Opinion
51	14	28	6	9	42	43	1	5	5	47	42	1	4
42	16	33	7	4	51	37	1	6	4	58	35	1	3
63	12	21	4	11	39	46	0	5	7	39	49	0	5
51	14	29	6	12	36	47	1	4	4	44	45	2	5
48	17	29	5	4	59	33	1	4	2	63	30	1	4
53	9	34	4	14	37	45	1	3	6	41	45	2	5
61	8	22	9	11	12	70	2	5	9	20	67	0	3
49	21	23	7	19	21	47	0	14	9	33	51	0	7
49	12	33	6	9	43	44	1	4	4	51	41	1	4
54	16	24	6	9	41	43	1	6	6	44	44	1	5
54	17	23	7	23	27	39	1	10	11	35	48	0	6
51	11	32	5	10	32	50	2	5	5	43	47	3	2
55	16	27	2	5	49	43	0	3	4	52	41	0	4
40	15	29	15	2	63	32	0	3	2	65	26	0	8
58	18	16	7	11	27	58	2	2	7	38	56	0	0
51	14	30	5	8	39	47	1	5	4	46	45	2	3
59	10	28	2	12	42	41	1	4	6	48	41	1	3
36	19	32	13	6	51	36	0	7	3	52	36	0	9
43	18	31	8	11	41	42	0	6	6	49	40	0	6
53	16	29	3	10	54	30	0	6	6	56	33	0	6
57	9	30	4	2	43	52	0	4	2	48	46	0	4
54	16	24	6	10	33	51	1	5	6	41	49	1	3

3. Do you feel that the commissioners' decision will deter other businesses from relocating to Flat Rock City?

4. Do you personally approve or disapprove or have no strong feelings either way about heterosexual couples who live together outside of marriage?

5. Do you personally approve or disapprove or have no strong feelings either way about gay or lesbian couples who live together?

TABLE 25 (Problem 48) **Materials included in municipal recycling programs, 1990**

Material	Cities Reporting	Percent
Newspaper	254	96.2
Glass	248	93.9
Aluminum	233	88.3
Plastic bottles/jugs	177	67.0
Corrugated paper/cardboard	160	60.6
Scrap metals	138	52.3
Leaves, wood, brush, yard wastes	125	47.3
Waste oil	122	46.2
High grade paper	109	41.3
Mixed paper	85	32.2
Other (batteries, tin)	40	15.2
All rigid plastics	29	11.0
Chip board	17	6.4

leader is Mr. Rene Duby, city manager. Mr. Duby explained to you that the city is considering starting a recycling program in response to widespread demands expressed by the citizenry. The problem is that no one in city government knows much about recycling. So the city wants you to help.

As Duby explained the city's need, "We don't think we should proceed with something as important as this without knowing what we're doing. So we'd like for you to help us. We think we can learn from the experiences of other cities. As you know, many have such programs. So we'd like you to get the information we need from them—perhaps through a survey. Find out what they're doing—especially what items they recycle. Find out how they promote their programs—what incentives they use, if any. And if they have encountered any special problems, have them point them out for us. It would help, too, if you determined whether their programs are mandatory or voluntary. Some of my council members are wary of anything mandatory."

With Duby's words in mind, you began to plan the project. First, you constructed a simple questionnaire—one designed to get the information Duby outlined for you. Then you built a mailing list of city managers from a directory that Duby had given you. Next, you mailed the questionnaires to the people on the list. To improve responses, you used a cover letter with Duby's signature on it, and you included return envelopes with Duby's office address on them. (Of course, you did this with Duby's approval.)

After a reasonable passage of time, you collected the returned questionnaires from the city manager's office. You are well pleased with the returns. Of the 320 questionnaires you mailed, 264 were returned. Then you tabulated the responses and arranged the totals neatly in tabular form (Tables 25–29).

TABLE 26	(Problem 48) **Importance of problems in municipal recycling programs (N = 264)**

Problem	Mean Score*	Rank
Finding markets for recyclables	4.15	1
Getting residents to participate in the program	3.70	2
Lack of sufficient state grants or other financial assistance	3.50	3
Securing adequate local government financial support	3.40	4
Obtaining information/technical assistance for recycling	2.83	5
Theft of recyclables	1.76	6

* 1 = Not important; 5 = Very important.

TABLE 27	(Problem 48) **Use of incentives to increase citizen participation in recycling (N = 264)**

Incentives	Number	Percent
Official recognition of recycling efforts	89	34.5
Contests with prizes	66	25.6
Campaigns by local scouts to encourage citizens to recycle	44	17.1
Discounts or rebates on disposal fees	30	11.7
Cash awards	26	10.1
Tax credits	2	0.8
Tax exemptions	2	0.8
Incentives listed by respondents		
Peer pressure by neighbors	20	
Increasing solid waste disposal fees for the use of more than one garbage can	11	
Having school age kids encourage their parents to recycle	11	
Fines for failure to recycle	6	

Now, with the tables before you, you are ready to begin the really important part of the assignment—organizing, analyzing, and presenting the findings in meaningful report form. You will use a report form appropriate for the occasion—perhaps with all the formal prefatory trappings. And you will use attractive graphics wherever they help communicate the report information. Although you suspect the report will be read by the council members and other dignitaries at city hall, you will address it to Mr. Duby. (For class purposes, if you need additional information on methodology, you may create it as long as it is logical and consistent with the information given in the assignment.)

49. **Reporting evaluation practices of sales managers to ASM directors.** At the annual meeting of the Association for Sales Managers (ASM), the directors discussed at length various projects that could be undertaken for the benefit of the membership. They selected one: "current practices of sales managers in evaluating performance of their salespeople." It would be helpful, they agreed, if the member-

TABLE 28   (Problem 48)   **Use of public information and education strategies (N = 264)**

Strategy	Number	Percent
Pamphlets, brochures, or bumper stickers	220	84.6
Speeches by officials to schools or local groups about recycling	179	68.8
Special educational programs about recycling in the public schools	169	65.0
Free newspaper public service notices	134	51.7
Paid newspaper advertisements	121	46.7
Neighborhood or community information meetings	121	46.5
Free radio public service announcements	82	31.5
Free television public service ads	77	29.6
Window displays or posted notices in neighborhoods	75	28.8
Paid radio commercials	40	15.4
Billboard advertisements	29	11.2
Contract with advertising firm(s) for multimedia promotion campaign	21	8.1
Paid television commercials	17	6.6
No educational or promotional materials are used	7	2.7
Publicity strategies listed by respondents as being successful		
Mail-outs about recycling with utility bills	20	
Public school programs that get kids to pressure their parents to recycle	11	
Block-leader programs	6	

TABLE 29   (Problem 48)   **Participation and diversion rates by program type (N = 264)**

Program Type	Mean Participation Rate	Mean Diversion Rate
Mandatory	74.3	21.6
All voluntary	39.7	12.2
With curbside pickup	48.6	12.3
With drop-off facilities only	24.6	10.8

ship knew how their fellow members do this important work. From the discussion, it became evident that opinions and practices concerning evaluation procedures vary widely. The directors agreed it would be good if the membership knew the extent of these variations. Such information should enable most of them to do a better job.

You, the executive secretary of ASM, are the person responsible for conducting the projects the directors select. Of course, you have easy access to the membership and usually have their good cooperation. So you decided to get the information needed through a random sample of the organization's 2,877 members. You began by constructing a questionnaire designed to get the information needed. Most of what you requested in it was suggested by the directors in their discussion, but you took the liberty to fill in a few voids. You are confident you have the subject covered thoroughly.

TABLE 30	(Problem 49) **Profile of respondents**

Type of Business	Percentage
Manufacturer of industrial goods	44
Manufacturer of consumer goods	16
Wholesaler	9
Retailer	4
Services	27
Total	100
Annual Dollar Sales Volume (in 000)	
Over $100,000	46
$51,000–$100,000	12
$11,000–$50,999	27
Under $11,000	15
Total	100
Sales Management Position	
Vice president sales	3
National sales manager	4
Regional sales manager	34
Zone sales manager	6
Field sales manager	37
Other sales management titles	16
Total	100

Next you mailed the questionnaires to a randomly selected sample of 500 members. Using a follow-up "prodding" letter to those slow in responding, you got what you believe is an excellent response of 416.

With the returned questionnaires in hand, you then began the chore of tabulating the information reported. From the demographic data you requested, you constructed a profile of respondents (Table 30). This information clearly shows that your sample is representative of the makeup of the membership.

You then recorded the information indicating how many used each of the conventional bases for evaluating performance, including both output (Table 31) and input (Table 32). These data show which of the work activities of salespeople the sales managers consider meaningful.

Next you recorded the qualitative bases the executives reported they use (Table 33). Based on perception and subjective evaluation, these bases nevertheless play a vital role in evaluating salespeople. Then, you compiled the data relating to the mechanics of evaluating—specifically the sources of information used (Table 35) and the frequency of evaluations (Table 34).

Although it is not actually a part of the evaluation procedure, the question of how sales objectives are set was included in your questionnaire. So you tabulated the responses to this question (Table 36). You believe the topic belongs in the

TABLE 31 (Problem 49)   Output bases used in performance evaluation

Base	Percent Using
Sales	
Sales volume in dollars	81
Sales volume to previous year's sales	78
Sales volume by product or product line	68
Amount of new account sales	58
Sales volume in units	54
Sales volume to dollar quota	54
Sales volume by customer	49
Sales volume to market potential	34
Sales volume to physical unit quota	24
Sales volume per order	15
Sales volume by outlet type	11
Sales volume per call	10
Percentage of sales made by telephone or mail	8
Market Share	
Market share per quota	19
Accounts	
Number of new accounts	71
Number of accounts lost	43
Number of accounts on which payment is overdue	22
Number of accounts buying the full line	16
Profit	
Net profit dollars	26
Return on investment	16
Net profit contribution	14
Gross margin	14
Gross margin per sales	13
New profit as a % of sales	13
Orders	
Order-call ratio	26
Net orders per repeat order	17
Number of canceled orders per orders booked	14

report. Sales objectives serve as a guide to performance measurement. How they are developed and their fairness is a highly controversial matter with sales managers and their salespeople.

With these data recorded and reduced to percentages, you are ready to begin the task of analyzing and organizing them for presentation. Then you will present the findings in clear and precise language. Although in time your findings will be sent to the membership in a newsletter, you will present the information to the

TABLE 32   (Problem 49)   **Input bases used in performance evaluation**

Base	Percent Using
Calls	
Calls per period	57
Number of calls per number of customers (by product class)	17
Selling Expense	
Selling expense to sales	41
Selling expense to quota	22
Average cost per call	13
Ancillary Activities	
Number of required reports turned in	44
Number of customer complaints	31
Training meetings conducted	28
Number of letters/phone calls to prospects	25
Number of demonstrations conducted	25
Number of service calls made	24
Number of dealer meetings held	15
Advertising displays set up	12

TABLE 33   (Problem 49)   **Qualitative bases used in performance evaluation**

Base	Percent Using
Attitude	90
Product knowledge	89
Selling skills	85
Appearance and manner	82
Communication skills	81
Initiative and aggressiveness	80
Planning ability	78
Time management	73
Knowledge of competition	72
Judgment	69
Creativity	61
Knowledge of company policies	59
Report preparation and submission	59
Customer goodwill generated	50
Degree of respect from trade and competition	34
Good citizenship	23

TABLE 34   (Problem 49)   **Frequency of performance review**

Frequency of Review	Percentage of Respondents
Weekly	5
Monthly	8
Quarterly	28
Semiannually	26
Annually	33

TABLE 35   (Problem 49)   **Sources of information used in salesperson evaluation**

Source	Percent Using
Printed form for performance evaluation	56
Analysis of computer printouts for each territory	50
Analysis of call reports	48
Other (supervisory calls, feedback from clients)	44

TABLE 36   (Problem 49)   **Participation of salespeople in setting standards or objectives**

Participation	Percent Using
Salespeople set their own objectives with no inputs from management	0
Salespeople set their own objectives with some inputs from management	3
Salespeople and management jointly set objectives	55
Management sets objectives with some inputs from salespeople	23
Management sets objectives with no inputs from salespeople	8
No response	11

directors in a formal report. The report will include the conventional prefatory parts appropriate for this relatively formal situation. It will use graphics wherever their appearance will help to communicate the report story. Address the report to the eleven directors, listing them by name. Tanya Krall is the chair.

50. **Comparing corporate energy conservation activities in the United States, Canada, and the United Kingdom.** For today's report writing assignment, assume you are director of research for the International Association of Manufacturing (IAM). It's your job to identify, research, and report on current and critical issues affecting the 9,456 IAM members. One topic that has occupied your mind for quite some time is the energy problem and how firms are dealing with it. Now, you are determined to find out more specifics about the energy problem in industry.

| **TABLE 37** | (Problem 50) | **Critical energy problems facing firms during the next 10 years** |

| | % Identifying Problem as Critical | | |
Critical Problems	Canada (206)*	U.K. (117)*	U.S. (321)*
Cost of energy	38.0	37.2	46.3
Cost of natural gas	4.0	5.1	1.5
Cost of electricity	1.4	2.1	1.4
Cost of petroleum	3.0	1.2	1.6
Cost of other fuels	13.4	8.8	1.0
Availability of electricity	17.7	7.9	20.3
Availability of energy in general	31.6	28.2	29.9
Availability of natural gas	13.1	6.1	33.0
Availability of petroleum	3.3	3.1	11.9
Changing to alternative fuels	7.4	14.4	14.0
Government regulation of energy	3.3	3.1	11.9
Capital investment for energy utilization/conservation	11.2	9.2	5.6
Energy curtailments and cutbacks	3.4	6.9	5.3
Energy-related inflation	17.1	16.7	5.4
Energy/environmental interface	3.4	1.1	5.2
Awareness	0.2	2.1	1.0
Present situation versus future situation	0.8	0.2	1.0

*Number of firms responding to survey.

To do that, you design a research study that will give you answers to many of the questions you have. Because you believe the energy topic has international dimensions, you decide to survey not only the United States, but Canada and the United Kingdom as well. In your questionnaire, you include questions about critical energy problems facing firms in the future, whether firms have energy policy plans, the components of the plans, organization of conservation, time spent on energy conservation activities by executives, and the executives' titles.

You send this rather extensive questionnaire to a random sample of manufacturing firms in the three countries—432 in Canada, 236 in the United Kingdom, and 651 in the United States. Because of the high interest in the topic, you receive a very high return rate of 206, 117, and 321 forms, respectively. After you process and edit the returned questionnaires, you enter them into your computer and print the results as shown in Tables 37–42. Now, you are ready to analyze the results and write up the report so that it can be available to your IAM members.

The report you will write will be a long, formal one with all the trappings that the situation calls for. You will have a title fly, title page, letter of transmittal, table of contents, executive summary, and the report proper. You will write in the third person and use graphics to support the text of your analysis. Throughout your report, you will remember that the quality of your writing is no better than the quality of your thinking in the analysis of the data that will form the foundation of the report.

TABLE 38   (Problem 50)   **The corporate energy policy plan**

	Percent Response		
Issue	Canada (206)	U.K. (117)	U.S. (321)
Does your company have a formal, written corporate energy policy/plan?			
Yes	39.5	28.0	69.0
No	60.5	72.0	31.0
Total	100.0	100.0	100.0
How long has your firm had a formal, written corporate energy policy/plan?			
No. of years			
1	30.3	6.6	15.4
2	37.1	11.9	16.3
3	22.6	43.9	26.7
4	2.5	23.6	20.8
5 or more	7.5	14.0	20.8
Total	100.0	100.0	100.0
Does your firm's energy plan apply to:			
Entire company	65.0	69.4	63.8
Manufacturing facilities only	25.0	18.4	15.5
Divisions only	7.9	8.2	10.7
Individual depts. only	2.1	4.0	10.0
Total	100.0	100.0	100.0

TABLE 39   (Problem 50)   **Components of the corporate energy policy/plan**

	Percent Response		
Components	Canada	U.K.	U.S.
Formation of energy conservation committees or policy teams	85.9	82.3	82.0
Guidelines for surveying current energy consumption	93.2	98.2	97.6
Customer allocation plans to be implemented when reduced energy supplies cause product shortages	15.3	25.5	19.9
Recommendations for reducing energy consumption	93.2	99.5	93.5
Suggested systems for measuring energy savings	94.7	93.6	89.5
Addition of energy-related responsibilities to existing job descriptions	67.6	80.0	93.5

You will publish the executive summary of your report in the next issue of *Manufacturing Update* sent to all IAM members. You will offer to send the entire report to those requesting it for the cost of duplication and mailing.

Write the report that will present and compare the information about energy activities in the three countries for IAM members.

| **TABLE 40** | (Problem 50) | **Organization of energy conservation activities** |

| | Percent Response | | |
Method of Organization	Canada	U.K.	U.S.
Centralized staff department	9.9	11.6	6.7
Separate functional activity within each division	15.2	19.7	10.3
Combination of divisional and centralized activities	41.4	50.7	58.6
Other	4.9	4.3	3.5
Not specified	28.6	13.7	20.9
Total	100.0	100.0	100.0

| **TABLE 41** | (Problem 50) | **Job title of senior energy executive** |

| | Percent Response | | |
Title	Canada	U.K.	U.S.
President or CEO	5.0	—	3.0
Assistant to president/CEO	3.0	3.1	3.2
Executive VP/Senior VP/Group VP	4.5	—	2.9
Vice president	10.8	—	21.7
Director	5.3	22.3	14.4
Manager/general manager	17.5	22.3	18.4
Coordinator	5.0	15.5	6.7
Engineer	8.9	17.5	5.7
Miscellaneous	3.4	10.0	2.9
Not specified	36.6	9.3	21.1
Total	100.0	100.0	100.0

51. Determining sales potential for computers in the small business market.
"We're missing a good market with those small business people. Why don't you find out about the market so we can see whether we can sell our product to them. Write up what you find in a report on the potential of this small business market for us."

These were the words of your boss, Mr. Raul Cerniglia of Computer Sales Company. When you met with him yesterday, his message was quite clear: investigate the small business market in terms of sales potential for computers. As you ponder the "how to" of Mr. Cerniglia's charge, you, sales manager for Computer Sales Company, begin to pinpoint the specific areas of information you will need to complete your report writing assignment.

To get facts about the small business market, you decide to conduct a survey. First, you purchase a list of small businesses from QuickInfo Services, a large marketer of lists that guarantees its listings to be 95 percent accurate. Then you draw a random sample of 562 from the list of 17,817 to whom you will send a

TABLE 42   (Problem 50) **Time spent on energy conservation by senior energy executive**

	Percent Response		
Percent of Time	Canada	U.K.	U.S.
1–10	50.3	46.8	31.0
11–20	6.3	11.6	14.0
21–30	6.9	6.3	6.3
31–40	.3	0.9	2.2
41–50	4.5	4.1	7.3
51–99	4.5	6.3	6.5
100	1.0	9.8	10.5
Not specified	26.2	14.2	22.2
Total	100.0	100.0	100.0

questionnaire about small business usage of computers. You will concentrate specifically on how small businesses use marketing information because you assume that most small businesses are in the marketing segment of the economy.

Next, you design a questionnaire to send to the sample you have selected. As you structure the questions on it, you decide to focus on three main areas: (*a*) characteristics of the small business market, (*b*) use of computers for keeping specific marketing information, and (*c*) use of computers for marketing control and planning. You design specific categories in each of these three areas in the construct of your questionnaire. Then you mail the completed instrument to the 562 businesses in your sample.

It has now been three weeks since your mailing and you have received 227 usable questionnaires (a 40.4 percent return). All statistical tests plus the design of your research project indicate that you have reliable and representative results. Thus, you tally the results of your work as shown in Tables 43, 44, and 45. These tables will provide the facts for the report you will prepare for Mr. Cerniglia.

As you begin to think about the report, you determine that it will be on the formal side. Thus, you will give special attention to the wording and appearance of the report. But this special attention will not substitute for the detail of analysis you will give to the facts. You will remember that you have two purposes in your report writing project: to report the facts about computer usage in the small business market and to interpret these facts in terms of sales potential for Mr. Cerniglia. In your report, you will make good use of graphics to accent the important points of your analysis.

With these points in mind, prepare the report for Mr. Cerniglia.

52. **Investigating franchising as a possible distribution policy for SeaCatch.** As research analyst for Datamatics, you just received a call from your newest client, Eunice Zimmerman. Ms. Zimmerman has had the idea of establishing a number of sushi bars throughout the United States and Canada. Several months ago, she

TABLE 43	(Problem 51) **Usage of microcomputers for marketing control and planning**					
Information Category and Item (A)	**No Response** (B)	**N/A** (C)	**Don't Keep Info** (D)	**Info Not on Micro** (E)	**Info Is on Micro** (F)	**Use Index*** (G)
Marketing control area						
Rank product sales by volume	1.9%	38.4%	18.7%	10.0%	31.0%	3.1
Analyze sales by geographic territory	1.5	36.8	28.8	7.3	25.6	3.5
Analyze sales by type of customer	1.5	36.8	29.8	9.8	23.1	2.4
Identify profitable products	0.7	34.4	16.6	17.3	31.0	1.8
Identify profitable customers	0.7	32.8	23.3	17.7	25.5	1.4
Evaluate productivity of sales force	1.5	49.6	22.8	15.7	10.4	0.7
Evaluate effect of sales promotion	1.9	42.3	19.8	22.3	58.3	2.6
Determine best ad media	0.7	40.4	14.6	27.9	26.4	0.9
Marketing planning areas						
Determine best timing for promotion efforts	1.4	37.1	16.2	32.2	13.1	0.4
Forecasting sales	1.5	25.6	13.6	31.2	38.1	1.2
Forecasting profitability	1.5	27.7	14.6	18.4	37.8	2.1
Identifying future customers	1.4	21.5	19.8	35.2	22.1	0.6
Setting sales quotas	1.7	31.6	18.9	23.4	24.4	1.0
Pinpointing new product needs	2.9	36.8	17.2	31.8	11.3	0.4
Deciding to drop current products/vendors	2.9	37.1	12.7	30.4	16.9	0.6

*Column (F) ÷ column (E)

incorporated under the title SeaCatch, so she has a legal entity for her new business. Now she wants to know how to market the individual fast-food outlets. With the current interest in low cholesterol diets, you believe that Ms. Zimmerman has a potentially successful concept. It should prove profitable, too, given the right distribution setup.

To answer Ms. Zimmerman's questions, you began researching the marketing literature. You found that franchising is the most frequently used distribution policy for fast-food operations. Interestingly, franchising began in the United States in 1863; so it is far from a new marketing plan. Today there are more than 540,000 franchises in the United States that employ more than 7.2 million people in 60 different industries. Sales for last year exceeded 758.5 billion, and the top foreign markets for franchises are Canada, Japan, and Europe.

Armed with this background information, you now decide to investigate the idea of franchising in more detail. Because of the widespread use of franchising, mailing lists of both franchisors and franchisees are readily available. You purchase one for fast-food convenience outlets in North America (7,214 franchisors; 15,635 franchisees) from Infomart, Inc. To both of these groups, you intend to send a questionnaire about franchise operations. In particular, you will ask questions about royalty and advertising fees; successful franchisee characteristics;

| TABLE 44 | (Problem 51) **Characteristics of respondents** |

Characteristic	Frequency	Percent
Industry		
Agricultural, fisheries, forestry	3	0.3
Transportation	3	0.3
Manufacturing durable goods	15	7.2
Utilities	5	2.3
Retail trade	35	11.2
Insurance	8	3.5
Nonprofit	9	4.1
Entertainment	15	6.6
Business and repair services	46	22.3
Mining	3	0.6
Communications	21	10.4
Manufacturing nondurable goods	7	4.9
Wholesale trade	6	2.8
Real estate	7	3.2
Financial services	12	5.4
Education/training	11	5.0
Personal services	21	9.9
Total	227	100.0
Position of respondent		
Owner	158	69.6
Manager	13	5.7
Marketing manager	2	0.9
Sales manager	1	0.4
General manager	13	5.7
Data processing manager	2	0.9
President	25	11.0
Vice president—marketing	9	4.0
Other	4	1.8
Total	227	100.0
Number of full-time employees		
No response	2	0.3
1–19	205	89.7
20–99	17	9.5
100–250	3	0.5
Total	227	100.0
Gender		
No response	3	0.5
Female	59	20.7
Male	165	78.8
Total	227	100.0
Last year's gross sales volume		
No response	3	3.7
Under $100,000	137	41.3
$100,000 to $249,999	39	18.2
$250,000 to $499,999	22	14.9
$500,000 to $1.0 million	11	9.2
$1.0 million to $1.5 million	9	6.8
$1.5 million to $2.0 million	6	5.9
Total	227	100.0

| TABLE 45 | (Problem 51) Use of microcomputers for keeping specific marketing information |

Information Category and Item (A)	No Response (B)	N/A (C)	Don't Keep Info (D)	Info Not on Micro (E)	Info Is on Micro (F)	Use Index* (G)
Customer information						
Name, address, telephone, etc.	0.2%	4.7%	2.7%	15.9%	76.5%	4.8
Classification (age, gender, type of business)	2.3	19.5	20.6	11.5	46.1	4.0
Credit rating	4.6	41.5	29.6	9.9	14.4	1.5
Purchase history	4.2	25.1	14.3	14.2	42.2	2.8
Product attribute preference (color, size, brand name, etc.)	4.6	43.3	18.9	6.0	27.2	4.5
Sales information						
Gross sales	0.7	14.2	3.4	16.1	65.6	4.1
Sales by product line	2.8	34.4	7.4	16.1	39.3	2.4
Sales by product item	4.2	36.7	8.6	16.2	34.3	2.1
Name of customer	1.2	10.4	1.4	13.1	73.9	5.6
Location of customer	1.2	10.3	3.4	10.0	75.1	7.5
Type of customer	3.2	24.7	9.9	7.8	70.0	9.0
Date of sale	1.7	14.0	3.9	17.6	62.8	3.6
Method of payment	1.6	25.9	14.5	17.7	40.3	2.3
Returned orders	2.4	50.9	7.9	17.6	21.2	1.2
Unfilled orders	2.9	55.6	6.4	15.2	19.9	1.3
Order cycle time	2.3	58.8	7.8	7.4	26.7	3.6
Names of salespersons	1.2	54.4	9.9	10.0	24.5	2.5
Inventory information						
Inventory on hand	0.7	48.7	3.9	17.6	29.1	1.7
Inventory on hand by product line	3.4	55.0	10.8	13.6	17.2	1.3
Inventory on hand by product item	1.7	60.2	7.0	12.7	18.4	1.4
Location of inventory	3.7	62.3	6.6	15.9	11.5	0.7
Date of inventory acquisition	1.2	55.6	10.8	17.6	14.8	0.8
Marketing costs						
Product (invoice) costs	2.3	29.4	5.6	15.7	47.0	3.0
Fixed marketing costs	1.3	35.4	3.2	14.9	45.2	3.0
Advertising expenses	1.2	23.4	1.8	18.0	55.6	3.0
Personal selling expenses	2.3	32.4	2.9	22.3	44.1	2.0
Sales promotion expenses	2.3	45.4	4.3	15.4	32.6	2.1
Packaging	3.2	57.6	9.7	17.6	11.9	0.7
Shipping	1.9	39.4	5.4	15.0	38.3	2.6
Theft/losses	2.9	52.2	7.7	12.2	18.6	1.5
Misc. (e.g., marketing research)	5.9	46.8	9.4	14.9	23.0	1.5

*Column (F) ÷ column (E).

TABLE 46   (Problem 52) **Royalty and advertising fees for franchises**

Royalty Range (as % of sales)	% Franchisees Reporting	% Franchisors Reporting
None	20	13
0–3%	7	8
3–6%	39	59
6–9%	26	16
More than 9%	8	4

Advertising Fee Range (as % of sales)	% Franchisees Reporting	% Franchisors Reporting
None	14	22
0–2%	41	30
2–4%	26	11
More than 4%	17	1
Negotiated	—	36

TABLE 47   (Problem 52) **Importance of characteristics required for success as viewed by franchisees and franchisors, in percentages**

Characteristic	Franchisees			Franchisors		
	Very Important	Important	Not Very Important	Very Important	Important	Not Very Important
Support from family	54	26	20	48	30	22
Strong people skills	65	30	5	66	32	2
Financial backing	73	25	2	69	25	6
Creativity	28	55	18	14	42	44
Willingness to work hard	94	6	0	95	4	1
Management ability	86	13	1	95	5	0
Desire to succeed	92	8	0	95	4	1
Previous experience in own business	14	44	42	18	45	37
Previous management experience in same industry	2	18	80	4	12	84

franchising advantages; initial ongoing services provided by franchisor/franchisee; and issues covered by a franchise agreement. Because regulatory laws differ by country, you will inquire also about areas where government regulation is needed in Canada.

From this preliminary thinking, you design a questionnaire instrument to measure the perceptions of a random sample of each group in the mailing list you purchased. (Assume that the procedure you use will give you reliable and representative findings.) The results from your survey are complete, and they are neatly tallied and arranged as shown in Tables 46–52.

TABLE 48   (Problem 52) **Advantages of franchising**

Advantage	Percentage of Franchisees Agreeing	Percentage of Franchisors Agreeing
You can develop a franchise more quickly than an independent business	90	84
You can make more money in a franchise than in an independent operation	49	45
A franchise offers the benefit of a known trade name	95	97
A franchise offers a proven business formula	81	97
A franchise offers more independence than salaried employment	90	81
A franchise is less risky than an independent business	76	86

TABLE 49   (Problem 52) **Initial services provided by franchisor and franchisee and degree of satisfaction with each**

Service	Franchisee Response				Franchisor Response			
	% Providing	Degree of Satisfaction %			% Providing	Degree of Satisfaction %		
		High	Med	Low		High	Med	Low
Market survey	66	35	43	28	81	61	41	5
Site selection	74	50	41	15	87	78	23	5
Lease negotiation	68	44	38	22	79	69	31	6
Store design	76	54	36	16	89	83	19	4
Management training programs	87	38	44	24	96	72	26	8
Operating manuals	91	47	40	19	95	66	33	5
Recognized trademark	98	76	24	4	99	72	26	6
Franchise financing	38	44	33	29	34	54	22	30
Equipment package	61	45	48	13	78	68	33	5

It is now your job to use these facts in a report directed to Ms. Zimmerman. The report will be a formal one in wording and physical appearance. More importantly, however, you will need to present the facts about franchising and interpret them in such a way as to relate to the distribution problems of SeaCatch. To interpret the data, you will need graphics to supplement your words.

Prepare the long, formal report about franchising for your client, Eunice Zimmerman.

53. **Interpreting how company administrators view people.** It's been 10 years since you last conducted a training seminar for Professional Software Company managers on human relations skills. But Julius Vanzant, president of Professional Software, believes that now is the time to offer one again. As he tells you, the vice president for human resources at Professional Software: "When I was head of production 10 years ago, I completely changed my management philosophy be-

TABLE 50	(Problem 52) **Ongoing services provided by franchisor and franchisee and degree of satisfaction with each**

| | Franchisee Response | | | | Franchisor Response | | | |
| | | Degree of Satisfaction % | | | | Degree of Satisfaction % | | |
Service	% Providing	High	Med	Low	% Providing	High	Med	Low
Advertising & promotion	95	37	43	26	99	52	36	15
Bookkeeping	33	26	46	34	36	39	50	17
Centralized purchasing	63	54	30	22	76	55	36	15
Operating assistance	66	28	42	36	99	60	38	2
Marketing research	60	33	51	23	61	48	42	16
Information bulletin	86	43	46	17	84	54	42	16
Inventory control	39	44	35	27	59	57	38	21

TABLE 51	(Problem 52) **Issues covered by franchise agreement**

Issue	Percentage of Franchisors Reporting	Percentage of Franchisees Reporting
Supply purchase	89	82
Quality control	94	78
Competing business	84	89
Renewal clause	83	84
Termination clause	98	95
Territory restrictions	92	77
Approved suppliers	80	71

cause of the training. It made me look at people differently. And I needed that back then. I think that others need it now as well. As I remember, we did a survey and based our Professional Software program on the results. Maybe you could repeat that process before we plan the seminars this time around.''

Back in your office, you begin searching the files for the survey that Mr. Vanzant referred to. You have been with the company only seven years; but the training and development department reports directly to you. So you ask them to help in the search of their records, too. It doesn't take long for you to find the survey completed 10 years ago.

The file on the survey that you locate indicates a relatively straightforward design to determining executive attitudes toward people and their behavior. First, there are questions about general behavior of people followed by questions about people's preferences for responsibility, leadership, change, and receptivity. Both of these sets of questions are phrased in multiple-choice format. In addition, there

TABLE 52   (Problem 52)   **Areas where government regulation is needed in Canada**

Issue	Percentage of Franchisors Reporting	Percentage of Franchisees Reporting
Length of term renewals	31	23
Terminations	56	50
Renewals	43	38
Suppliers	26	31
Territory restrictions	42	30
No regulations needed	64	72
Disclosure	74	88
Tying purchase arrangements	36	52

are nine true/false questions that seek additional opinions about people's behavioral disposition. All told, 267 respondents from a total mailing of 658 replied to the survey 10 years ago (a 40.6 percent return rate).

Because you believe the design is a good one, you decide to use the same format in the survey you will conduct this year. There will be one difference, however—the addition of various demographics that will tell you about the respondents. To begin the study, you purchase a mailing list of managers from throughout the United States and Canada from Datamatics, Inc. From this list, you stratify a sample of 1,870 to reflect the demographics of age, span of control, experience, type of organization, and level of management. Then you send the questionnaire along with a cover letter to the managers in the sample.

Today, you have 751 returns (a 40.2 percent return rate); the results of the surveys are tallied in Table 53. You will use the results as the basis for a report to Mr. Vanzant. You will also use conventional long report format. In the report, you will need to compare many relationships—the results 10 years ago with those for this year as well as the differences between Canada and U.S. managers. You will derive conclusions with a human relations training program in mind. Throughout the report, you will need to use graphics to support the text.

Write the report for Mr. Vanzant.

54. **Determining Whether Gifts/Entertainment Will Stimulate Sales At Leander Industries.** Today's assignment finds you working as research specialist for Solution Research, Inc. After working with the company for five years, you know that hard work and clear thinking are the keys to producing good results for clients. And these characteristics are the underpinnings of effective reports too. You will need them both in the long report you are going to prepare for Leander Industries.

Solution Research has been retained to conduct a survey for Leander, which is considering using gifts and entertainment to stimulate lagging sales. This client is convinced that a strong connection exists between these two variables—sales

| **TABLE 53** | (Problem 53) **Attitudes toward people and their behavioral dispositions** | | | |

	10 Years Ago (Total) 267	This Year (U.S.) 458	This Year (Canada) 293	This Year (Total) 751
Part I				
The behavior of most people in general is most influenced by				
a. economic factors	7%	3%	4%	3%
b. social factors	5	7	5	6
c. a combination of social, economic, psychological, and biological factors	88	90	91	91
Most people naturally tend to be most concerned with				
a. the desire to help others	1	1	1	1
b. their own needs and desires	77	77	77	77
c. a combination of both	22	22	22	22
Most people				
a. have no ambition	1	1	1	1
b. have a lot of ambition	18	13	29	20
c. fall somewhere between the extremes	81	86	69	79
What is your opinion about the brightness of people?				
a. people in general are very bright	17	14	14	14
b. people in general are not very bright	8	4	13	8
c. people in general fall between these extremes	75	82	73	78
Part II				
How do most people react when given responsibility?				
a. they prefer to assume a great deal of responsibility	25%	19%	18%	19%
b. they dislike responsibility	22	19	34	27
c. they fall between the extremes	53	62	48	54
Most people				
a. prefer to be leaders	20	14	27	19
b. prefer to be followers	37	41	41	41
c. fall between the extremes	43	45	32	40
Most people				
a. tend to resist change	85	86	81	84
b. welcome change	1	0	2	1
c. fall between the extremes	14	14	17	15
Most people				
a. are very gullible	30	19	33	25
b. are very hardheaded	7	5	16	9
c. fall between the extremes	63	76	51	66
Part III: True / False				
a. Behavior of people is influenced by psychological, social, biological, and economic factors	95% / 5	94% / 6	98% / 2	96% / 4

TABLE 53 (Problem 53) *continued*	10 Years Ago (Total) 267	This Year (U.S.) 458	This Year (Canada) 293	This Year (Total) 751
Part III: *continued* True / False				
b. People want to do what's right, but are blocked by their personalities, childhood experiences, and circumstances beyond their control	83 / 17	71 / 29	89 / 11	78 / 22
c. People tend to be concerned about their own needs and objectives	96 / 4	92 / 8	91 / 9	91 / 9
d. Some people lack ambition, dislike responsibility, and prefer to be led, some are the opposite, and most fall somewhere in between	73 / 27	88 / 12	82 / 18	85 / 15
e. People tend to be resistant to change	97 / 3	97 / 3	91 / 9	94 / 6
f. People are gullible at first but most catch on quickly	58 / 42	70 / 30	70 / 30	70 / 30
g. People are not very bright	12 / 88	8 / 92	20 / 80	12 / 88
h. People easily fall prey to charlatans & demagogues	34 / 66	25 / 75	41 / 59	31 / 69
i. Most people are bright enough	67 / 33	88 / 12	81 / 19	85 / 15
Part IV				
Your age:				
a. under 25	—	1%	4%	2%
b. 25–35	—	25	42	32
c. 36–45	—	35	32	34
d. over 45	—	39	22	32
No. of persons reporting to you directly:				
a. 1–3	—	40	26	34
b. 4–6	—	23	34	28
c. 7–12	—	20	18	19
d. 13 or more	—	17	22	19
No. of years you have managed people:				
a. 1–3	—	18	27	21
b. 4–6	—	16	22	19
c. 7–10	—	17	24	20
d. 11 or more	—	49	27	40
Your type of enterprise:				
a. finance	—	8	5	7
b. commercial	—	7	13	9

| | **TABLE 53** | (Problem 53) *concluded* | | | | |

	10 Years Ago (Total) 267	This Year (U.S.) 458	This Year (Canada) 293	This Year (Total) 751
Part IV *continued*				
c. health services	—	2	2	2
d. government	—	7	0	4
e. manufacturing	—	48	42	46
f. high-technology	—	10	12	10
g. other businesses	—	16	20	18
h. other institutional	—	2	6	4
Your organizational level:				
a. top (report to or are the top manager)	—	26	28	26
b. middle (if not a or c)	—	60	53	58
c. 1st level (directly supervise nonmanagement)	—	14	19	16

Country of which I am a citizen
U.S., 59%; Non-U.S., 41% of this year total

Country where I live presently
U.S., 61%; Non-U.S., 39% of this year total

Country in which I was born
U.S., 57%; Non-U.S., 43% of this year total

and gifts/entertainment expense. Moreover, they believe that more aggressive giving and entertaining behavior will produce a more aggressive sales effort for potential customers. Before they move operationally on these ideas, however, they need more facts about gifts and entertainments so they can design appropriate policies to guide promotion strategy. And that's where you enter the picture.

In order to get Leander the facts they need, you designed a questionnaire and pretested it. The instrument itself contained gifts/entertainment activities and a five-point rating scale asking respondents to assess each one of the activities based on how important the activity was in successful selling. Also, you asked for selected demographics of respondents.

After making adjustments based on the pretest, you mailed the questionnaire to 850 salespersons drawn from a larger list of 4,500 names that you purchased from a mailing list broker. Both the 4,500 and 850 names were randomly selected and represented different industries throughout the United States.

From the initial mailing, you have received 210 returned usable questionnaires—a 24.71 percent response. Of these 210 returns, 147 (70 percent) were from industrial salespersons and 63 (30 percent) from consumer salespersons. For the study, you defined industrial salespeople as those who sold to other businesses for business purposes and consumer salespeople as those who sold to consumers for personal use.

TABLE 54   (Problem 54)   **Products sold by salespeople**

Product	Frequency
Consumer products	23
Automotive	20
Real estate	19
Business supplies	15
Food products	14
Industrial products	13
Electrical supplies	10
Pharmaceuticals/medical	8
Advertising	7
Paper products	7
Building materials	6
Agricultural chemicals	6
Ladies' apparel	6
Computers	5
Petroleum products	5
Investments	5
Hardware	4
Alcoholic beverages	4
Fire apparatus	3
Shipping containers	3
Telecommunications	3
Men's apparel	3
Insurance	3
Transportation	3
Graphic arts	2
Sporting goods	2
Printing	2
Trucking	2
Storage	2
Tobacco	1
Home improvement	1
Scientific	1
Cable TV	1
Educational careers	1
Total	210

After tallying and editing the results, you now have them arranged for your analysis and interpretations. As shown in Tables 54, 55, and 56, the demographics of the respondents should tell you specifics about their background, customers, and selling efforts in general. More important to your study, however, are those facts shown in Table 57. Here you have the ratings the respondents gave to the gifts/entertainment activities, per se. These facts are the ones that will provide the meat of your analysis.

TABLE 55   (Problem 54)   **Years of selling experience**

Years	Number	%
1	62	29.5
2–4	24	11.4
5–9	18	8.6
10 or more	99	47.2
No answer	7	3.3
Total	210	100.0

TABLE 56   (Problem 54)   **Primary customers**

Type	Number	%
Final consumers	63	30.0
Business manufacturers	4	1.9
Business wholesalers	2	1.0
Industrial distributors	2	1.0
Businesses	135	64.2
No answer	4	1.9
Total	210	100.0

Now, you must analyze the data and present them in a meaningful report to Leander Industries. Your report will be on the long side of the physical format continuum—title fly, title page, table of contents, executive summary plus report proper. Also, you will need graphics to help tell the story. Your report will include recommendations for the use of gifts/entertainment at Leander.

Address the report to Ms. Tracey Hebranson at Leander Industries. You will write the report formally without first and second person pronouns.

55. **Constructing a patient profile for Addicare.** As an independent researcher specializing in survey research, you have been hired by Addicare, a drug treatment facility. Addicare offers inpatient treatment to substance abuse clients for 60 days. The program is holistic in that it treats the total person—physically, emotionally, psychologically, socially, etc. Located in a large metropolitan area, the facility handles referrals from area hospitals, physicians, and businesses through employee assistance programs.

Erwin Schweers, the chief administrator at Addicare, wants to know how successful the drug rehabilitation product that Addicare offers truly is. On the surface, you have enough patients entering the program to make operations profitable. And referrals seem to be continuing at consistent to slightly increasing rates. From a short run and tactical view, the facility seems to be effective.

But from a longer run behavior change vantage point, Addicare wants to know the success of the facility in terms of rehabilitation (i.e., do people quit their

TABLE 57	(Problem 54) **General importance and differences between consumer and industrial salespeople concerning gift/entertainment activities**

Gift/Entertainment Item	Overall Average*	Consumer Average*	Industrial Average*
Taking a client to lunch	3.51	2.86	3.57
Taking a client to dinner (evening)	3.30	2.91	3.30
Taking a client to breakfast	2.96	2.68	3.11
Giving a client free product samples for personal use	2.85	2.74	2.85
Playing golf with a client and paying the client's way	2.84	2.70	2.91
Paying a client's travel expenses to visit a product demonstration	2.74	2.62	2.80
Giving a client a work-related gift (i.e., desk pen set)	2.55	2.47	2.61
Buying a client alcoholic beverages at a cocktail lounge	2.51	2.21	2.64
Playing tennis with a client and paying the client's way	2.50	2.54	2.48
Inviting a client to your home for entertainment purposes	2.35	2.26	2.31
Taking a client to a sporting event	2.28	1.94	2.39
Playing handball with a client and paying the client's way	2.22	2.15	2.22
Taking a client to a night club show	2.13	1.99	2.13
Inviting a client to a private party	2.10	2.29	1.99
Taking a client to a cultural event (i.e., theater)	1.97	1.99	1.95
Giving a client a non-work-related gift (i.e., golf bag)	1.95	1.67	2.00
Providing a client with lodging	1.94	2.04	1.88
Giving a client a recreational trip	1.77	1.66	1.74
Providing a client with social companionship	1.75	1.77	1.70
Providing a client with a car to use	1.53	1.95	1.33
Taking a client to a movie	1.46	1.64	1.35
Giving a client a monetary gift	1.37	1.44	1.31

*1 = not important; 5 = very important

drug habits after treatment, for how long, at what price, and such). In order to help answer these questions about program effectiveness, you were retained to construct a profile of drug patients to serve as a guide to the facility's staff. The guide could be used for training other staff members, identifying program strengths and weaknesses, improving on services offered, pinpointing needed treatment areas, and the like. It is a logical follow-up to the usual financial and market data that often are used to assess organizational success.

To address these longer run issues of treatment success, you prepared an extensive questionnaire and sent it to 725 patients whom Addicare had served over the past five years. Your cover letter to the questionnaire invited the patients to participate in the study on an anonymous basis. The questionnaire which accompanied the letter was designed to capture patients' perceptions of different dimensions of the program's success. More specifically, you wanted to know how often patients used drugs at the beginning of their treatment, after one year from the program, and between one and two years. These before-after measures you hoped would give you the long-term measures of program success you needed.

| **TABLE 58** | (Problem 55) | **Drug usage at beginning of program treatment** |

Usage	Cocaine	Alcohol	Marijuana
More than once a day	31.5%	17.0	14.0
Once a day	14.6	19.2	12.3
2–6 days/week	30.3	33.4	15.5
Once a week	10.1	12.8	13.1
2–3 times/month	3.5	4.4	6.2
Once a month	1.8	3.3	10.6
Less than once a month	1.7	2.7	8.5
Never (not using now)	3.6	6.6	19.2

| **TABLE 59** | (Problem 55) | **Cocaine usage at three time periods** |

Usage	Beginning of Treatment	Within 1 Year	1 to 2 Years
More than once a day	31.5%	2.4%	.5%
Once a day	14.6	.2	.4
2–6 days/week	30.3	4.1	4.0
Once a week	10.1	1.9	.3
2–3 times/month	3.5	2.8	.3
Once a month	1.8	3.2	.3
Less than once a month	1.7	12.2	6.8
Never (not using now)	3.6	75.6	88.9

In addition, you asked questions about various patient symptoms before and after treatment as well. And you asked about patient attitudes about drug use and changes in quality of life. These specific parts of success formed the basis of your approach to determining the long-run effectiveness of Addicare's program.

Today you have received 350 usable returns (48.38 percent). To assure that the returns were representative, you telephoned selectively some of the nonresponding patients. A majority of them could not be located—a typical expectancy given the nature of the problem. The ones you did contact, however, indicated they had forgotten to respond. When questioned by phone, they confirmed generally the results you obtained through the usable returns. These official results, presented in Tables 58 to 70, will provide the facts for a long formal report you will prepare for Addicare. Because the results are extensive, you will need to organize them logically before you interpret them. Also, you will need to use graphics to convey the findings. Prepare the report for Addicare. It will include the prefatory dressings of title fly, title page, table of contents, and executive summary before the actual report. You will write the report in third person to give it a tone of formality that the situation demands. Your report should do more than

TABLE 60   (Problem 55)   **Alcohol usage at three time periods**

Usage	Beginning of Treatment	Within 1 Year	1 to 2 Years
More than once a day	17.0%	2.7%	2.3%
Once a day	19.2	5.9	2.2
2–6 days/week	33.4	9.1	17.0
Once a week	12.8	8.4	10.3
2–3 times/month	4.4	17.7	6.6
Once a month	3.3	5.9	15.8
Less than once a month	2.7	7.5	14.6
Never (not using now)	6.6	43.4	33.2

TABLE 61   (Problem 55)   **Marijuana usage at three time periods**

Usage	Beginning of Treatment	Within 1 Year	1 to 2 Years
More than once a day	14.0%	2.3%	1.9%
Once a day	12.3	3.6	.5
2–6 days/week	15.5	5.2	2.6
Once a week	13.1	5.6	2.1
2–3 times/month	6.2	3.6	4.1
Once a month	10.6	2.7	2.2
Less than once a month	8.5	10.5	6.3
Never (not using now)	19.2	68.2	81.7

recite the facts. It should relate the facts to the evaluation of the treatment program of Addicare.

56. **Solving a problem on your campus.** (Requires research) Certain problems exist on many college campuses. At least, they exist in the minds of many of the faculty, students, and staff. From the following list of such problems, select one that you think needs attention at your college:

Library operation

Campus security

Policies on sales of tickets to athletic events

Regulation of social activities

Student government

Registration procedure

Faculty-student relations

Orientation program for freshmen

| TABLE 62 | (Problem 55) **Caffeinated coffee usage at three time periods** |

Usage	Beginning of Treatment	Within 1 Year	1 to 2 Years
More than once a day	33.8%	23.1%	26.8%
Once a day	23.6	10.8	20.2
2–6 days/week	12.5	7.7	8.9
Once a week	7.7	5.6	4.1
2–3 times/month	3.5	4.0	.3
Once a month	2.6	.5	0.0
Less than once a month	2.9	2.7	2.2
Never (not using now)	12.0	44.3	37.1

| TABLE 63 | (Problem 55) **Nicotine usage at three time periods** |

Usage	Beginning of Treatment	Within 1 Year	1 to 2 Years
More than once a day	45.2%	52.1%	43.8%
Once a day	16.0	.7	2.2
2–6 days/week	5.5	2.6	2.2
Once a week	1.8	.9	.2
2–3 times/month	.9	1.9	4.3
Once a month	1.6	.2	.1
Less than once a month	1.3	.5	0.0
Never (not using now)	26.5	38.4	47.1

Curriculum improvement

Increasing enrollments

Scholastic honesty

Campus crime

Improving cultural atmosphere on campus

Class attendance policies

Scholastic probation policies

Parking, traffic control

Grade inflation

Student government

Emphasis on athletics

Campus beautification

Fire prevention

Computer facilities

Bookstore operation

TABLE 64   (Problem 55)   **Physical symptoms at three time periods**

Symptom	Beginning of Treatment	Within 1 Year	1 to 2 Years
Loss of energy	37.6%	13.8%	4.6%
Physical deterioration	31.2	9.6	2.5
Sinus problems	24.1	13.1	12.1
Insomnia	21.8	10.8	2.8
Headaches	20.9	8.3	6.1
General health failure	16.3	6.8	2.5
Heart palpitations	13.8	6.5	2.3
Lost sex drive	13.5	6.2	4.5
Sore throat	13.1	7.6	4.2
Shaking	13.0	4.3	2.2

TABLE 65   (Problem 55)   **General psychological symptoms at three time periods**

Symptom	Beginning of Treatment	Within 1 Year	1 to 2 Years
Depression	40.0%	25.6%	14.3%
Irritability	38.3	22.1	16.2
Anxiety	37.8	26.3	8.8
Fears	28.1	16.8	6.5
Paranoia	26.6	8.1	4.2
Concentration problems	27.3	12.2	6.3
Loss of interest in friends	26.1	5.8	6.2
Loss of interest in nondrug activities	25.6	3.3	4.4
Memory problems	24.4	14.8	10.4
Suspiciousness	21.8	7.8	4.4

You will first gather all the significant facts regarding the problem you select. When you are thoroughly acquainted with them, you will gather authoritative opinions concerning the solution. Obtaining such information may involve looking through bibliographic sources to find out what has been done on other campuses. It may involve interviewing people on campus who are attempting to deal with the problem. Next you will carefully analyze your program in light of all you have learned about it. Then you will develop a solution to the problem.

To make the situation appear realistic, place yourself in the proper role at your school. Write a formal report, with all the conventional prefatory parts. Address the report to the appropriate administrator.

TABLE 66   (Problem 55) **States of mind about drug use at three time periods**

State of Mind	Beginning of Treatment	Within 1 Year	1 to 2 Years
Think I am addicted	43.5%	31.6%	9.8%
Feel I cannot refuse drug/s of choice	39.9	9.8	8.1
Feel loss of control over drug use	38.5	8.1	6.5
Feel like binge using	34.2	4.0	4.3
Feel unable to stop using drugs	33.6	7.3	8.2
Prefer drugs to food	30.5	7.5	4.1
Feel a real need for drugs	29.5	11.5	4.7
Prefer drugs to family activities	28.3	5.7	2.2
Fear of being discovered as a user	28.0	8.6	2.2
Feel depressed when using	27.2	8.5	2.1

TABLE 67   (Problem 55) **Social symptoms about drug use at three time periods**

Social Symptom	Beginning of Treatment	Within 1 Year	1 to 2 Years
I miss work due to my drug use	41.9%	9.1%	.5%
I make excuses due to my drug use	39.9	7.5	2.6
Other people object to my drug use	33.3	9.6	4.7
There is fighting or arguing due to my drug use	31.5	9.5	4.5
My spouse objects to my drug use	30.5	9.3	4.1
I borrow money due to my drug use	28.2	4.0	.5
I have used 50% or more of my savings due to my drug use	26.3	7.6	2.2
I am in debt due to my drug use	25.4	12.8	6.1
Breakup of my family is threatened due to drug use	24.2	8.8	4.3
I have no money left due to my drug use	22.2	4.4	4.2

57. **Determining what business will be like in the months ahead.** (Requires research) Roland A. Anderson, president of Northern Lights Energy Company, has assigned you, his assistant, to write a consensus business forecast for presentation at next Wednesday's meeting of the board of directors. Northern Lights, an oil and gas exploration company, does not employ an economist; Anderson does not believe in such frills. "Why should we pay for one," he says, "when the current business periodicals give us free forecasts by all the leading economists?"

Since Anderson's instructions were—as usual—quite vague, much of what you do will depend on your good judgment. All Anderson said was that he wanted you to survey the predictions of the leading economic forecasters for the months ahead and to present your findings in a clear and meaningful report to the board. And he wanted the forecasts consolidated—that is, he did not want

TABLE 68   (Problem 55)   **Goals about future drug use at three time periods**

Goals	Beginning of Treatment	Within 1 Year	1 to 2 Years
Don't know	2.2%	1.2%	2.8%
100% clean	67.1	75.4	70.2
Continue alcohol, cocaine, and/or marijuana	6.4	1.8	0.0

TABLE 69   (Problem 55)   **Long-term attitude changes about drug use at two time periods**

Changes in attitudes	Within 1 Year	1 to 2 Years
No change	3.1%	.3%
Change:		
Want more drugs	1.2	0.0
Want less	11.5	4.8
Don't want	27.1	60.2
Other specific changes	59.6	35.2
(Increased awareness of negative effects of drugs; lowered tolerance of other drug users; increased awareness of one's own addiction)		

TABLE 70   (Problem 55)   **Changes in quality of life measures at two time periods**

Changes	Within 1 Year		1 to 2 Years	
	Better	Much Better	Better	Much Better
In emotions	12.7%	62.1%	22.0%	66.7%
In social life	11.9	52.2	22.1	46.7
In family life	12.9	55.1	26.6	61.3
In energy level	17.8	58.1	7.9	89.1
In eating habits	15.5	56.0	28.8	46.7
In sleep patterns	7.7	65.7	12.5	71.2

a mere succession of individual forecasts. Your report, covering the entire economy, will, of course, be largely general in nature. But you will give special emphasis to forecasts pertaining to the oil and gas industry.

The report will be in a form appropriate for the board. Because the board members will want to get at the most important material quickly, be sure to include a fast-moving executive summary. Address the report to President Anderson, who also chairs the board.

Topic Suggestions for Intermediate-Length and Long Reports

Following are suggestions for additional report problems ranging from the simple to the highly complex. You can convert them into realistic business problems by supplying details and/or adapting them to real-life business situations. For most of these problems, you can obtain the needed information through library research. The topics are arranged by business field, although many of them cross fields.

☐ Accounting

1. Report on current depreciation accounting practices and recommend depreciation accounting procedures for Company X.

2. Design an inventory control system for X Company.

3. Report to Company X executives on how tax court decisions handed down over the past six months will affect their firm.

4. What security measures should Company X take with access to its accounting data?

5. Advise the managers of X Company on the accounting problems that they can anticipate when the company begins overseas operations.

6. Analyze break-even analysis as a decision-making tool for X Company.

7. Explain to potential investors which sections in Company X's most recent annual report they should review most carefully.

8. Analyze the relative effects on income of the FIFO and LIFO methods of inventory valuation during a prolonged period of inflation.

9. Write a report for the American Accounting Association on the demand for accountants with computer systems training.

10. Develop for accounting students at your college information that will help them choose between careers in public accounting and careers in private accounting.

11. Advise the management of X Company on the validity of return on investment as a measure of performance.

12. Report on operations research as a decision-making tool for accountants and managers.

13. Report to the management of X Company on trends in the content and design of corporate annual reports.

14. Report to an association of accountants the status of professional ethics in accounting.

15. Report to management of X Company on the communication skills important to accounting.

16. Advise the founders of new Company X on income tax considerations in the selection of a form of business organization.

17. Review for Company X the pros and cons of installing a computerized accounting system.

☐ GENERAL BUSINESS

18. Evaluate the adequacy of current college programs for developing business leadership.

19. Which business skills should schools and colleges teach, and which should companies teach?

20. What should be the role of business leaders in developing courses and curricula for business schools?

21. Examine and report on the current status of education for business.

22. How does business assess the content and quality of college-level business education?

23. Report on the advisability of including business internships in a business degree program.

24. What images of business and businesspersons do current business textbooks convey?

25. How does today's business community regard the Master of Business Administration degree?

26. Evaluate the contribution that campus business and professional clubs make to business education.

27. How effective is computer-based training in education for business?

28. Should education for business be specialized, or should it provide a generalized, well-rounded education?

☐ LABOR

29. For the executives of the National Association of Manufacturers (or some such group), report on the outlook for labor-management relations in the next 12 months.

30. For the officers of a major labor union, research and report progress toward decreasing job discrimination against minorities.

31. For X Union, project the effects that technology will have on traditionally unionized industries by the year 20XX.

32. Advise the management of X Company on how to deal with Y Union, which is attempting to organize the employees of X Company.

33. Evaluate the effectiveness of mediation in resolving labor-management disputes.

34. Interpret the change in the number of union members over the past _____ years.

35. Report on the successes and failures of employee-run businesses.

36. Report on the status and effects of "right to work" laws.

37. Report on the potential impact of "comparable worth" on X Company (or _____ industry).

38. Evaluate the effects of a particular strike (your choice) on the union, the company, the stockholders, and the public. Write the report for a government investigating committee.

39. For Union X, prepare an objective report on union leadership in the nation during the past decade.

40. Layoffs based on seniority are causing a disproportionate reduction in the number of women and minority workers at Company X. Investigate alternatives that the company can present to the union.

41. Investigate recent trends relative to the older worker and the stands that unions have taken in this area.

42. Review the appropriateness of unionizing government workers, and recommend to a body of government leaders the stand they should take on this issue.

43. Report on the role of unions (or managements) in politics, and recommend a course for them to follow.

☐ FINANCE

44. As a financial consultant, evaluate a specific form of tax shelter for a client.

45. Review the customer-relations practices of banks, and recommend customer relations procedures for Bank X.

46. Review current employee loan practices and recommend whether Company X should make employee loans.

47. Report on what Company X needs to know about financial matters in doing business with _____ (foreign country).

48. Give estate planning advice to a client with a unique personal situation.

49. Advise X Company on whether it should lease capital equipment or buy it.

50. Advise Company X on whether it should engage in a joint venture with a company overseas or establish a wholly owned foreign subsidiary.

51. Compare the costs for X Company of offering its workers child-care or elder-care benefits.

52. Should Company X accept national credit cards or set up its own credit card system?

53. Advise Company X on how to avoid a hostile takeover.

54. Advise Company X on whether it should list its stock on a major stock exchange.

55. Advise Company X, which is having problems with liquidity, on the pros and cons of factoring accounts receivable.

56. Recommend the most feasible way to finance newly formed X Company.

□ **MANAGEMENT**

57. Develop for Company X a guide to ethics in its highly competitive business situation.

58. After reviewing pertinent literature and experiences of other companies, develop a plan for selecting and training administrators for an overseas operation on Company X.

59. Survey the current literature and advise Company X on whether its management should become politically active.

60. After reviewing the pros and cons, advise X Company on whether it should begin a program of hiring the handicapped or disadvantaged.

61. Report on the behavioral and psychological effects of introducing wellness programs to Company X.

62. The executives of X Company (a manufacturer of automobile and truck tires) want a report on recent court decisions relating to warranties. Include any recommendations that your report justifies.

63. Report on the problems involved in moving company X headquarters from _____ (city) to _____ (city).

64. After reviewing current practices with regard to worker participation in management, advise Company X on whether it should permit such participation.

65. Should Company X contract for _____ (service) or establish its own department?

66. Review the advantages and disadvantages of rotating executive jobs at Company X, and then make a recommendation.

67. What should be Company X's policy on office romances?

68. Develop an energy conservation or recycling plan for X Company.

69. Evaluate internal communications in the X Company and make specific suggestions for improvement.

70. Design a security system for preventing computer espionage at Company X, a leader in the highly competitive _____ industry.

71. Evaluate the various methods for determining corporate performance and select the one most appropriate for Company X.

72. Advise X Company on the procedures for incorporating in _____ (state or province).

73. Survey the literature to find meaningful criteria for selecting executives for foreign service for X Company.

74. Report to Company X on the civil and criminal liabilities of its corporate executives.

75. As a consultant for a citizens' group, investigate the pros and cons of attracting a nuclear plant to your geographic area.

76. Determine for a legislative committee the extent of minority recruiting, hiring, and training in the _____ industry.

77. As a consultant for an association of farmers, evaluate the recent past and project the future of growing or raising _____ (your choice—cattle, poultry, wheat, soybeans, or the like).

78. Develop a plan for reducing employee turnover for Company X.

79. Report to a labor union on recent evidence of sexual harassment, and recommend steps that the union should take to correct any problems you find.

80. Investigate the feasibility of hiring older workers for part-time work for X Company.

☐ **PERSONNEL/HUMAN RESOURCES ADMINISTRATION**

81. Report on and interpret for X Company the effects of recent court decisions on the testing and hiring of employees.

82. Survey company retirement practices and recommend retirement policies for Company X.

83. Report on practices in compensating key personnel in overseas assignments and recommend for X Company policies for the compensation of such personnel.

84. Report on what personnel executives look for in application letters and résumés.

85. Report on the advantages and disadvantages of Company X's providing on-site day care for children of employees.

86. After reviewing the legal and ethical questions involved, make a recommendation concerning the use of honesty tests in employee hiring.

87. Review what other companies are doing about employees suffering from drug or alcohol abuse, and recommend a policy on the matter for Company X.

88. Report on effective interviewing techniques used to identify the best people to hire.

☐ **MARKETING**

89. Review the available literature and advise Company X on whether it should franchise its _____ business.

90. Select a recent national marketing program and analyze why it succeeded or failed.

91. Advise the advertising vice president of Company X on whether the company should respond to or ignore a competitor's direct attack on the quality of its product.

92. Review the ethical considerations involved in advertising directed to children and advise X Company on the matter.

93. Determine for Company X the social and ethical aspects of pricing for the market.

94. Explore the possibilities of trade with _____ (a foreign country) for X Company.

95. Determine for a national department store chain changing trends in the services that customers expect.

96. Prepare a report to help a contingent of your legislature decide whether current regulation of advertising should be reduced.

97. Determine the problems X Company will encounter in introducing a new product to its line.

98. Report on the success of rebates as a sales stimulator and advise Company X on whether it should use rebates.

99. Should Company X rent or lease trucks for distributing its products?

100. Determine the trends in packaging in the _____ industry.

101. Should X Company establish its own sales force, use manufacturers' agents, or use selling agents?

102. How should Company X evaluate the performance of its salespeople?

103. Determine for X Company how it can evaluate the effectiveness of its advertising.

104. Select the best channel of distribution for new product Y and justify your choice.

105. Should X Company establish its own advertising department or use an advertising agency?

106. Make a market study of _____ (city) to determine whether it is a suitable location for _____ (a type of business).

107. Report to X Company on telemarketing and recommend whether it should use telemarketing to increase sales.

☐ **COMPUTER APPLICATIONS**

108. Develop a plan for converting Company X's administration operations from a manual system to a computerized system.

109. Recommend a notebook computer for use by the salespeople of Company X when they are traveling.

110. Advise Company X about the steps it can take to protect its computerized files from sabotage.

111. Determine whether Company X should purchase or lease its computer equipment.

112. Should Company X use integrated software, or should it select word processing, spreadsheet, database, and graphics software separately?

113. Explain for Company X the advantages and disadvantages of electronic mail, and advise the company on whether to use it.

114. Report to the president of Company X the copyright and contract laws that apply to the use of computer programs.

115. What are the potential applications of artificial intelligence in the _____ industry?

116. What are the advantages and disadvantages of allowing employees of Company X to do computer-related work in their homes, rather than requiring them to do all computer-related work at the office?

117. Report to the International Organization of Business Communications on the impact of electronic technology on business communication.

118. Report on the future developments of robotics in the _____ industry.

119. Review and rank for possible adoption three software packages that Company X might use for its _____ work (name the field of operations).

120. Determine for Company X the factors it should consider in selecting computer insurance.

121. Report on the types of training available to X Company for its staff when upgrading its current word processing software.

☐ **BUSINESS EDUCATION**

122. Evaluate the effect of remodeling your new office site to take on a more homey look.

123. Report on why office romances still result in job losses.

124. Analyze the possibility of instituting company-wide training on etiquette, covering everything from handling telephone calls, to sexual harassment, to dining out.

125. Advise management on the importance of the air quality in the offices.

126. Investigate ways to improve the retrieval time and accuracy of information at X Company.

127. Evaluate the reprographic services and practices at your school from an environmental perspective.

128. Report on ways to hire and keep the best employees in the word processing center.

ORAL REPORT PROBLEMS

The following situations offer you realistic opportunities to present information, analysis, conclusions, and recommendations orally to a specific audience. Immerse yourself in the role assigned and apply the principles of effective oral reporting (Chapter 17) as effectively as you can.

Note also that with appropriate invention or adaptation of details, many of the written report topics listed above can be used for oral presentations as well. Consult with your instructor to select and adjust a topic, define the audience, and establish additional specifics necessary to create a true-to-life and challenging situation.

1. Survey the major business publications for information about the outlook for the national (or world) economy for the coming year. Then present a summary report to the directors of Allied Department Stores, Inc.

2. As a student leader on your campus, you have been asked by the faculty senate (or a comparable faculty group) to report to its members on the status of faculty-student relations. You will include recommendations on what can be done to improve those relations.

3. Report to a meeting of a wildlife-protection organization on the status of an endangered species in your area. You will need to gather the facts through research, probably in wildlife publications.

4. A national chain of _____ (your choice) is opening an outlet in your city. You have been assigned the task of reviewing site possibilities. Gather the pertinent information, and make an oral recommendation to the board of directors.

5. The Future Business Leaders Club at your old high school has asked you to report to it on the nature and quality of business study at your college. You will cover all the factors that you think high school students need to know. Include a graphic in your presentation.

6. As representative of a travel agency, present a travel package on _____ (place or places of your choice) to the members of the Adventurer Travel Club. You will describe places to be visited, and you will cover all the essential details—dates, hotels, guide service, meals, costs, manner of travel, and so on.

7. Report to a meeting of Consumers' Alliance (a consumer-protection organization) on the economics of renting telephones from the telephone company versus buying telephones. You will need to gather facts through research.

8. Look through current newspapers, magazines, and so on, and get the best available information on the job outlook for this year's college graduates. You will want to look at each major field separately. You may also want to show variations by geographic area, degree, and schools. Present your findings in a well-organized and illustrated oral report.

9. Present a plan for improving some phrase of operation on your campus (registration, scholastic honesty, housing, grade appeals, library, cafeteria, traffic, curricula, athletics, and so on).

10. Present an objective report on some legislation of importance to business (right-to-work laws, environmental controls, taxes, and the like). Take care to present evidence and reasoning from all the major viewpoints. Support your presentation with facts, figures, and so on whenever they will help. Prepare graphic supports.

11. Assume that you are being considered by a company of your choice for a job of your choice. Your prospective employer has asked you to make a _____-

minute (your instructor will specify) report on your qualifications. You may project your education to the date you will be in the job market, making assumptions that are consistent with your record to date.

12. Prepare and present an informative report on how individuals may reduce their federal or state income tax payments. You will probably want to emphasize the most likely sources of tax savings—such as tax sheltering and avoiding common errors.

13. Make a presentation to a hypothetical group of investors that will get you the investment money you need for a purpose of your choice. Your purpose could be to begin a new business, to construct a building, to develop land—whatever interests you. Make your presentation as real (or realistic) as you can. And support your appeal with graphics.

14. As chairperson of the site-selection committee of the National Federation of Business Executives, present a report on your committee's recommendation. The committee has selected a city and a convention hotel (you may choose each). Your report will give your recommendation and the reasons that support it. For class purposes, you may make up whatever facts you may need about the organization and its convention requirements and about the hotel. But use real facts about the city.

15. As a buyer of men's (or women's) clothing, report to the sales personnel of your store on the fashions for the coming season. You may get the necessary information from publications in the field.

16. The top administrators of your company have asked you to look into the matter of whether the company should own automobiles, rent automobiles, or pay mileage costs on employee-owned automobiles. (Automobiles are used by sales personnel.) Gather the best available information on the matter, and report it to the top administrators. You may make up any company facts you need; but make them realistic.

17. In a group designated or approved by your instructor, present a persuasive presentation proposing that your school make more computing equipment available for student use. Be sure to cover all aspects of such a decision including cost, access, security, etc.

18. Choose a graphics package most of your classmates could use to prepare visuals for oral reports. Report on the features, documentation, and cost. Feel free to use graphic aids to support your report.

A Grading Checklist for Reports

The following checklist serves two purposes. It is first a guide to preparing reports, and second, an aid to grading reports. (Your instructor can use the symbols to mark errors.) The checklist covers all types of reports—from the simple memorandums to the long, analytical reports. For each report type, you need use only the items that apply.

Title (T)

T   1   Complete? The title should tell what the reader may expect to find in the report. Use the five Ws as a check for completeness (*who, what, where, when, why*—sometimes *how*).

T   2   Too long. This title is longer than it needs to be. Check it for uneconomical wording or unnecessary information.

Letter of Transmittal (LT)

LT   1   More directness is needed in the opening. The letter should present the report right away.

LT   2   Content of the letter needs improvement. Comments that help the reader to understand or appreciate the report are appropriate.

LT   3   Do not include findings unless the report has no executive summary.

LT   4   A warm statement of your attitude toward the assignment is appropriate—often expected. You either do not make one, or the one you make is weak.

LT   5   A friendlier, more conversational style would improve the letter.

Executive Summary (ES)

ES   1   (If direct order assigned) Begin directly—with a statement of finding, conclusion, or recommendation.

ES   2   (If indirect order assigned) Begin with a brief review of introductory information.

ES 3 The summary of highlights should be in proportion and should include major findings, analyses, and conclusions. Your coverage here is (*a*) scant or (*b*) too detailed.

ES 4 Work for a more interesting and concise summary.

ORGANIZATION—OUTLINE (O)

O 1 This organization plan is not the best for this problem. The main sections should form a logical solution of the problem.

O 2 The order of the parts of this outline is not logical. The parts should form a step-by-step route to the goal.

O 3 These parts overlap. Each part should be independent of other parts. Although some repetition and relating of parts may be desirable, outright overlap is a sign of bad organization.

O 4 More subparts are needed here. The subparts should cover all the information covered by the major part.

O 5 This subpart does not fit logically under this major part.

O 6 These parts are not equal in importance. Do not give them equal status in the outline.

O 7 (If talking captions assigned) These captions do not talk well.

O 8 Coordinate captions should be parallel in grammatical structure.

O 9 This caption is too long. These captions are too long.

O 10 Vary the wording of the captions to avoid monotonous repetition.

INTRODUCTION (I)

I 1 This introduction does not cover exactly what the reader needs to know. Although the needs vary by problem, these topics usually are important: (*a*) origin of the problem, (*b*) statement of the problem, (*c*) methods used in researching the problem, and (*d*) preview of the presentation.

I 2 Coverage of this part is (*a*) scant or (*b*) too detailed.

I 3 Important information has been left out.

I 4 Findings, conclusions, and other items of information are not a part of the introduction.

COVERAGE (C)

C 1 The coverage here is (*a*) scant or (*b*) too detailed.

C 2 More analysis is needed here.

C 3 Here you rely too heavily on a graphic aid. The text should cover the important information.

C 4   Do not lose sight of the goal of the report. Relate the information to the problem.

C 5   Clearly distinguish between fact and opinion. Label opinion as opinion.

C 6   Your analyses and conclusions need the support of more fact and authoritative opinion.

WRITING (W)

W 1   This writing should be better adapted to your readers. It appears to be (*a*) too heavy or (*b*) too light.

W 2   Avoid the overuse of passive voice.

W 3   Work for more conciseness. Try to cut down on words without sacrificing meaning.

W 4   For this report more formal writing is appropriate. Write consistently in impersonal (third person) style.

W 5   A more personal style is appropriate for this report. Use personal pronouns (I's, we's, you's).

W 6   The change in thought is abrupt here.
   a.   Between major parts, use introductions, summaries, and conclusions to guide the reader's thinking.
   b.   Use transitional words, phrases, or sentences to relate minor parts.

W 7   Your paragraphing is questionable. Check the paragraphs for unity. Look for topic sentences.

GRAPHIC AIDS (GA)

GA 1   You have (*a*) not used enough graphic aids or (*b*) used too many graphic aids.

GA 2   For the information presented, this graphic aid is (*a*) too large or (*b*) too small.

GA 3   This type of graphic aid is not the best for presenting this information.

GA 4   Place the graphic aid as near as is practical to the place where its contents are discussed.

GA 5   The appearance of this graphic aid needs improvement. It does not make a good impression on the reader.

GA 6   Refer the readers to the graphic aids at the times they should look at them.

GA 7   Preferably make the references to the graphic aids incidental, as subordinate parts of sentences that comment on the content of the graphic aids [for example " . . . , as shown in Figure 5," or (see Figure 5)].

LAYOUT AND MECHANICS (LM)

LM 1   The layout of this page is (*a*) too fat, (*b*) too skinny, or (*c*) too low, high, or off center (as marked).

LM 2   Neatness? Smudges, erasures, and such detract from the message.

LM   3   Make the margins straighter. The roughness here offends the eye.

LM   4   The spacing here needs improvement. (*a*) Too much space here. (*b*) Not enough space here.

LM   5   Your page numbering is not the best. See the text for the specific instructions.

LM   6   This page appears (*a*) choppy or (*b*) heavy.

LM   7   Your selection of type and position for the captions is not the best.

LM   8   This item of form is not generally acceptable.

Statistical Techniques for Determining Sample Size and Reliability

The cumulative frequency test is a useful way to measure the adequacy of your sample and the reliability of your results. However, the standard error of the percentage and the standard error of the mean are more accurate.

As you learned from your study of primary research, you must verify the adequacy of your sample and the reliability of your results before you attempt to draw conclusions from your survey data. The cumulative frequency test described in Chapter 5 is one of the less technical means of verification and adequate for some research. However, when you need a more accurate measure, you may want to use one of the statistical techniques described in the following paragraphs. The first, the standard error of the percentage, is used when the findings are recorded in percentage form. And the second, the standard error of the mean, is used when you are concerned with a population average or mean. Both are adaptations of the standard deviation, which is a measure of the spread of the normal distribution.

Each of these two basic formulas may be used to determine either the sample size or the measure of error. But each application of either formula tests only one characteristic of the study at a time. Thus, in determining the desired size of a sample within a prescribed error range, you may need to use the appropriate formula several times—enough times to assure a reasonable degree of reliability for the study as a whole. A 10-question survey, therefore, does not necessarily require 10 separate applications of the appropriate formula. But it will require, in addition to an initial test, as many applications as you, the researcher, need to make sure your results are as representative and accurate as they can or need to be.

This formula computes the standard error of the percentage.

The standard error of the percentage is expressed in the following formula:

$$\sigma_p = \sqrt{\frac{pq}{N}}$$

where

σ_p is the standard error of the percentage,
p is the frequency of the occurrence of the phenomenon measured, expressed as a percentage of the whole,
q is $(1 - p)$, and
N is the number of the cases in the sample.

And this version of the same formula computes the required sample size.

If you need to obtain the number required for a given allowable error, rather than the standard error, you use this version of the formula to determine the size of the sample, or N:

$$N = \frac{pq}{\sigma_p^2}$$

Working the formula for two standard errors results in greater accuracy.

The sample size computed by this formula gives results within the limits of error specified about 68 out of 100 times. For greater accuracy, you could work the formula for two standard errors, which ensures that the answer has a 95 out of 100 chance of being within the error allowed. The formula then becomes:

$$N = \frac{pq}{\left(\frac{\sigma_p}{2}\right)^2}$$

Consider the following practical application of the standard error of the percentage formula. Assume you are conducting a consumer preference of a new soap. One of your questions is, "What do you think of the scent of the soap?" The answers are: Like it; Do not like it; and No opinion. On the basis of early returns, you estimate 60 percent (0.60 in decimal form) of the respondents will answer they like the scent and 40 percent (0.40) will indicate they dislike it or have no opinion. You decide you can tolerate a 5 percent error in your results. If you want to be 95 percent sure the answers will be within the 5 percent error, what size should your sample of responses be?

To find the answer, first identify the known values in the formula. The percentage of those indicating they like the scent is p, and $(1 - p)$ or q is the percentage of those indicating they dislike the scent or have no opinion. The standard error of percentage (σ_p) is .05. The problem thus becomes:

$$N = \frac{0.60 \times 0.40}{\left(\frac{0.05}{2}\right)^2} = \frac{0.24}{0.000625} = 384$$

That is, in order to meet the reliability requirements you have set, you will have to review 384 responses.

If you would have been satisfied with 68 percent certainty, you would have solved the problem as follows:

$$N = \frac{0.60 \times 0.40}{(.05)^2} = \frac{0.24}{0.0025} = 96$$

Use this formula to compute the standard error of the mean.

The standard error of the mean formula is what you use when you want to determine the error of findings expressed as a mean as well as the sample size needed to obtain such findings. It is expressed as follows:

$$\sigma_{\bar{x}} = \frac{\sigma}{\sqrt{N}}$$

where

N is the size of the sample,
σ is the standard deviation of the items in the sample, and
$\sigma_{\bar{x}}$ is the standard error of the mean.

Compute the standard deviation or estimate it to be one-sixth of the range of values in your sample.

Here you have to determine values for two unknowns, the standard deviation (σ) and the standard error of the mean ($\sigma_{\bar{x}}$). If you are familiar with statistics, you can compute the standard deviation by using the conventional statistical formula.[1] But if you do not know statistics, you can estimate the standard deviation to be one-sixth of the range (R) of the values—that is, one-sixth of the difference between the largest and smallest items in the sample. If you use this approximate method and adapt the formula to determine sample size, the formula becomes:

$$\sqrt{N} = \frac{\frac{R}{6}}{\sigma_{\bar{x}}}$$

For $\sigma_{\bar{x}}$, the standard error of the mean, simply decide how much error (in units in which your data are given) you can permit and still have satisfactory results.

Assume, for example, you are studying average weekly incomes of factory workers. In a preliminary survey, you find incomes ranging from $200 to $290. Although this information is scant, you have something to work with; so you assume a range of $90, which is $290 less $200. You decide you want the mean value of the sample to be no more than $1 away from the true mean value. When you apply these values for R and $\sigma_{\bar{x}}$, the formula becomes:

$$\sqrt{N} = \frac{\frac{R}{6}}{\sigma_{\bar{x}}} = \frac{\frac{90}{6}}{1} = \frac{15}{1}$$

$$N = 15^2 = 225$$

Thus, you will need a sample of 225 to get the accuracy you want—with 68 percent certainty that the sample's response will reflect the response of the population as a whole. If you want to be 95 percent certain, divide the standard error by 2. In this

---

[1] The formula for the standard deviation is

$$\sigma = \sqrt{\frac{\Sigma x^2}{N}}$$

Σx^2 is the summation of the deviations from the mean squared. N is the number of units.

case the standard error of 1, divided by 2, is 0.5. Computing with this new value will result in $N = 900$. That is, you will need a sample of 900 to be 95 percent sure the average salary you calculate for the sample is accurate within \$1 of the actual average salary of the factory workers you are studying.

These illustrations lead to two general observations. First, when the estimates of sample size are based on scant preliminary information, as these estimates are, it is a good idea to apply the appropriate formula again as you collect more survey information. Second, improving the certainty of your estimates from 68 to 95 percent requires you to reduce the range of error by half and quadruple the size of your required sample. (Recall that the required sample for the soap survey increased from 96 to 384 responses and the required number of factory workers in the weekly wage survey went from 225 to 900.) The fourfold increases are evident in the table below.

Table for determining sample size* (sample size necessary to ensure, with 95 percent certainty, that the survey proportions are within a given number of percentage points of the true value)

Maximum Percentage Error Either Way	Frequency with Which Phenomenon Occurs					
	5 or 95 Percent	10 or 90 Percent	20 or 80 Percent	30 or 70 Percent	40 or 60 Percent	50 Percent
0.5	7,600	14,400	25,600	33,600	38,400	40,000
1.0	1,900	3,600	6,400	8,400	9,600	10,000
2.0	475	900	1,600	2,100	2,400	2,500
3.0	211	400	711	933	1,067	1,111
4.0	119	225	400	525	600	625
5.0	76	144	256	336	384	400
10.0	19	36	64	84	96	100

*When findings are expressed in percentage form.

For a detailed explanation of statistical techniques, consult a statistics textbook.

If you need more detailed information about statistical techniques for determining sample size and reliability, you are well advised to review a text on the subject. Also available are a number of computer software packages that will compute standard statistical formulas and present error and frequency options in tabular or chart form.

The Gunning Fog Index

Products of the readability studies discussed in Chapter 2 are formulas for measuring readability. Perhaps the easiest to use and the most popular is the Gunning Fog Index. This index, or a similar one, is included with most computer style-analyzing software packages.

STEPS IN APPLYING THE INDEX

The index indicates the grade level of education the reader should have to read the material easily.

The ease with which the Gunning Fog Index is used is obvious from a review of the simple steps listed below. Its ease of interpretation is also obvious in that the index computed from these simple steps is in grade level of education. For example, an index of seven means that the material tested is easy reading for one at the seventh-grade level. An index of 12 indicates high school graduate level of readability. And an index of 16 indicates the level of the college graduate.

The simple steps for computing the index are as follows:

Here are the steps for computing the index.

1. *Select a sample.* For long pieces of writing use at least 100 words. As in all sampling procedure, the larger the sample, the more reliable the results will be. So, in measuring readability for a long manuscript one would be wise to select a number of samples at random throughout the work.

2. *Determine the average number of words per sentence.* First count words and sentences in a sample selected. Then divide the total number of words by the total of sentences.

3. *Determine the percentage of hard words in the sample.* Words of three syllables or longer are considered to be hard words. But do not count as hard words: (1) words that are capitalized, (2) combinations of short, easy words (*grasshopper, businessperson, bookkeeper*), or (3) verb forms made into three-syllable words by adding *ed* or *es* (*repeated, caresses*).

4. *Add the two factors computed above and multiply by 0.4.* The product is the minimum grade level at which the writing is easily read.

Application of the Gunning Fog Index is illustrated with the following paragraph.

431

In *general, construction* of *pictograms* follows the *general procedure* used in *constructing* bar charts. But two special rules should be followed. First, all of the picture units used must be of equal size. The *comparisons* must be made wholly on the basis of the number of *illustrations* used and never by *varying* the *areas* of the *individual* pictures used. The reason for this rule is *obvious*. The human eye is grossly *inadequate* in *comparing areas* of *geometric* designs. Second, the pictures or symbols used must *appropriately* depict the *quantity* to be *illustrated*. A *comparison* of the navies of the world, for *example,* might make use of *miniature* ship drawings. Cotton *production* might be shown by bales of cotton. *Obviously,* the drawings used must be *immediately interpreted* by the reader.

The grade level of readership for this selection is 13.2.

Inspection of the paragraph reveals these facts. It has 10 sentences and 129 words for an average sentence length of 13. Of the total of 129 words, 26 are considered to be hard words. Thus, the percentage of hard words is 20. From these data, the Gunning Fog Index is computed as follows.

Average sentence length	13
Percentage of hard words	20
Total	33
Multiply by	0.4
Grade level of readership	13.2

CRITICAL APPRAISAL OF THE FORMULAS

Readability formulas are a convenient measure of writing. That is why they are so popular.

Readability formulas are widely used in business today. Perhaps the reason for their popularity is the glitter of their apparent mathematical exactness. Or perhaps they are popular because they reduce to simple and workable formulas the most complex work of writing. Whatever the reason, the wise writer will look at the formulas objectively.

Unquestionably, these formulas have been a boon to improving clarity in business report writing. And they provide a convenient check and measure of the level of one's writing. But they also have some limitations.

But if you overuse them, you will write in a primer style. Short sentences comprised exclusively of simple words can make dull reading.

The most serious limitation of the formulas is the primer style of writing that can result from a slavish use of them. Overly simple words and a monotonous succession of short sentences make dull reading. Dull reading doesn't hold the reader's attention. And without the reader's attention, there can be little communication.

Use readability formulas, therefore, primarily as a guide.

Perhaps the formulas are most useful to the unskilled writers. By intelligent use of the formulas, they may at least be able to improve the communication quality of their work. Their writing styles, which were poor to begin with, do not suffer. Skilled writers, on the other hand, can violate the formulas and still communicate. Charles Dickens, for example, was a master in communicating in clear yet long sentences. So was William Faulkner. And so are some business writers. Because most business report writers fall somewhere between these extremes of writing ability, the wisest course for them is to use the formulas as general guides. But never will a formula replace the clear and logical thinking that is the underpinning of all clear writing.

Index